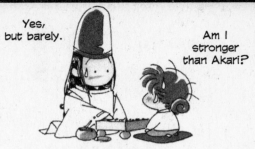

Yes,
but barely.

Am I
stronger
than Akari?

Yumi Hotta

With this volume, *Hikaru no Go* will have
been serialized for a full two years. Yet I
still struggle to come up with ideas for the
story. So nothing's really changed from
how things were when we first began. And
during those times I still mutter the same
thing under my breath—"It's okay, Obata
Sensei will come up with something!"

—Yumi Hotta

It all began when Yumi Hotta played a pick-up game of go with
her father-in-law. As she was learning how to play, Ms. Hotta
thought it might be fun to create a story around the
traditional board game. More confident in her storytelling
abilities than her drawing skills, she submitted the beginnings of
Hikaru no Go to **Weekly Shonen Jump**'s Story King Award.
The Story King Award is an award that picks the best story, manga,
character design and youth (under 15) manga submissions every
year in Japan. As fate would have it, Ms. Hotta's story (originally
named, "*Kokonotsu no Hoshi*"), was a runner-up in the "Story"
category of the Story King Award. Many years earlier, Takeshi Obata
was a runner-up for the Tezuka Award, another Japanese manga
contest sponsored by **Weekly Shonen Jump** and **Monthly
Shonen Jump**. An editor assigned to Mr. Obata's artwork came
upon Ms. Hotta's story and paired the two for a full-fledged manga
about go. The rest is modern go history.

HIKARU NO GO VOL. 11
The SHONEN JUMP Manga Edition

This manga contains material that was originally published in English from
SHONEN JUMP #56 to #60. Artwork in the magazine may have been
slightly altered from that presented here.

STORY BY YUMI HOTTA
ART BY TAKESHI OBATA
Supervised by YUKARI UMEZAWA (5 Dan)

Translation & English Adaptation/Andy Nakatani
English Script Consultant/Janice Kim (3 Dan)
Touch-up Art & Lettering/Inori Fukuda Trant
Cover & Interior Design/Courtney Utt
Additional Touch-up/Josh Simpson & Rachel Lightfoot
Editors/Yuki Takagaki & Annette Roman

Editor in Chief, Books/Alvin Lu
Editor in Chief, Magazines/Marc Weidenbaum
VP of Publishing Licensing/Rika Inouye
VP of Sales/Gonzalo Ferreyra
Sr. VP of Marketing/Liza Coppola
Publisher/Hyoe Narita

Printed in the U.S.A.

Published by VIZ Media, LLC
P.O. Box 77010
San Francisco, CA 94107

SHONEN JUMP Manga Edition
10 9 8 7 6 5 4 3 2 1
First printing, January 2008

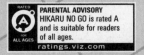

www.viz.com

THE WORLD'S
MOST POPULAR MANGA

www.shonenjump.com

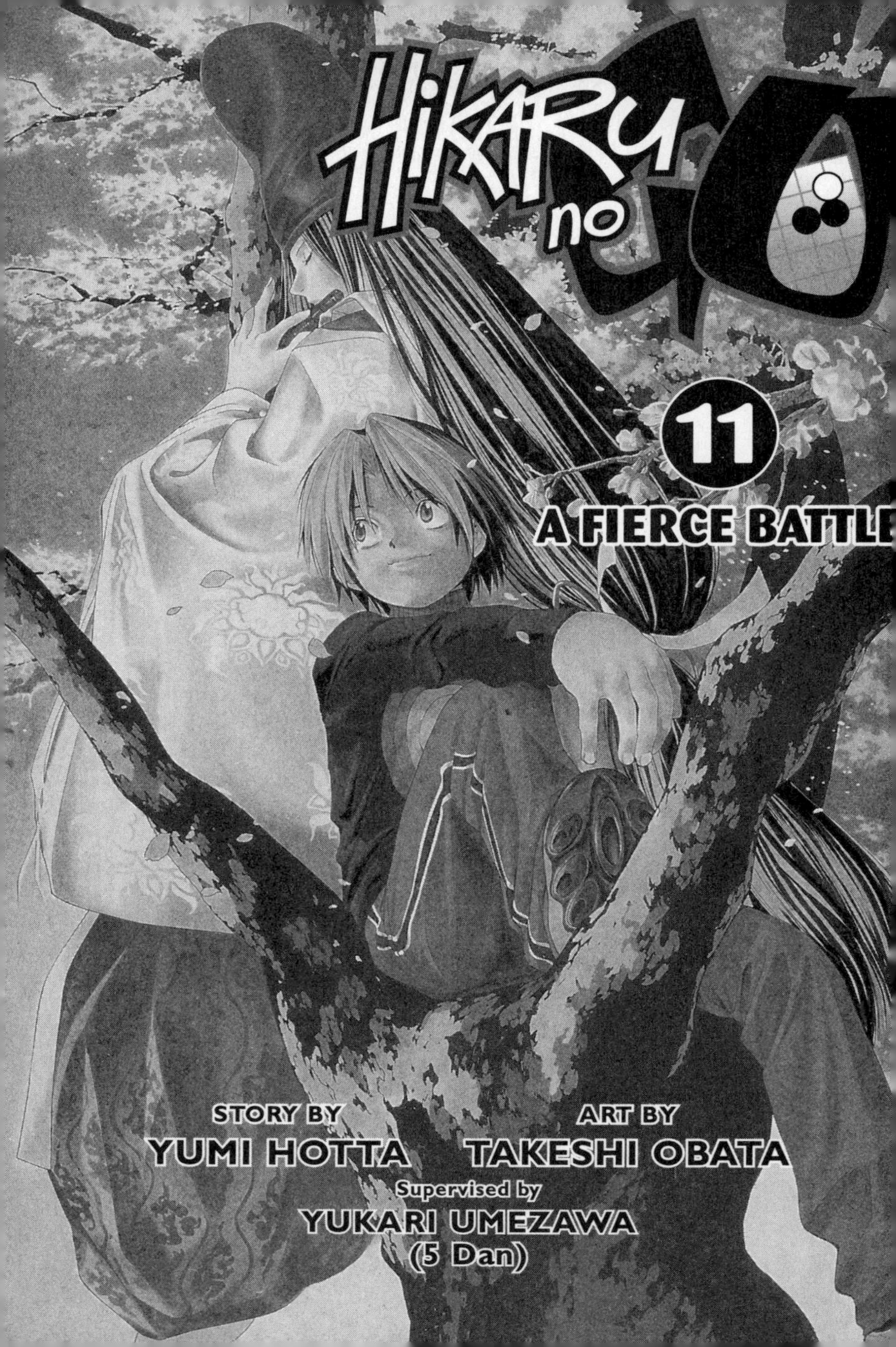
HIKARU no GO
11
A FIERCE BATTLE
STORY BY
YUMI HOTTA
ART BY
TAKESHI OBATA
Supervised by
YUKARI UMEZAWA
(5 Dan)

Character Introductions

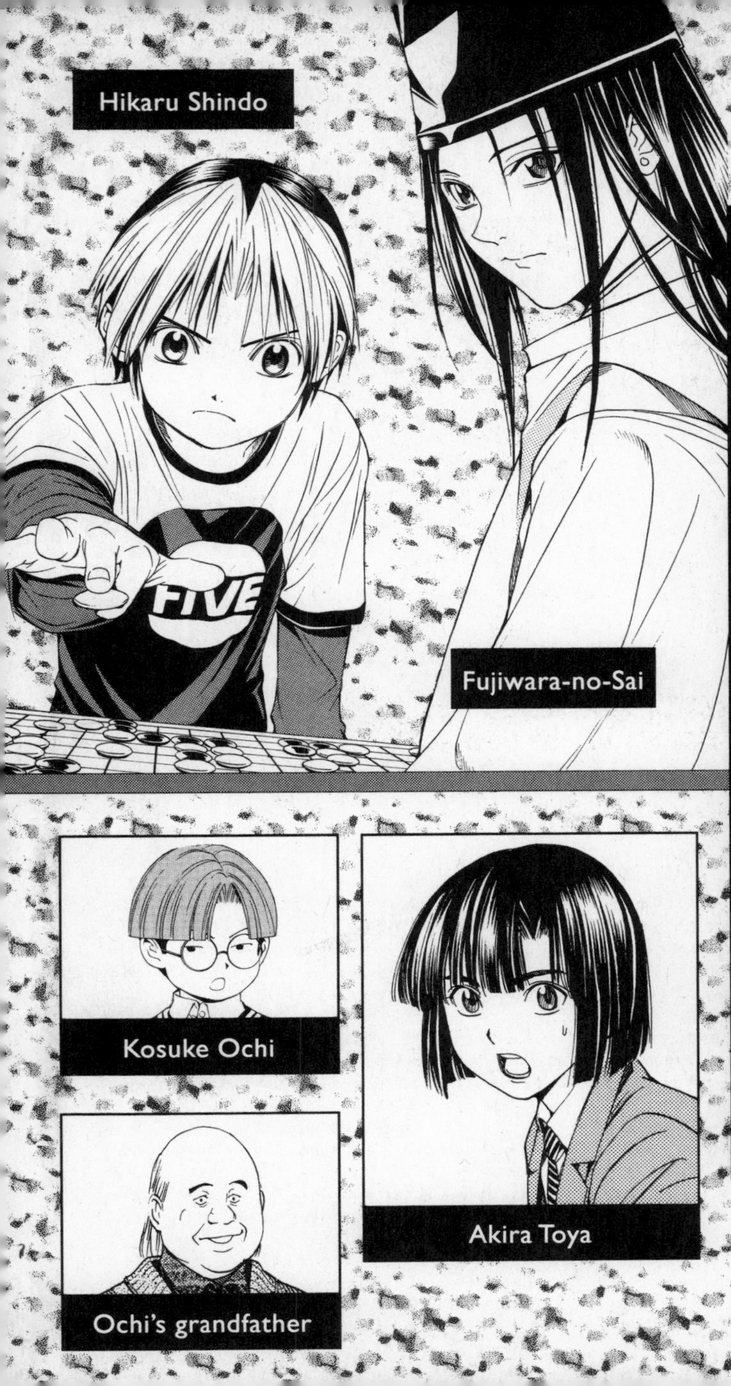

Fujiwara-no-Sai
Hikaru Shindo
Akira Toya
Kosuke Ochi
Ochi's grandfather

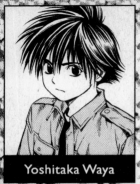

Ryo Iijima
Yuta "Fuku" Fukui
Yoshitaka Waya
Asumi Nase
Shinichiro Isumi
Morishita 7 Dan
Toshinori Honda

Story Thus Far

Hikaru Shindo discovers an old go board one day up in his grandfather's attic. The moment Hikaru touches the board, the spirit of Fujiwara-no-Sai, a genius go player from Japan's Heian Era, enters his consciousness. Sai's love of the game inspires Hikaru, as does a meeting with the child prodigy Akira Toya—son of go master Toya Meijin. With his interest in go awakened, Hikaru now dreams of becoming a professional player.

After the preliminary rounds of the pro test, Hikaru visits several go salons and gains even more skill and experience. Now come the main rounds—out of 27 rounds only the top three players will move on to join the pros. Hikaru takes a loss in game 10, but manages to keep up with top players Ochi, Isumi and Waya. In game 12, Hikaru faces Isumi, who is undefeated up to this point, but a misplaced stone forces Isumi to resign. The incident throws both players off for a few rounds. By game 21, Ochi has one loss, Waya has two, both Isumi and Hikaru have three, and Honda has four. For the rest of the pro test, Ochi studies under Akira Toya to prepare for his final game with Hikaru. Ochi is shocked to learn the extent of Hikaru's strength before he became an insei when Akira shows him a game he lost to Hikaru two years ago.

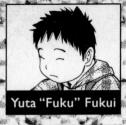

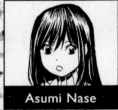

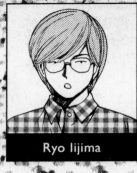

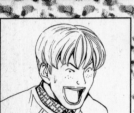

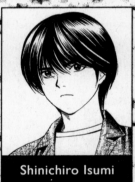

CONTENTS

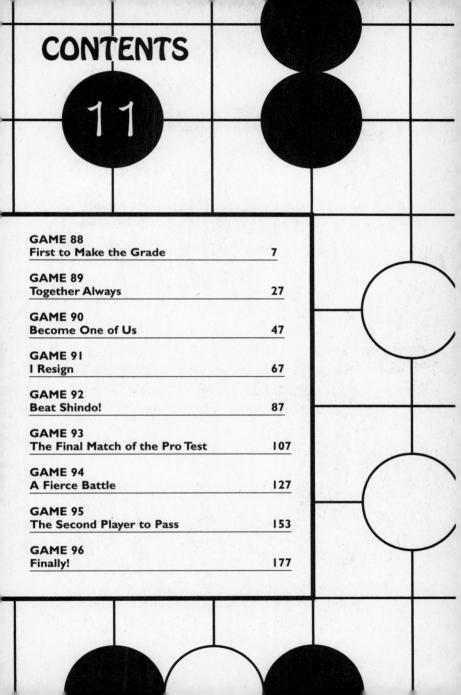

11

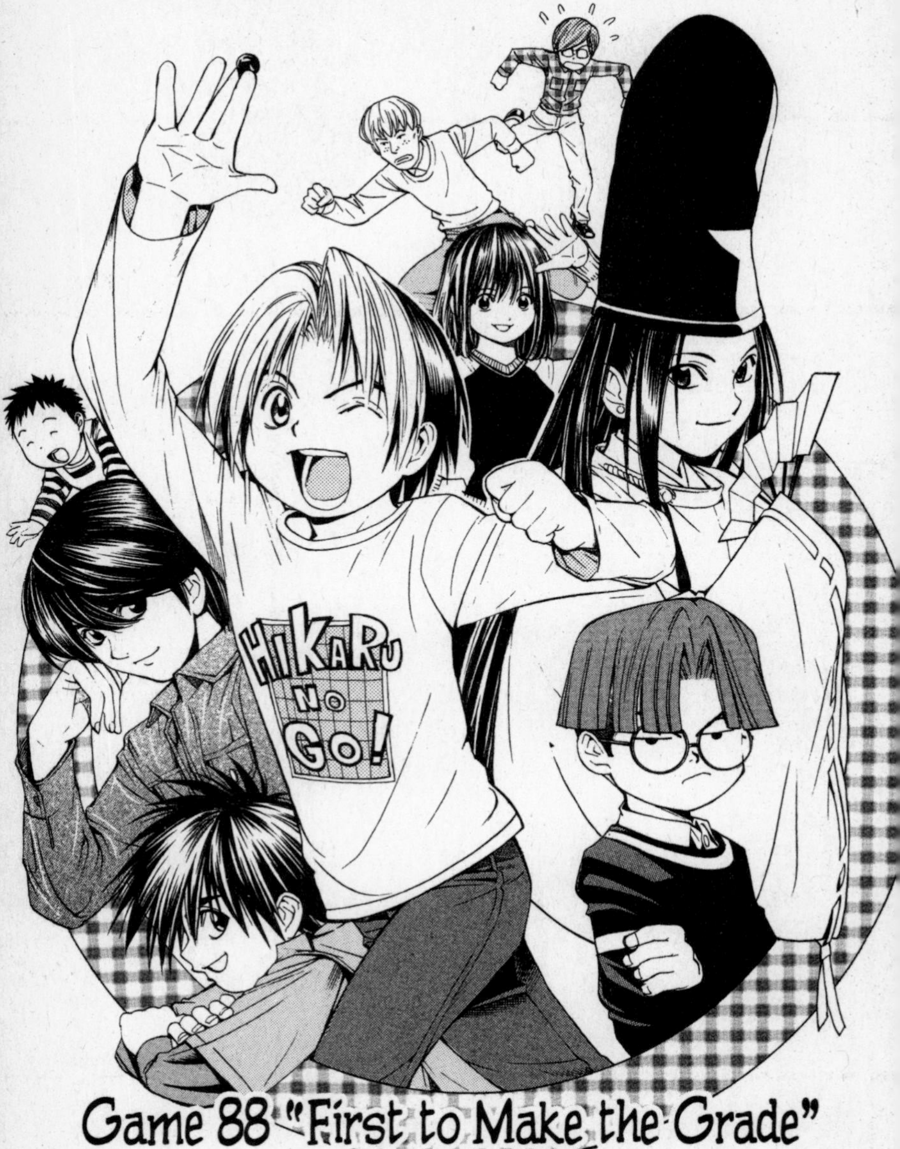
HIKARU
NO
GO!

Game 88 "First to Make the Grade"

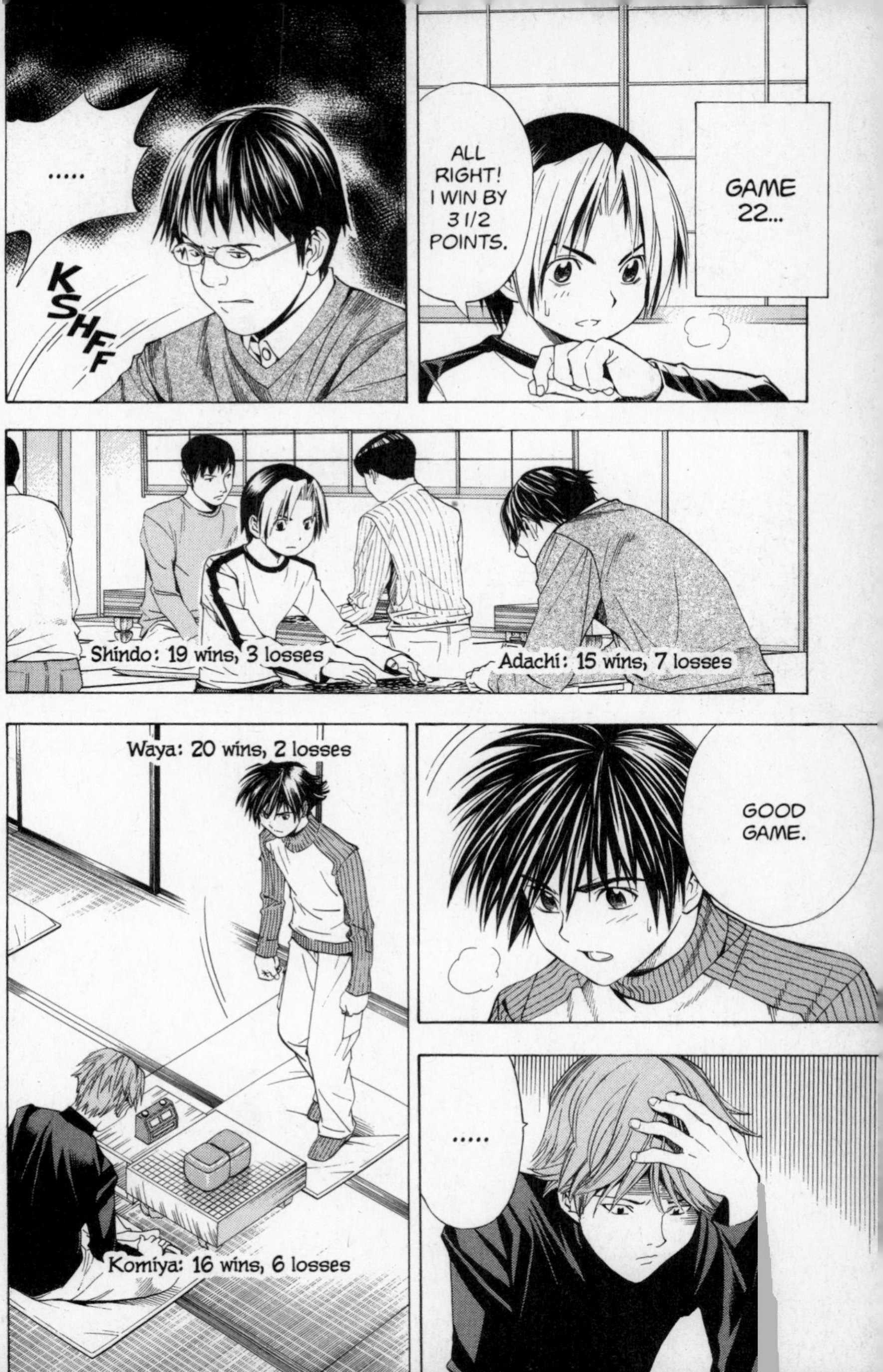
GAME 22...
ALL RIGHT! I WIN BY 3 1/2 POINTS.
.....
KSHFF
Adachi: 15 wins, 7 losses
Shindo: 19 wins, 3 losses
GOOD GAME.
.....
Waya: 20 wins, 2 losses
Komiya: 16 wins, 6 losses

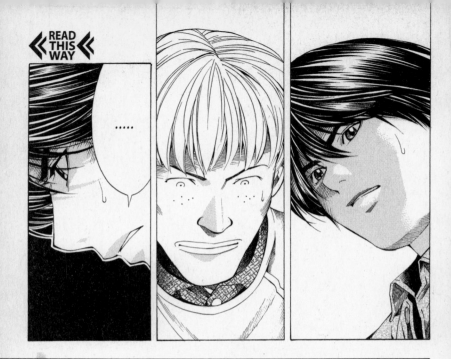

.....

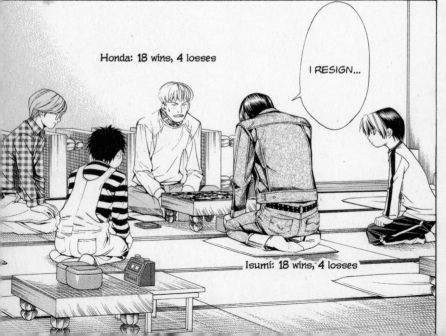

Honda: 18 wins, 4 losses

I RESIGN...

Isumi: 18 wins, 4 losses

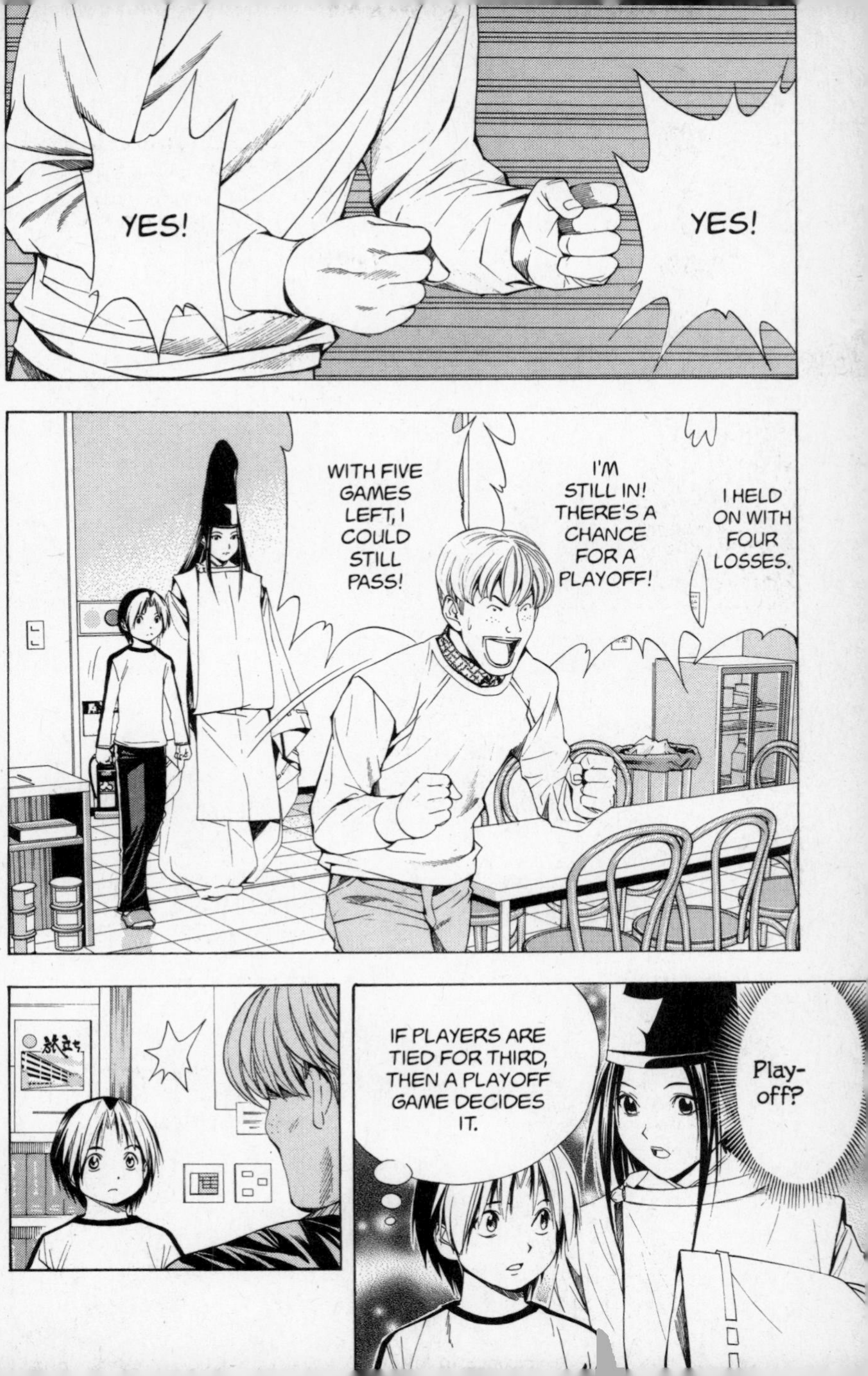
YES!
YES!
I HELD ON WITH FOUR LOSSES.
I'M STILL IN! THERE'S A CHANCE FOR A PLAYOFF!
WITH FIVE GAMES LEFT, I COULD STILL PASS!
Play-off?
IF PLAYERS ARE TIED FOR THIRD, THEN A PLAYOFF GAME DECIDES IT.

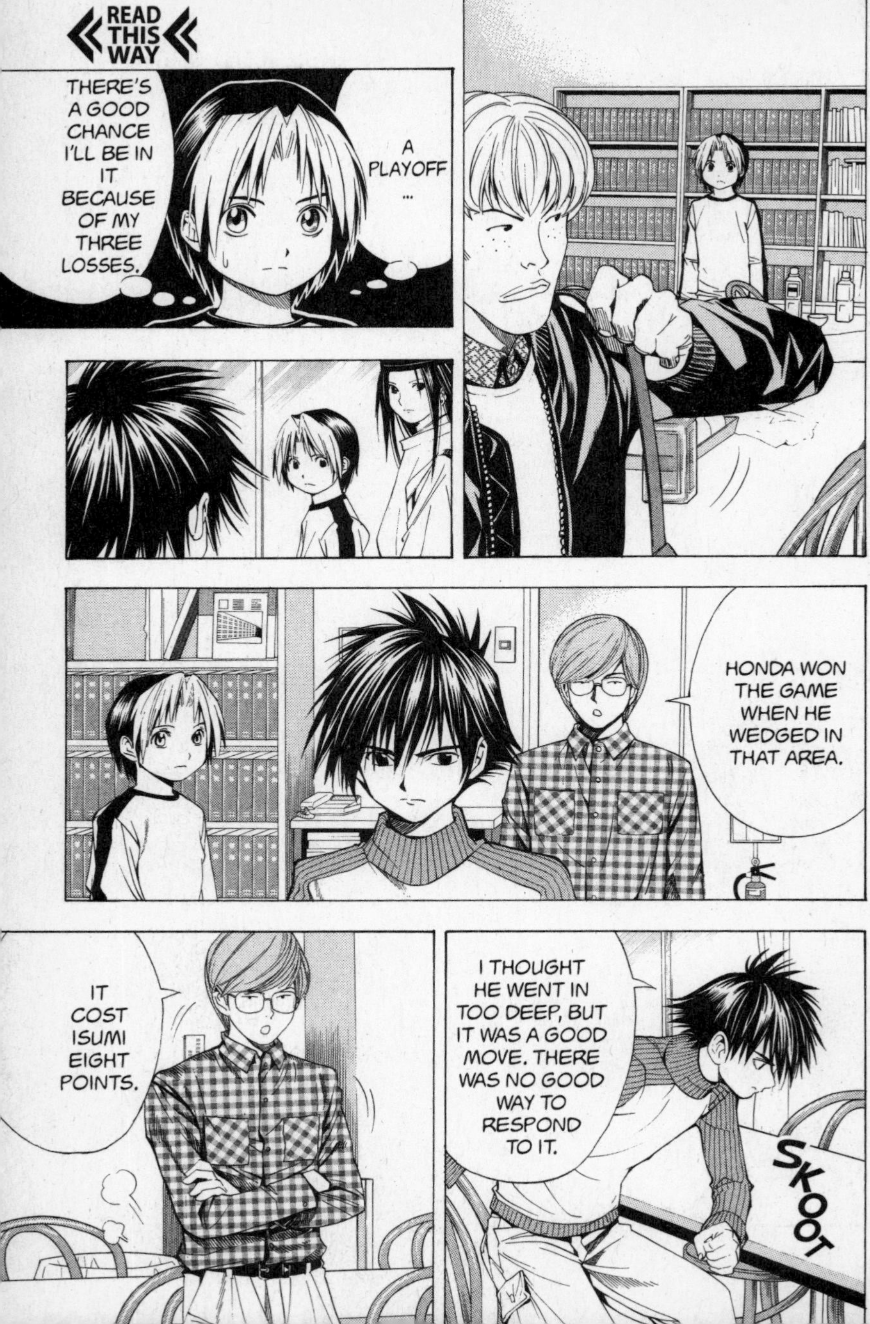
READ THIS WAY
A PLAYOFF ...
THERE'S A GOOD CHANCE I'LL BE IN IT BECAUSE OF MY THREE LOSSES.
HONDA WON THE GAME WHEN HE WEDGED IN THAT AREA.
I THOUGHT HE WENT IN TOO DEEP, BUT IT WAS A GOOD MOVE. THERE WAS NO GOOD WAY TO RESPOND TO IT.
SKOOT
IT COST ISUMI EIGHT POINTS.

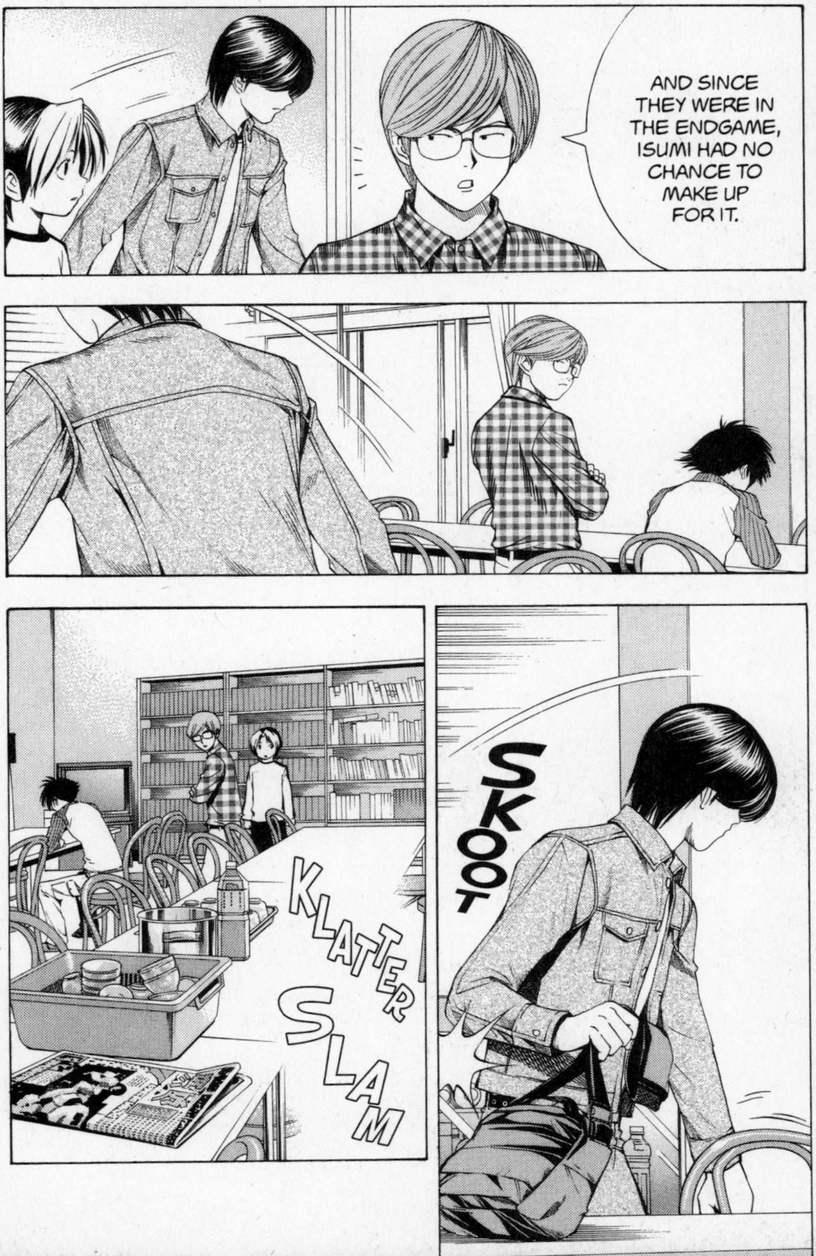
AND SINCE THEY WERE IN THE ENDGAME, ISUMI HAD NO CHANCE TO MAKE UP FOR IT.
SKOOT
KLATTER
SLAM

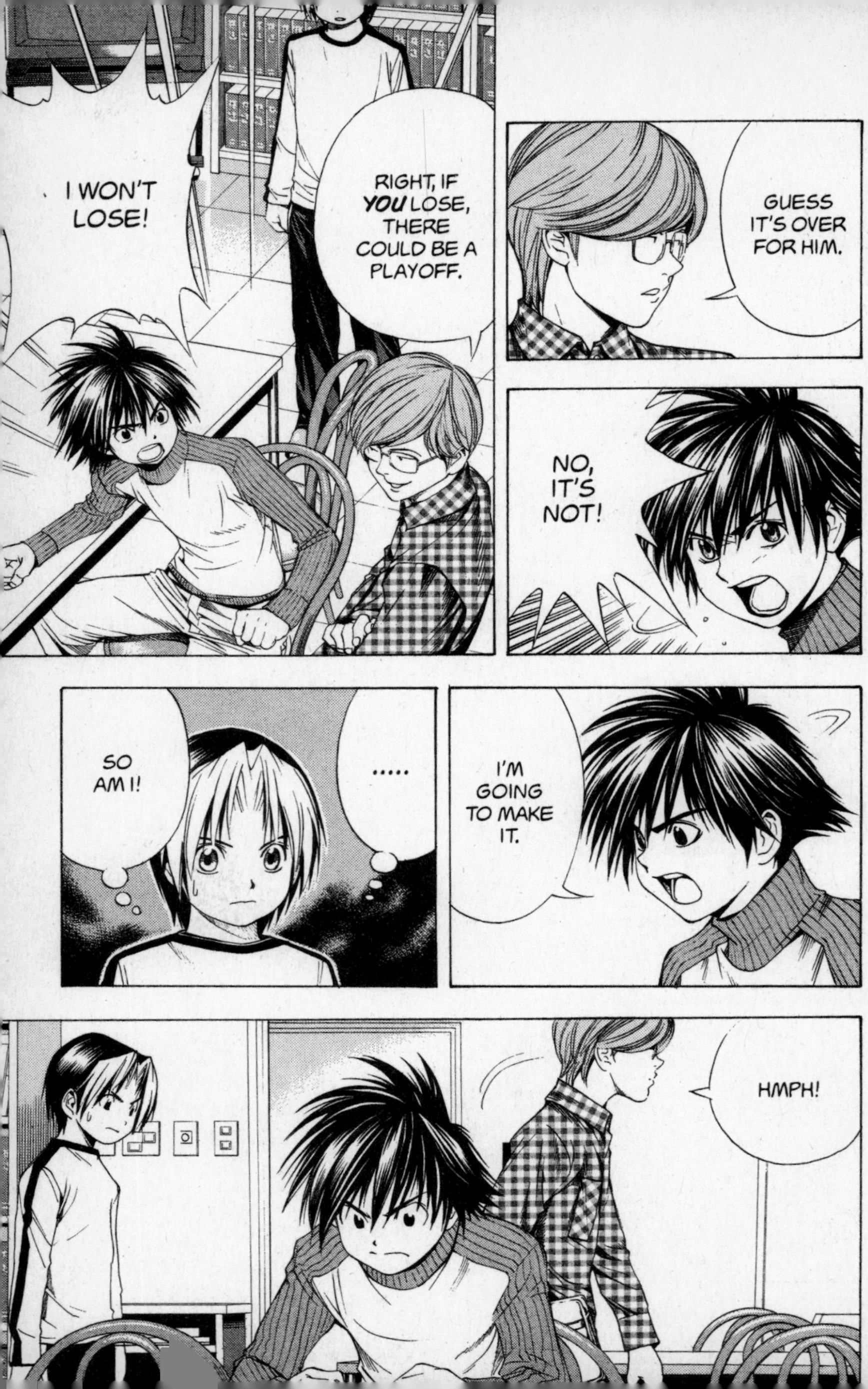
GUESS IT'S OVER FOR HIM.
NO, IT'S NOT!
RIGHT, IF YOU LOSE, THERE COULD BE A PLAYOFF.
I WON'T LOSE!
I'M GOING TO MAKE IT.
.....
SO AM I!
HMPH!

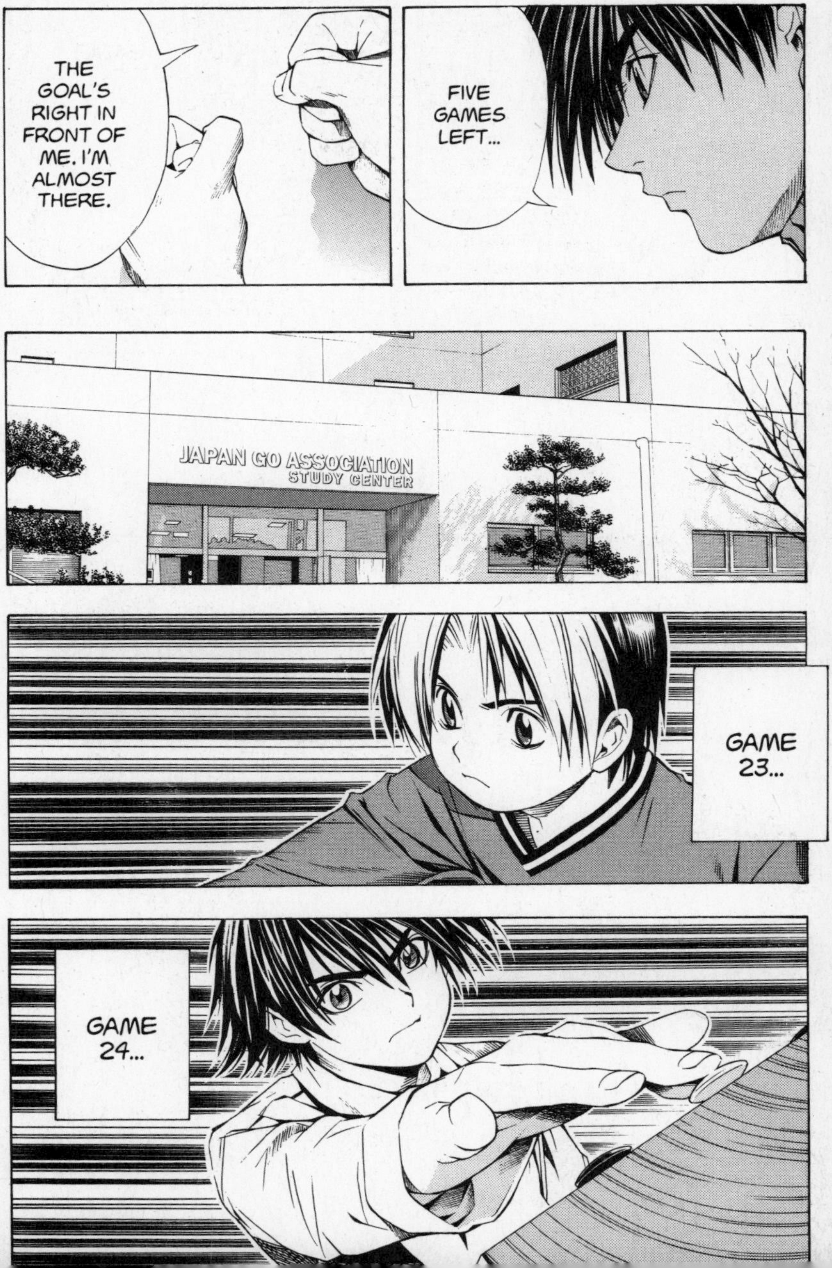
FIVE GAMES LEFT...
THE GOAL'S RIGHT IN FRONT OF ME. I'M ALMOST THERE.
JAPAN GO ASSOCIATION
STUDY CENTER
GAME 23...
GAME 24...

READ THIS WAY

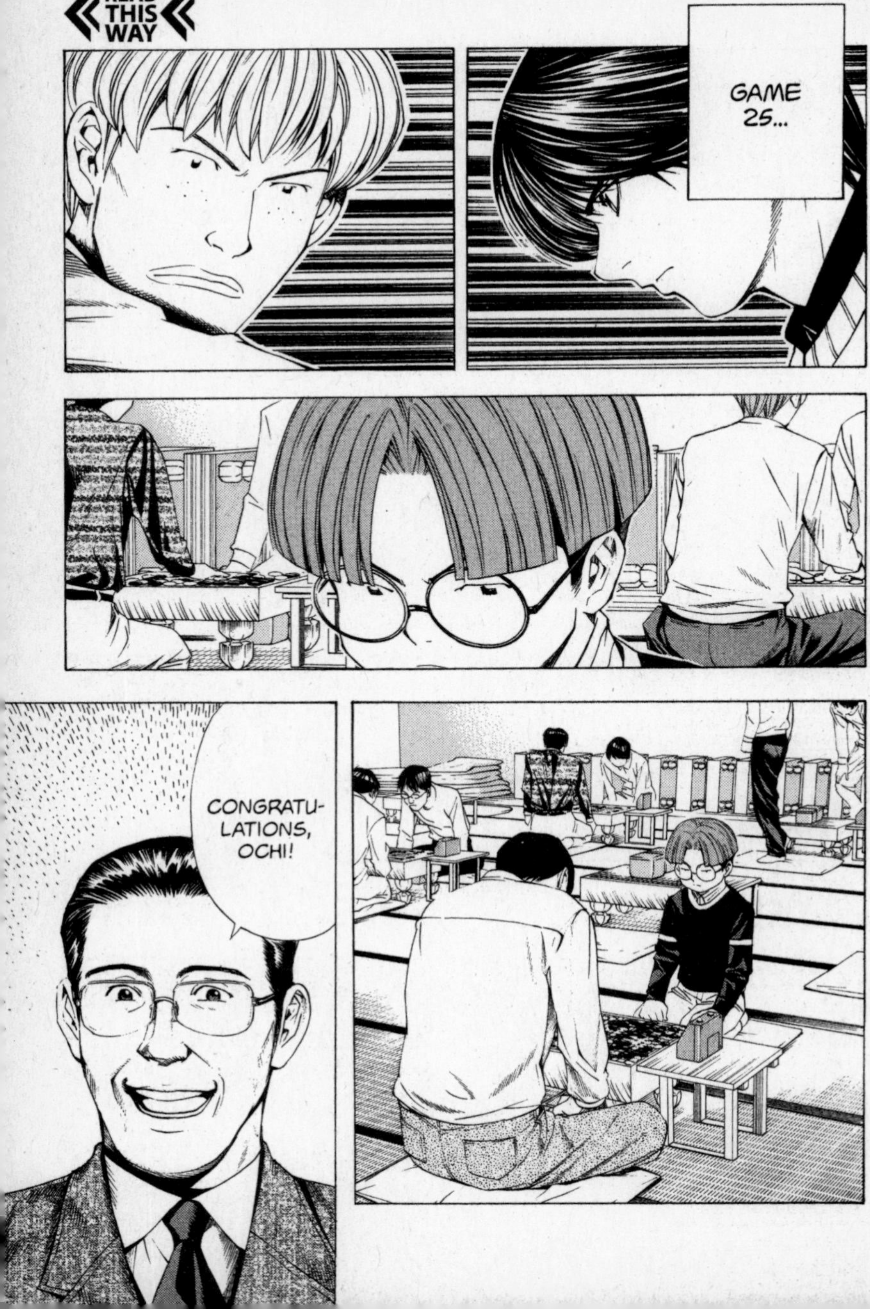
GAME 25...
CONGRATU-LATIONS, OCHI!

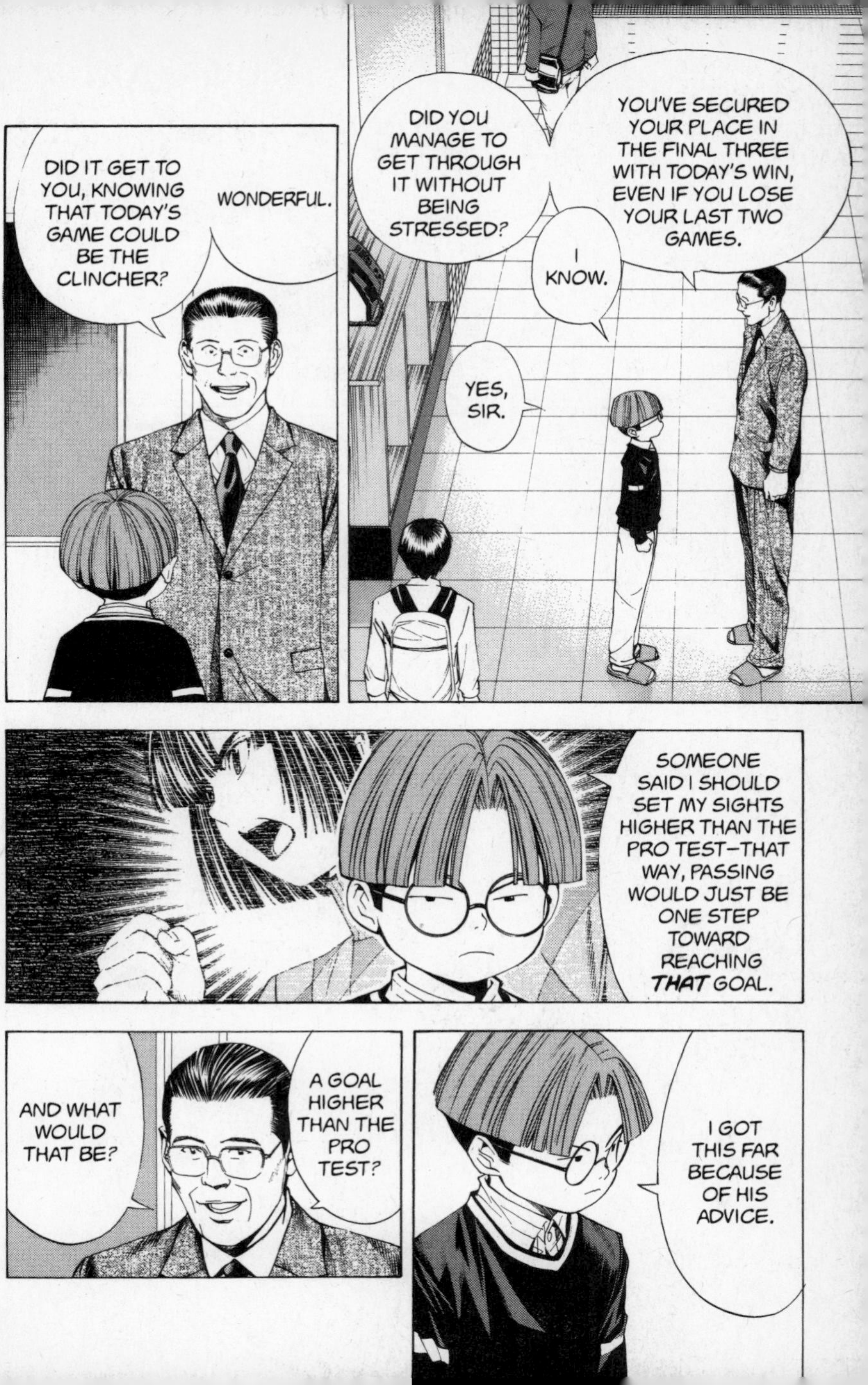
YOU'VE SECURED YOUR PLACE IN THE FINAL THREE WITH TODAY'S WIN, EVEN IF YOU LOSE YOUR LAST TWO GAMES.
DID YOU MANAGE TO GET THROUGH IT WITHOUT BEING STRESSED?
I KNOW.
YES, SIR.
WONDERFUL.
DID IT GET TO YOU, KNOWING THAT TODAY'S GAME COULD BE THE CLINCHER?
SOMEONE SAID I SHOULD SET MY SIGHTS HIGHER THAN THE PRO TEST—THAT WAY, PASSING WOULD JUST BE ONE STEP TOWARD REACHING *THAT* GOAL.
I GOT THIS FAR BECAUSE OF HIS ADVICE.
A GOAL HIGHER THAN THE PRO TEST?
AND WHAT WOULD THAT BE?

READ THIS WAY

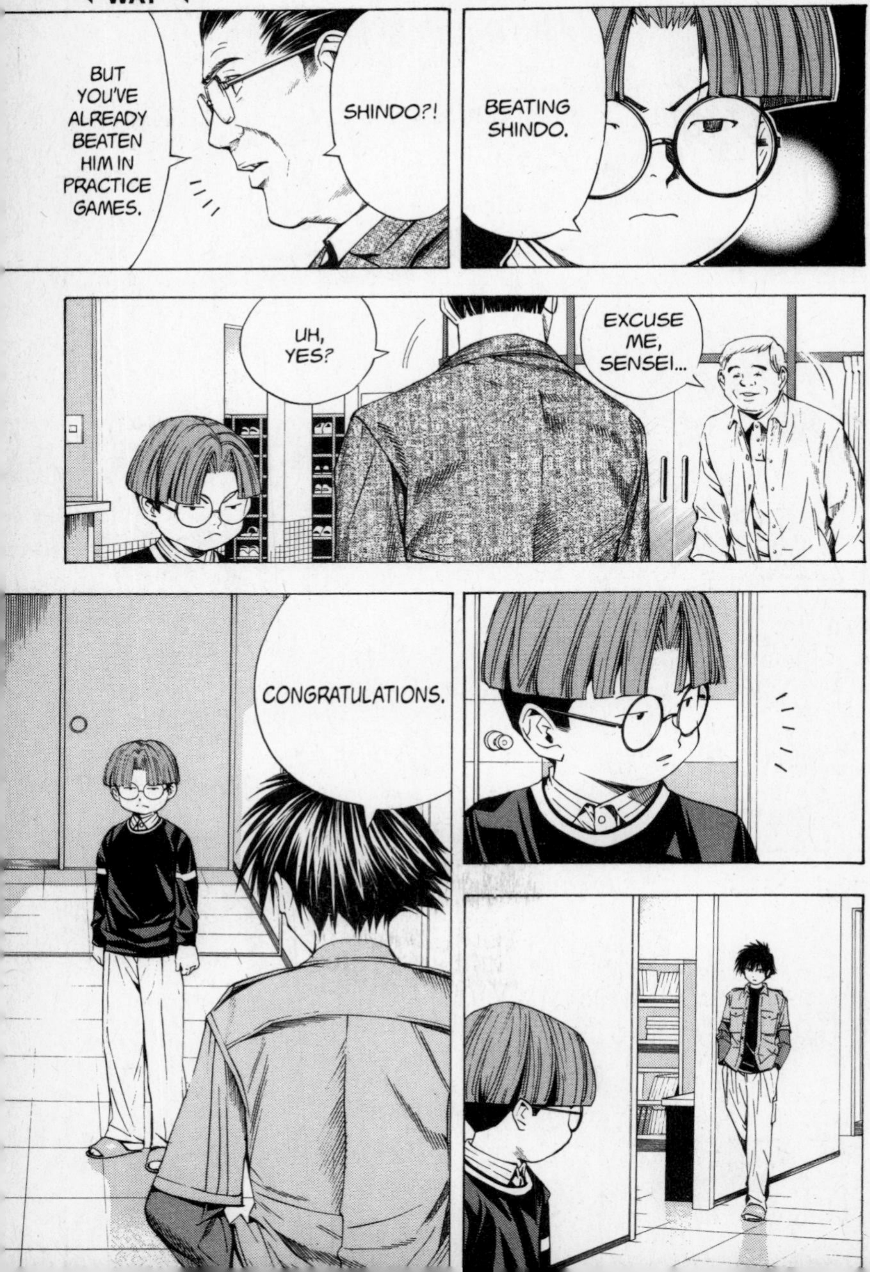
BEATING SHINDO.
SHINDO?!
BUT YOU'VE ALREADY BEATEN HIM IN PRACTICE GAMES.
EXCUSE ME, SENSEI...
UH, YES?
CONGRATULATIONS.

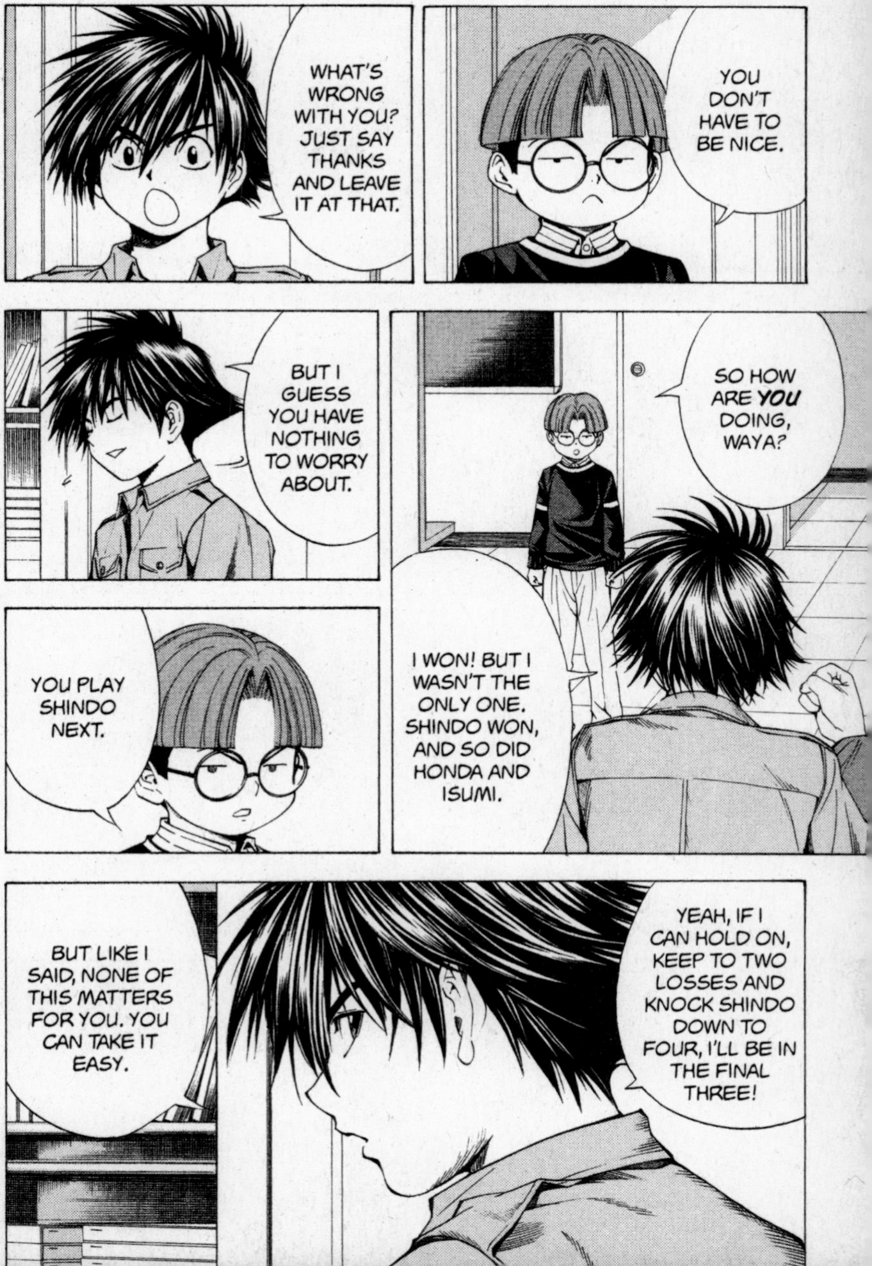
YOU DON'T HAVE TO BE NICE.
WHAT'S WRONG WITH YOU? JUST SAY THANKS AND LEAVE IT AT THAT.
SO HOW ARE *YOU* DOING, WAYA?
I WON! BUT I WASN'T THE ONLY ONE. SHINDO WON, AND SO DID HONDA AND ISUMI.
BUT I GUESS YOU HAVE NOTHING TO WORRY ABOUT.
YOU PLAY SHINDO NEXT.
YEAH, IF I CAN HOLD ON, KEEP TO TWO LOSSES AND KNOCK SHINDO DOWN TO FOUR, I'LL BE IN THE FINAL THREE!
BUT LIKE I SAID, NONE OF THIS MATTERS FOR YOU. YOU CAN TAKE IT EASY.

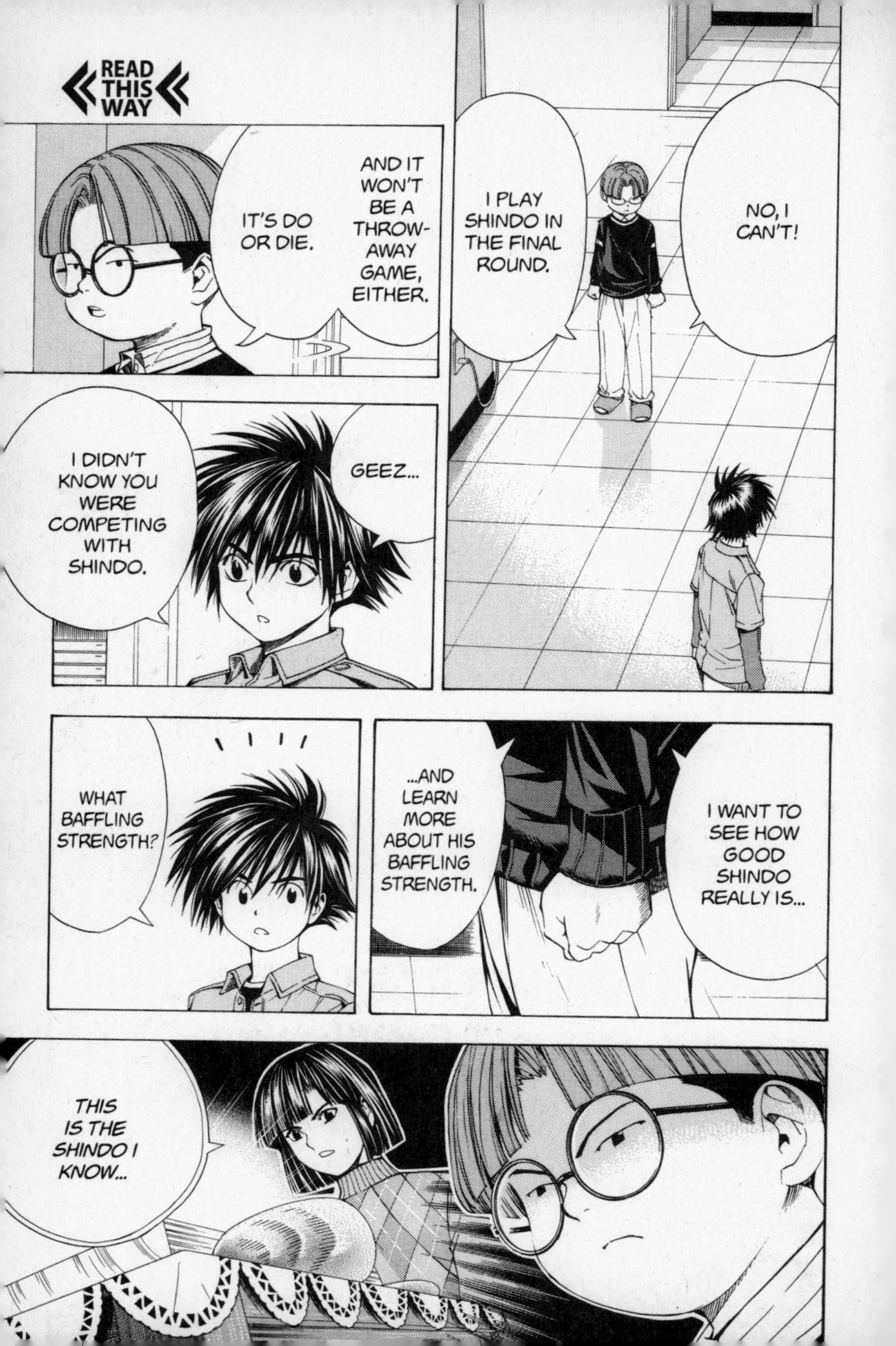
READ THIS WAY
NO, I CAN'T!
I PLAY SHINDO IN THE FINAL ROUND.
AND IT WON'T BE A THROW-AWAY GAME, EITHER.
IT'S DO OR DIE.
GEEZ...
I DIDN'T KNOW YOU WERE COMPETING WITH SHINDO.
I WANT TO SEE HOW GOOD SHINDO REALLY IS...
...AND LEARN MORE ABOUT HIS BAFFLING STRENGTH.
WHAT BAFFLING STRENGTH?
THIS IS THE SHINDO I KNOW...

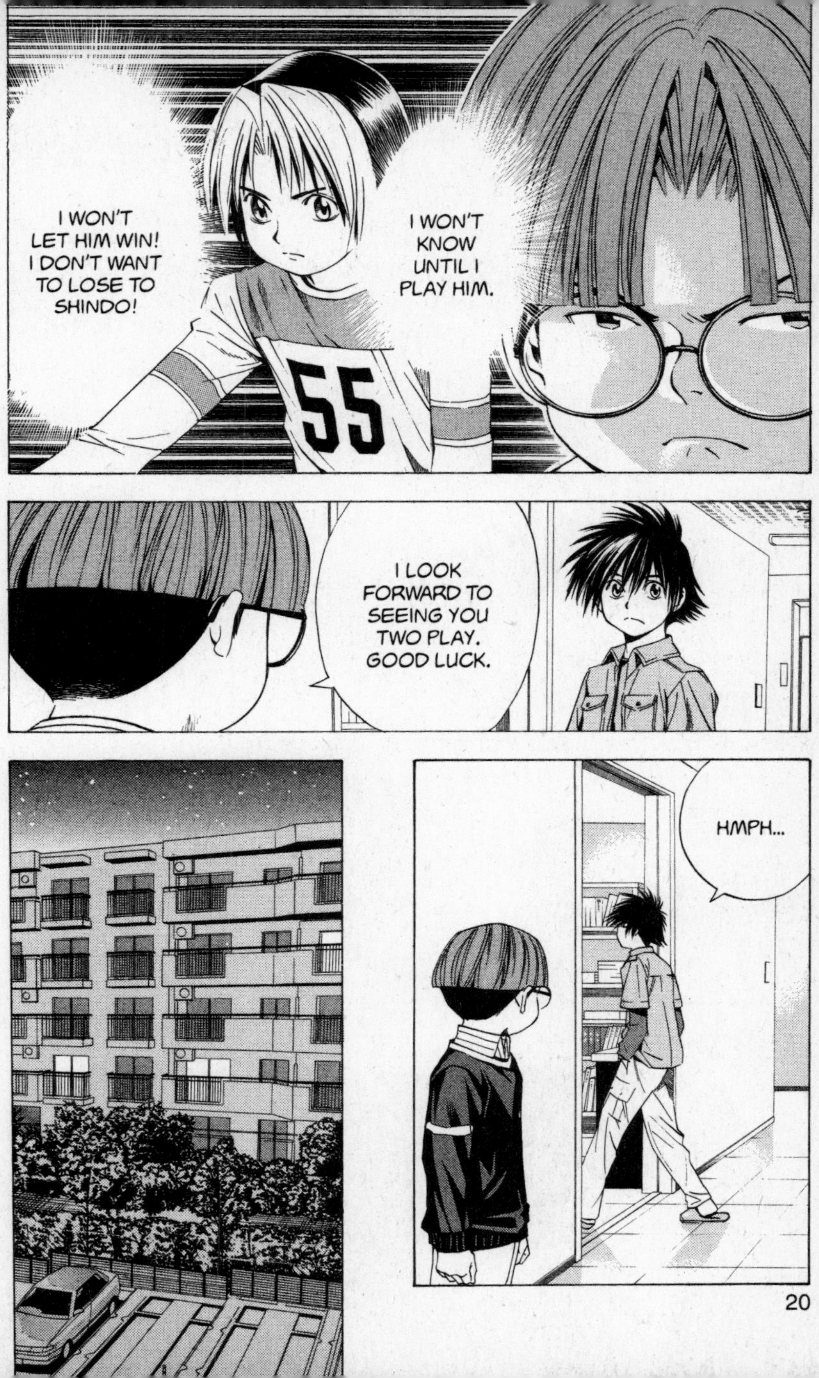
I WON'T KNOW UNTIL I PLAY HIM.
I WON'T LET HIM WIN! I DON'T WANT TO LOSE TO SHINDO!
I LOOK FORWARD TO SEEING YOU TWO PLAY. GOOD LUCK.
HMPH...

READ THIS WAY

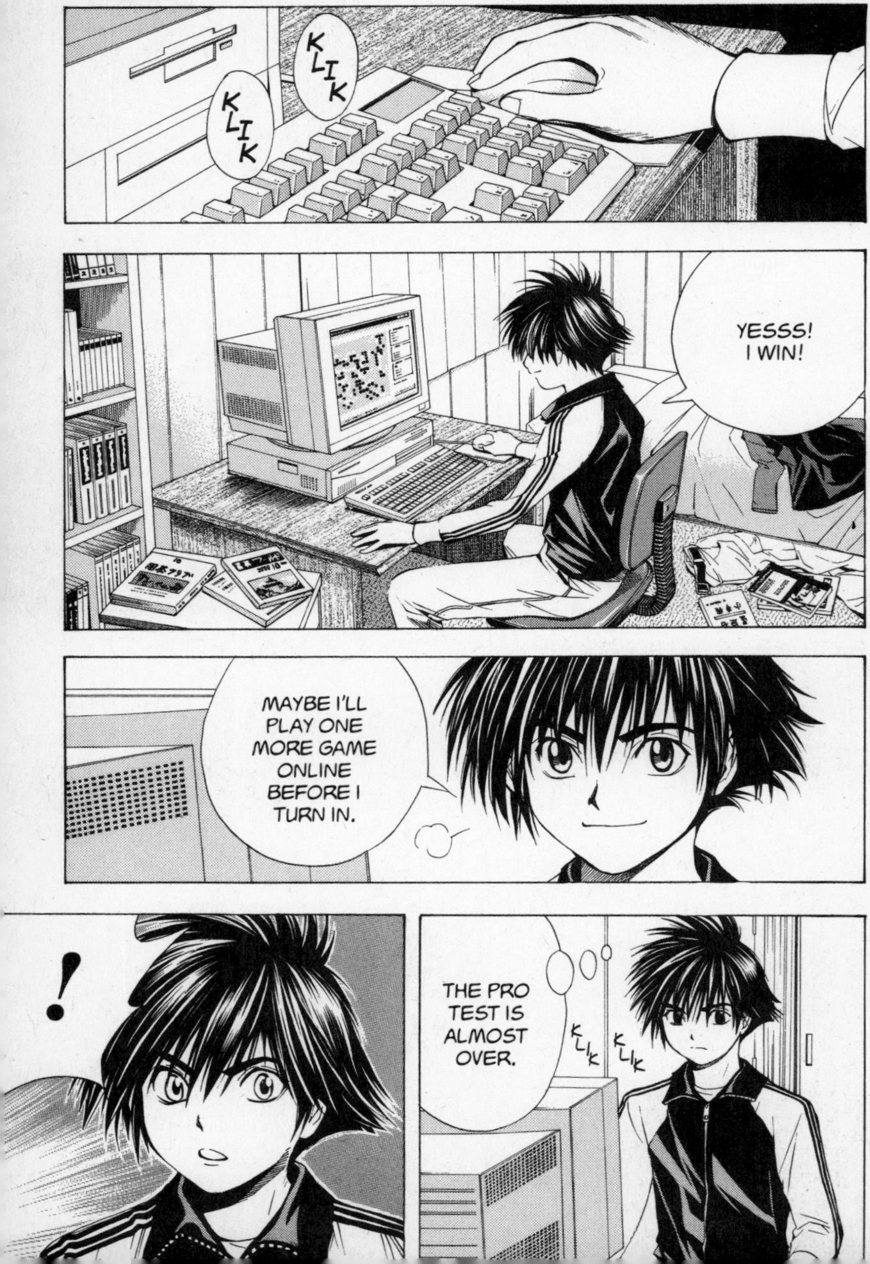
KLIK
KLIK
YESSS! I WIN!
MAYBE I'LL PLAY ONE MORE GAME ONLINE BEFORE I TURN IN.
THE PRO TEST IS ALMOST OVER.
KLIK
KLIK
!

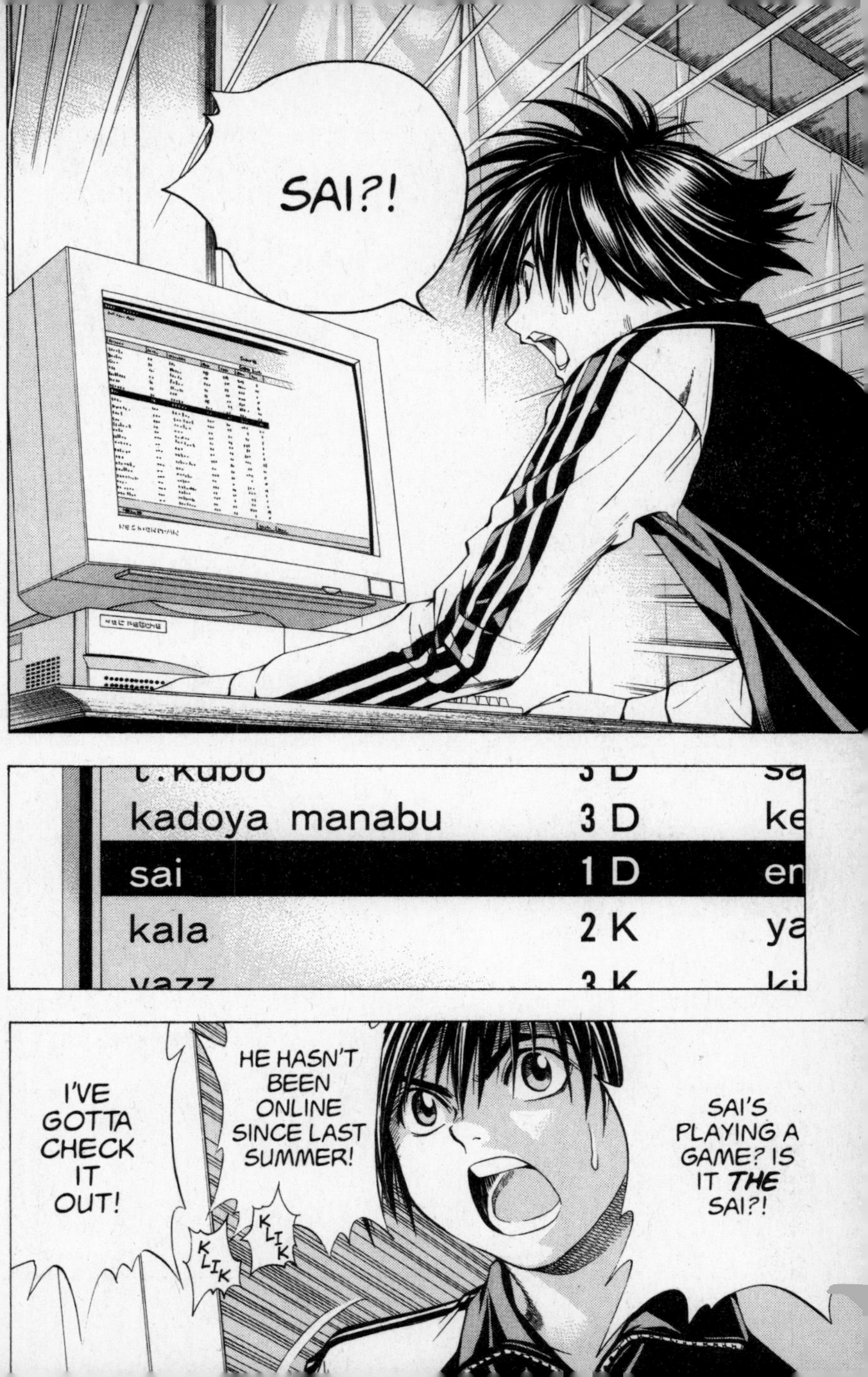
SAI?!
kadoya manabu 3 D
sai 1 D
kala 2 K
SAI'S PLAYING A GAME? IS IT *THE* SAI?!
HE HASN'T BEEN ONLINE SINCE LAST SUMMER!
KLIK
KLIK
I'VE GOTTA CHECK IT OUT!

READ THIS WAY

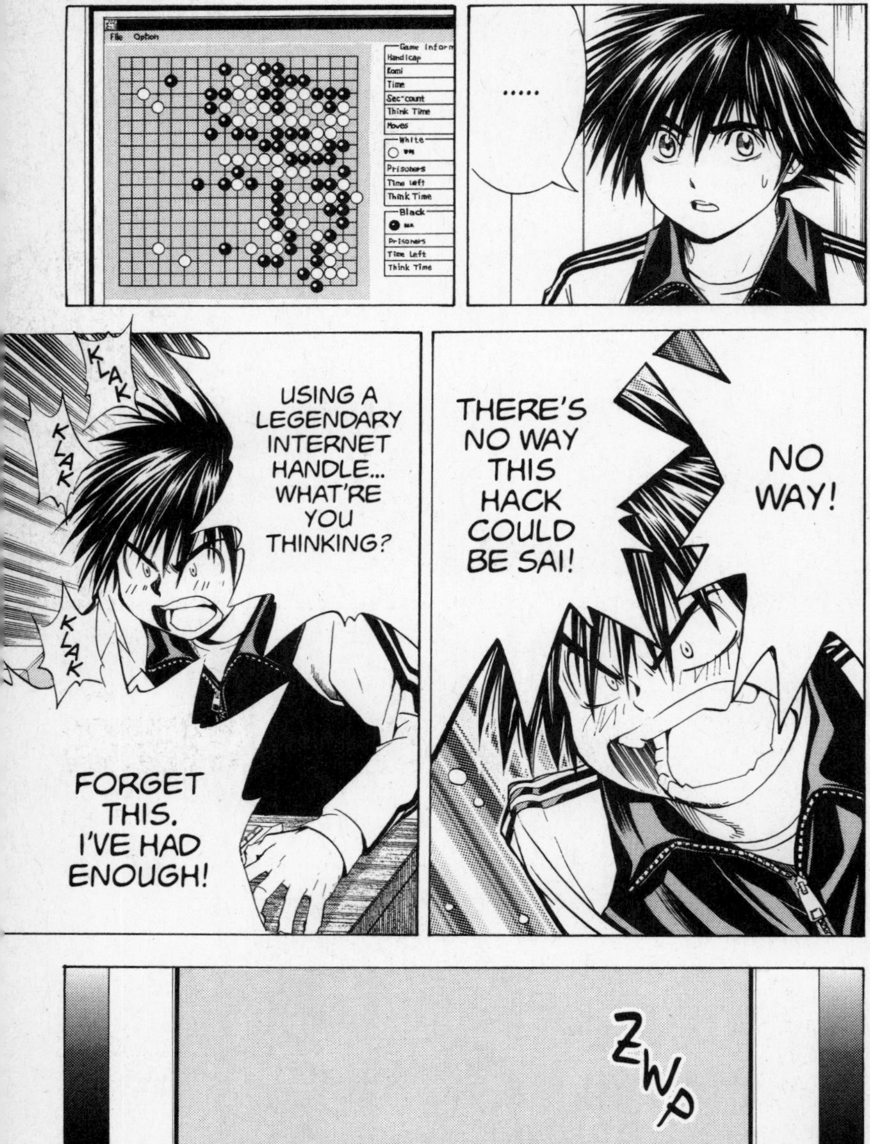
.....
File Option
Game Inform
Handicap
Komi
Time
Sec-count
Think Time
Moves
White
Prisoners
Time left
Think Time
Black
Prisoners
Time Left
Think Time
NO WAY!
THERE'S NO WAY THIS HACK COULD BE SAI!
KLAK KLAK KLAK
USING A LEGENDARY INTERNET HANDLE... WHAT'RE YOU THINKING?
FORGET THIS. I'VE HAD ENOUGH!
ZWP

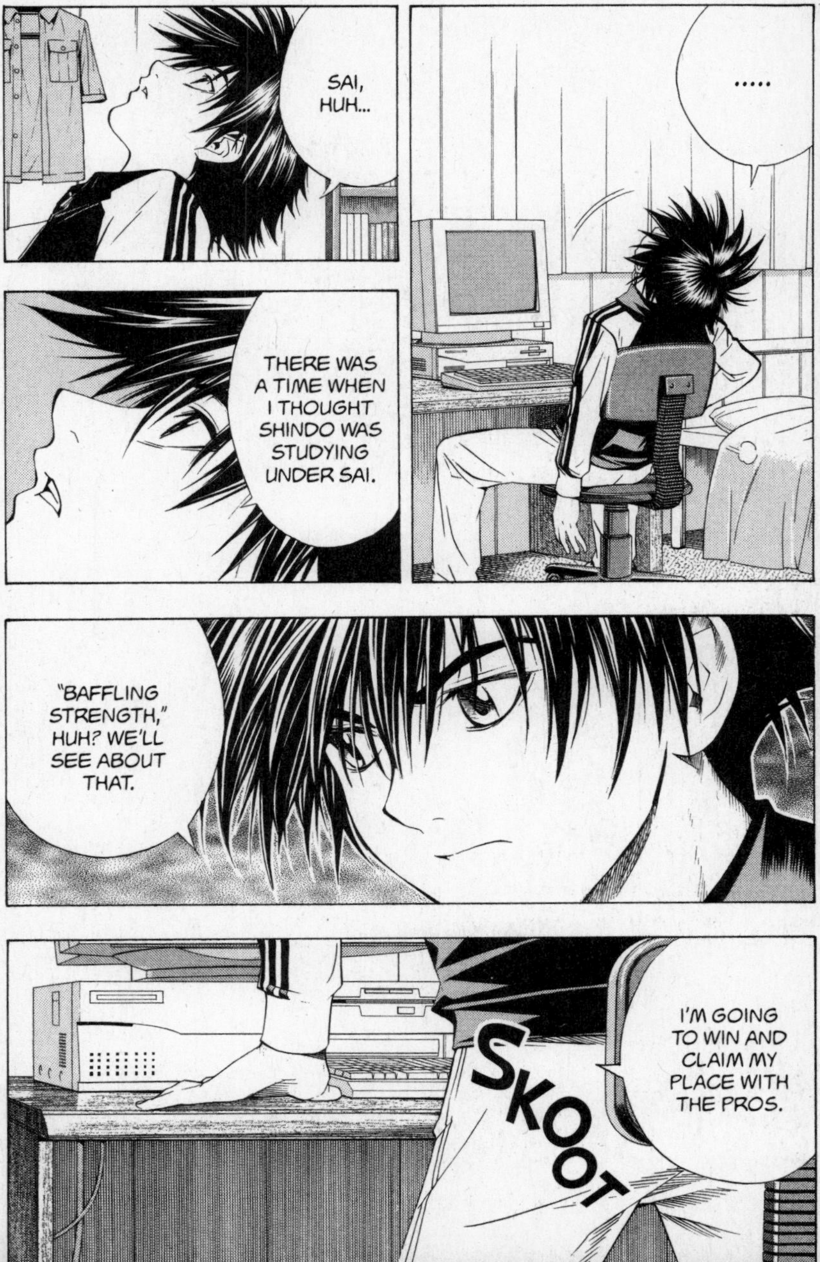
.....
SAI, HUH...
THERE WAS A TIME WHEN I THOUGHT SHINDO WAS STUDYING UNDER SAI.
"BAFFLING STRENGTH," HUH? WE'LL SEE ABOUT THAT.
I'M GOING TO WIN AND CLAIM MY PLACE WITH THE PROS.
SKOOT

READ THIS WAY

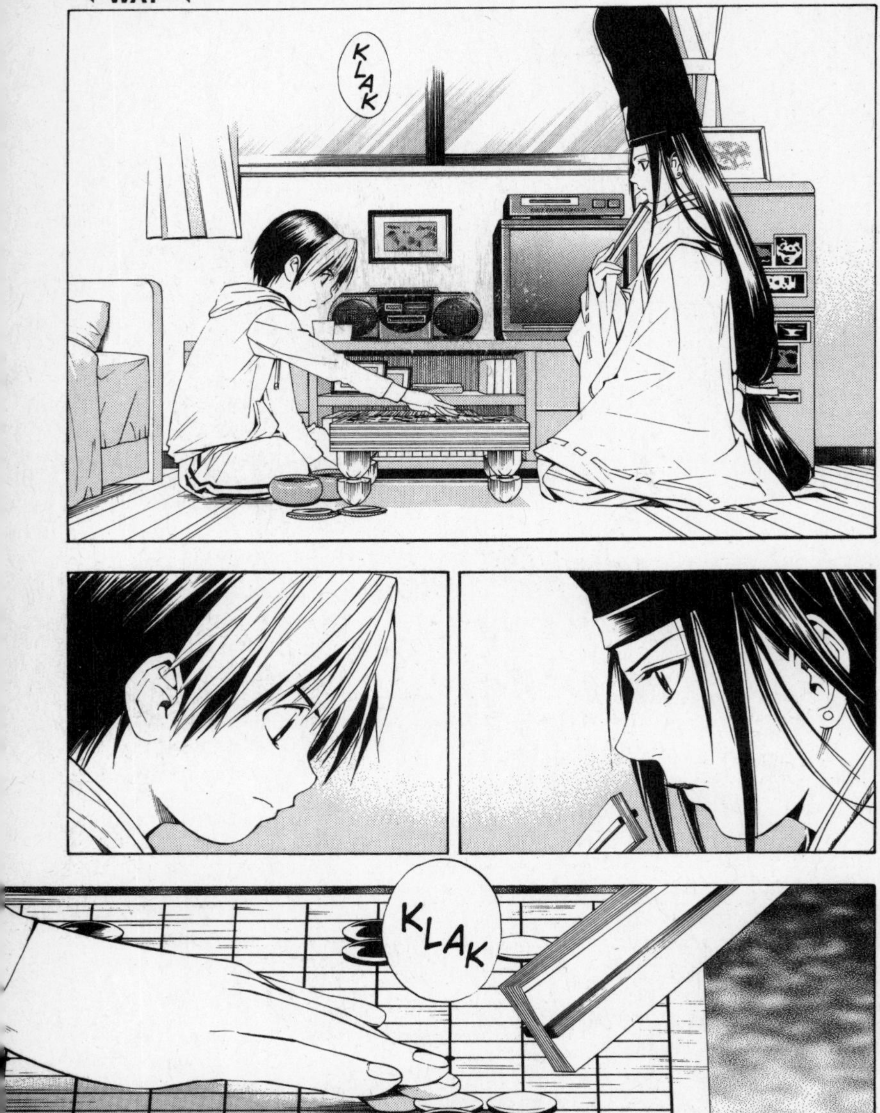
KLAK
KLAK

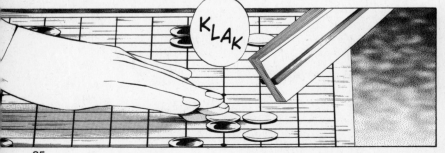

HIKARU NO GO STORYBOARDS

㉙

YUMI HOTTA

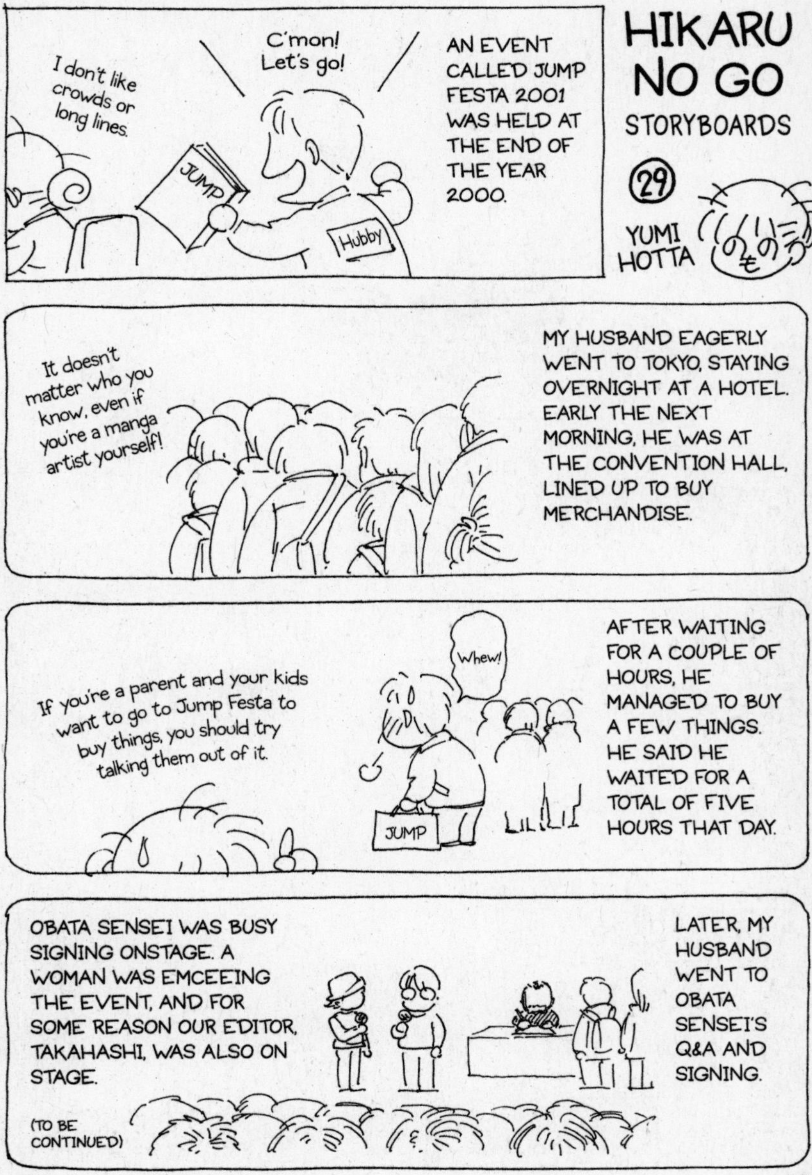
AN EVENT CALLED JUMP FESTA 2001 WAS HELD AT THE END OF THE YEAR 2000.
C'mon! Let's go!
JUMP
Hubby
I don't like crowds or long lines.
MY HUSBAND EAGERLY WENT TO TOKYO, STAYING OVERNIGHT AT A HOTEL. EARLY THE NEXT MORNING, HE WAS AT THE CONVENTION HALL, LINED UP TO BUY MERCHANDISE.
It doesn't matter who you know, even if you're a manga artist yourself!
AFTER WAITING FOR A COUPLE OF HOURS, HE MANAGED TO BUY A FEW THINGS. HE SAID HE WAITED FOR A TOTAL OF FIVE HOURS THAT DAY.
Whew!
JUMP
If you're a parent and your kids want to go to Jump Festa to buy things, you should try talking them out of it.
LATER, MY HUSBAND WENT TO OBATA SENSEI'S Q&A AND SIGNING.
OBATA SENSEI WAS BUSY SIGNING ONSTAGE. A WOMAN WAS EMCEEING THE EVENT, AND FOR SOME REASON OUR EDITOR, TAKAHASHI, WAS ALSO ON STAGE.
(TO BE CONTINUED)

Game 89 "Together Always"

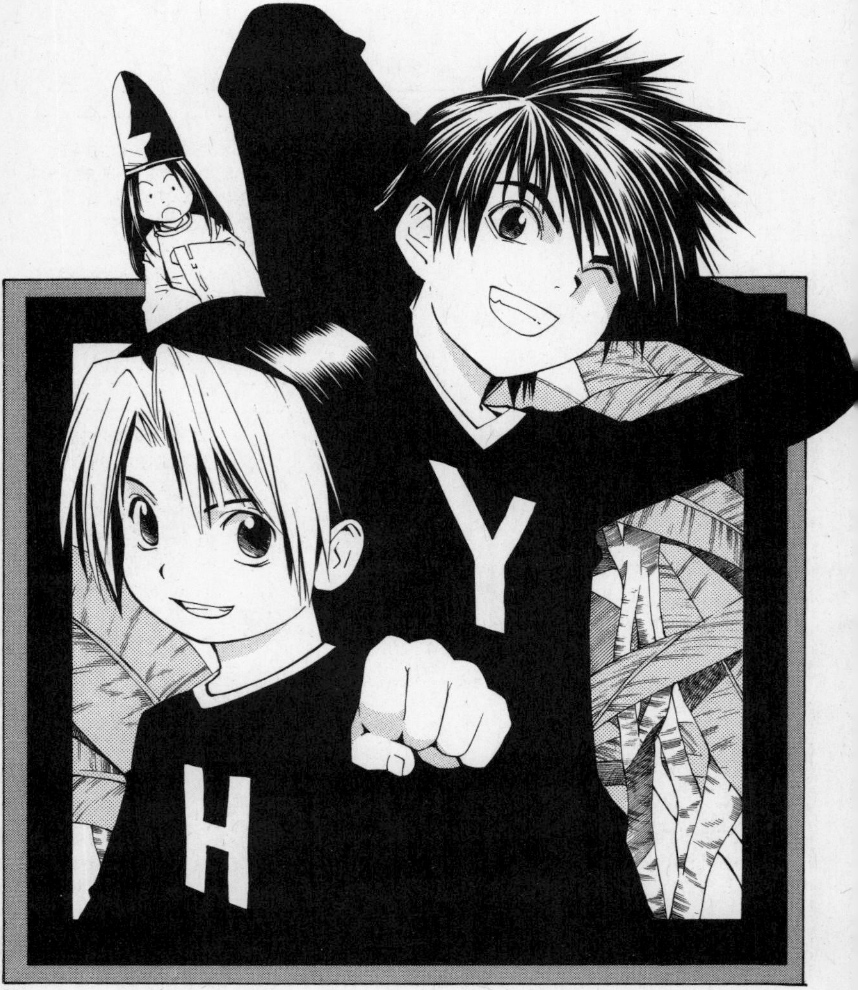

Y
H

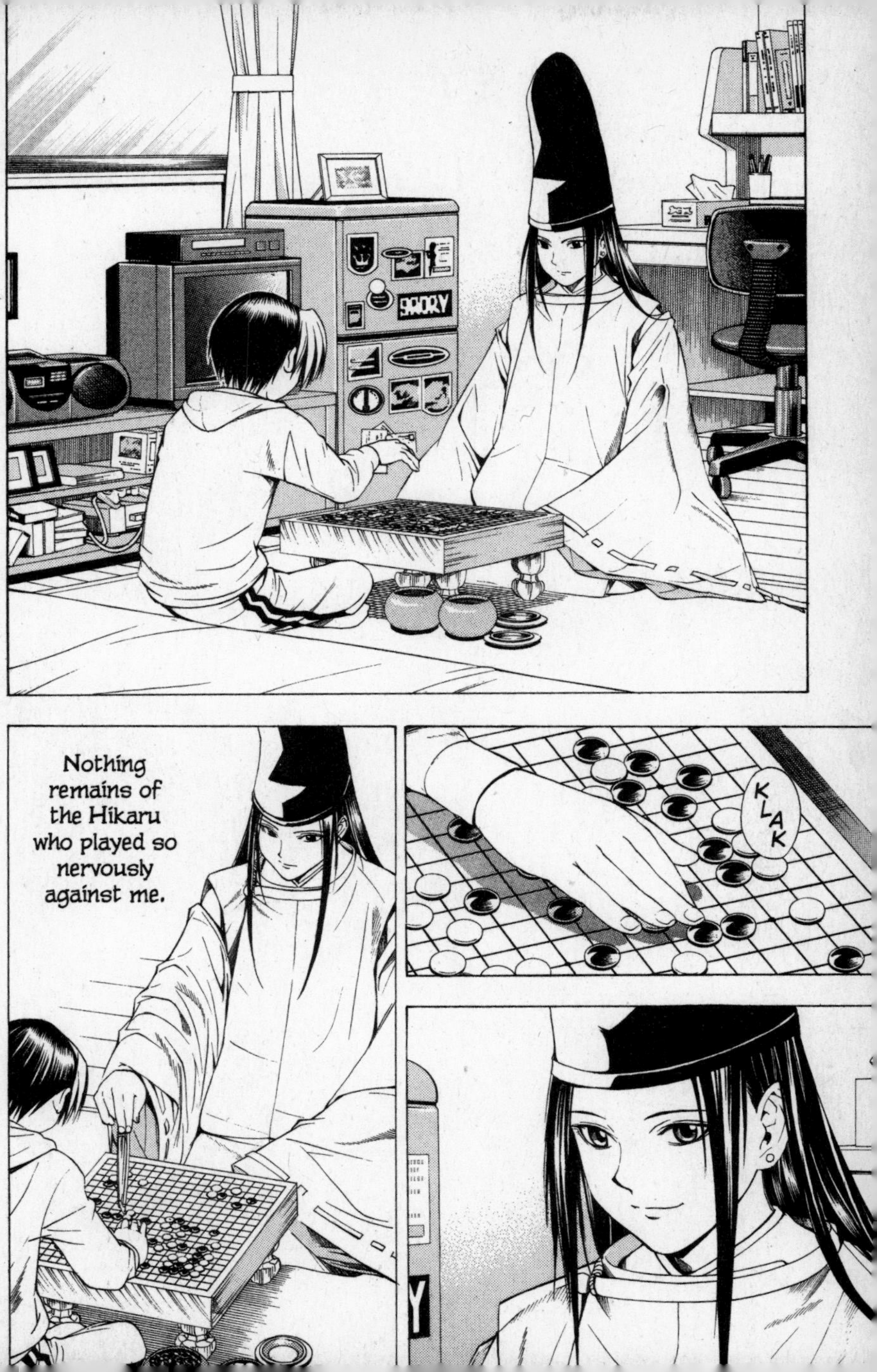
KLAK
Nothing remains of the Hikaru who played so nervously against me.

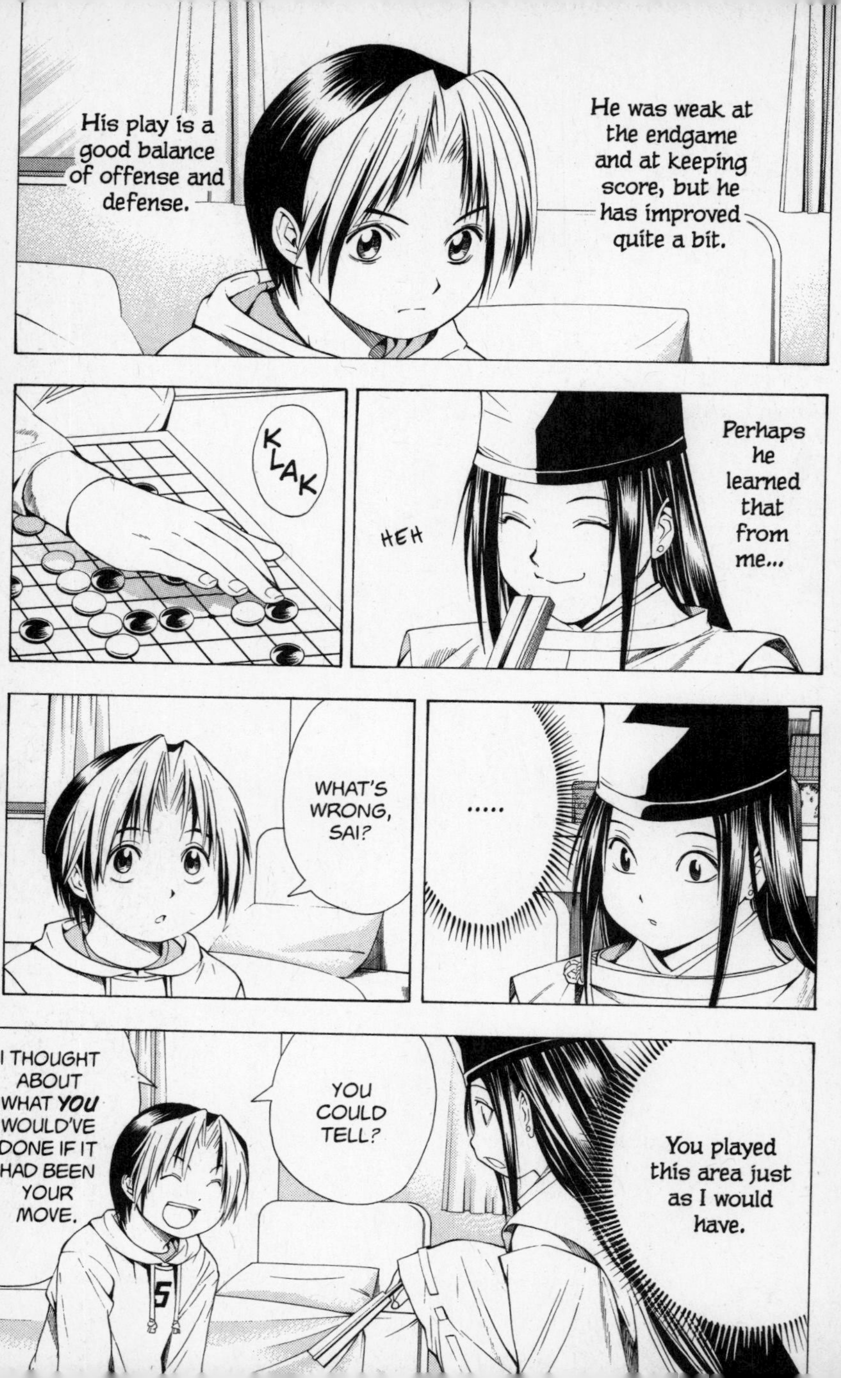
He was weak at the endgame and at keeping score, but he has improved quite a bit.
His play is a good balance of offense and defense.
Perhaps he learned that from me...
HEH
KLAK
.....
WHAT'S WRONG, SAI?
You played this area just as I would have.
YOU COULD TELL?
I THOUGHT ABOUT WHAT YOU WOULD'VE DONE IF IT HAD BEEN YOUR MOVE.

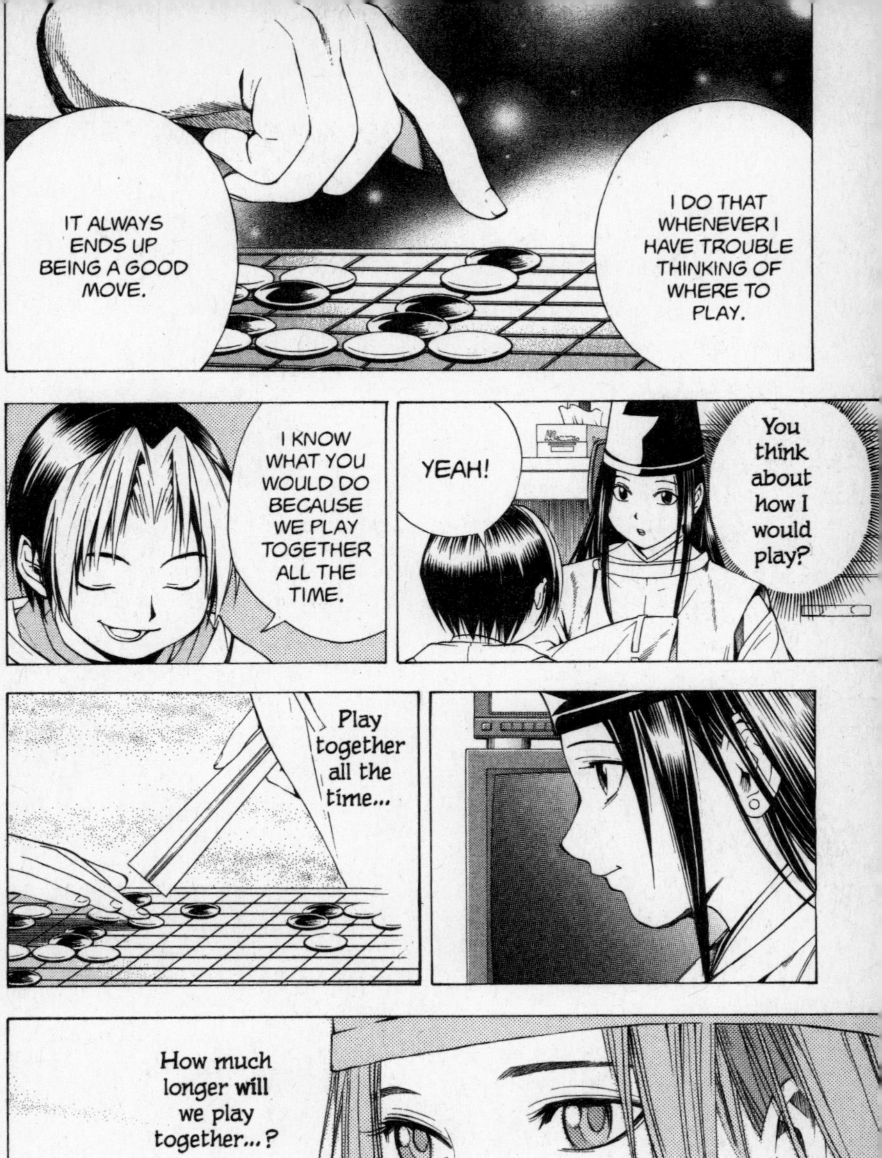
I DO THAT WHENEVER I HAVE TROUBLE THINKING OF WHERE TO PLAY.
IT ALWAYS ENDS UP BEING A GOOD MOVE.
You think about how I would play?
YEAH!
I KNOW WHAT YOU WOULD DO BECAUSE WE PLAY TOGETHER ALL THE TIME.
Play together all the time...
How much longer will we play together...?

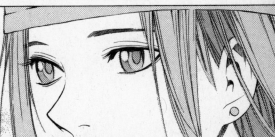

READ THIS WAY

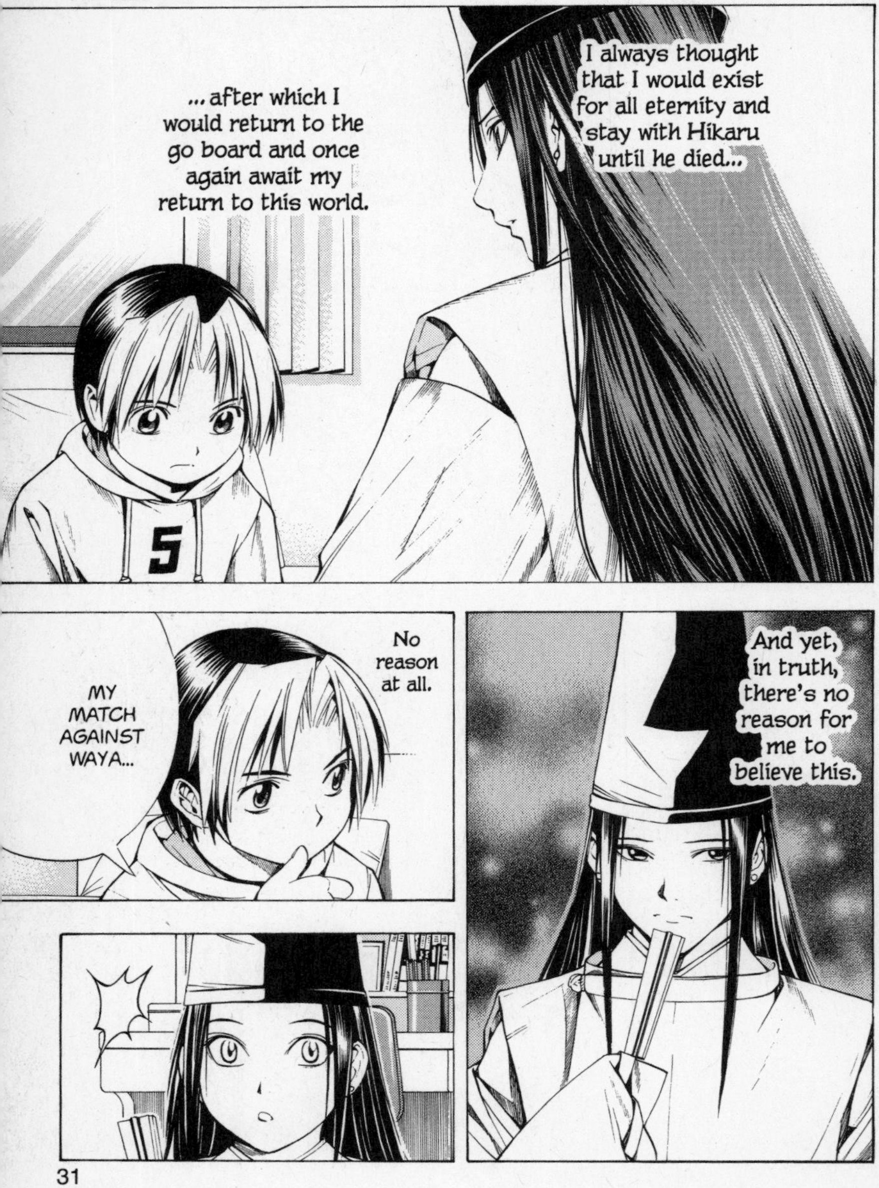
I always thought that I would exist for all eternity and stay with Hikaru until he died...
...after which I would return to the go board and once again await my return to this world.
And yet, in truth, there's no reason for me to believe this.
No reason at all.
MY MATCH AGAINST WAYA...

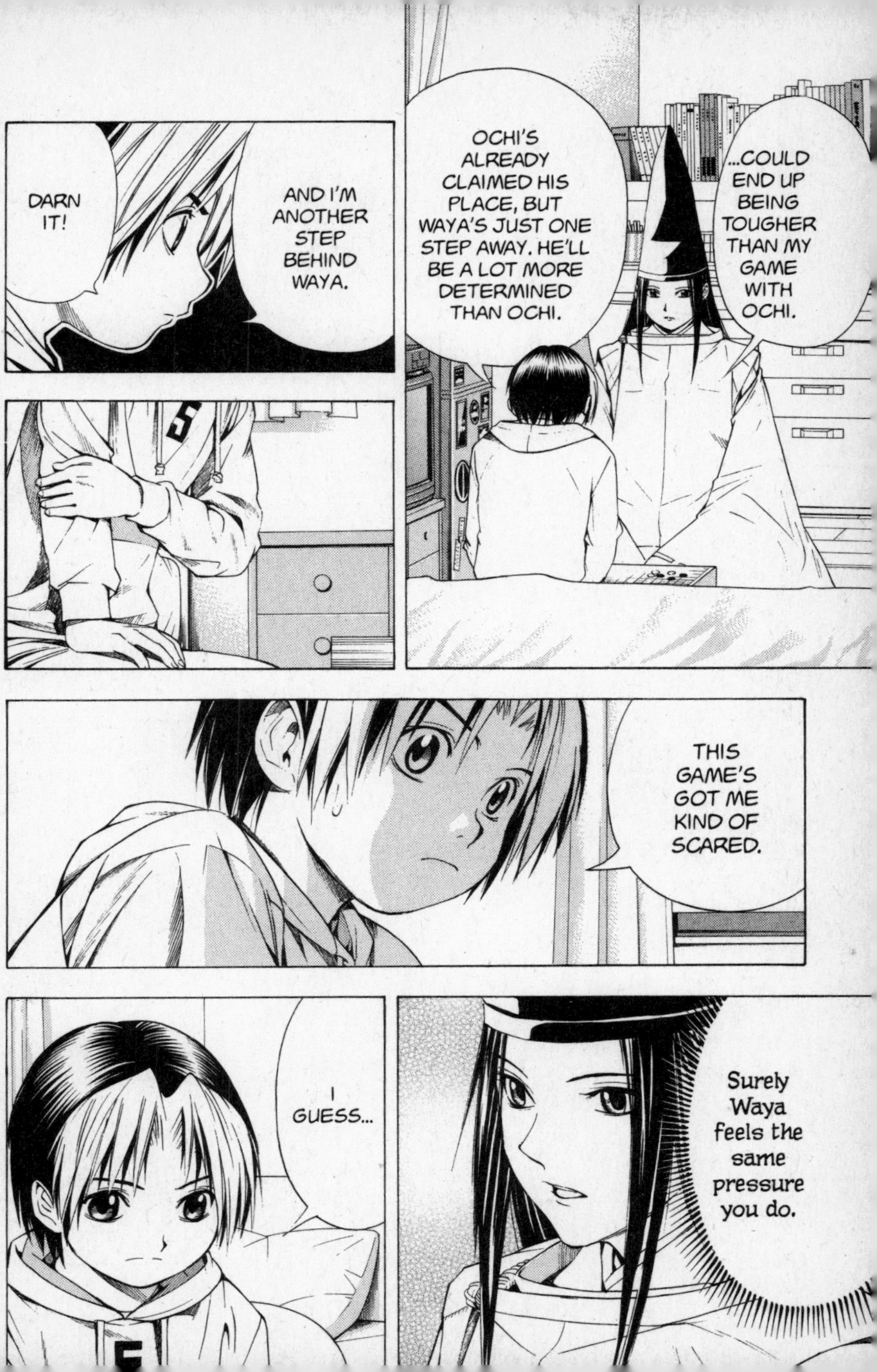
...COULD END UP BEING TOUGHER THAN MY GAME WITH OCHI.
OCHI'S ALREADY CLAIMED HIS PLACE, BUT WAYA'S JUST ONE STEP AWAY. HE'LL BE A LOT MORE DETERMINED THAN OCHI.
AND I'M ANOTHER STEP BEHIND WAYA.
DARN IT!
THIS GAME'S GOT ME KIND OF SCARED.
Surely Waya feels the same pressure you do.
I GUESS...

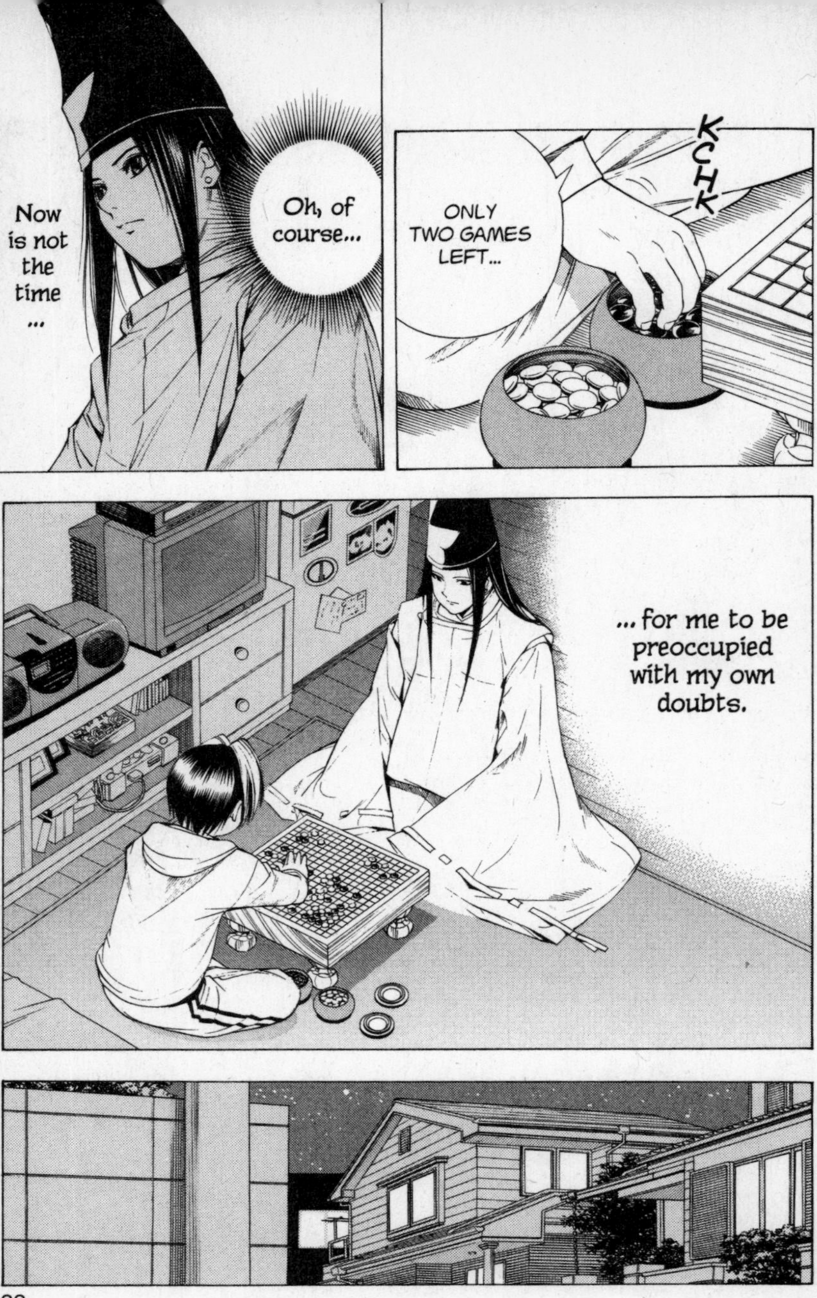
KCHK
ONLY TWO GAMES LEFT...
Oh, of course...
Now is not the time ...
... for me to be preoccupied with my own doubts.

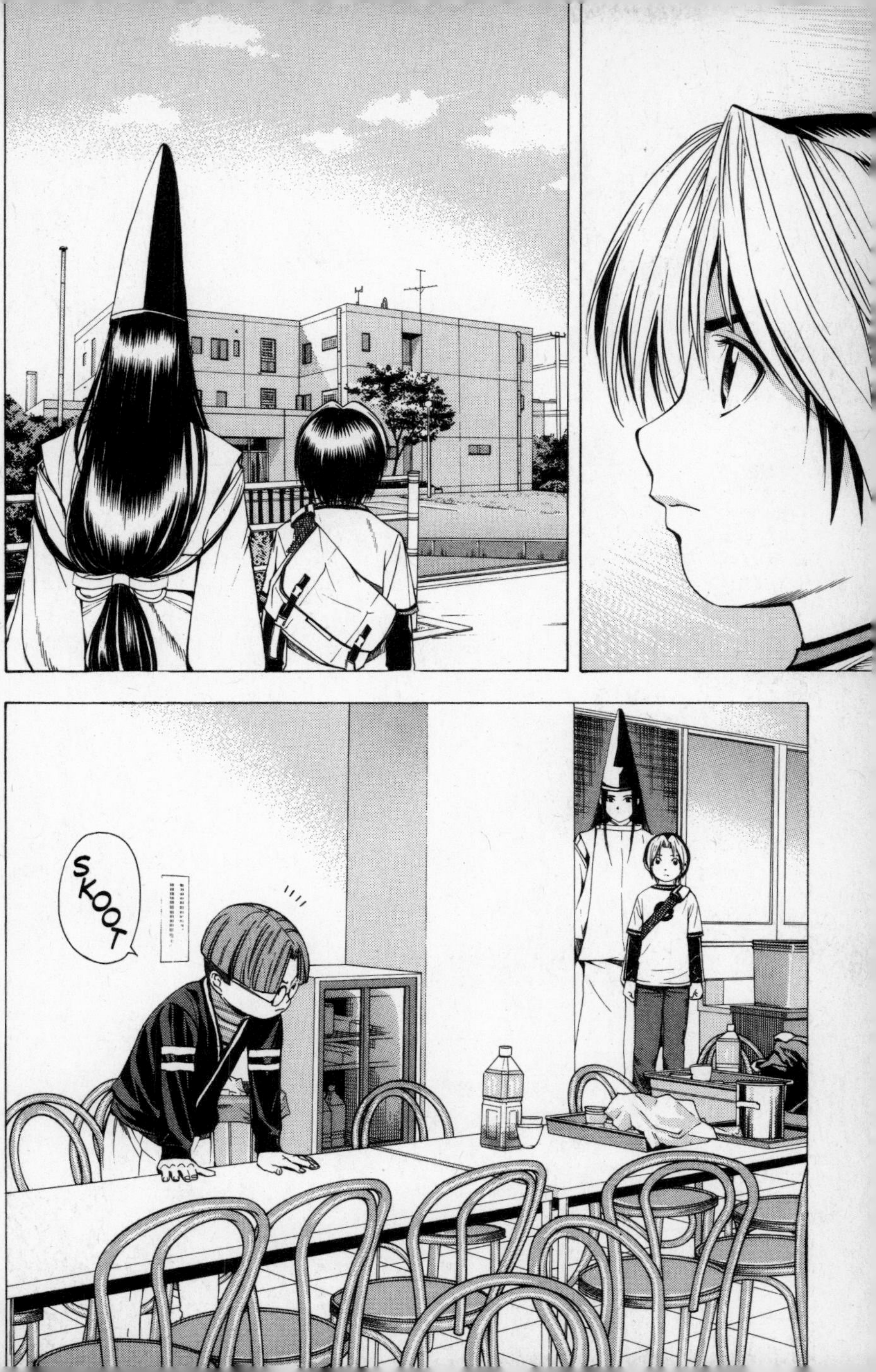
SKOOT

READ THIS WAY

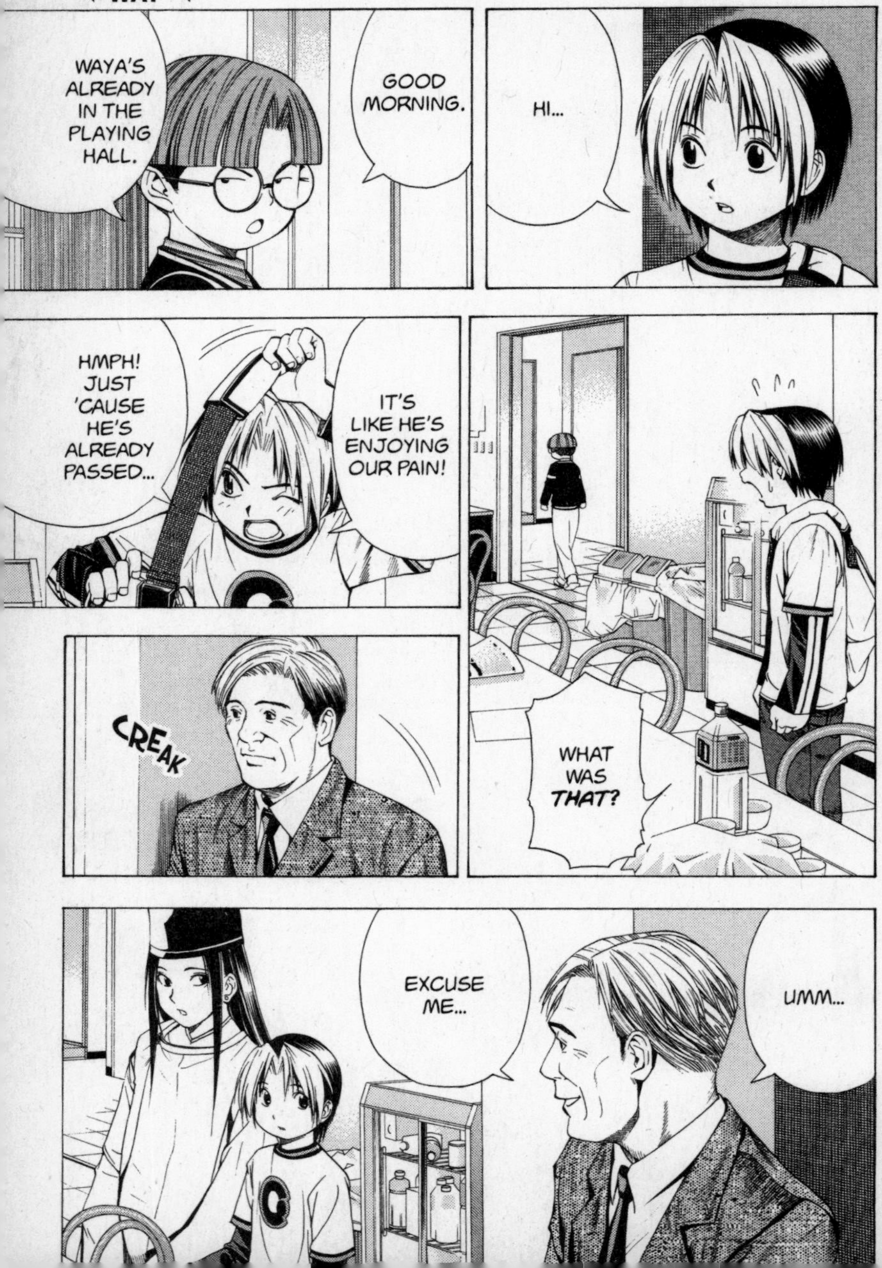
HI...
GOOD MORNING.
WAYA'S ALREADY IN THE PLAYING HALL.
WHAT WAS THAT?
IT'S LIKE HE'S ENJOYING OUR PAIN!
HMPH! JUST 'CAUSE HE'S ALREADY PASSED...
CREAK
UMM...
EXCUSE ME...

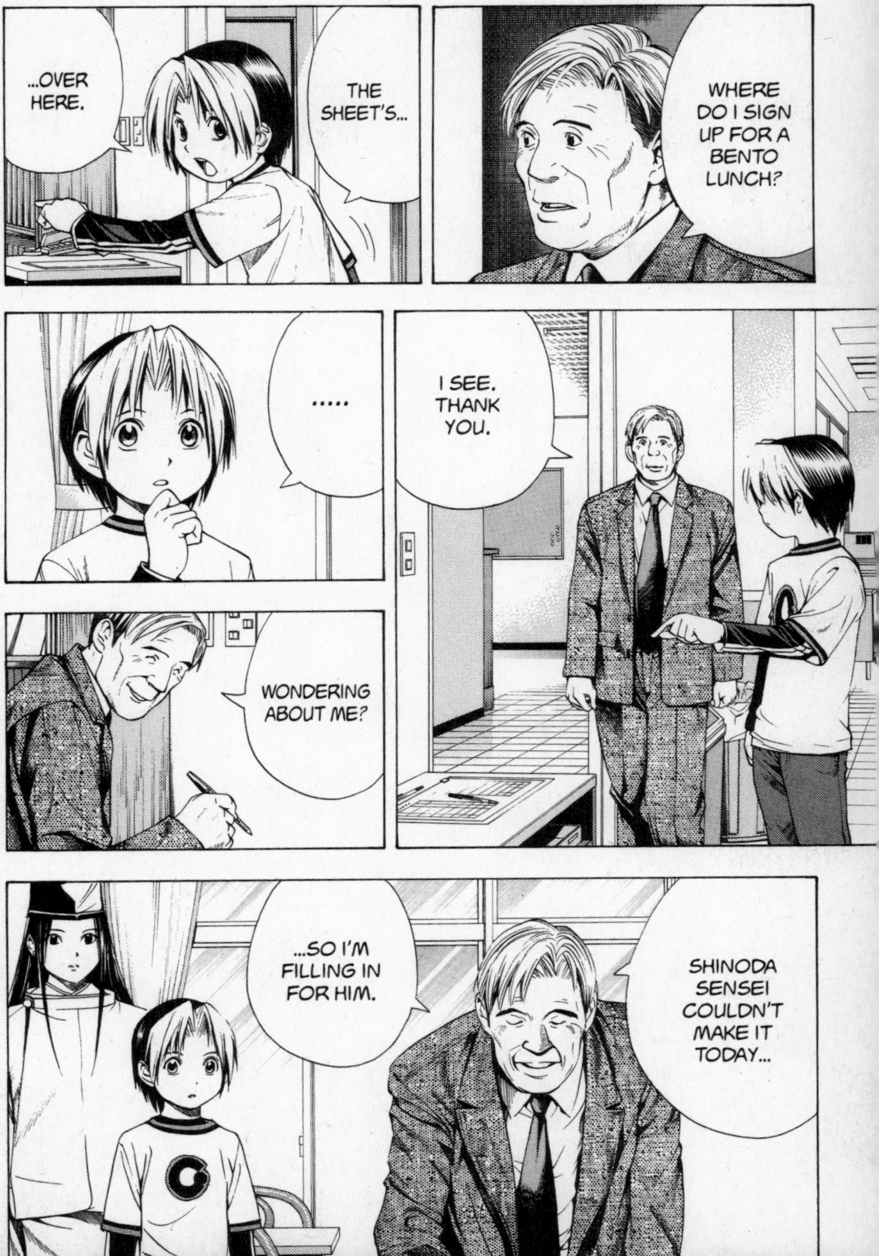
WHERE DO I SIGN UP FOR A BENTO LUNCH?
THE SHEET'S...
...OVER HERE.
I SEE. THANK YOU.
.....
WONDERING ABOUT ME?
SHINODA SENSEI COULDN'T MAKE IT TODAY...
...SO I'M FILLING IN FOR HIM.

READ THIS WAY

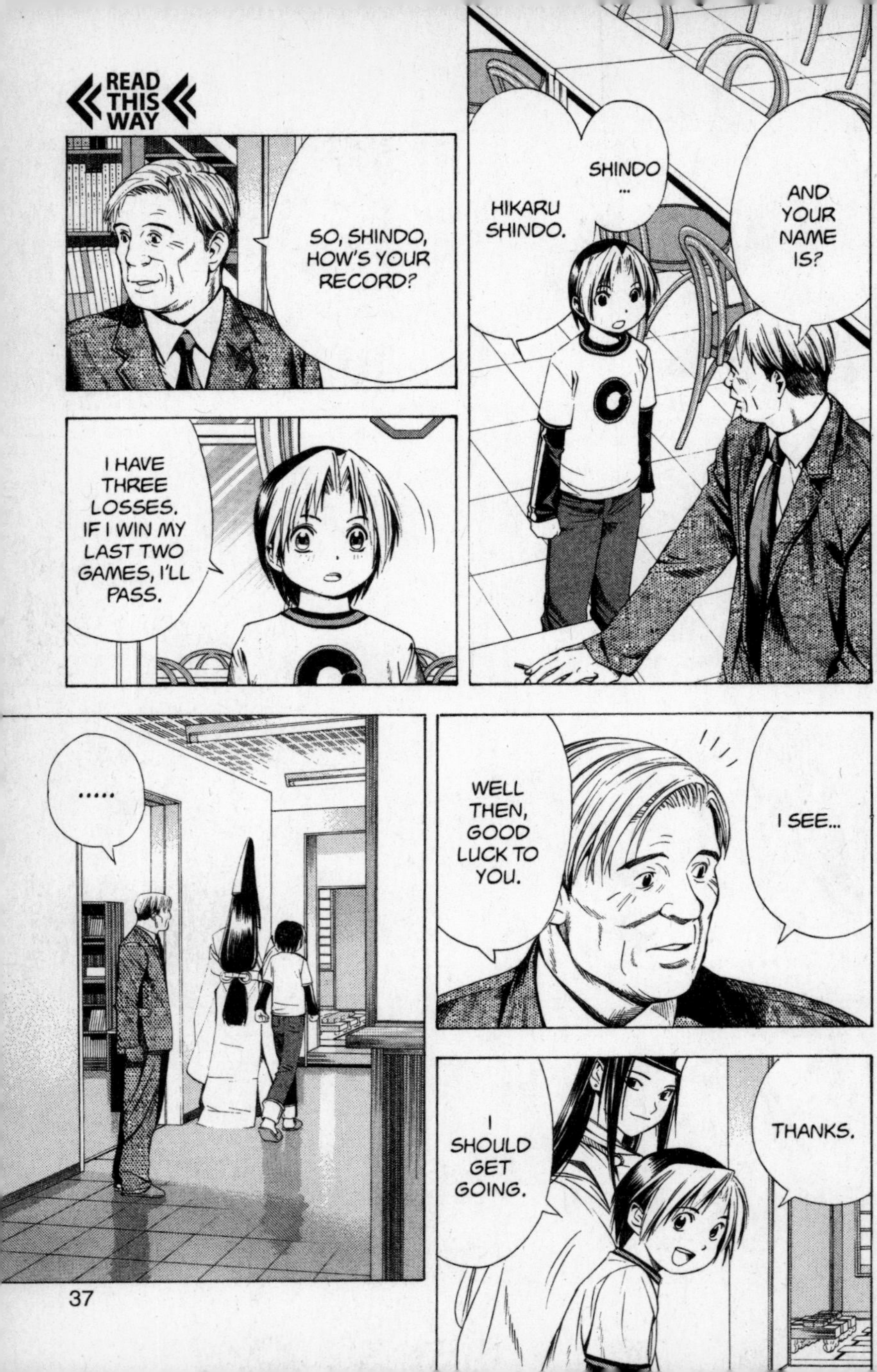
AND YOUR NAME IS?
SHINDO ...
HIKARU SHINDO.
SO, SHINDO, HOW'S YOUR RECORD?
I HAVE THREE LOSSES. IF I WIN MY LAST TWO GAMES, I'LL PASS.
I SEE...
WELL THEN, GOOD LUCK TO YOU.
THANKS.
I SHOULD GET GOING.
.....

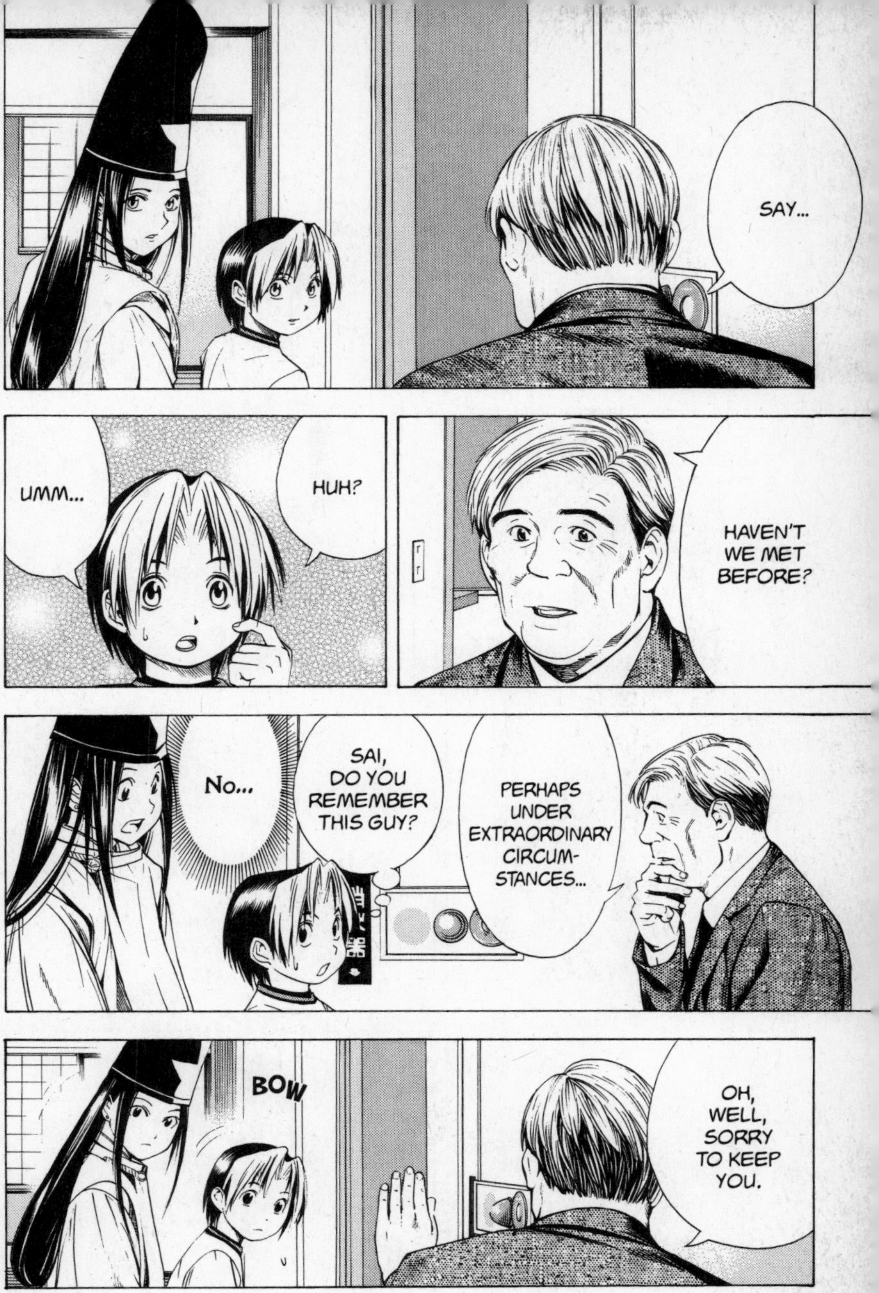
SAY...
HAVEN'T WE MET BEFORE?
HUH?
UMM...
PERHAPS UNDER EXTRAORDINARY CIRCUM-STANCES...
SAI, DO YOU REMEMBER THIS GUY?
No...
OH, WELL, SORRY TO KEEP YOU.
BOW

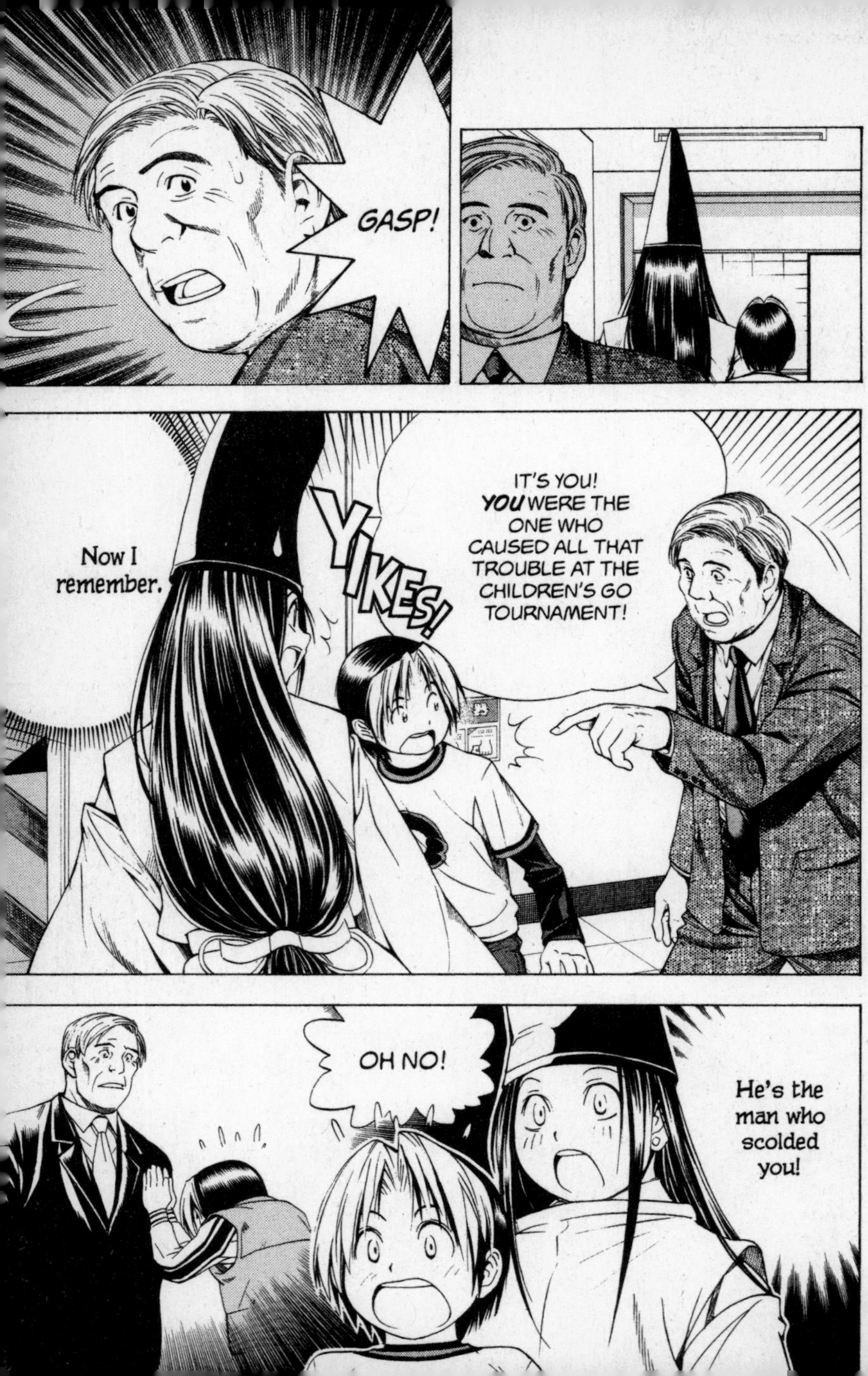
GASP!
IT'S YOU! YOU WERE THE ONE WHO CAUSED ALL THAT TROUBLE AT THE CHILDREN'S GO TOURNAMENT!
YIKES!
Now I remember.
He's the man who scolded you!
OH NO!

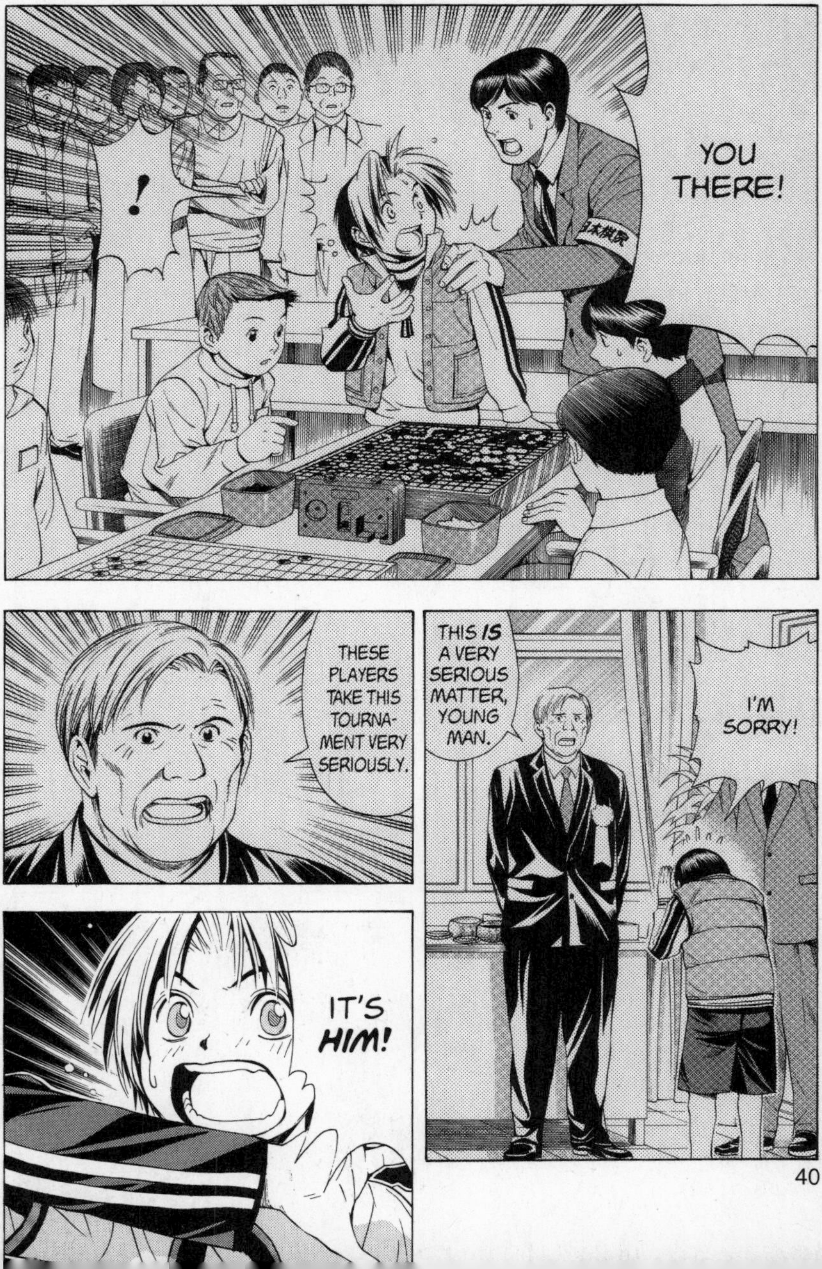
YOU THERE!
!
THIS *IS* A VERY SERIOUS MATTER, YOUNG MAN.
I'M SORRY!
THESE PLAYERS TAKE THIS TOURNAMENT VERY SERIOUSLY.
IT'S *HIM!*

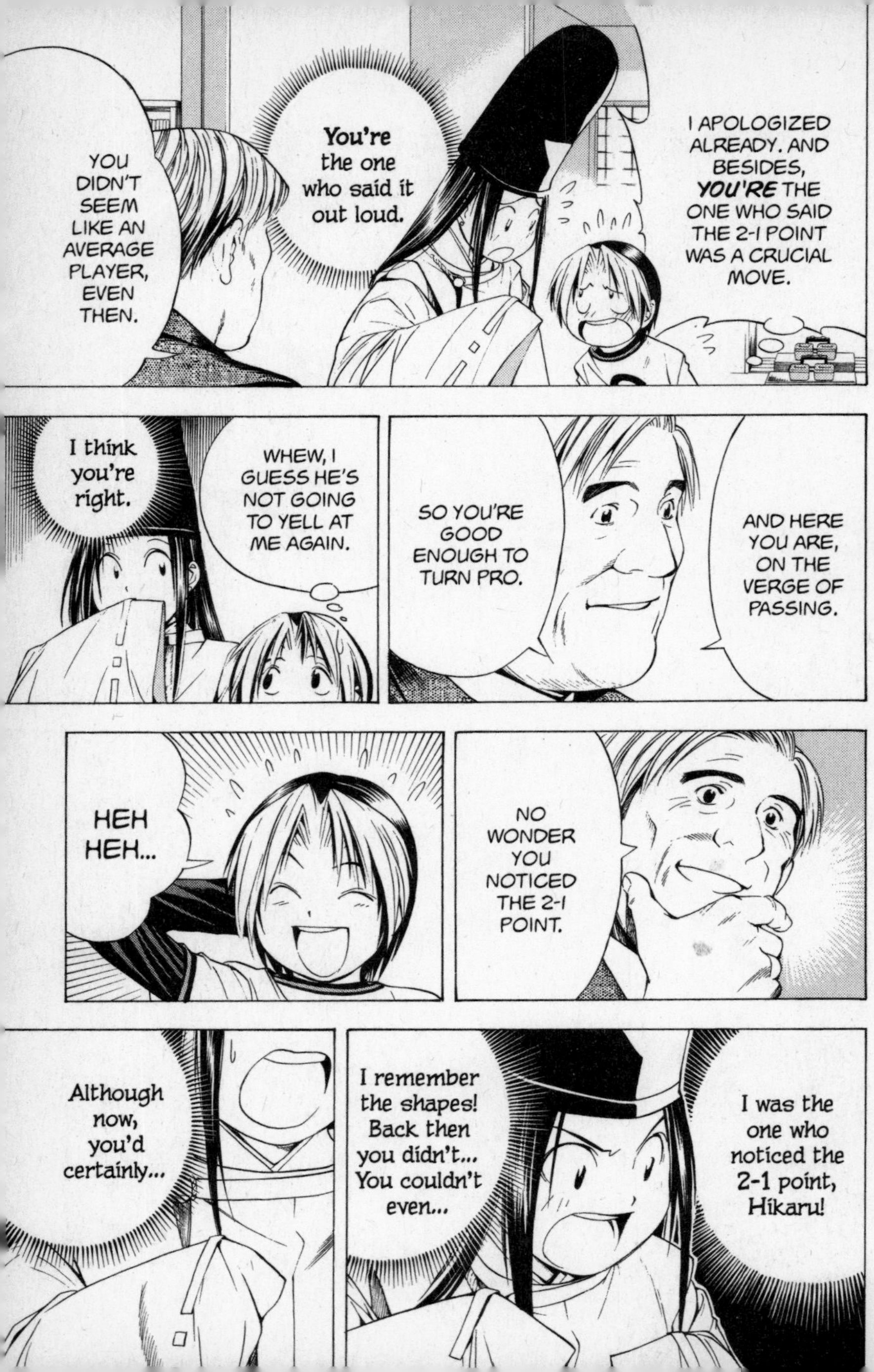
I APOLOGIZED ALREADY. AND BESIDES, ***YOU'RE*** THE ONE WHO SAID THE 2-1 POINT WAS A CRUCIAL MOVE.
You're the one who said it out loud.
YOU DIDN'T SEEM LIKE AN AVERAGE PLAYER, EVEN THEN.
AND HERE YOU ARE, ON THE VERGE OF PASSING.
SO YOU'RE GOOD ENOUGH TO TURN PRO.
WHEW, I GUESS HE'S NOT GOING TO YELL AT ME AGAIN.
I think you're right.
NO WONDER YOU NOTICED THE 2-1 POINT.
HEH HEH...
I was the one who noticed the 2-1 point, Hikaru!
I remember the shapes! Back then you didn't... You couldn't even...
Although now, you'd certainly...

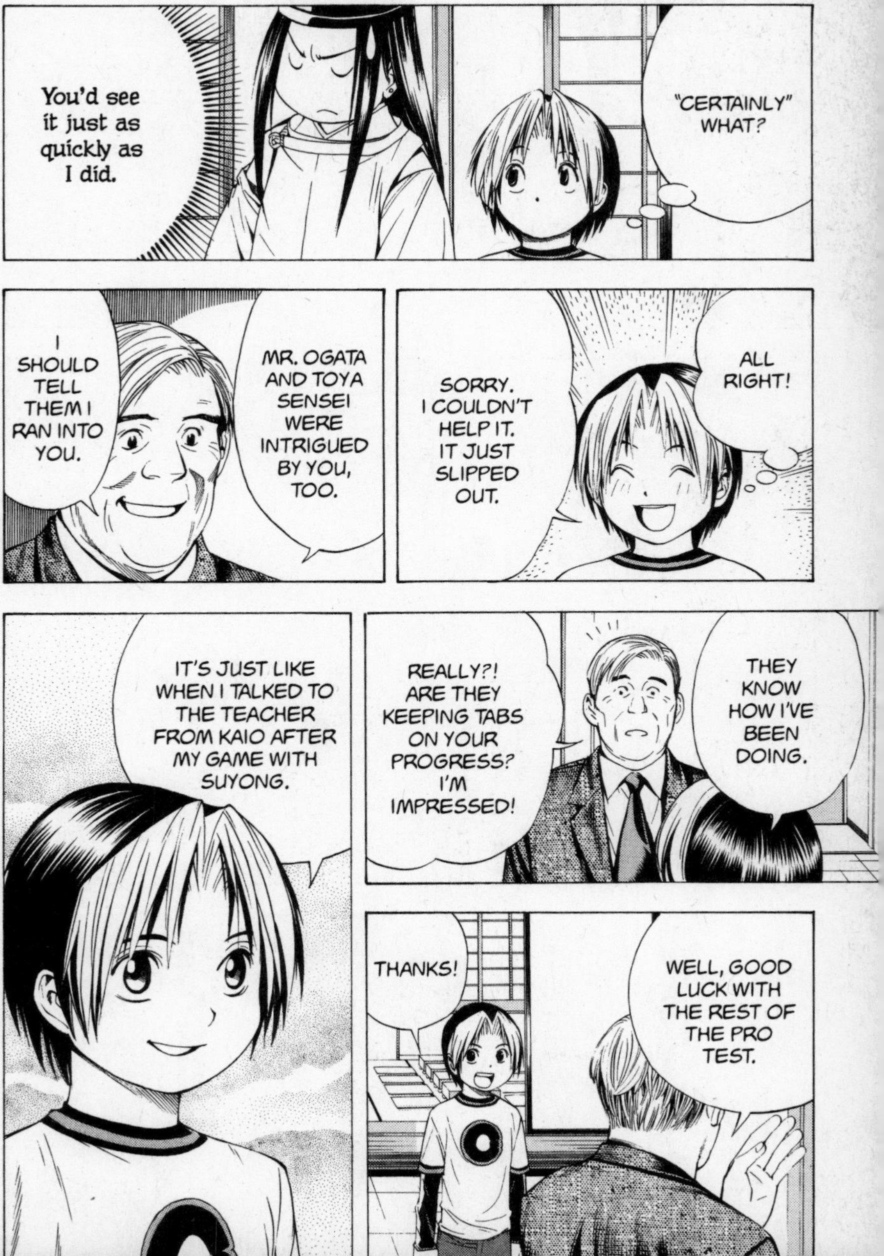
"CERTAINLY" WHAT?
You'd see it just as quickly as I did.
ALL RIGHT!
SORRY. I COULDN'T HELP IT. IT JUST SLIPPED OUT.
MR. OGATA AND TOYA SENSEI WERE INTRIGUED BY YOU, TOO.
I SHOULD TELL THEM I RAN INTO YOU.
THEY KNOW HOW I'VE BEEN DOING.
REALLY?! ARE THEY KEEPING TABS ON YOUR PROGRESS? I'M IMPRESSED!
WELL, GOOD LUCK WITH THE REST OF THE PRO TEST.
THANKS!
IT'S JUST LIKE WHEN I TALKED TO THE TEACHER FROM KAIO AFTER MY GAME WITH SUYONG.

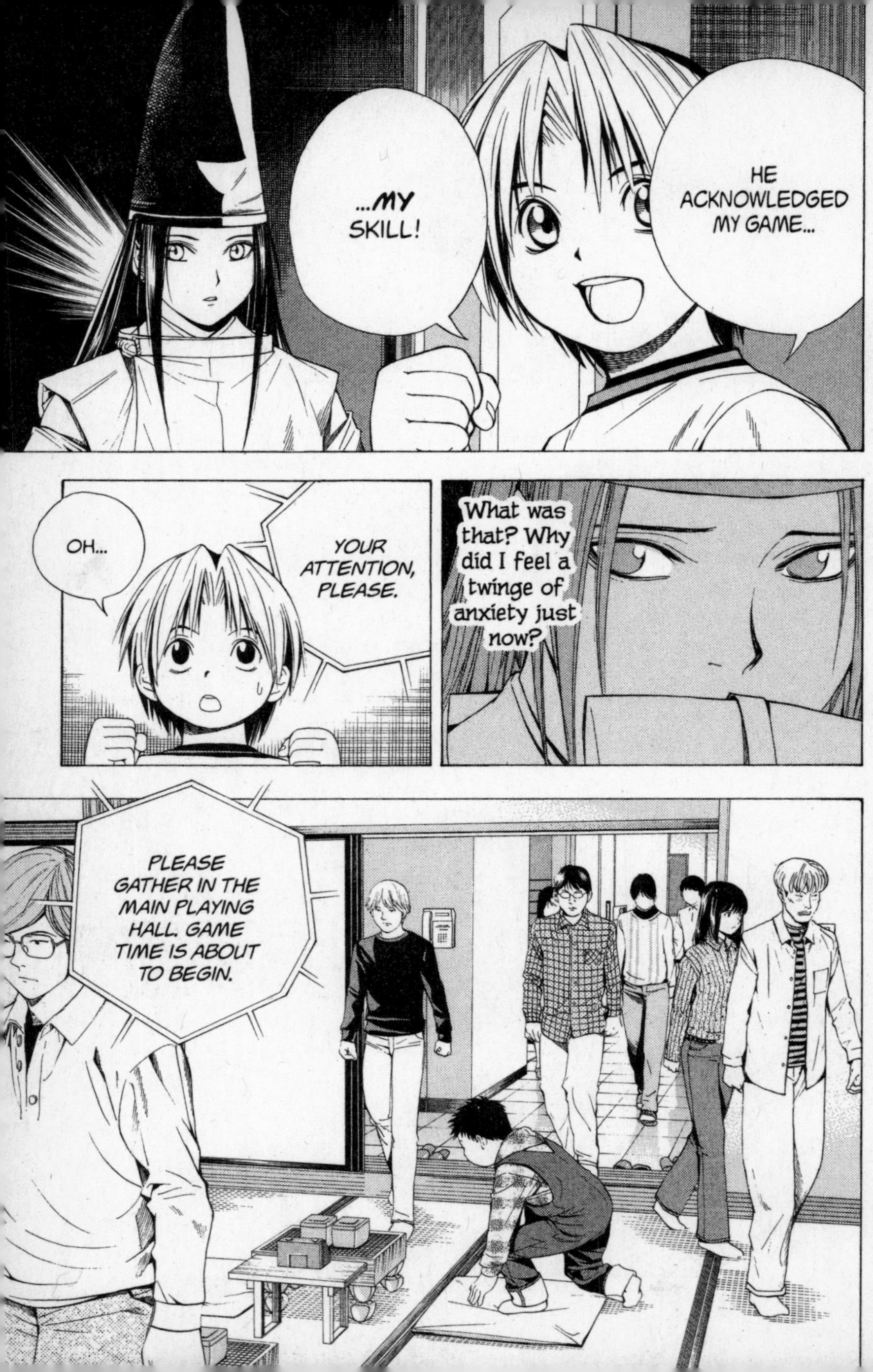
HE ACKNOWLEDGED MY GAME...
...MY SKILL!
What was that? Why did I feel a twinge of anxiety just now?
YOUR ATTENTION, PLEASE.
OH...
PLEASE GATHER IN THE MAIN PLAYING HALL. GAME TIME IS ABOUT TO BEGIN.

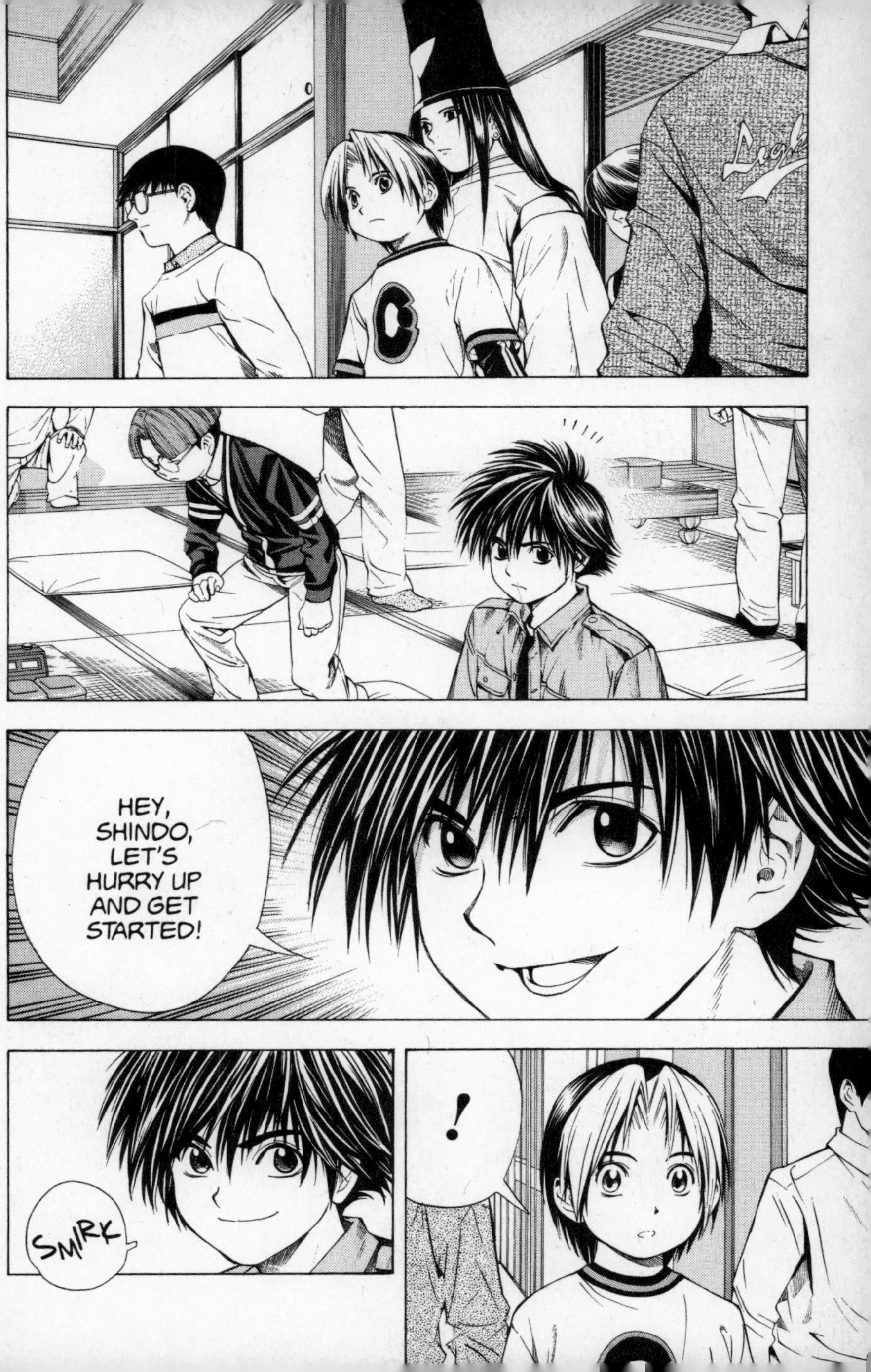
HEY, SHINDO, LET'S HURRY UP AND GET STARTED!
!
SMIRK

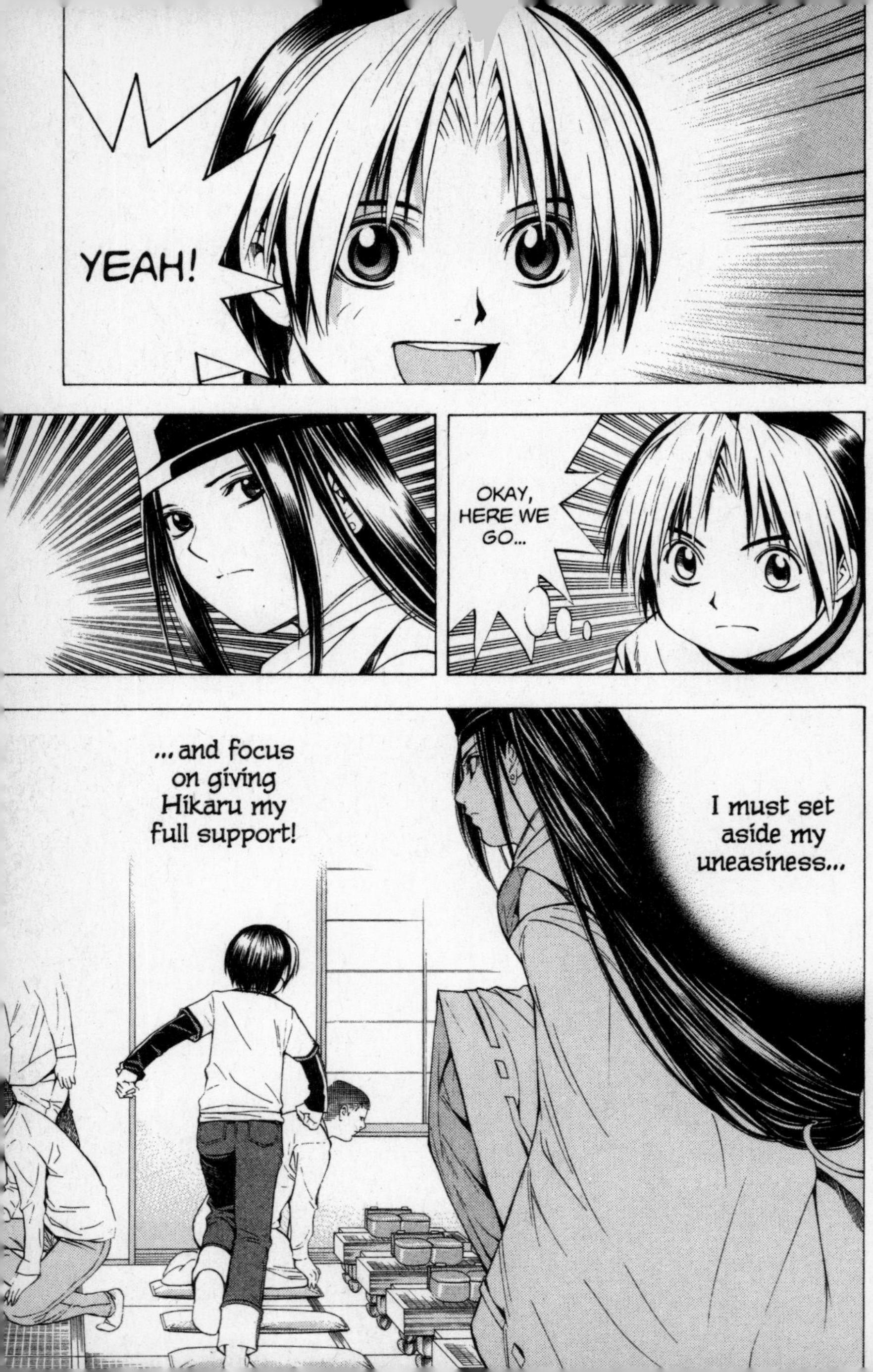
YEAH!
OKAY, HERE WE GO...
I must set aside my uneasiness...
...and focus on giving Hikaru my full support!

HIKARU NO GO

STORYBOARDS

30

YUMI HOTTA

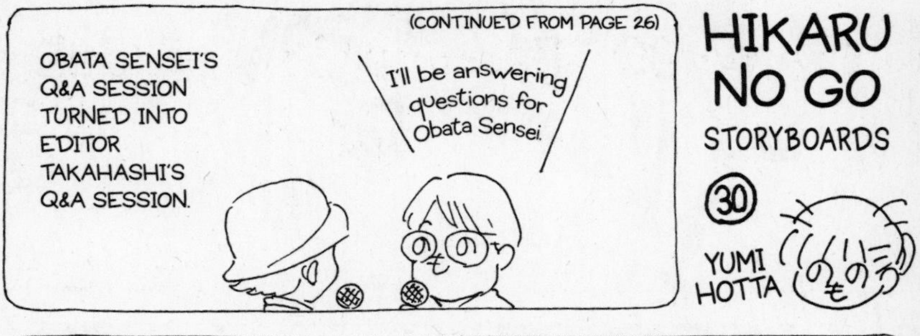

(CONTINUED FROM PAGE 26)
I'll be answering questions for Obata Sensei.
OBATA SENSEI'S Q&A SESSION TURNED INTO EDITOR TAKAHASHI'S Q&A SESSION.

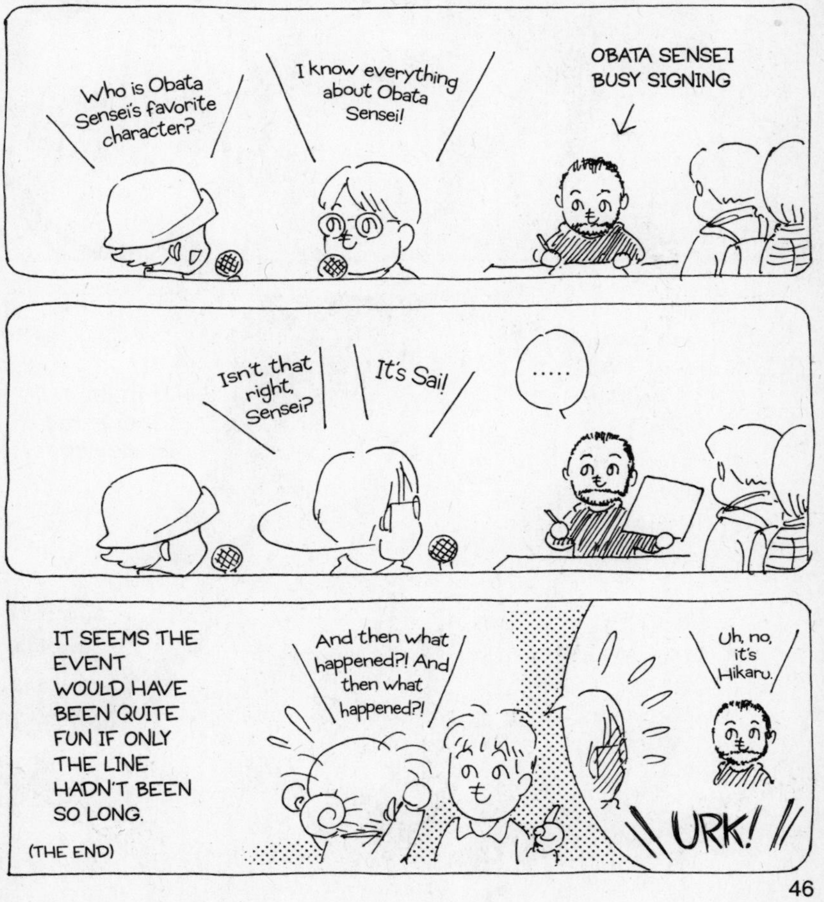

OBATA SENSEI BUSY SIGNING
I know everything about Obata Sensei!
Who is Obata Sensei's favorite character?
.....
It's Sai!
Isn't that right, Sensei?
Uh, no, it's Hikaru.
URK!
And then what happened?! And then what happened?!
IT SEEMS THE EVENT WOULD HAVE BEEN QUITE FUN IF ONLY THE LINE HADN'T BEEN SO LONG.
(THE END)

Game 90 "Become One of Us"

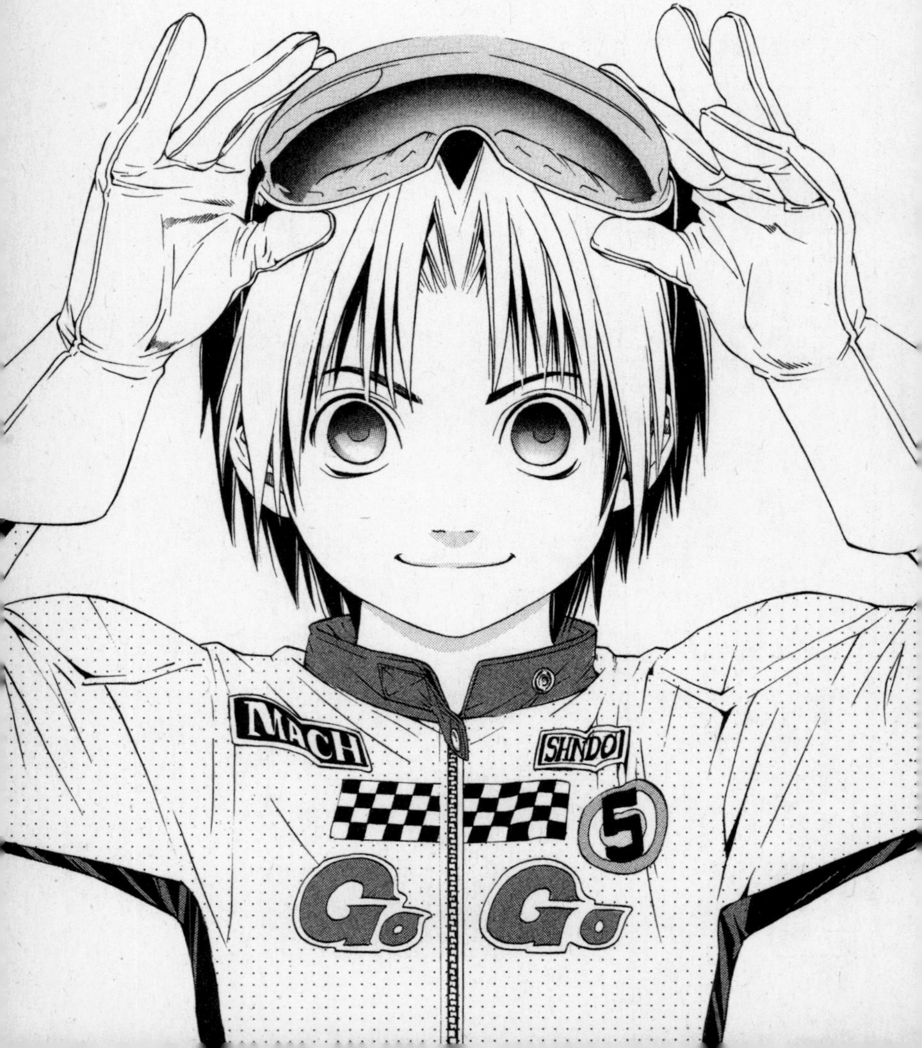

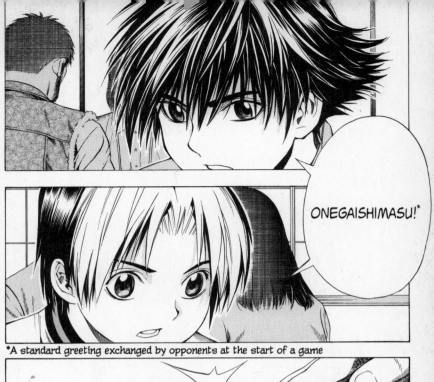

ONEGAISHIMASU!*

*A standard greeting exchanged by opponents at the start of a game

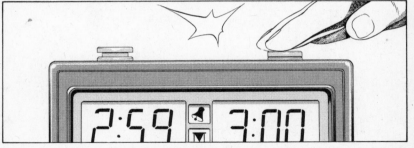

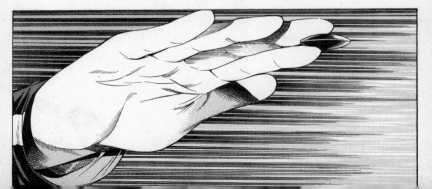

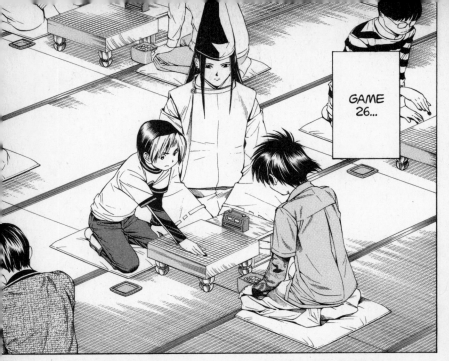

GAME 26...

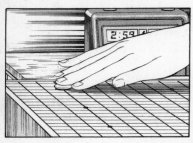

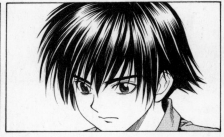

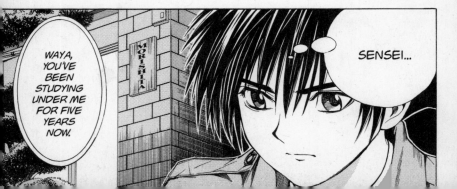

WAYA, YOU'VE BEEN STUDYING UNDER ME FOR FIVE YEARS NOW.

SENSEI...

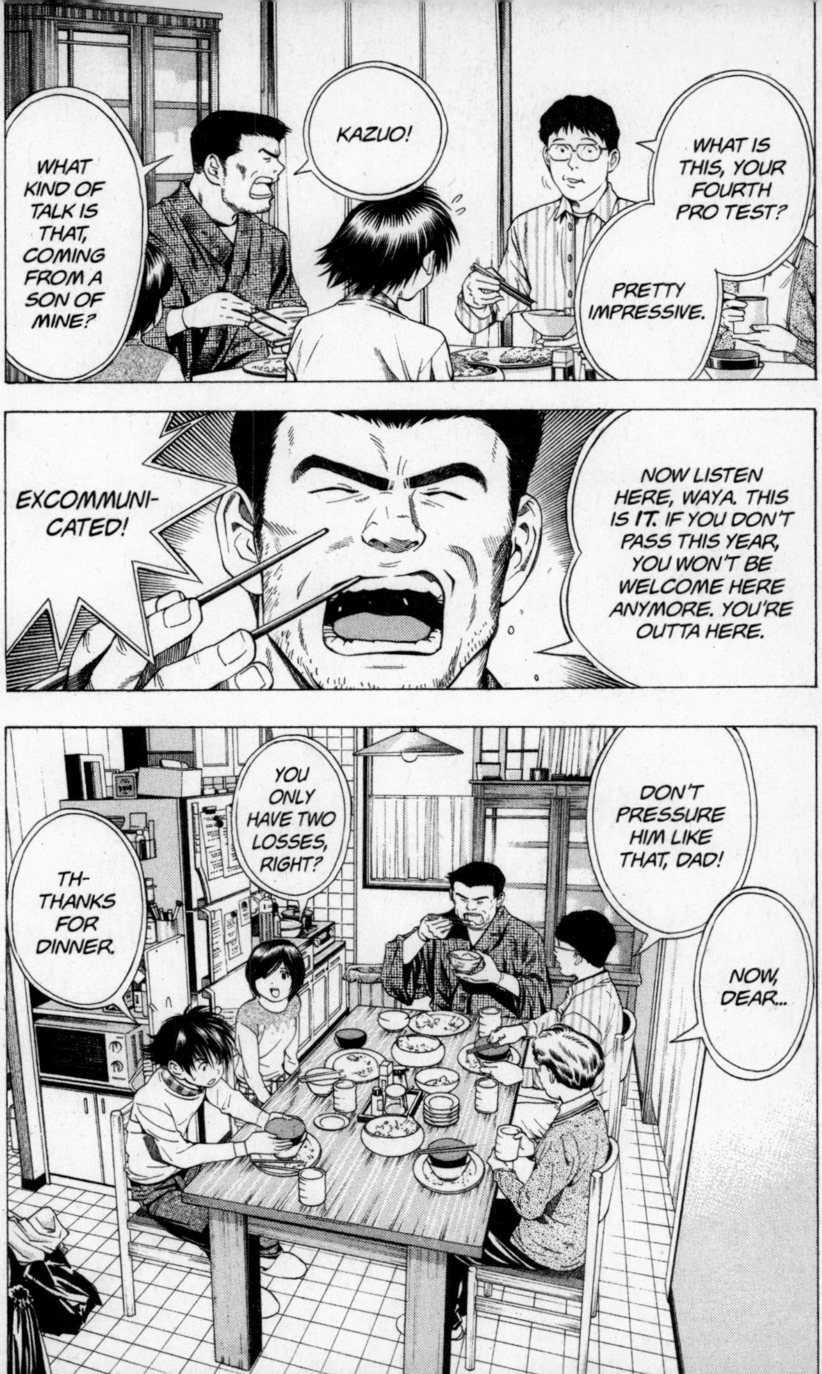
WHAT IS THIS, YOUR FOURTH PRO TEST?
PRETTY IMPRESSIVE.
KAZUO!
WHAT KIND OF TALK IS THAT, COMING FROM A SON OF MINE?
NOW LISTEN HERE, WAYA. THIS IS IT. IF YOU DON'T PASS THIS YEAR, YOU WON'T BE WELCOME HERE ANYMORE. YOU'RE OUTTA HERE.
EXCOMMUNI-CATED!
DON'T PRESSURE HIM LIKE THAT, DAD!
NOW, DEAR...
YOU ONLY HAVE TWO LOSSES, RIGHT?
TH- THANKS FOR DINNER.

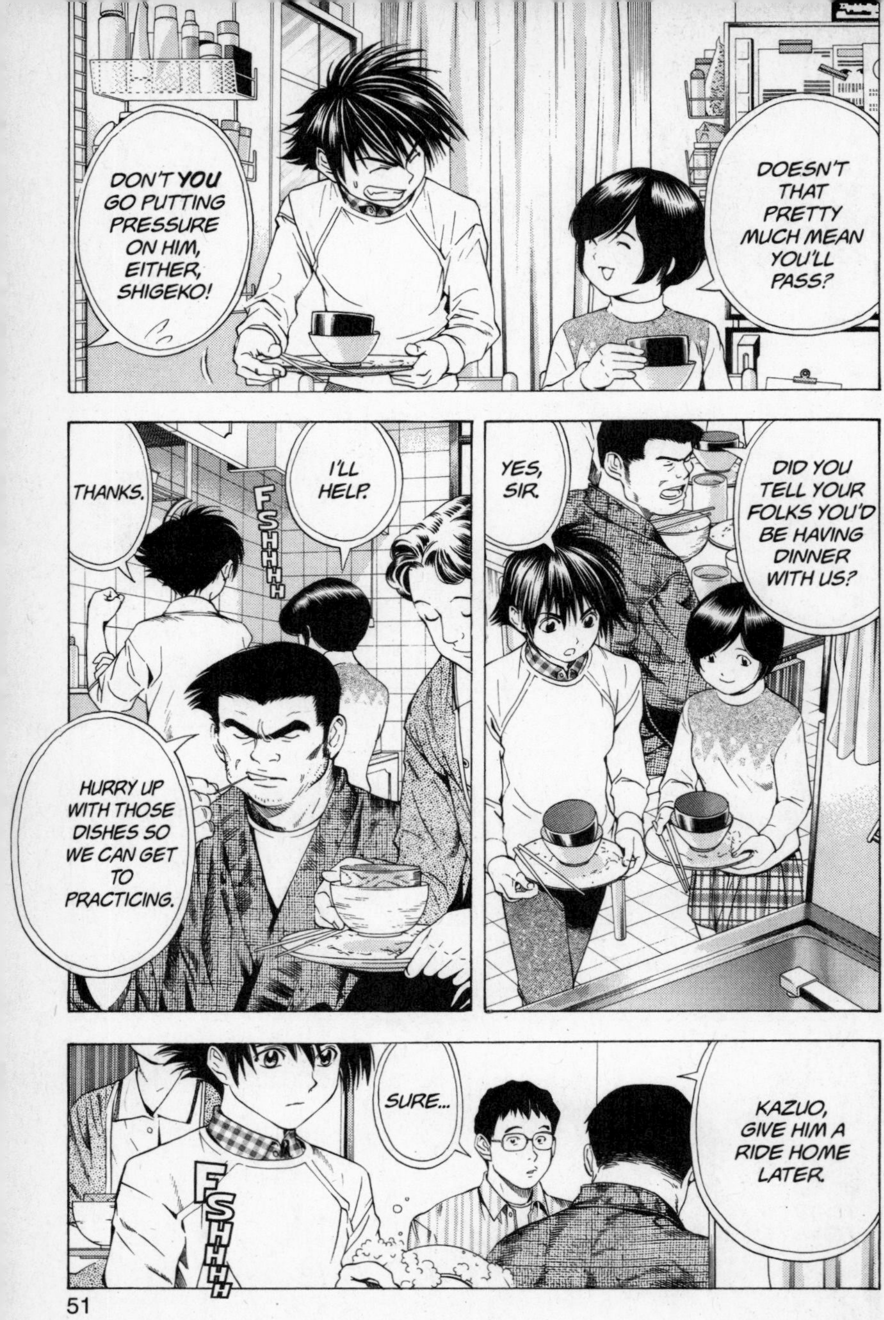
DOESN'T THAT PRETTY MUCH MEAN YOU'LL PASS?
DON'T **YOU** GO PUTTING PRESSURE ON HIM, EITHER, SHIGEKO!
DID YOU TELL YOUR FOLKS YOU'D BE HAVING DINNER WITH US?
YES, SIR.
I'LL HELP.
THANKS.
FSHHHH
HURRY UP WITH THOSE DISHES SO WE CAN GET TO PRACTICING.
KAZUO, GIVE HIM A RIDE HOME LATER.
SURE...
FSHHHH

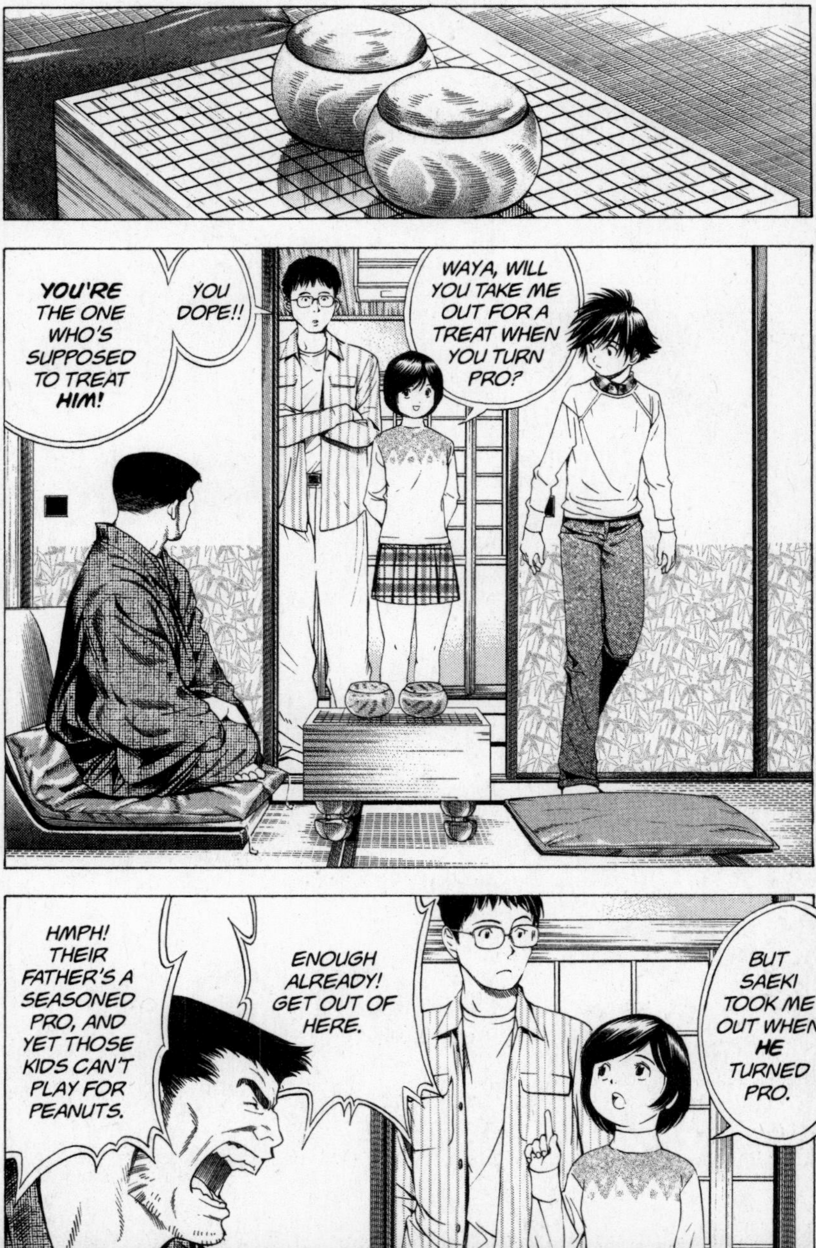
WAYA, WILL YOU TAKE ME OUT FOR A TREAT WHEN YOU TURN PRO?
YOU DOPE!!
YOU'RE THE ONE WHO'S SUPPOSED TO TREAT HIM!
BUT SAEKI TOOK ME OUT WHEN HE TURNED PRO.
ENOUGH ALREADY! GET OUT OF HERE.
HMPH! THEIR FATHER'S A SEASONED PRO, AND YET THOSE KIDS CAN'T PLAY FOR PEANUTS.

READ THIS WAY

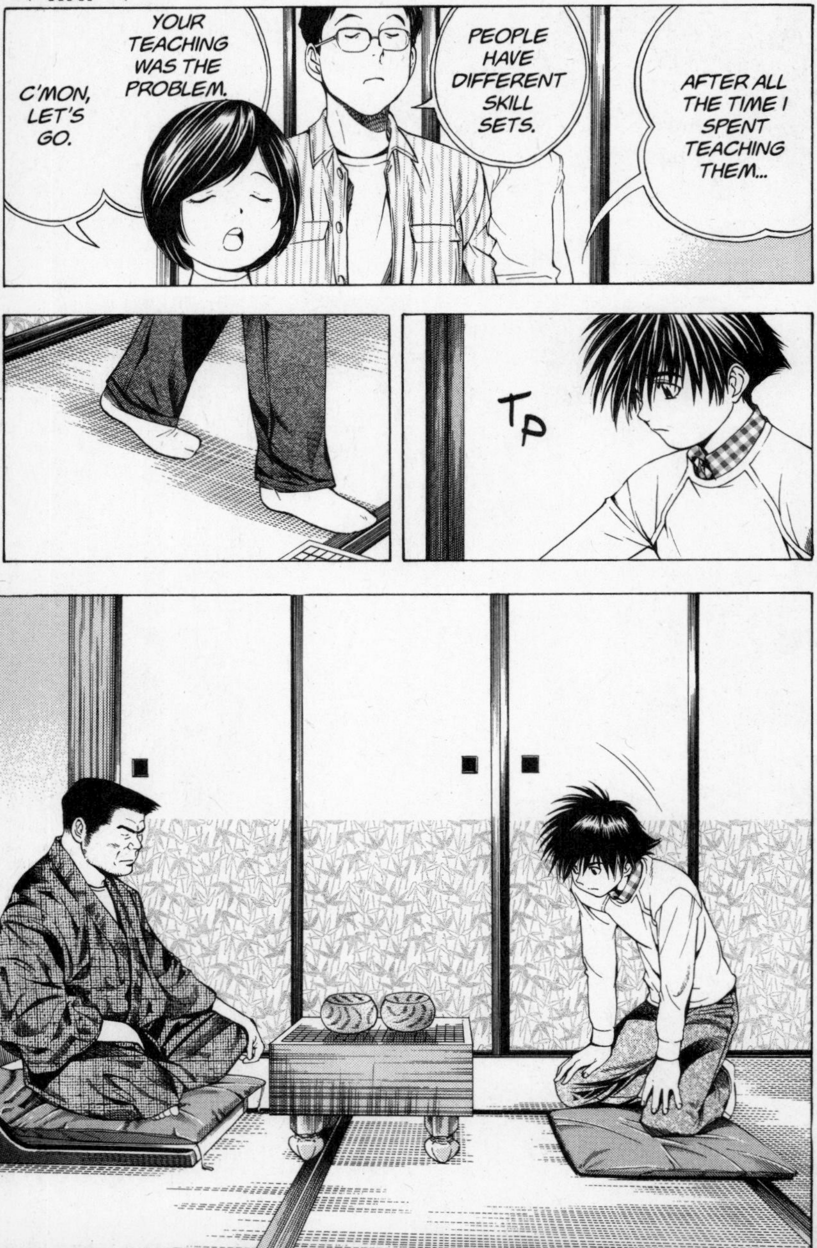
AFTER ALL THE TIME I SPENT TEACHING THEM...
PEOPLE HAVE DIFFERENT SKILL SETS.
YOUR TEACHING WAS THE PROBLEM.
C'MON, LET'S GO.
TP

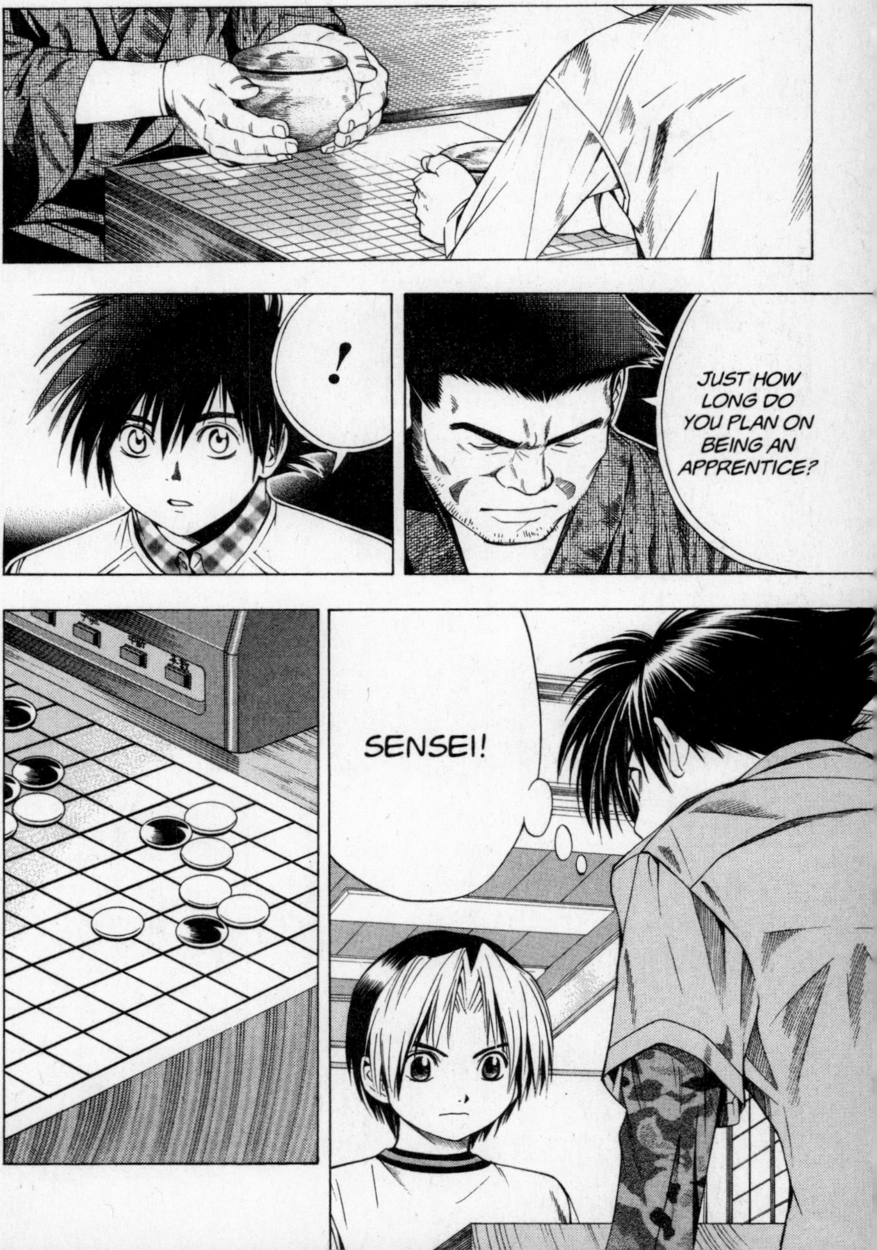
JUST HOW LONG DO YOU PLAN ON BEING AN APPRENTICE?
!
SENSEI!

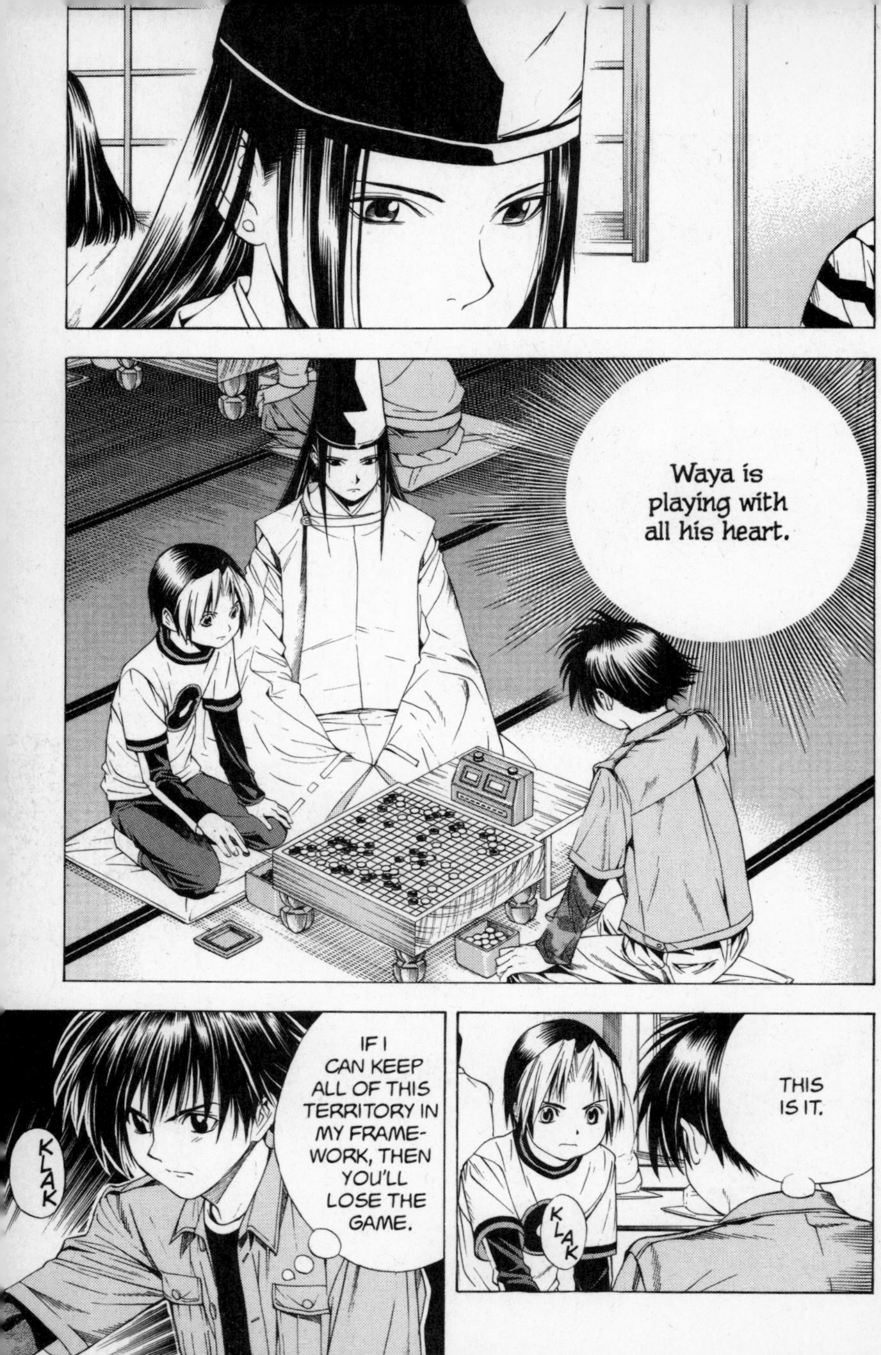
Waya is playing with all his heart.
THIS IS IT.
KLAK
IF I CAN KEEP ALL OF THIS TERRITORY IN MY FRAMEWORK, THEN YOU'LL LOSE THE GAME.
KLAK

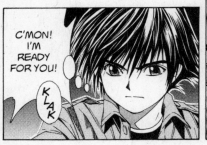

YOU HAVE NO CHOICE. YOU **HAVE** TO INVADE.
KLAK
C'MON! I'M READY FOR YOU!
KLAK
KLAK

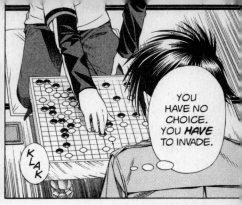

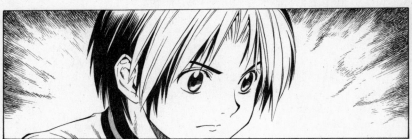

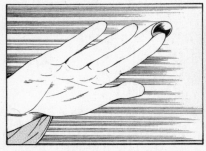

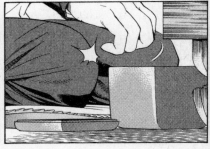

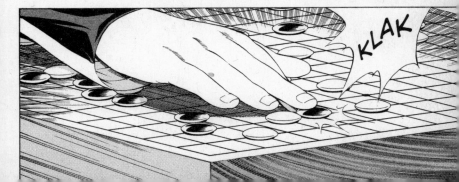

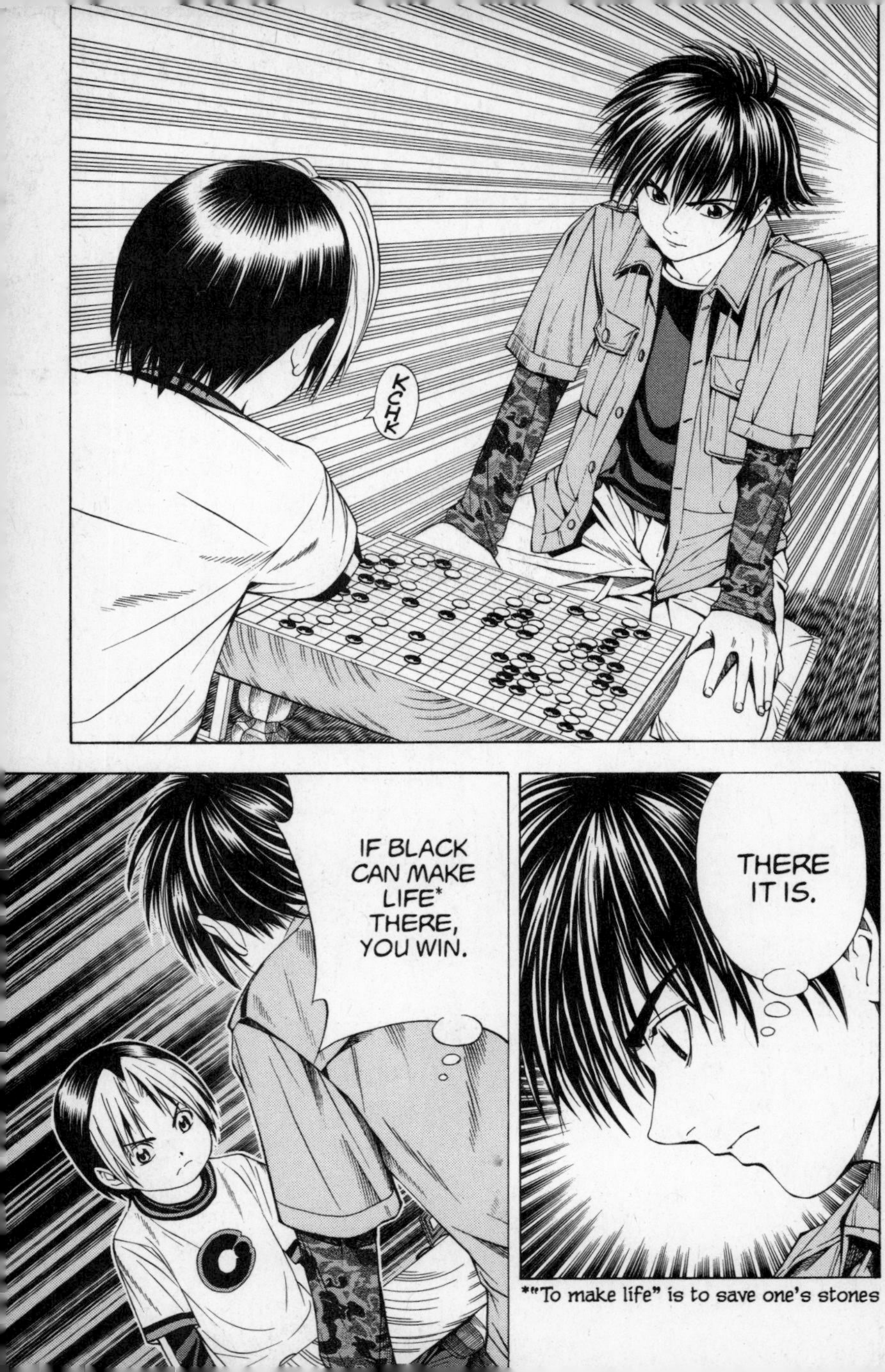
KCHK
THERE IT IS.
IF BLACK CAN MAKE LIFE* THERE, YOU WIN.

*"To make life" is to save one's stones

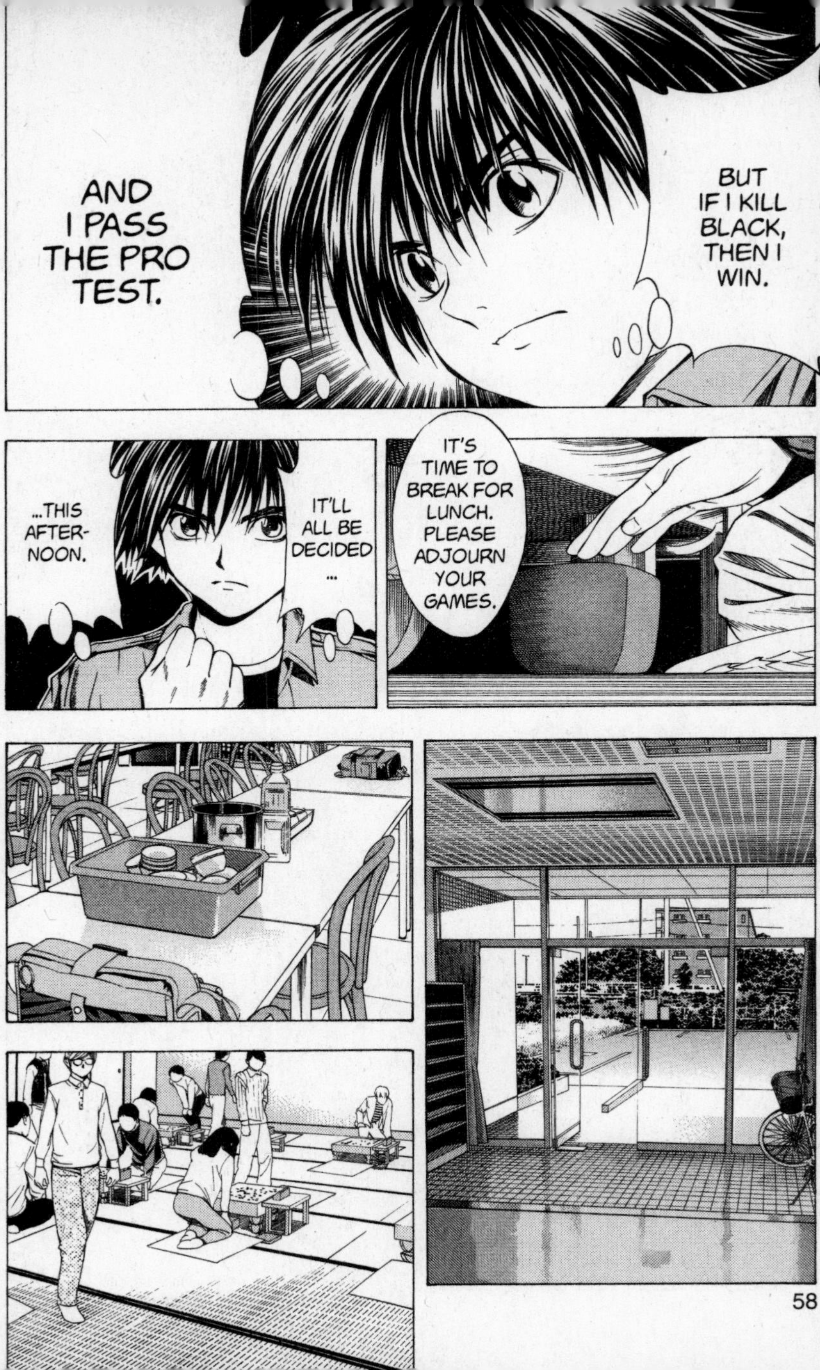
BUT IF I KILL BLACK, THEN I WIN.
AND I PASS THE PRO TEST.
IT'S TIME TO BREAK FOR LUNCH. PLEASE ADJOURN YOUR GAMES.
IT'LL ALL BE DECIDED ...
...THIS AFTERNOON.

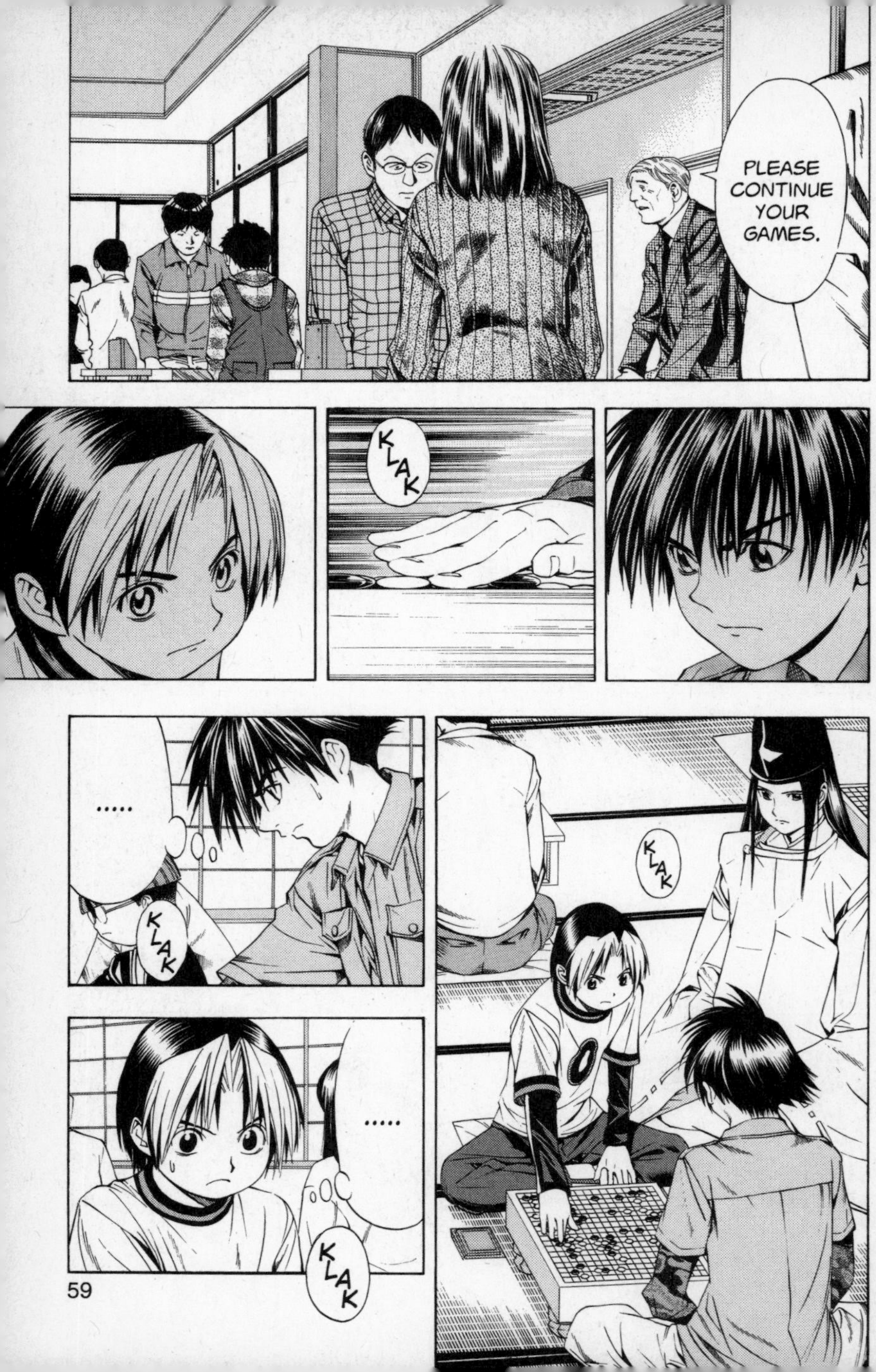
PLEASE CONTINUE YOUR GAMES.
KLAK
KLAK
.....
KLAK
.....
KLAK

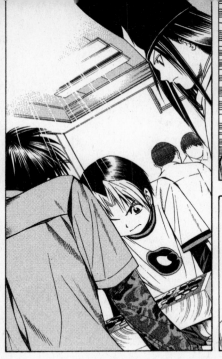

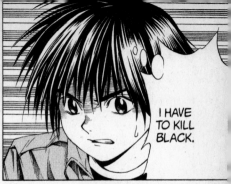

I HAVE TO KILL BLACK.

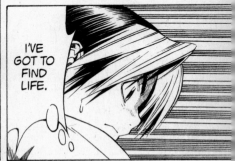

I'VE GOT TO FIND LIFE.

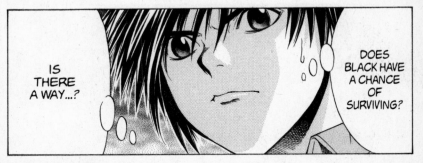

IS THERE A WAY...?

DOES BLACK HAVE A CHANCE OF SURVIVING?

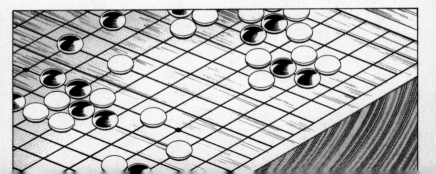

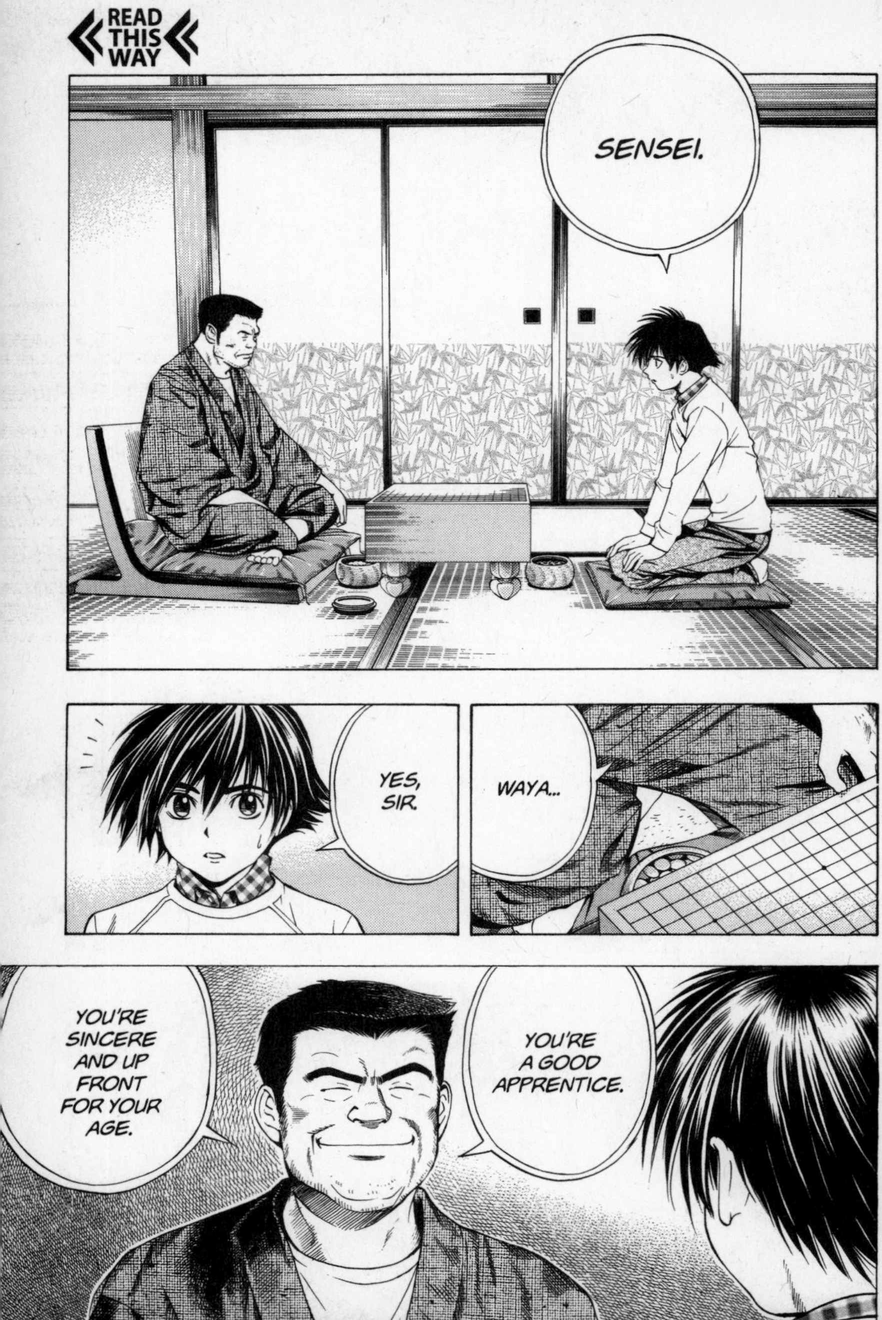
READ THIS WAY
SENSEI.
WAYA...
YES, SIR.
YOU'RE A GOOD APPRENTICE.
YOU'RE SINCERE AND UP FRONT FOR YOUR AGE.

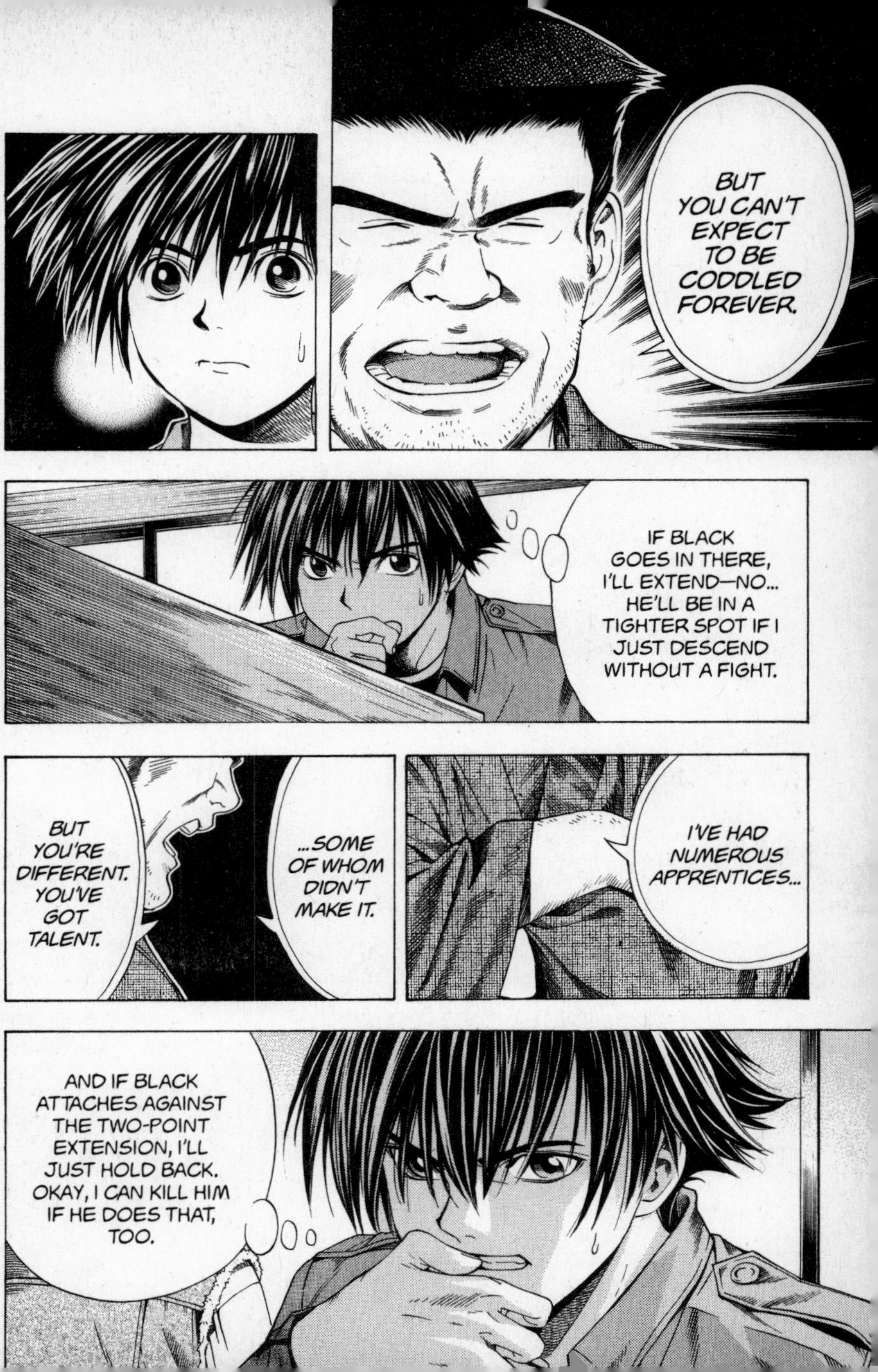
BUT YOU CAN'T EXPECT TO BE CODDLED FOREVER.
IF BLACK GOES IN THERE, I'LL EXTEND—NO... HE'LL BE IN A TIGHTER SPOT IF I JUST DESCEND WITHOUT A FIGHT.
I'VE HAD NUMEROUS APPRENTICES...
...SOME OF WHOM DIDN'T MAKE IT.
BUT YOU'RE DIFFERENT. YOU'VE GOT TALENT.
AND IF BLACK ATTACHES AGAINST THE TWO-POINT EXTENSION, I'LL JUST HOLD BACK. OKAY, I CAN KILL HIM IF HE DOES THAT, TOO.

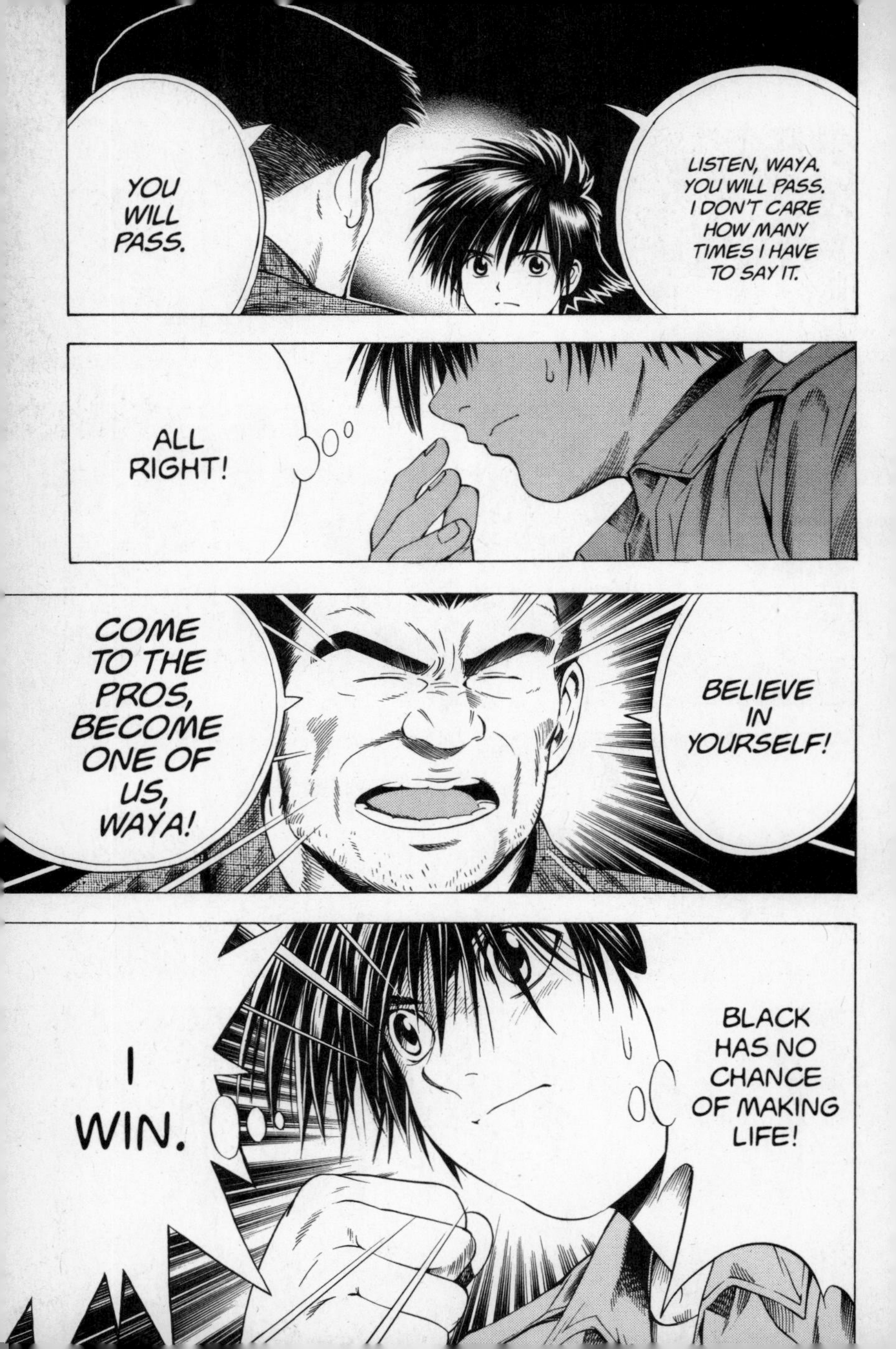
LISTEN, WAYA. YOU WILL PASS. I DON'T CARE HOW MANY TIMES I HAVE TO SAY IT.
YOU WILL PASS.
ALL RIGHT!
BELIEVE IN YOURSELF!
COME TO THE PROS, BECOME ONE OF US, WAYA!
BLACK HAS NO CHANCE OF MAKING LIFE!
I WIN.

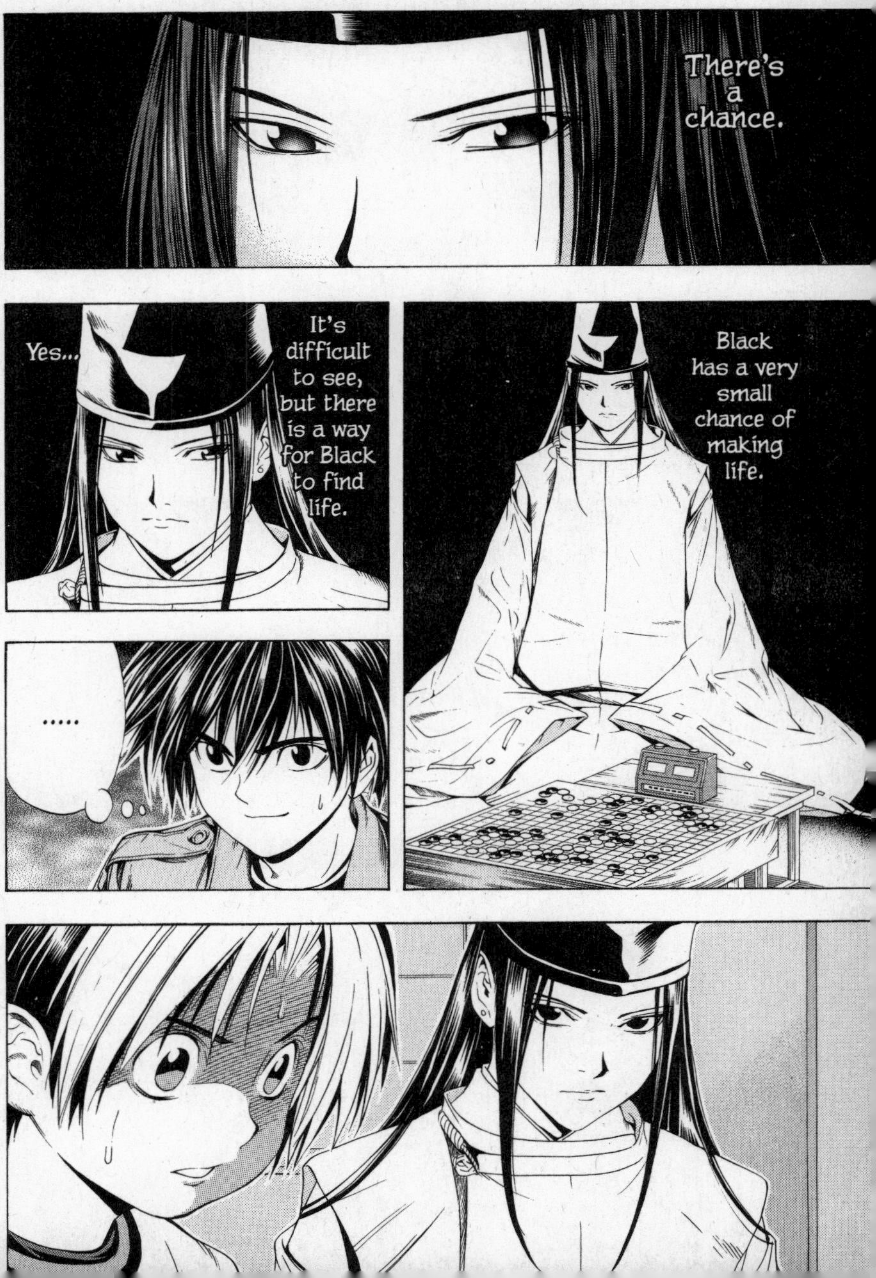
There's a chance.
Black has a very small chance of making life.
It's difficult to see, but there is a way for Black to find life.
Yes...
.....

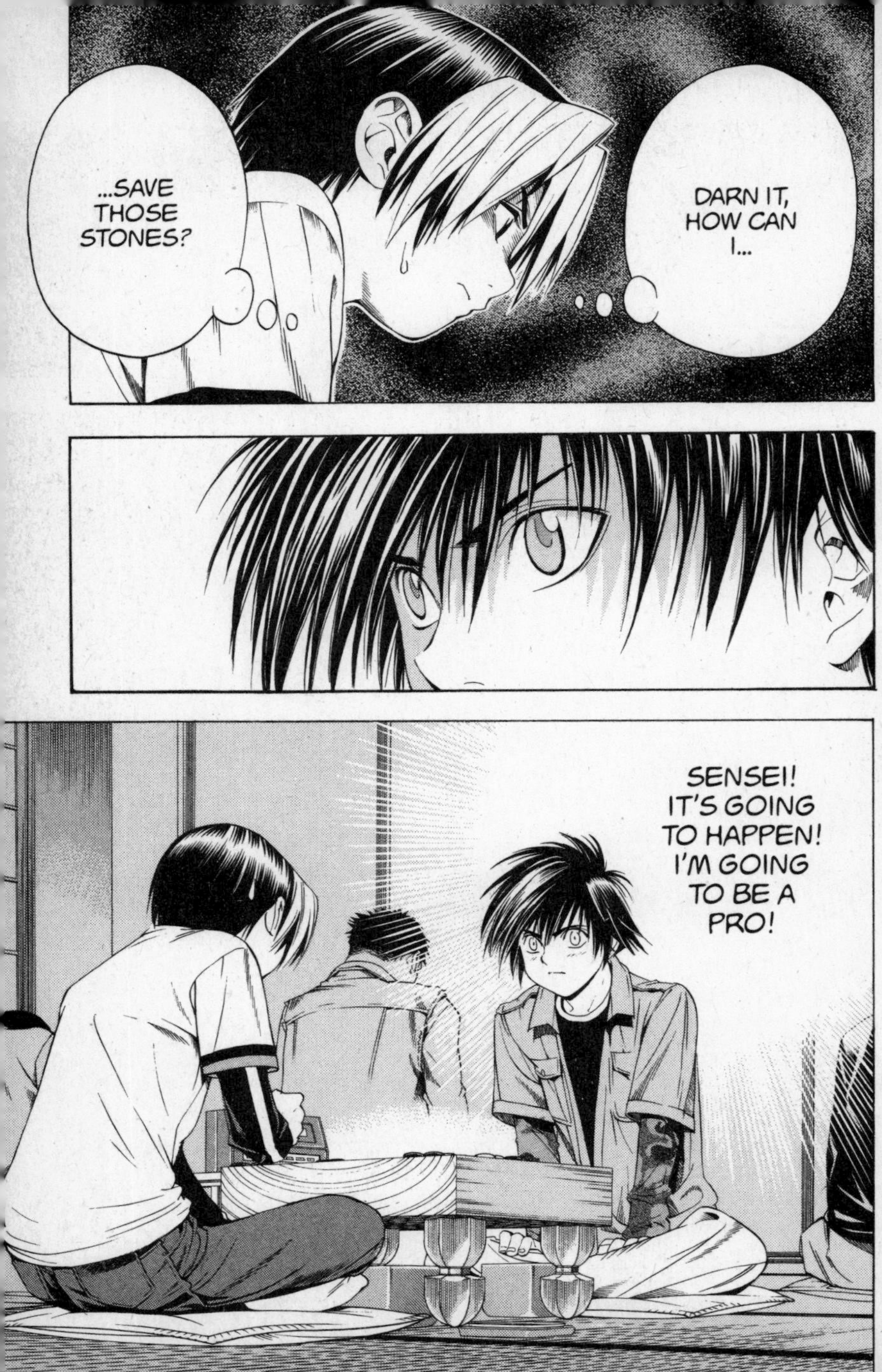
DARN IT, HOW CAN I...
...SAVE THOSE STONES?
SENSEI! IT'S GOING TO HAPPEN! I'M GOING TO BE A PRO!

A WORD ABOUT HIKARU NO GO

KOMI

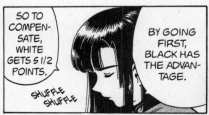

THE KOMI COUNTS FOR 5 1/2 POINTS.
KOMI?
Komi?
BY GOING FIRST, BLACK HAS THE ADVANTAGE.
SO TO COMPENSATE, WHITE GETS 5 1/2 POINTS.
SHUFFLE SHUFFLE
IF THE END SCORE IS 50 TO 50, THEN WHITE WINS BY 5 1/2 POINTS.
What? By 5 1/2 points?
DIDN'T YOU KNOW ABOUT THIS, SAI?

CURRENTLY, KOMI GIVES BLACK A FIVE-AND-A-HALF POINT HANDICAP FOR GOING FIRST. IN THE PAST, IT USED TO BE FOUR-AND-A-HALF POINTS. THERE ARE SIGNS THAT THE HANDICAP MAY GO UP TO SIX-AND-A-HALF POINTS IN THE NOT-SO-DISTANT FUTURE.*

THERE ARE PROFESSIONAL PLAYERS WHO SAY THAT THEY WOULD PREFER TO PLAY BLACK, EVEN WITH A SEVEN-AND-A-HALF POINT HANDICAP, AND THERE ARE THOSE SAY THAT A FIVE-AND-A-HALF POINT HANDICAP IS JUST RIGHT.

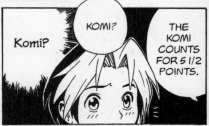

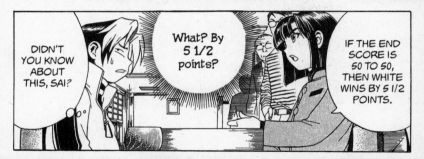

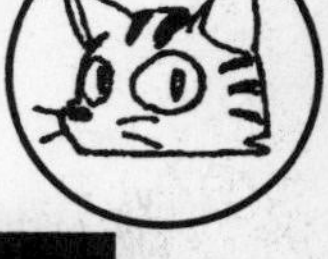

*THE HANDICAP HAS RISEN TO SIX-AND-A-HALF POINTS SINCE VOLUME 11 WAS FIRST PUBLISHED IN JAPAN. –ED.

Game 91 "I Resign"

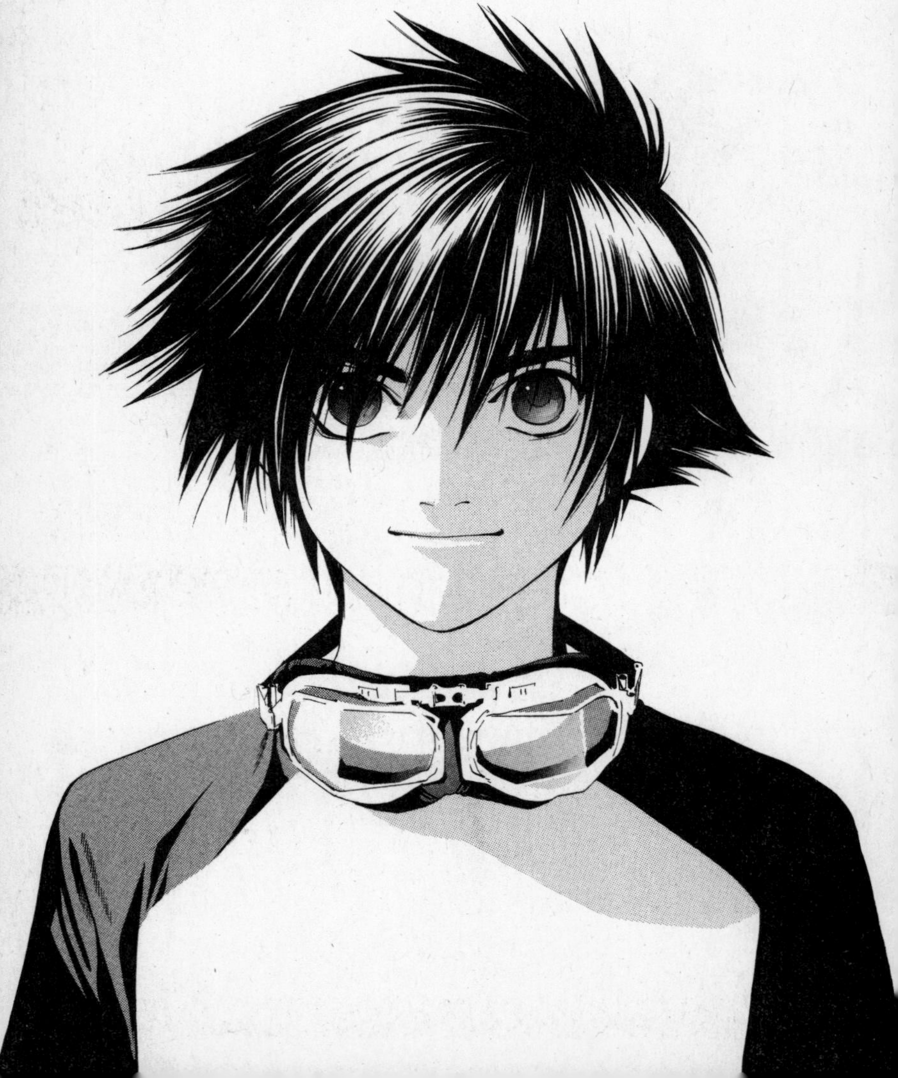

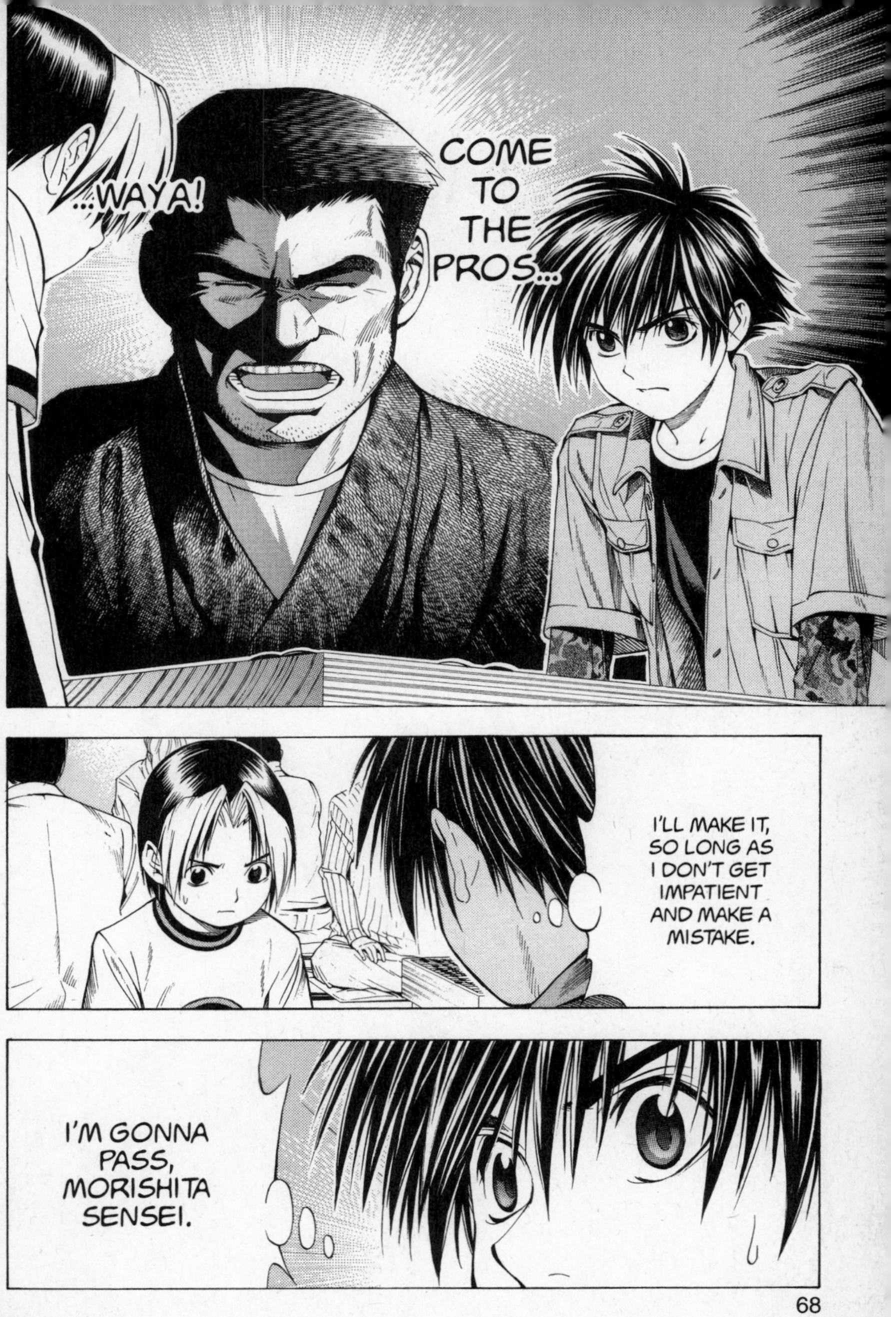
COME TO THE PROS...
...WAYA!
I'LL MAKE IT, SO LONG AS I DON'T GET IMPATIENT AND MAKE A MISTAKE.
I'M GONNA PASS, MORISHITA SENSEI.

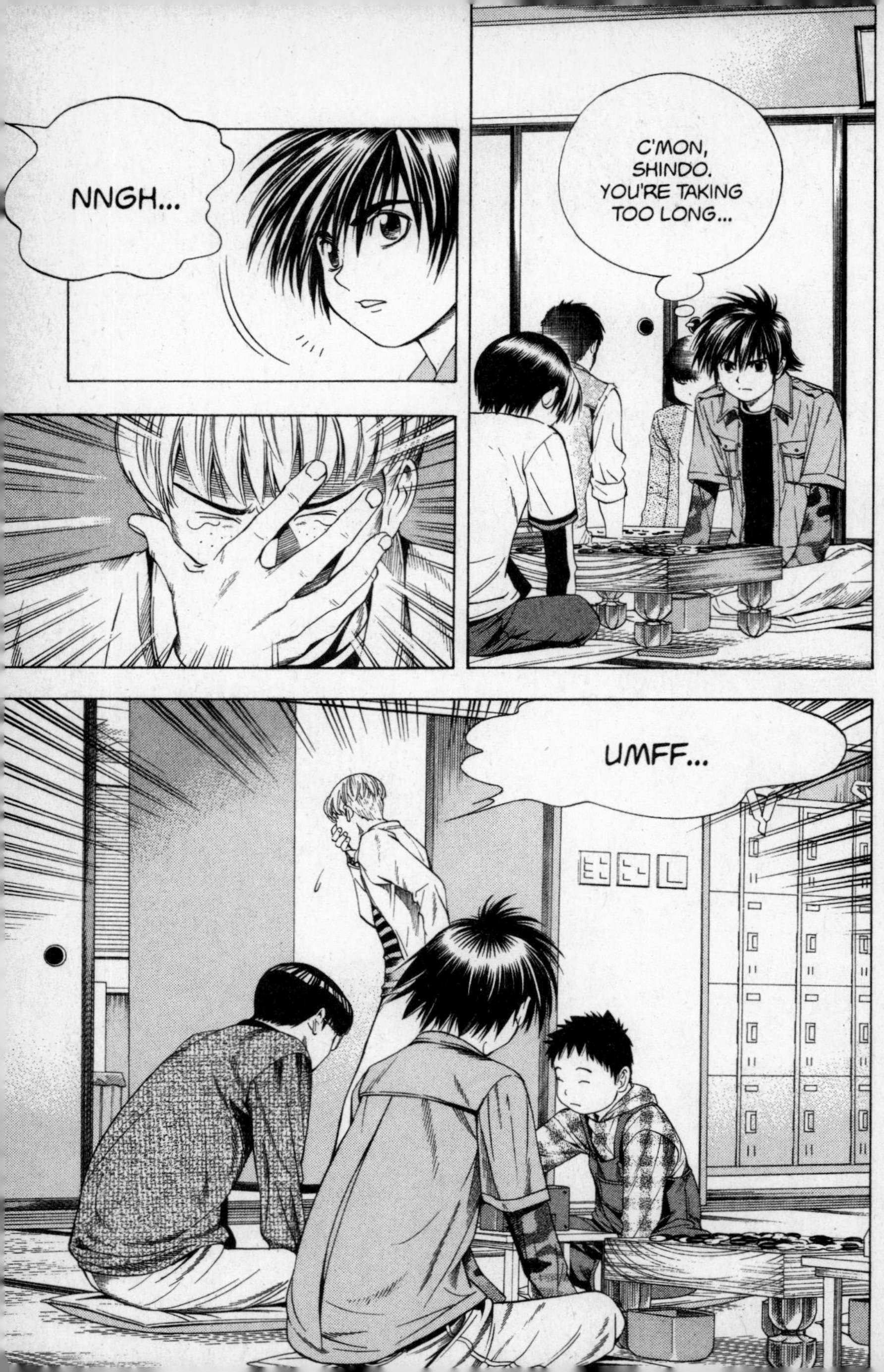
C'MON, SHINDO. YOU'RE TAKING TOO LONG...
NNGH...
UMFF...

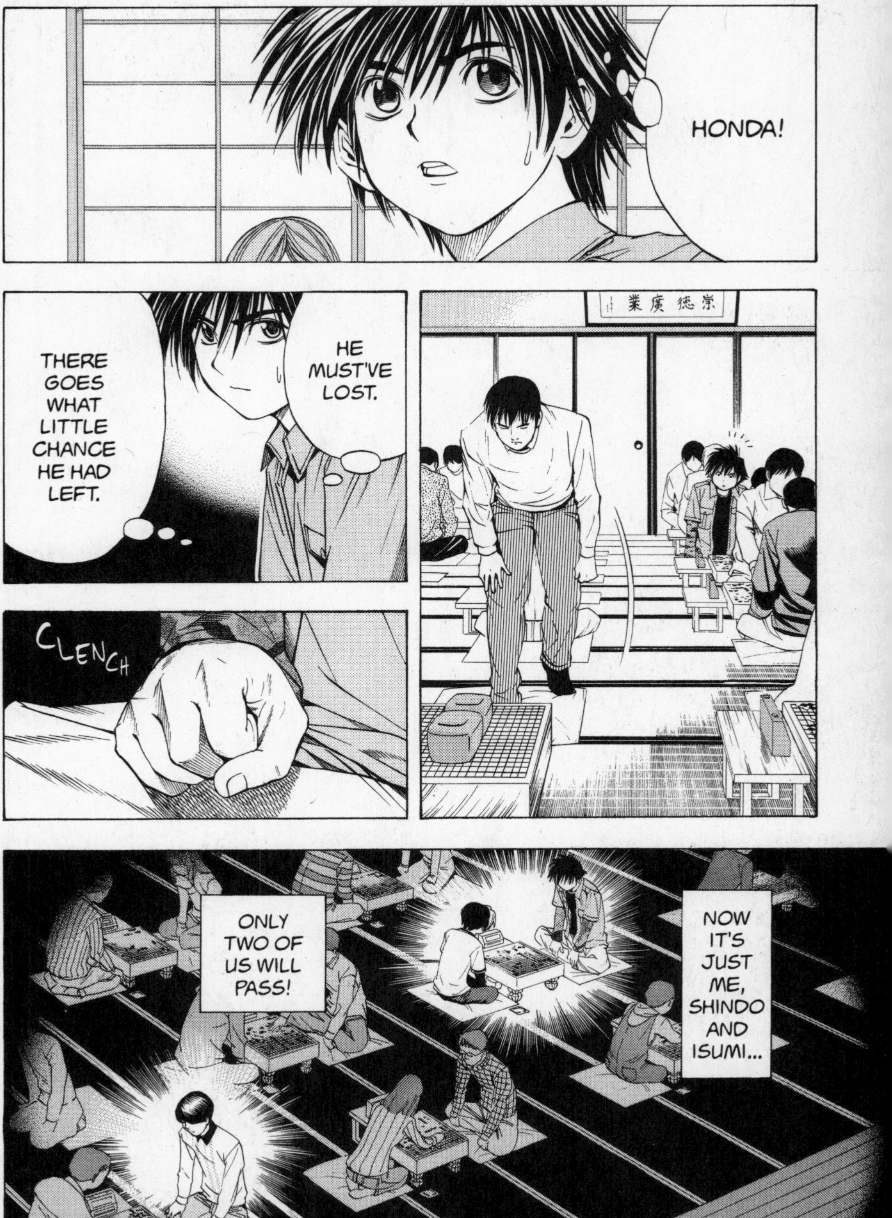
HONDA!
宗徳廣業
HE MUST'VE LOST.
THERE GOES WHAT LITTLE CHANCE HE HAD LEFT.
CLENCH
NOW IT'S JUST ME, SHINDO AND ISUMI...
ONLY TWO OF US WILL PASS!

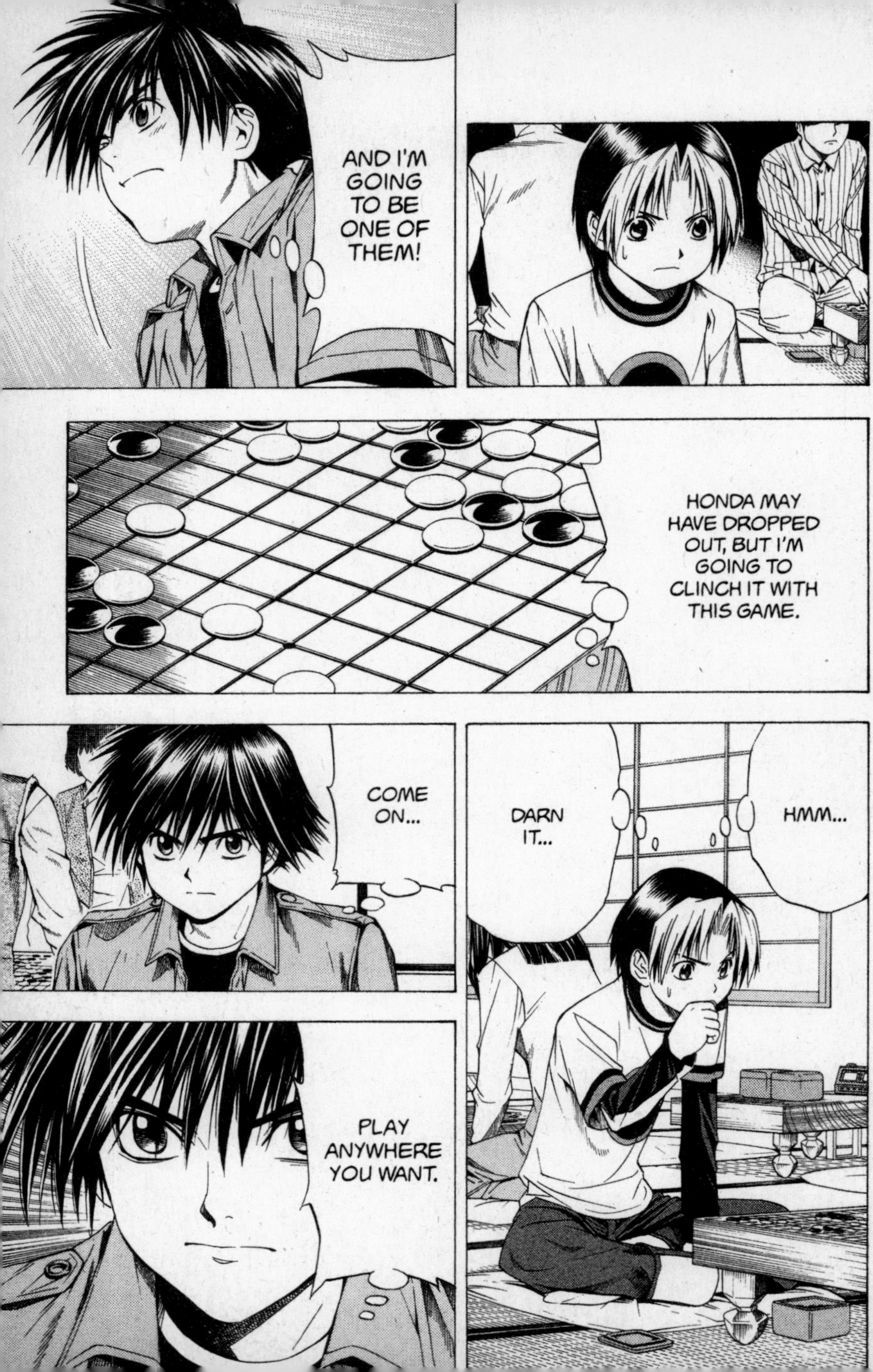
AND I'M GOING TO BE ONE OF THEM!
HONDA MAY HAVE DROPPED OUT, BUT I'M GOING TO CLINCH IT WITH THIS GAME.
HMM...
DARN IT...
COME ON...
PLAY ANYWHERE YOU WANT.

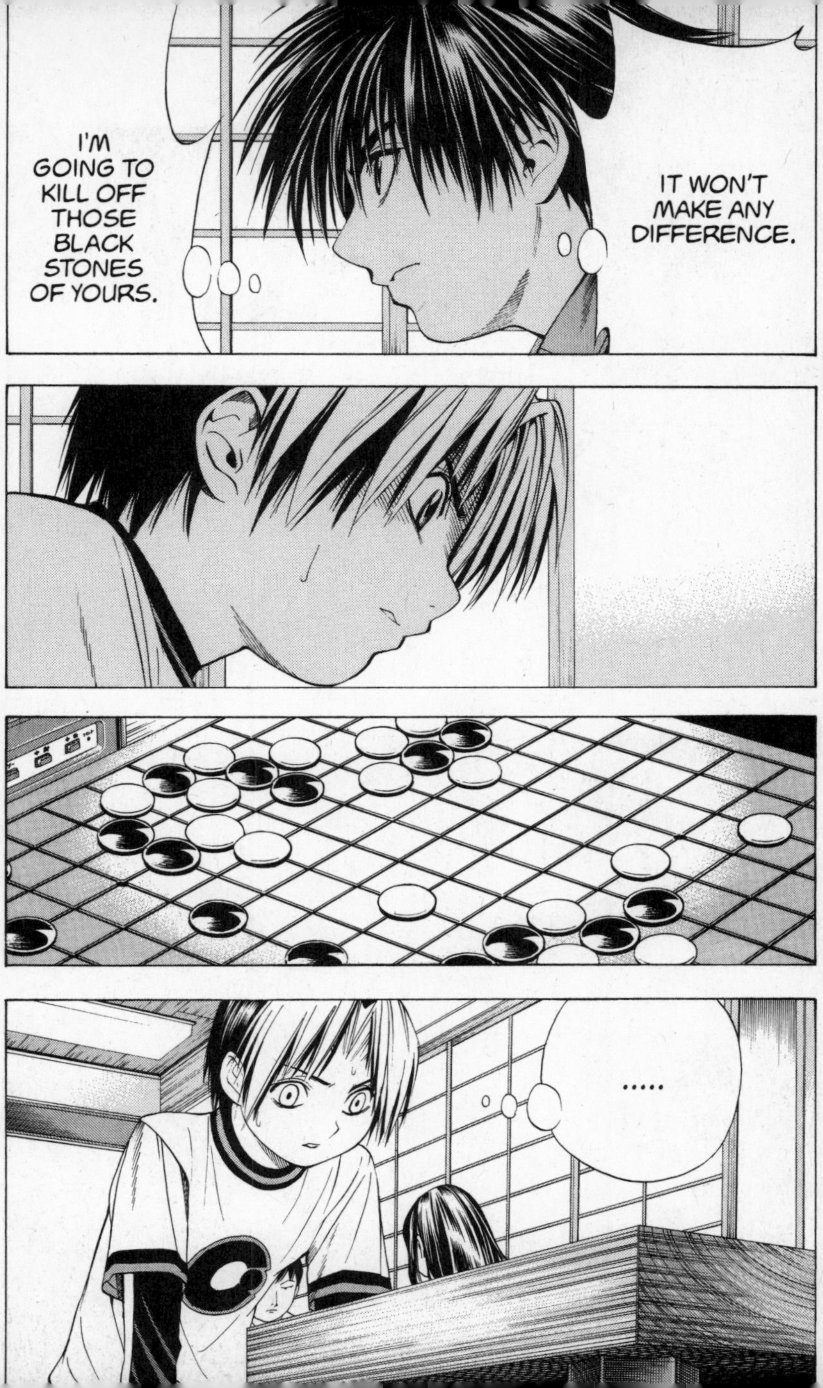
IT WON'T MAKE ANY DIFFERENCE.
I'M GOING TO KILL OFF THOSE BLACK STONES OF YOURS.
.....

READ THIS WAY

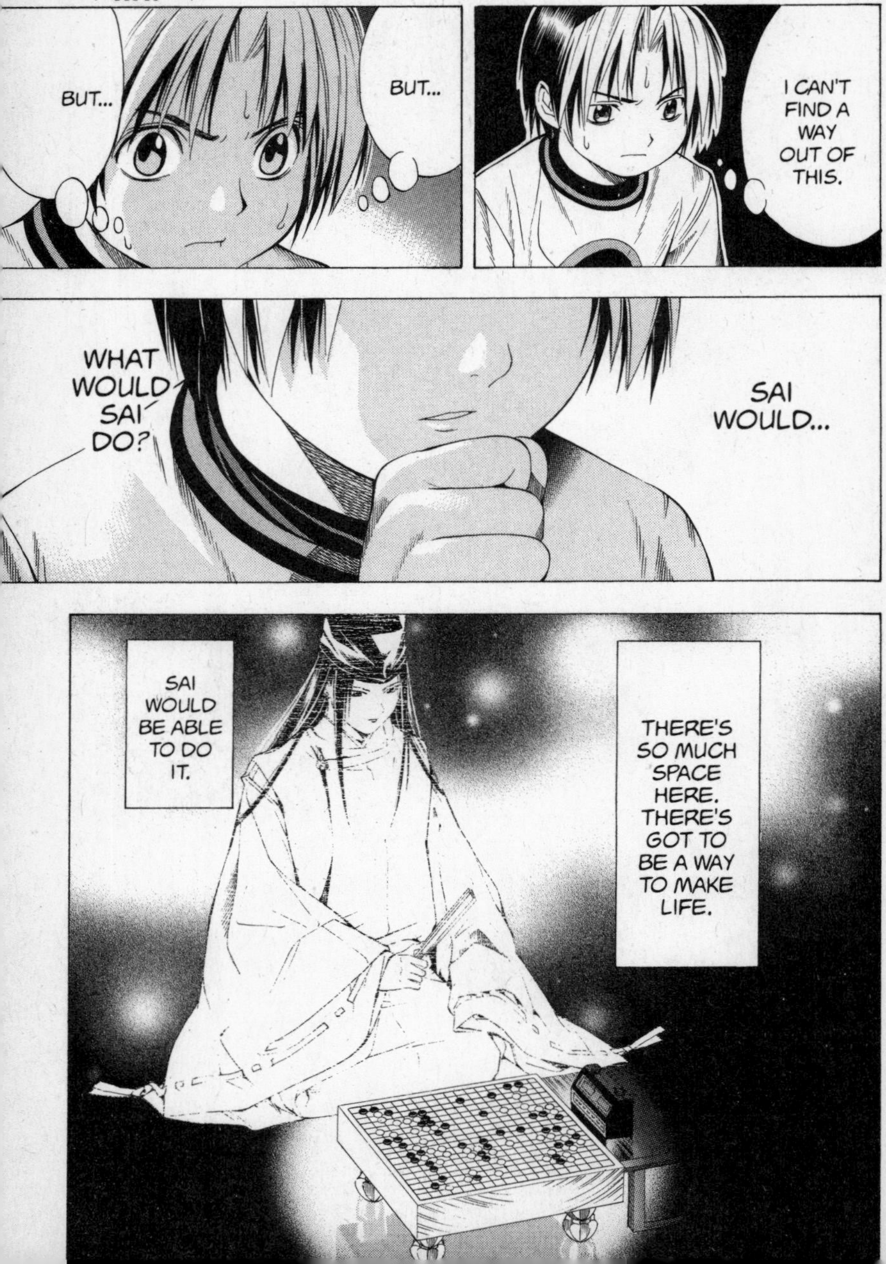
I CAN'T FIND A WAY OUT OF THIS.
BUT...
BUT...
SAI WOULD...
WHAT WOULD SAI DO?
THERE'S SO MUCH SPACE HERE. THERE'S GOT TO BE A WAY TO MAKE LIFE.
SAI WOULD BE ABLE TO DO IT.

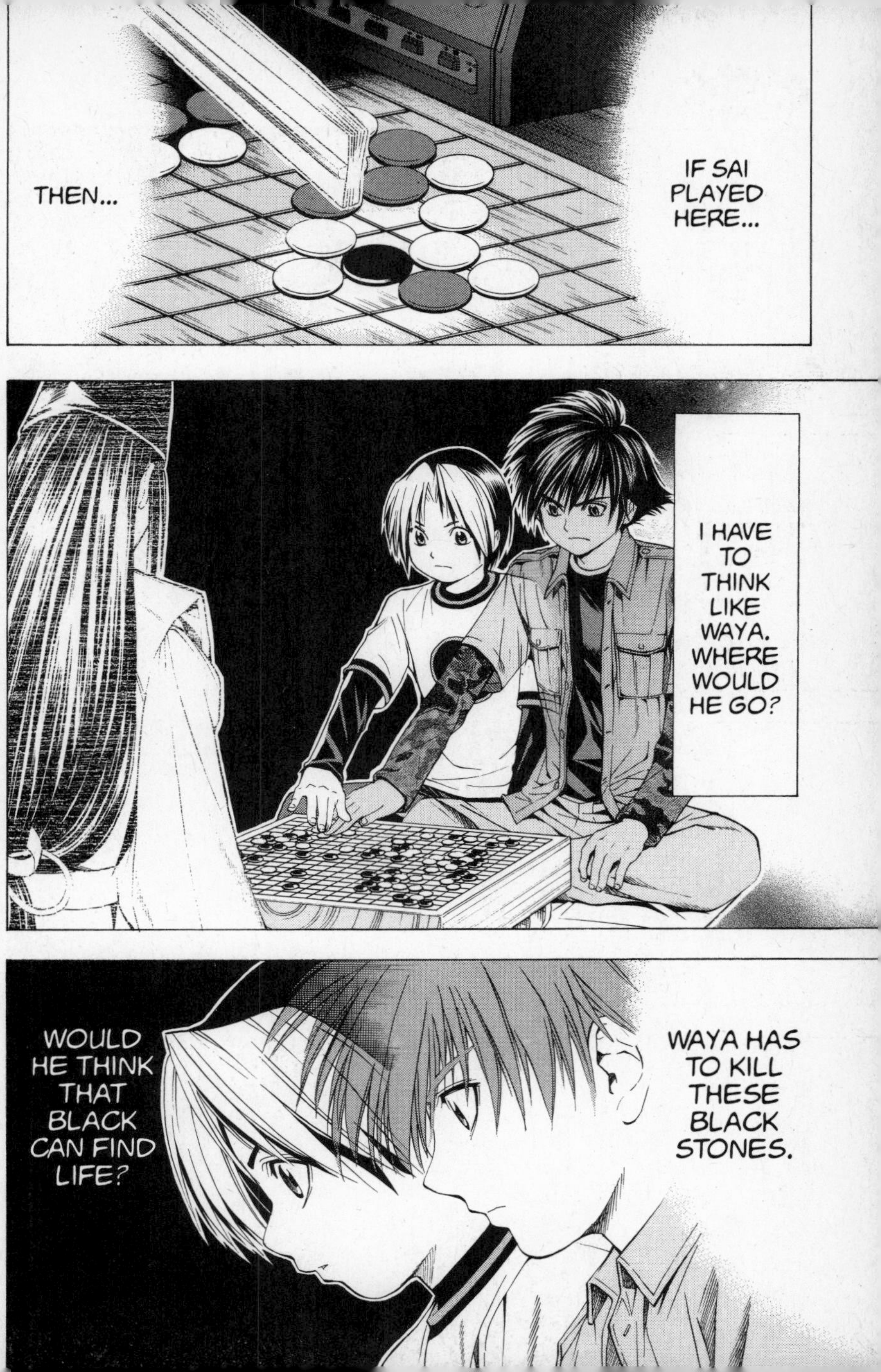
IF SAI PLAYED HERE...
THEN...
I HAVE TO THINK LIKE WAYA. WHERE WOULD HE GO?
WAYA HAS TO KILL THESE BLACK STONES.
WOULD HE THINK THAT BLACK CAN FIND LIFE?

READ THIS WAY

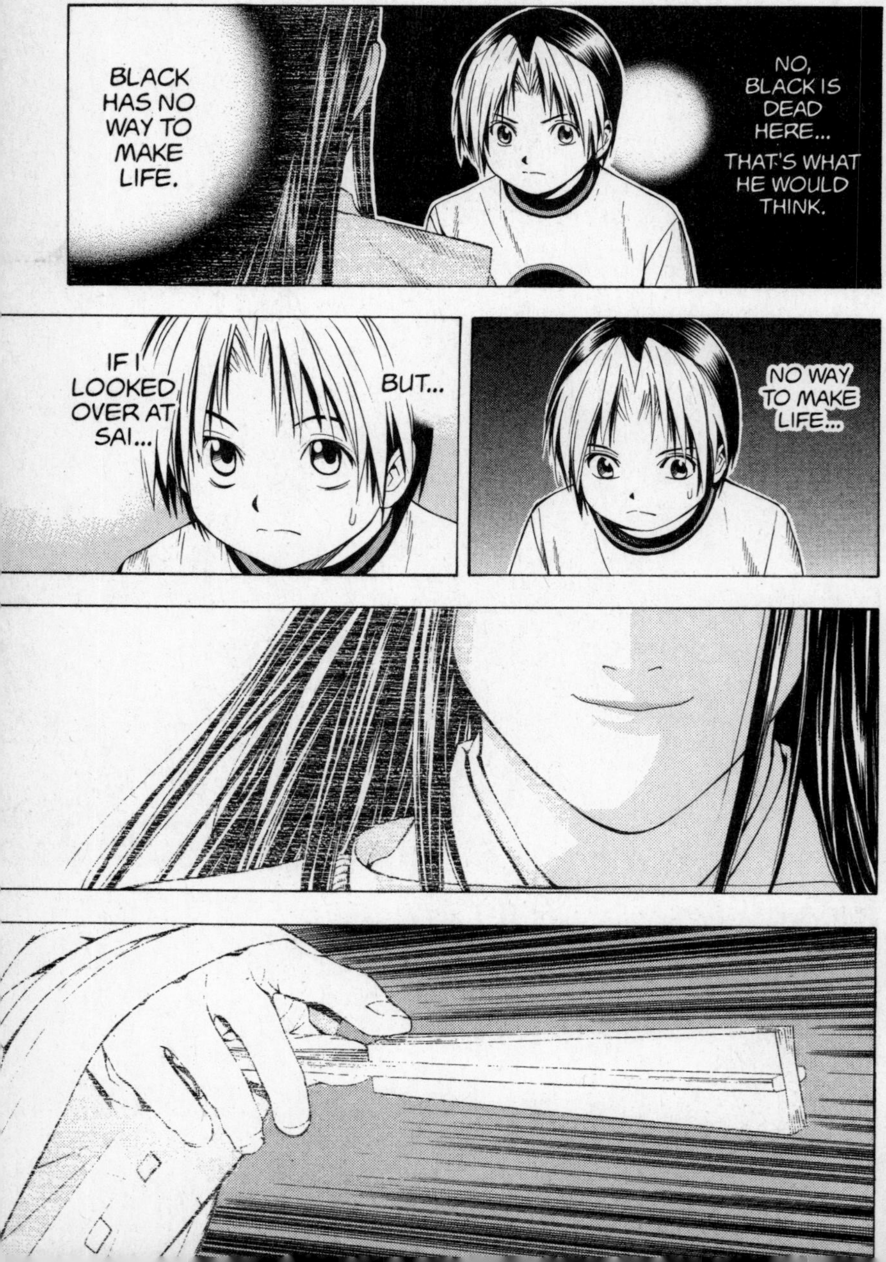
NO, BLACK IS DEAD HERE...
THAT'S WHAT HE WOULD THINK.
BLACK HAS NO WAY TO MAKE LIFE.
NO WAY TO MAKE LIFE...
BUT...
IF I LOOKED OVER AT SAI...

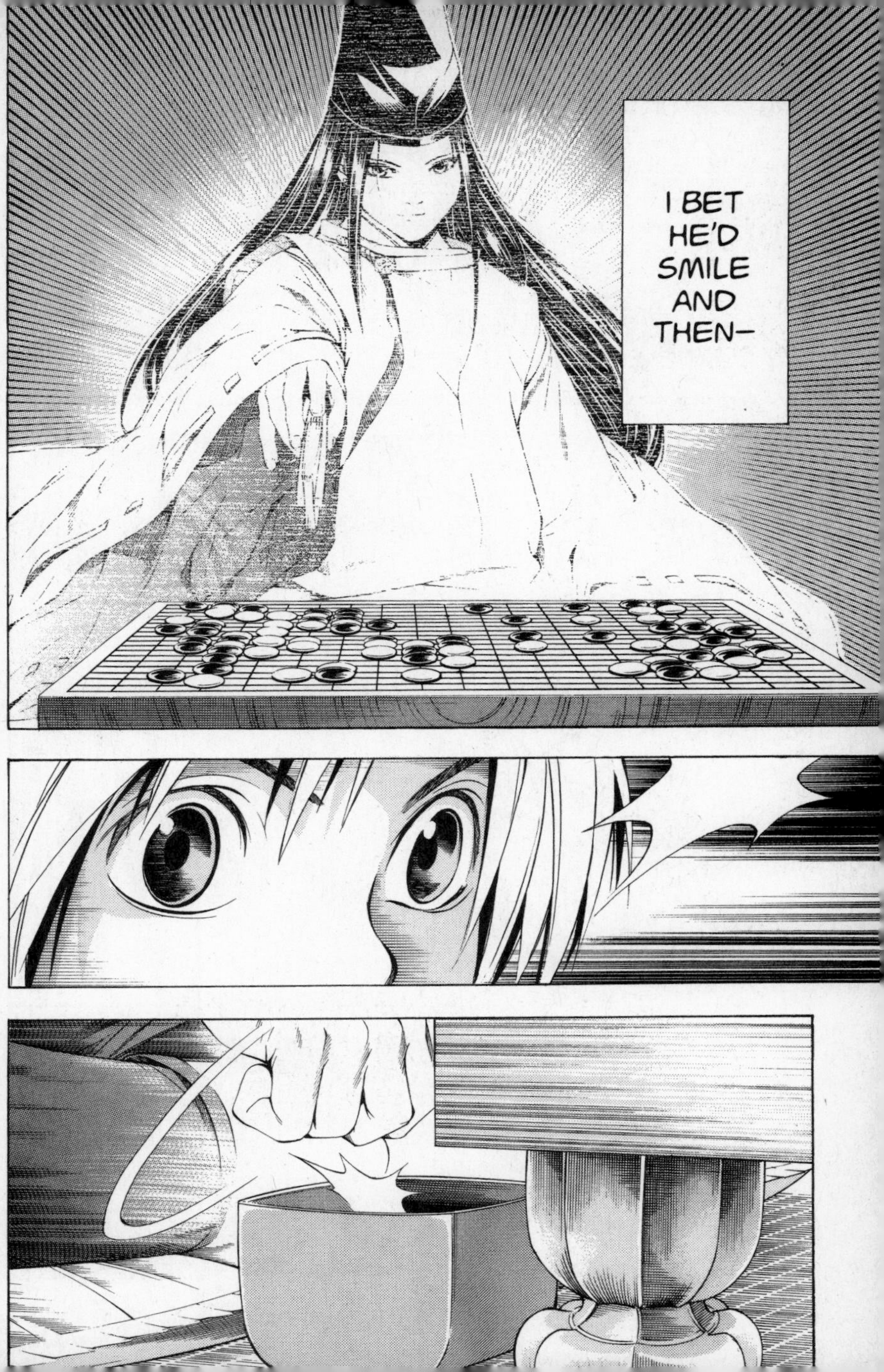
I BET HE'D SMILE AND THEN–

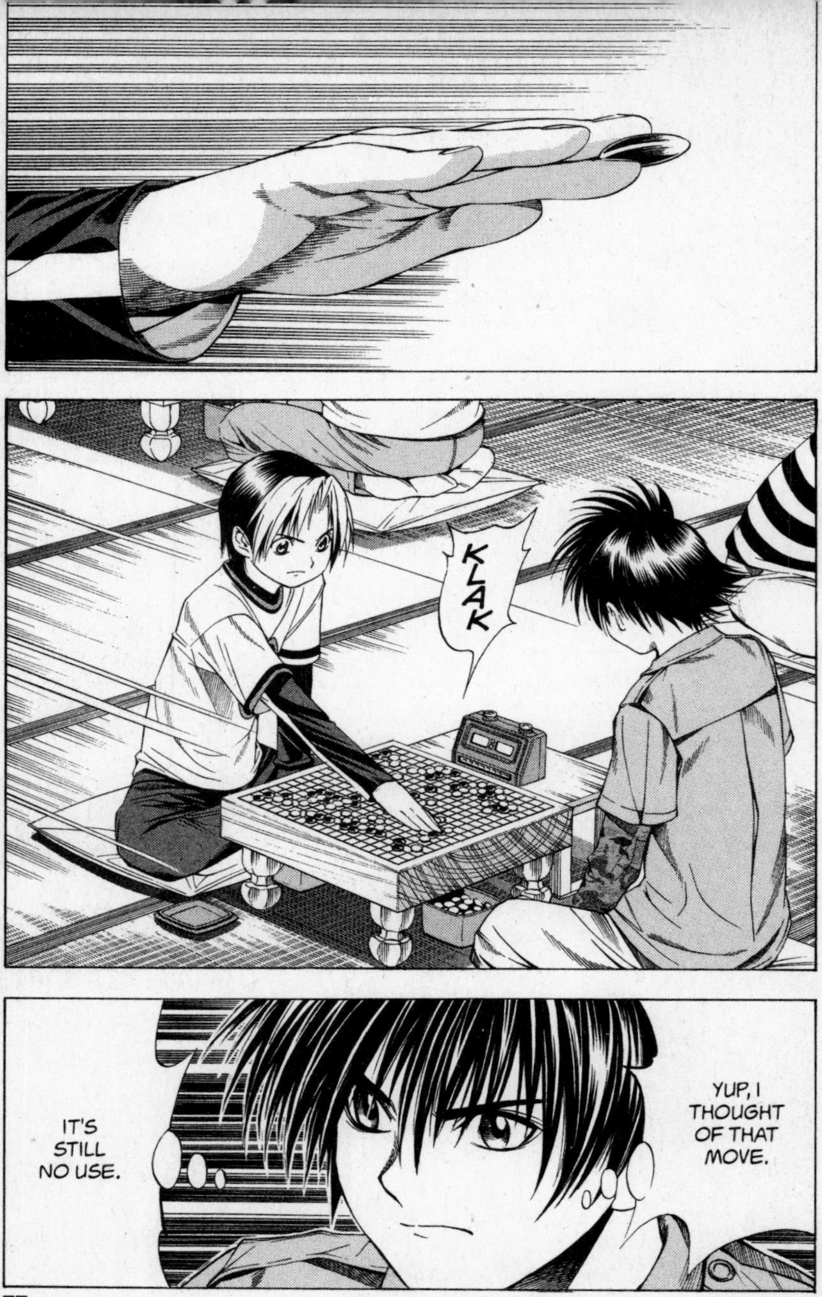
KLAK
YUP, I THOUGHT OF THAT MOVE.
IT'S STILL NO USE.

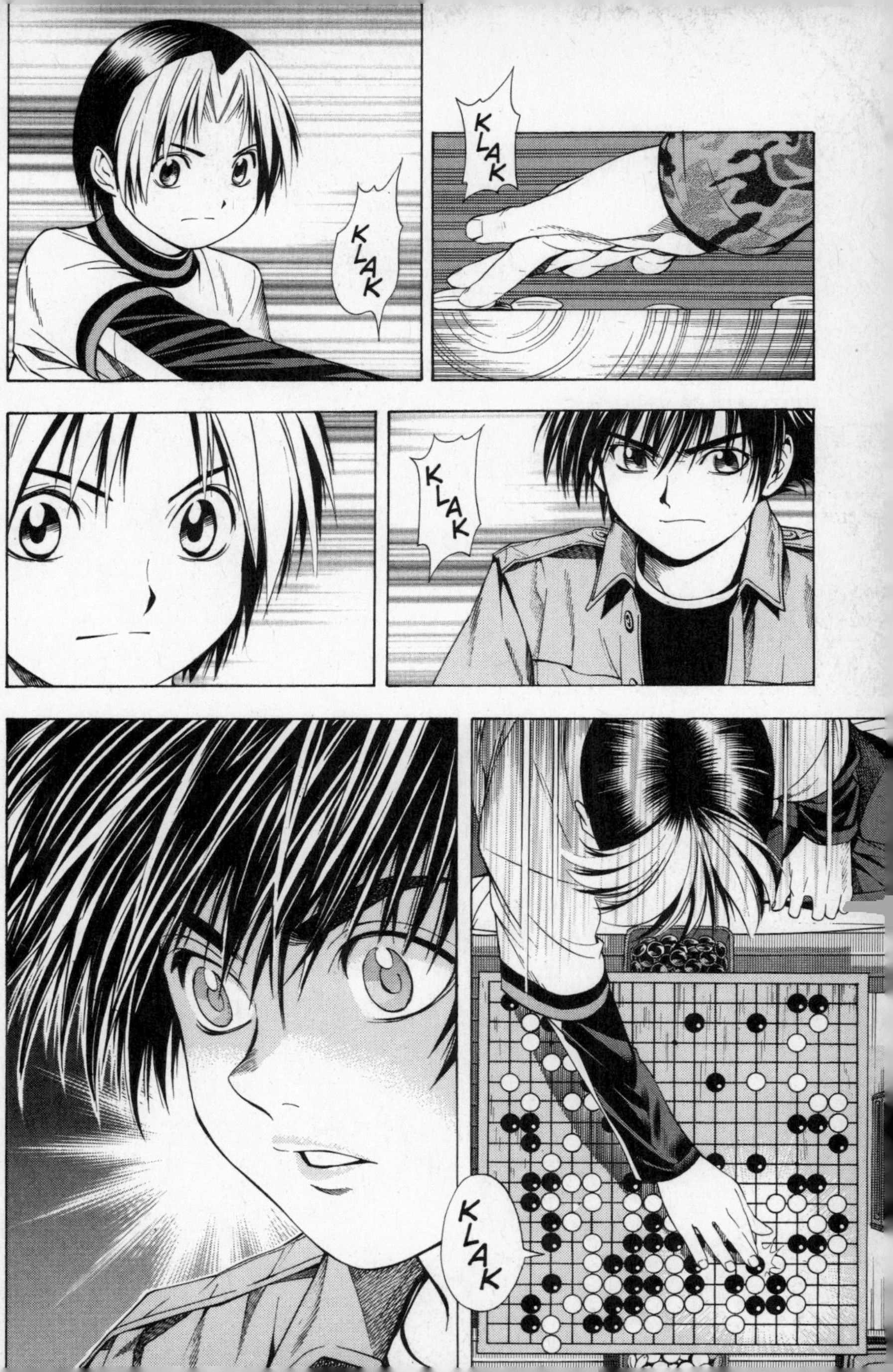
KLAK
KLAK
KLAK
KLAK

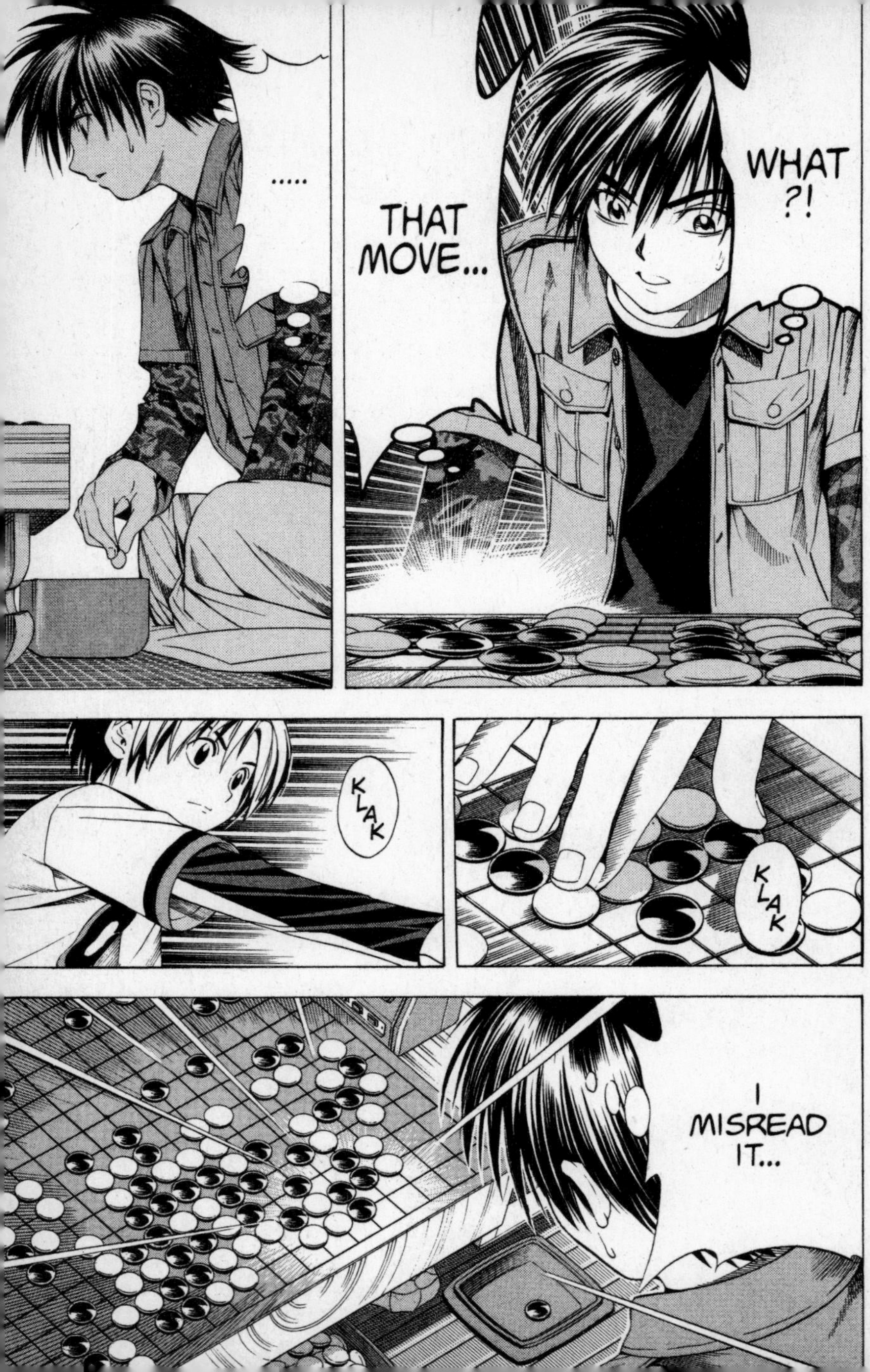
WHAT ?!
THAT MOVE...
.....
KLAK
KLAK
I MISREAD IT...

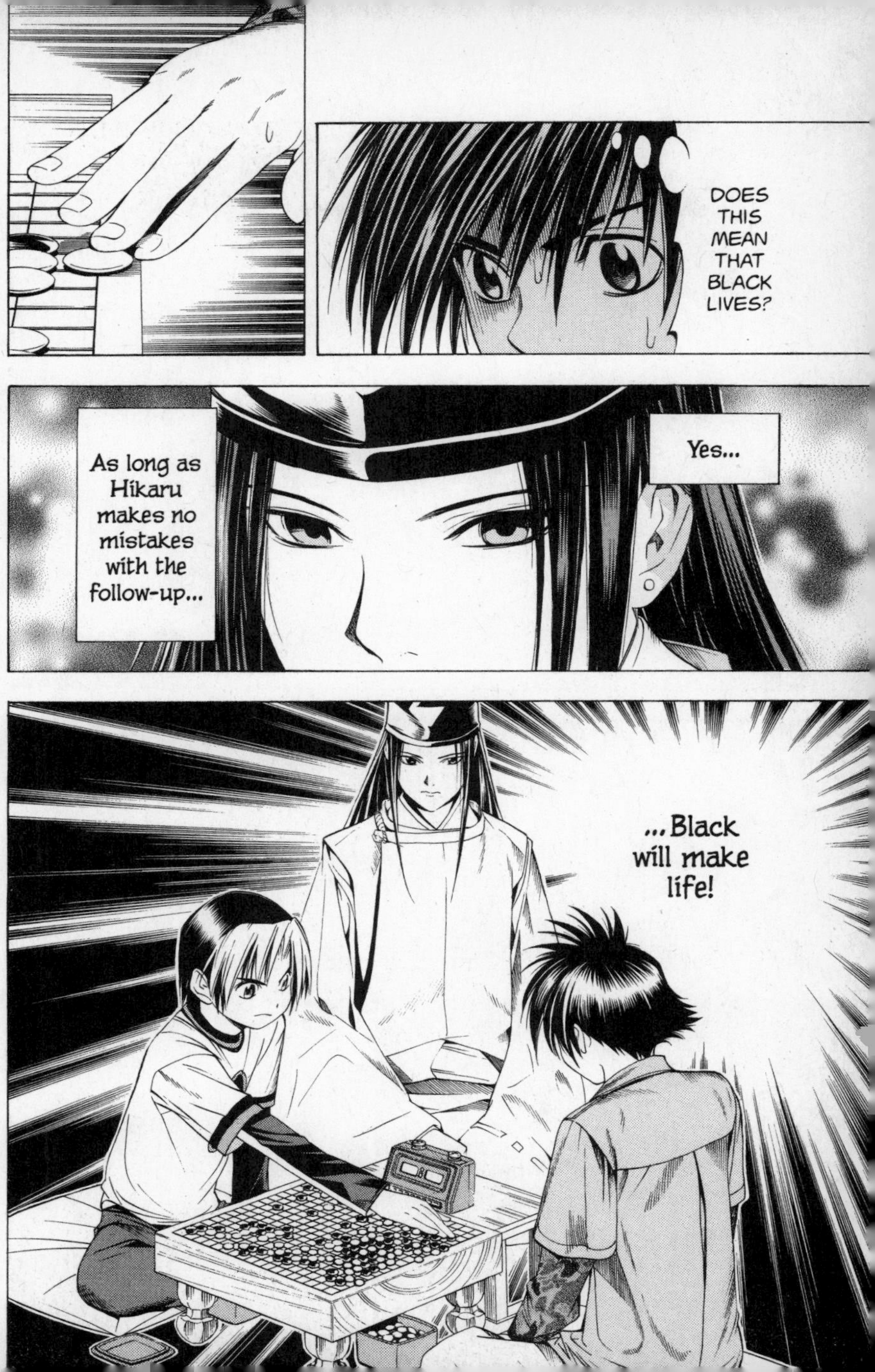
DOES THIS MEAN THAT BLACK LIVES?
Yes...
As long as Hikaru makes no mistakes with the follow-up...
...Black will make life!

READ THIS WAY

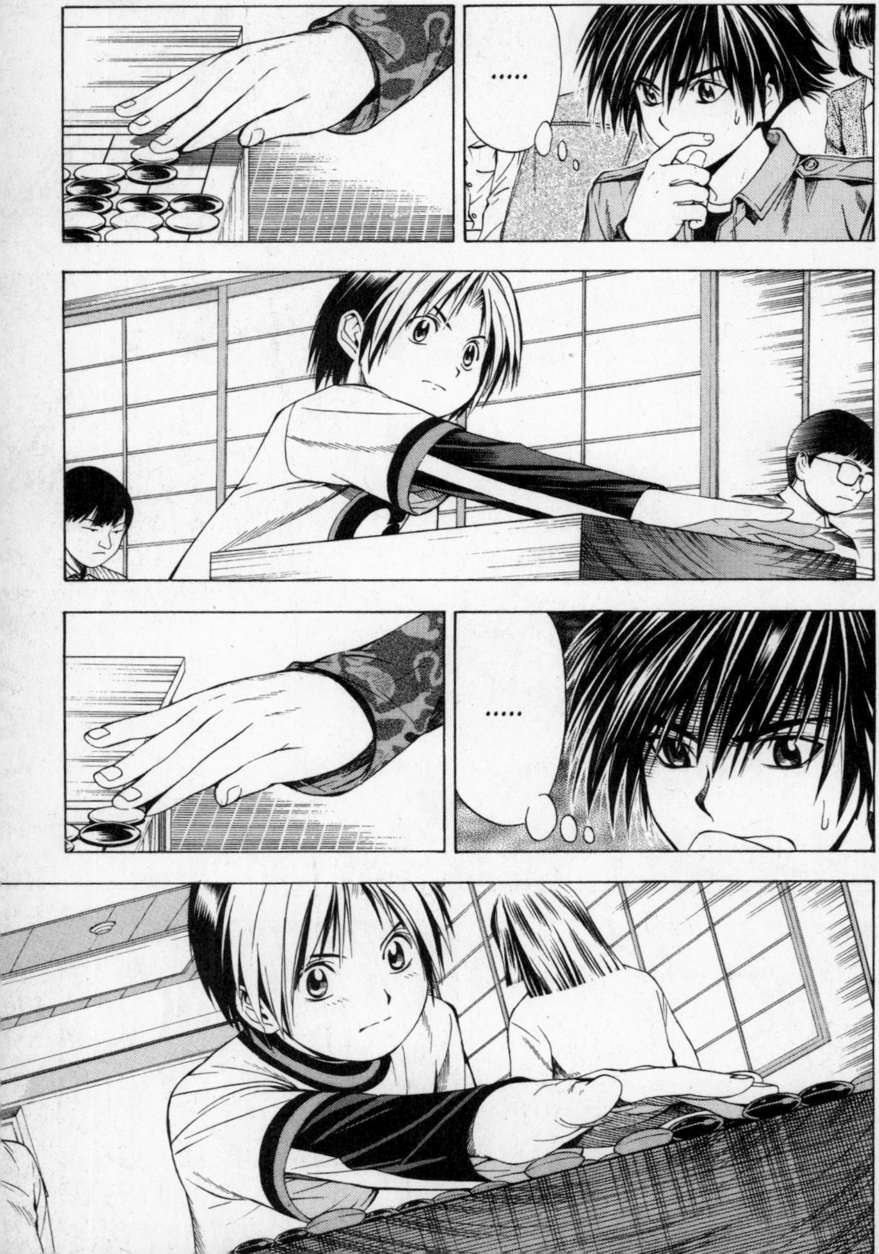
.....
.....

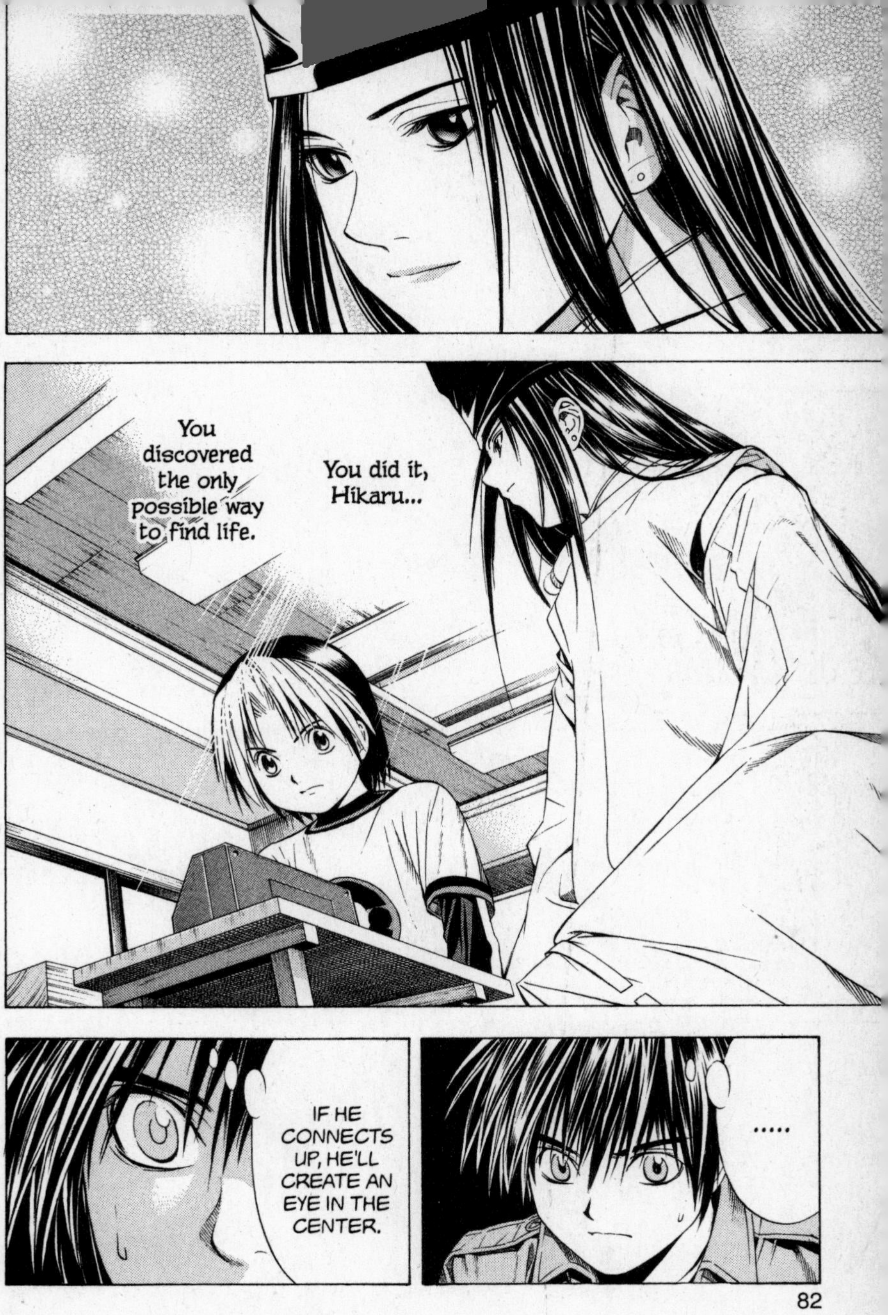
You did it, Hikaru...
You discovered the only possible way to find life.
.....
IF HE CONNECTS UP, HE'LL CREATE AN EYE IN THE CENTER.

READ THIS WAY

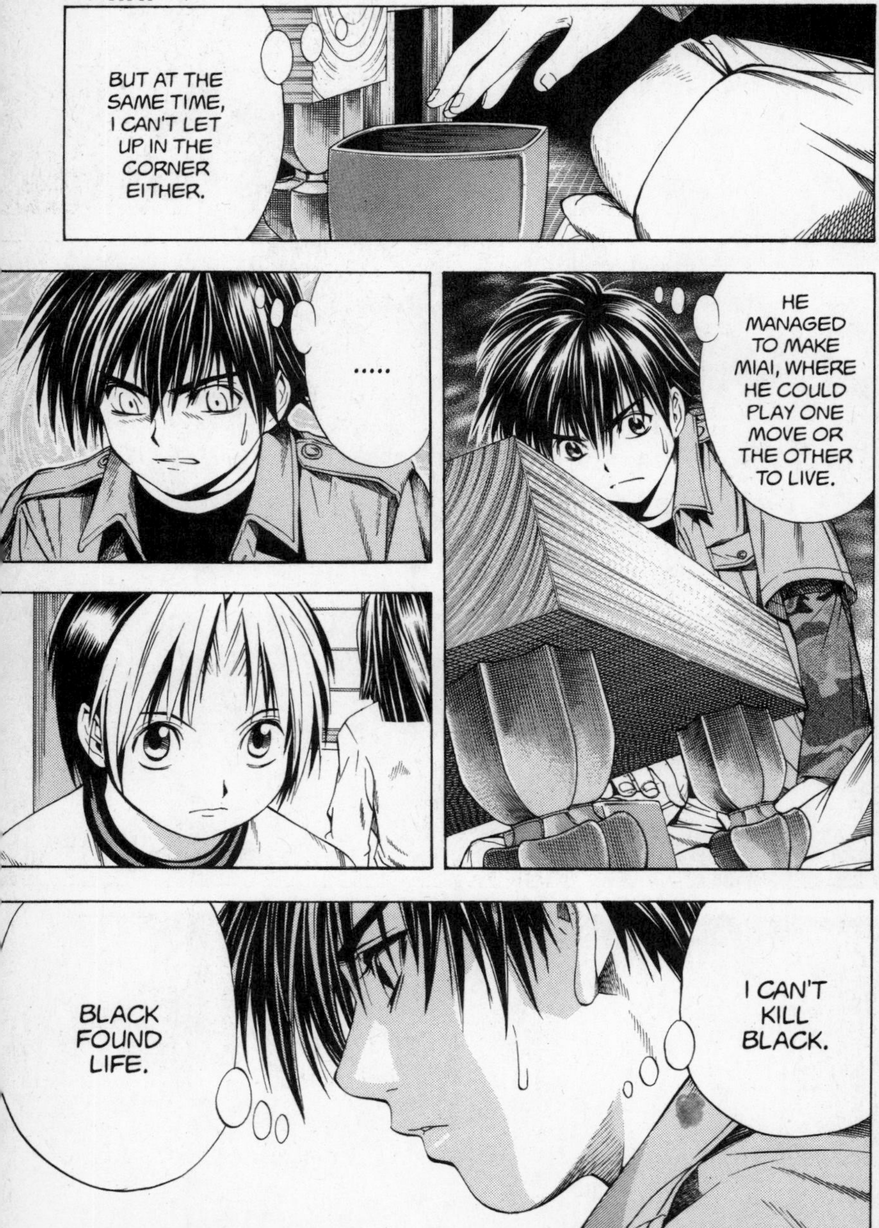
BUT AT THE SAME TIME, I CAN'T LET UP IN THE CORNER EITHER.
HE MANAGED TO MAKE MIAI, WHERE HE COULD PLAY ONE MOVE OR THE OTHER TO LIVE.
.....
I CAN'T KILL BLACK.
BLACK FOUND LIFE.

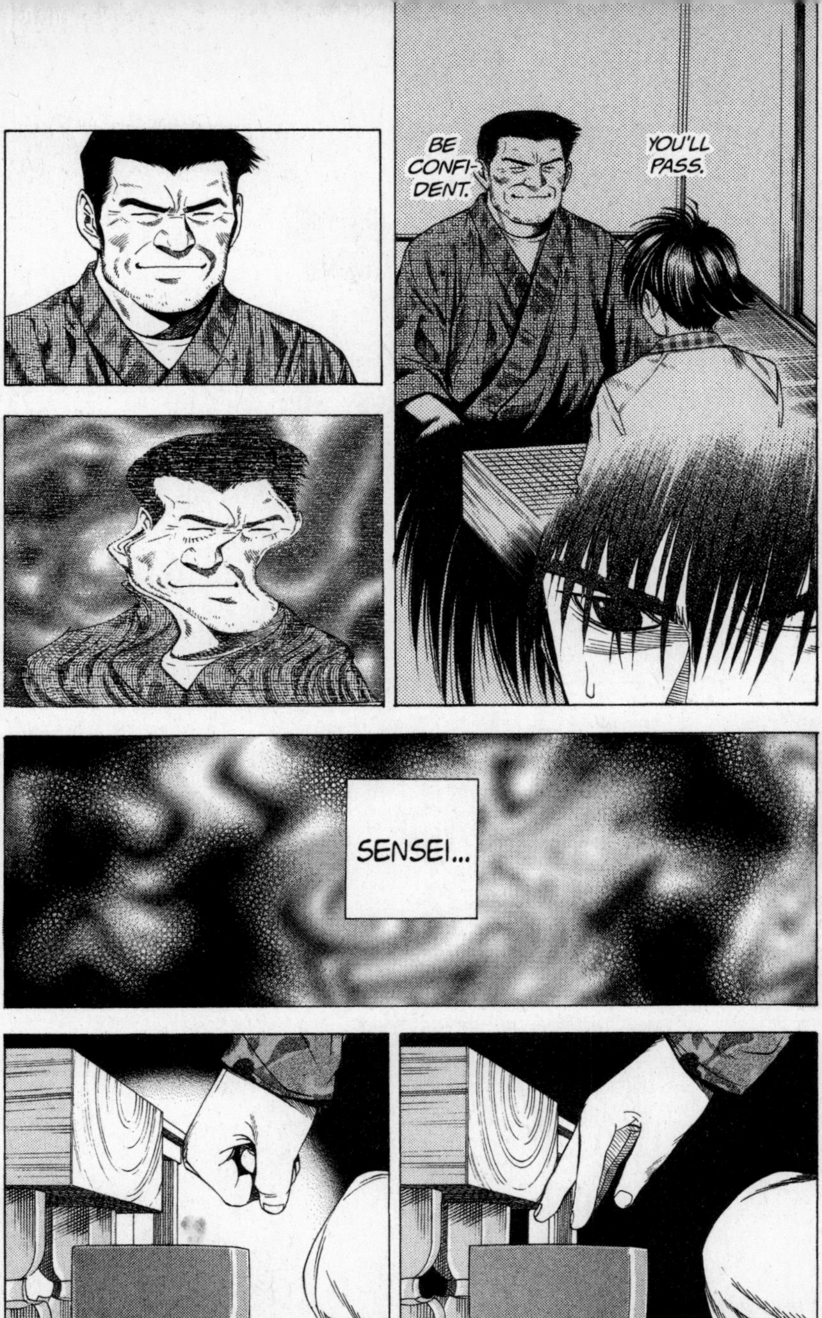
YOU'LL PASS.
BE CONFI-DENT.
SENSEI...

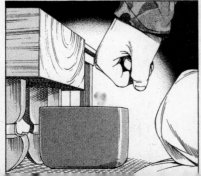

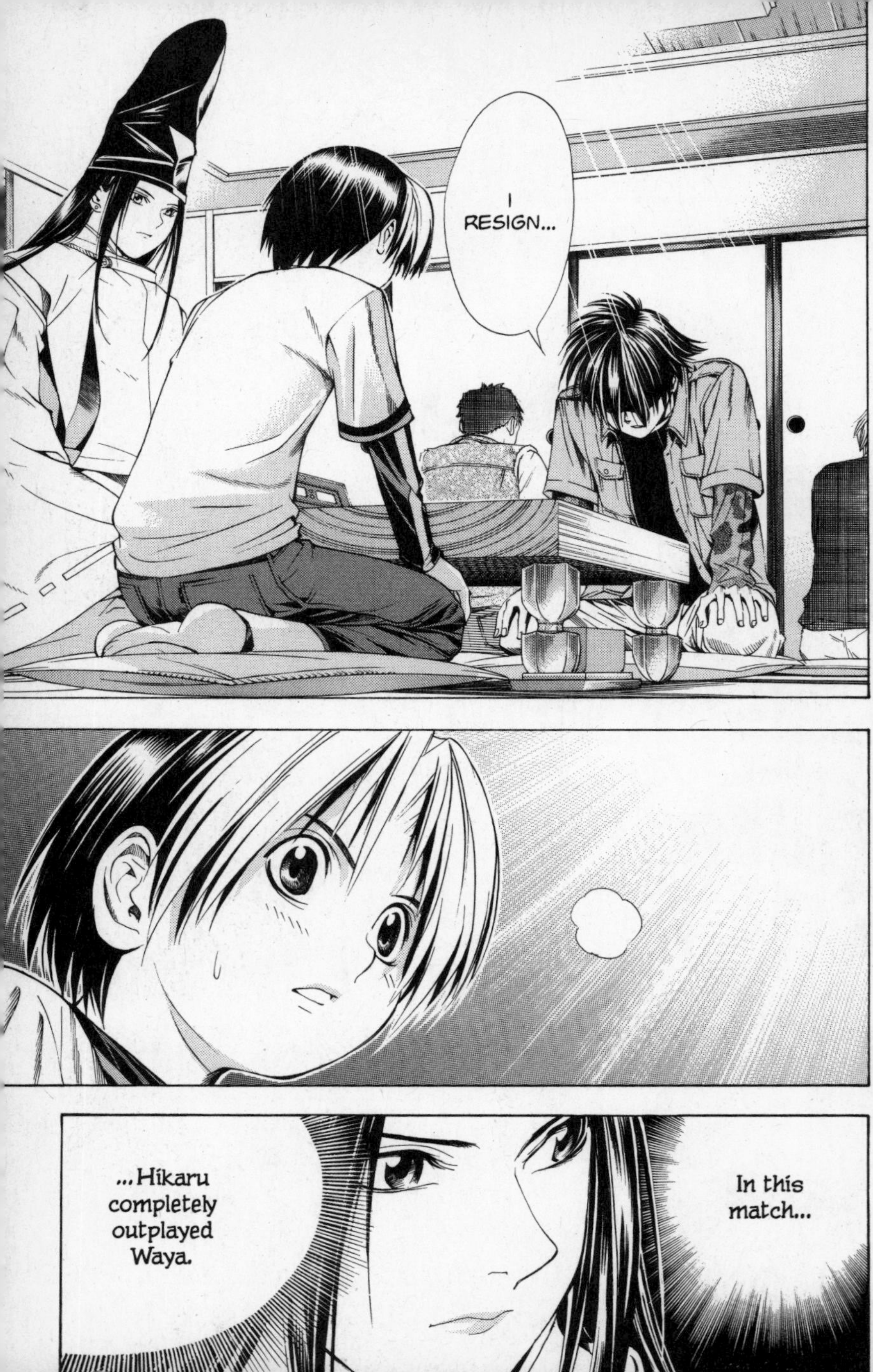
I RESIGN...
In this match...
...Hikaru completely outplayed Waya.

THE HONG KONG EDITION LOOKS JUST LIKE THE JAPANESE ONE, ONLY IT DOESN'T USE HONORIFICS!

*EACH CHARACTER IS JUST SAYING THE OTHER CHARACTER'S NAME!

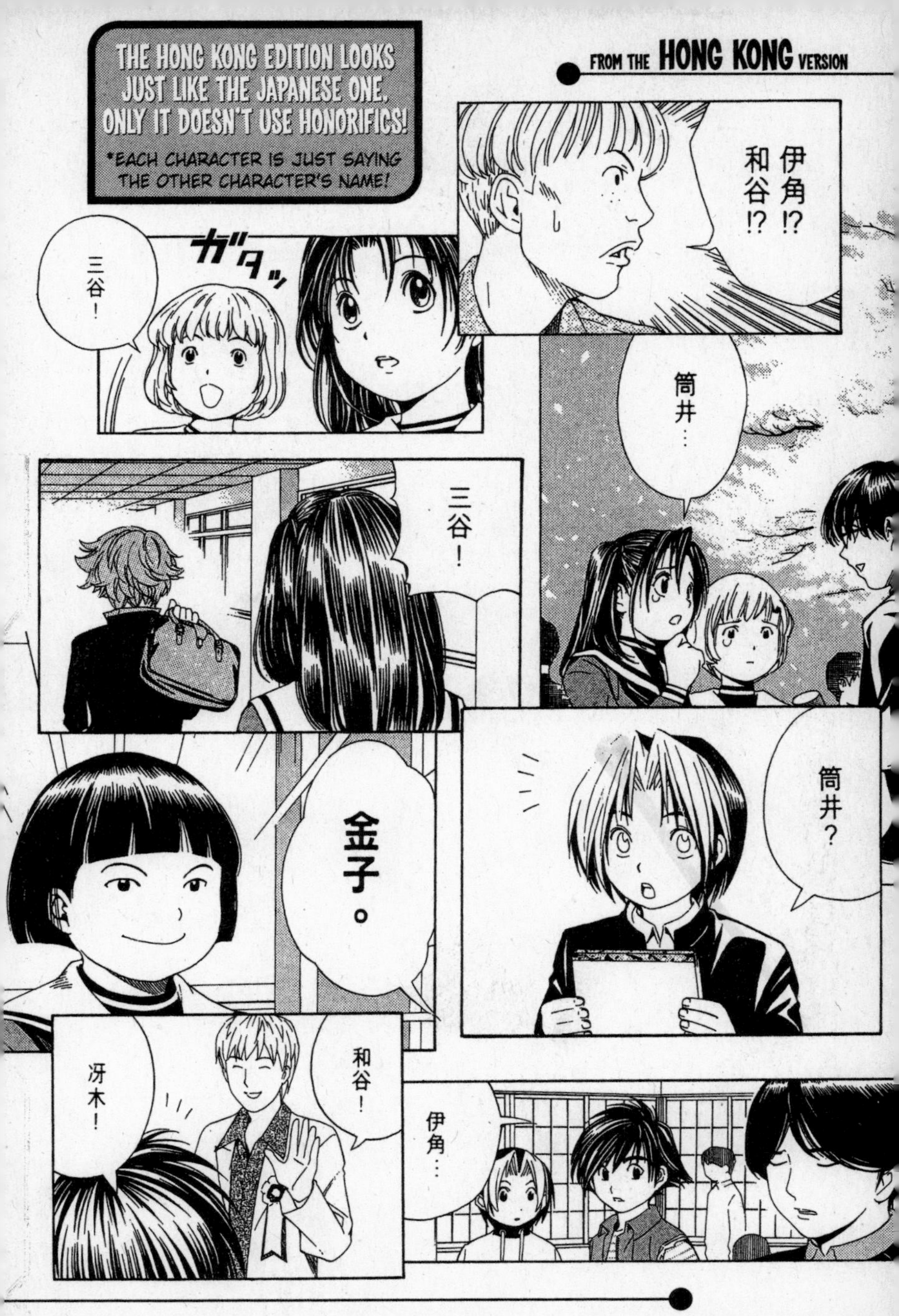
伊角!?
和谷!?
ガタッ
三谷!
筒井…
三谷!
筒井?
金子。
伊角…
和谷!
冴木!

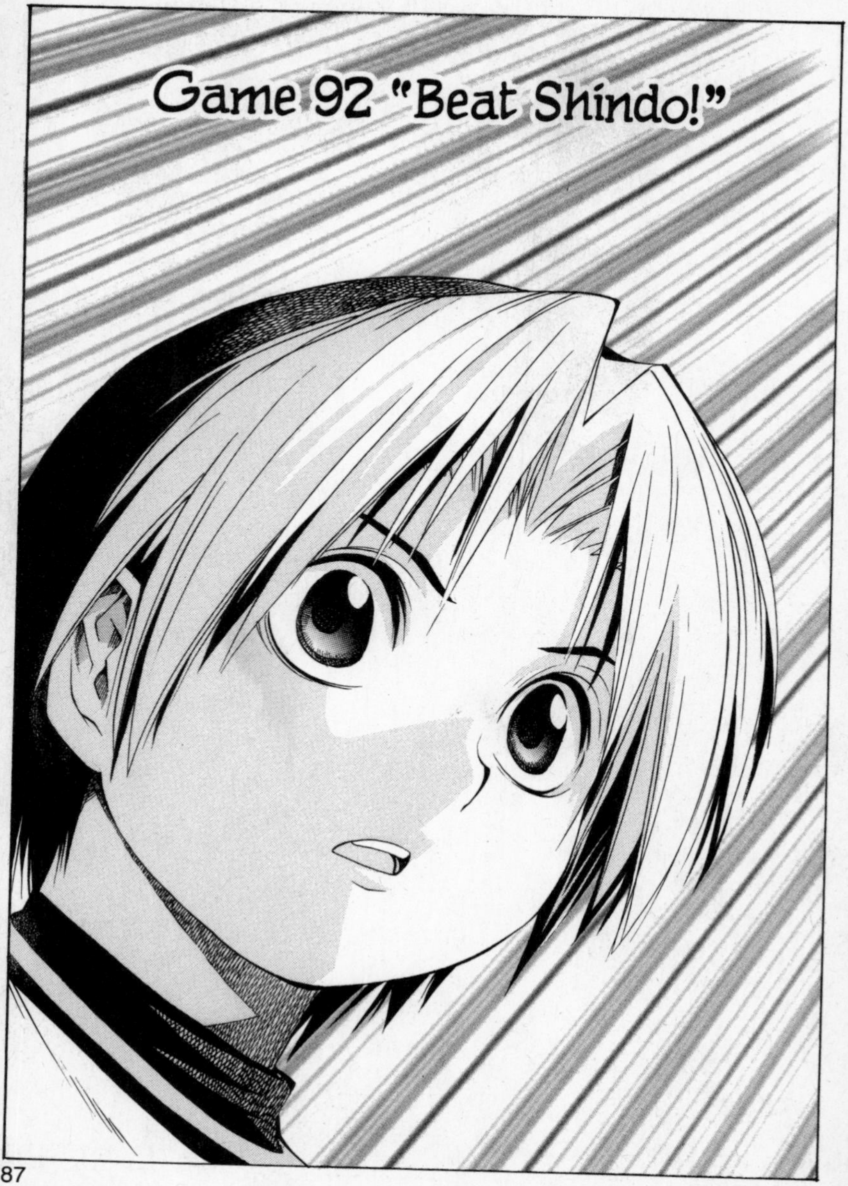
Game 92 "Beat Shindo!"

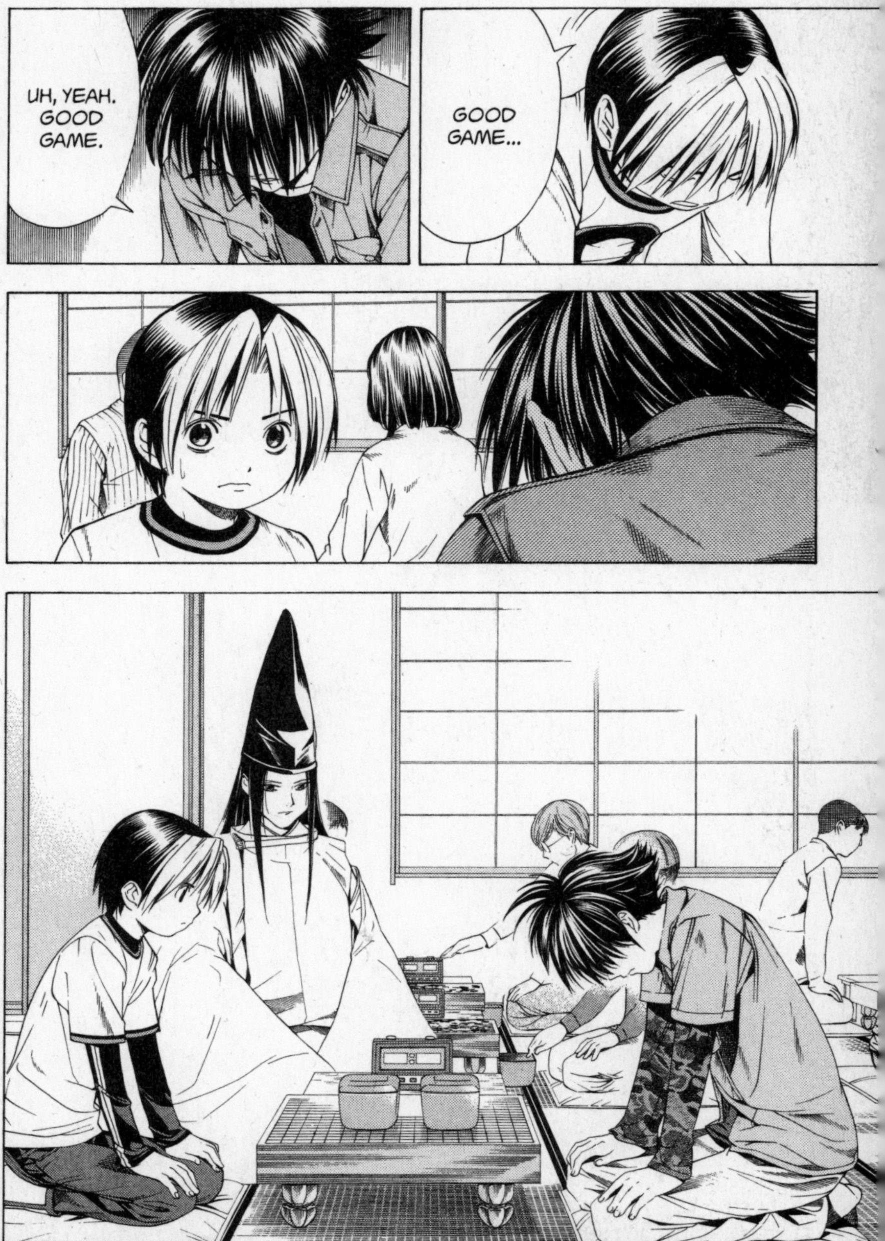
GOOD GAME...
UH, YEAH. GOOD GAME.

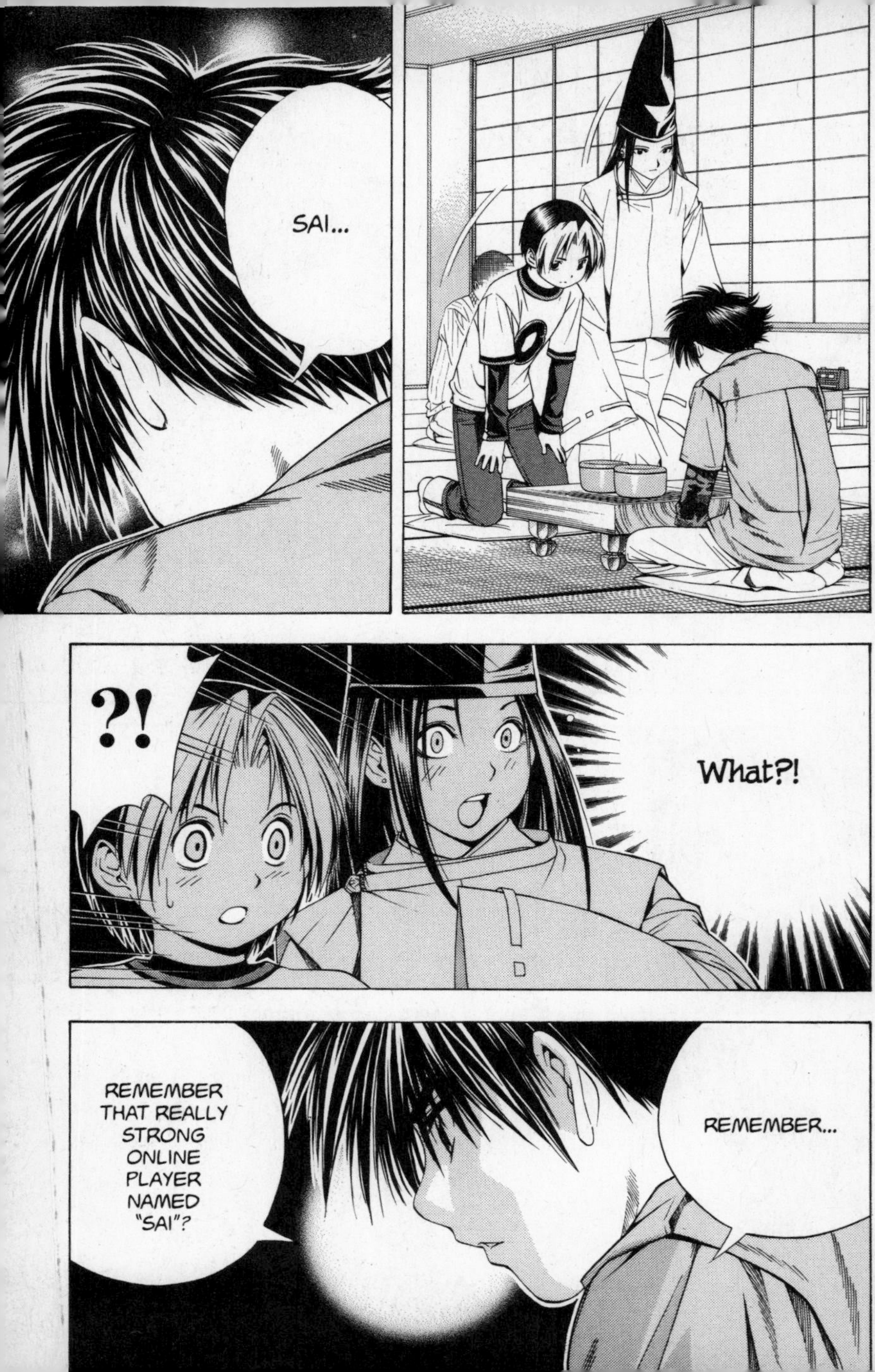
SAI...
What?!
?!
REMEMBER...
REMEMBER THAT REALLY STRONG ONLINE PLAYER NAMED "SAI"?

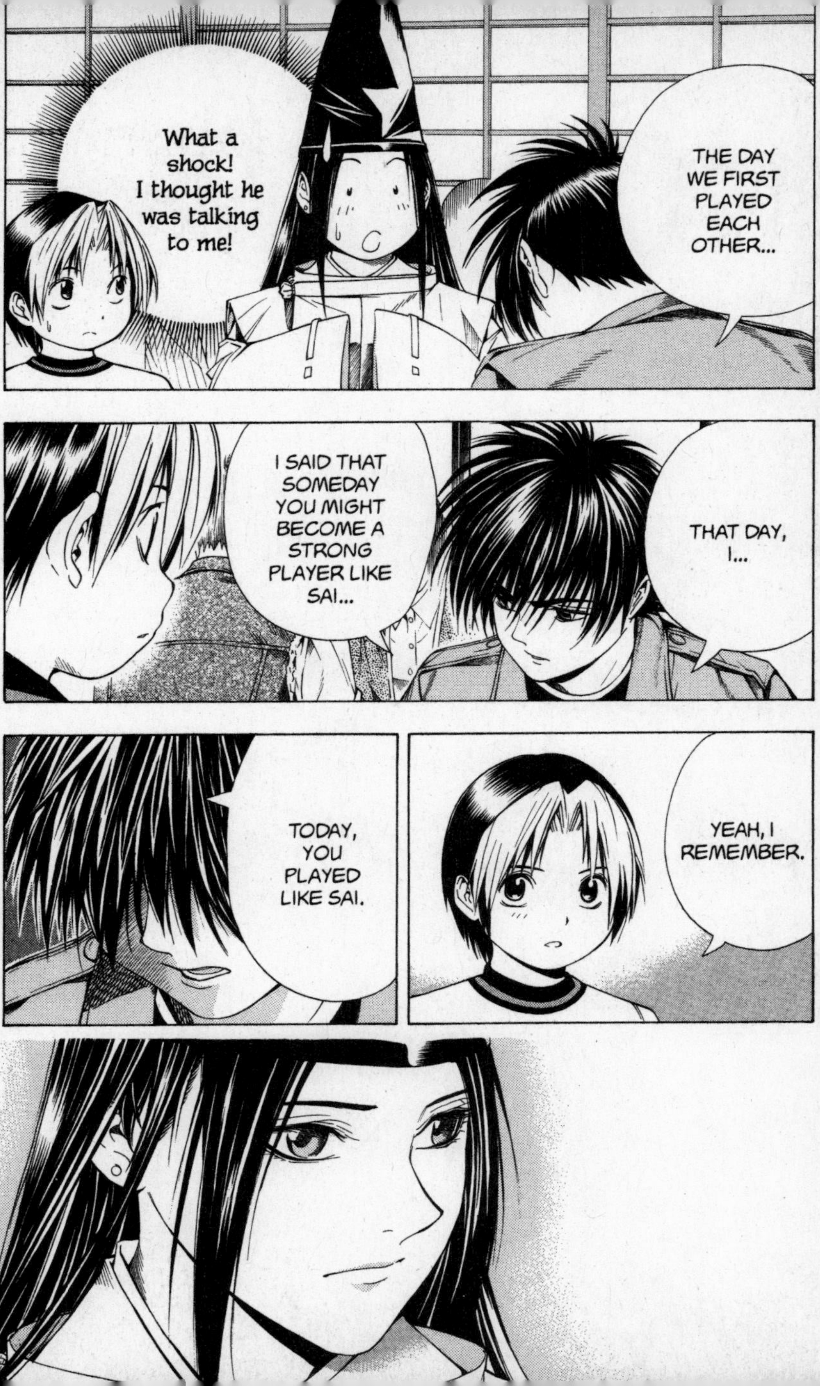
THE DAY WE FIRST PLAYED EACH OTHER...
What a shock! I thought he was talking to me!
THAT DAY, I...
I SAID THAT SOMEDAY YOU MIGHT BECOME A STRONG PLAYER LIKE SAI...
YEAH, I REMEMBER.
TODAY, YOU PLAYED LIKE SAI.

READ THIS WAY

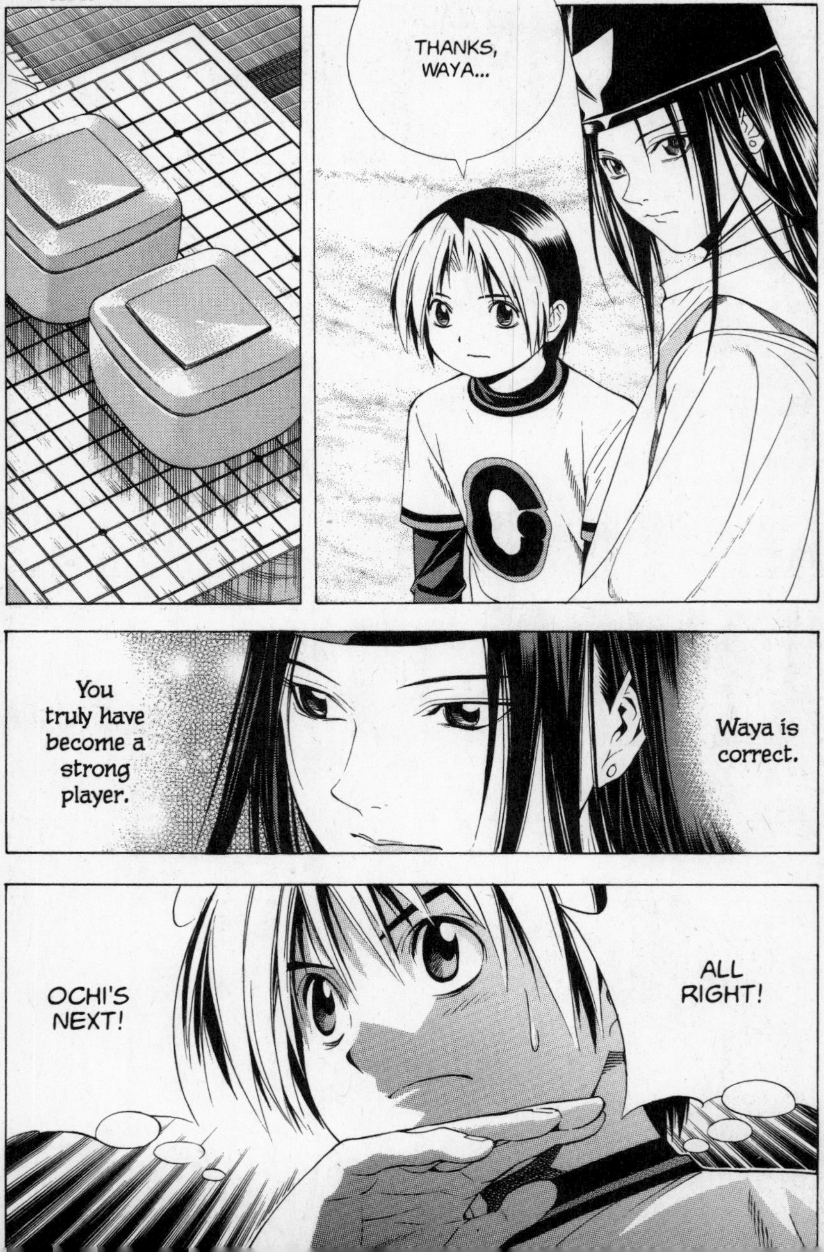
THANKS, WAYA...
Waya is correct.
You truly have become a strong player.
ALL RIGHT!
OCHI'S NEXT!

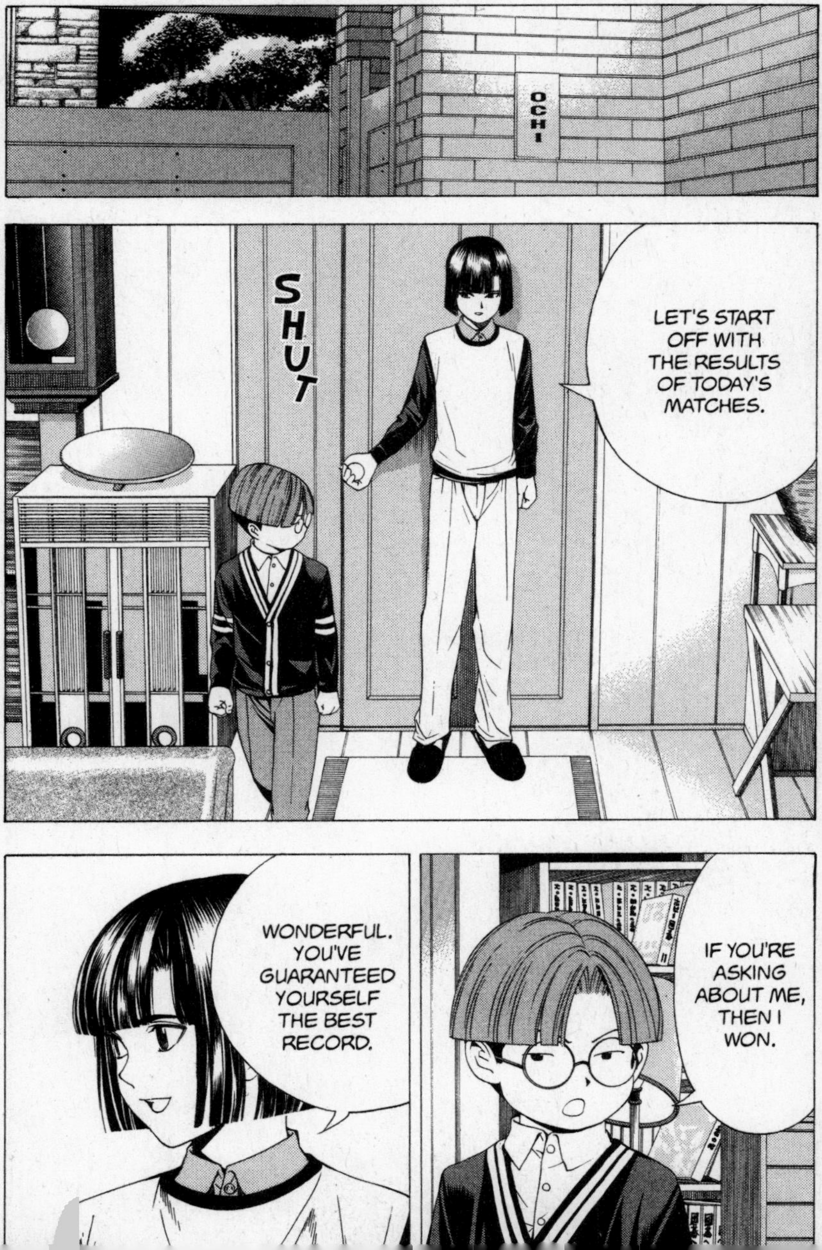
OCHI
SHUT
LET'S START OFF WITH THE RESULTS OF TODAY'S MATCHES.
IF YOU'RE ASKING ABOUT ME, THEN I WON.
WONDERFUL. YOU'VE GUARANTEED YOURSELF THE BEST RECORD.

READ THIS WAY

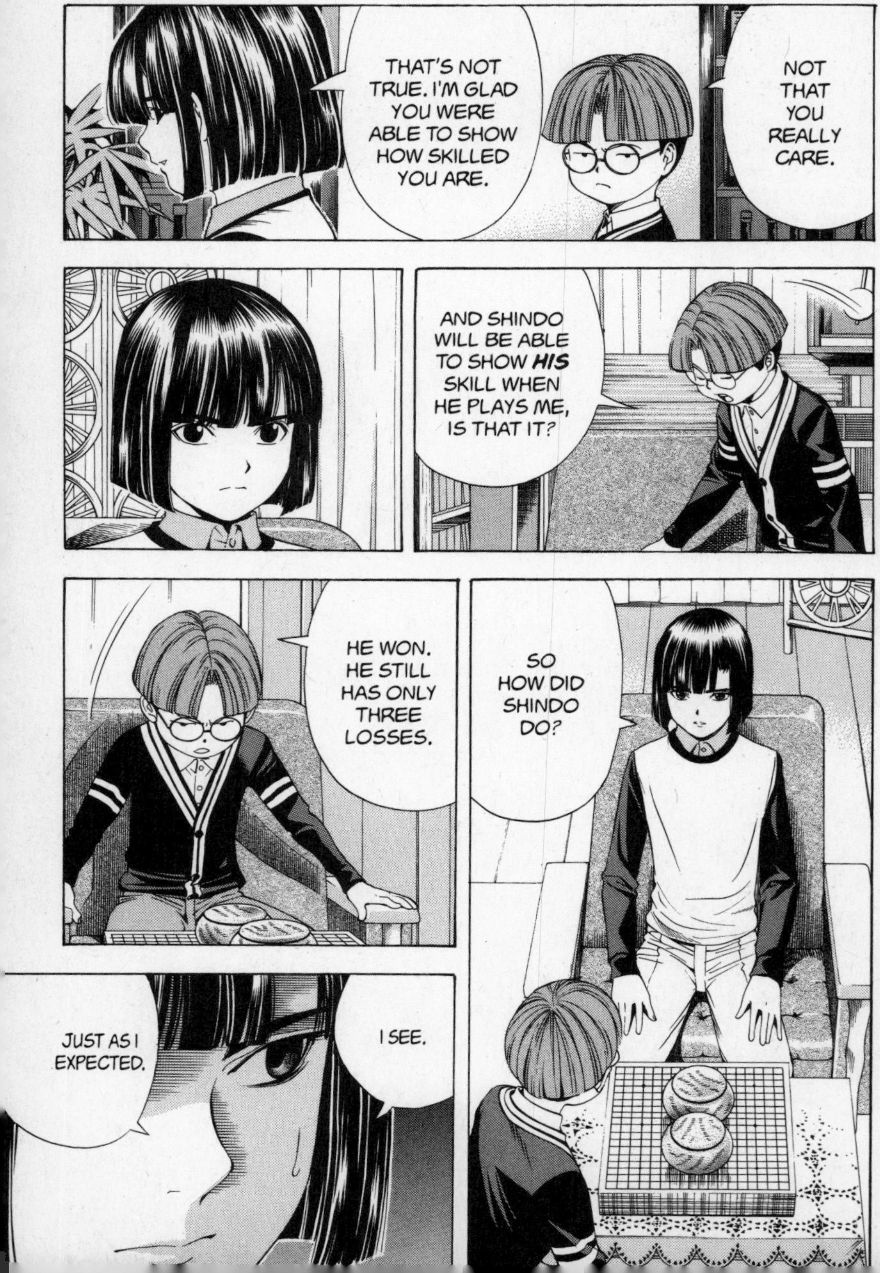
NOT THAT YOU REALLY CARE.
THAT'S NOT TRUE. I'M GLAD YOU WERE ABLE TO SHOW HOW SKILLED YOU ARE.
AND SHINDO WILL BE ABLE TO SHOW *HIS* SKILL WHEN HE PLAYS ME, IS THAT IT?
SO HOW DID SHINDO DO?
HE WON. HE STILL HAS ONLY THREE LOSSES.
I SEE.
JUST AS I EXPECTED.

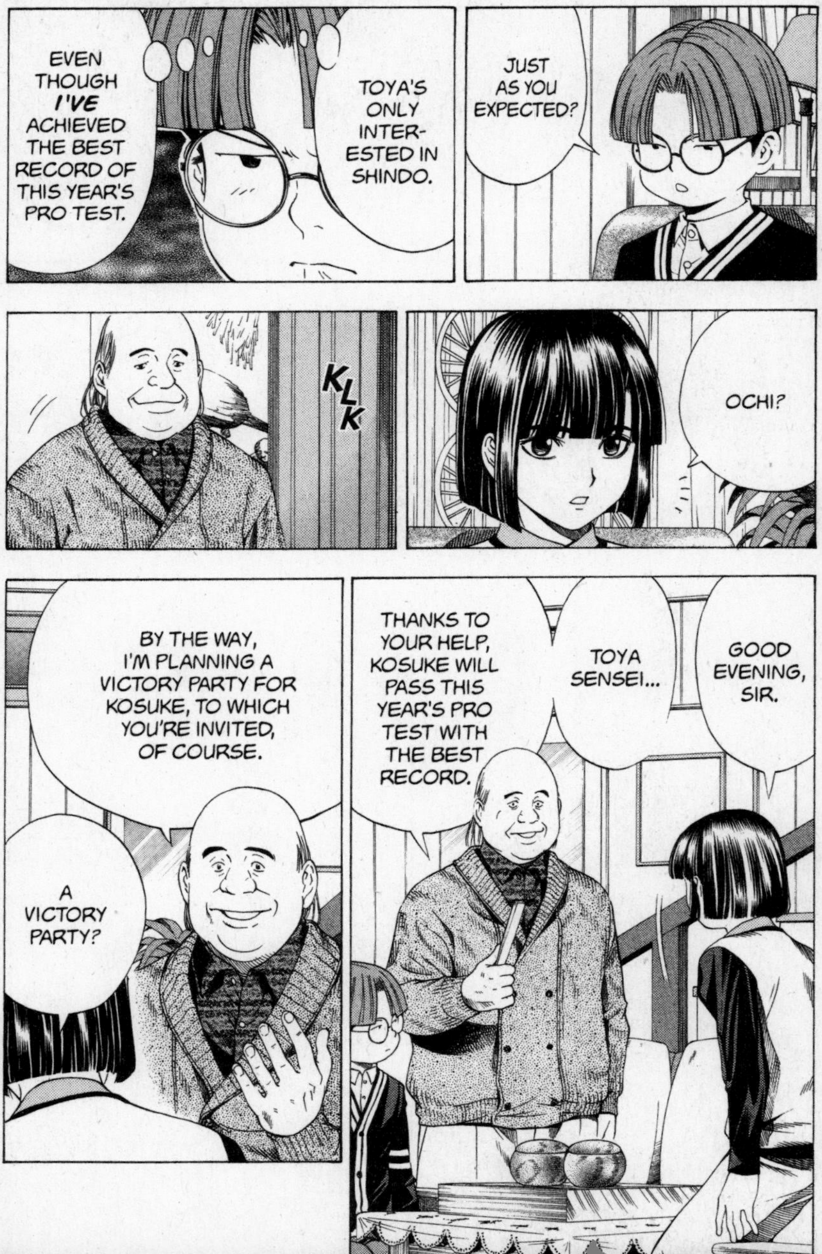
JUST AS YOU EXPECTED?
TOYA'S ONLY INTER-ESTED IN SHINDO.
EVEN THOUGH *I'VE* ACHIEVED THE BEST RECORD OF THIS YEAR'S PRO TEST.
OCHI?
KLK
GOOD EVENING, SIR.
TOYA SENSEI...
THANKS TO YOUR HELP, KOSUKE WILL PASS THIS YEAR'S PRO TEST WITH THE BEST RECORD.
BY THE WAY, I'M PLANNING A VICTORY PARTY FOR KOSUKE, TO WHICH YOU'RE INVITED, OF COURSE.
A VICTORY PARTY?

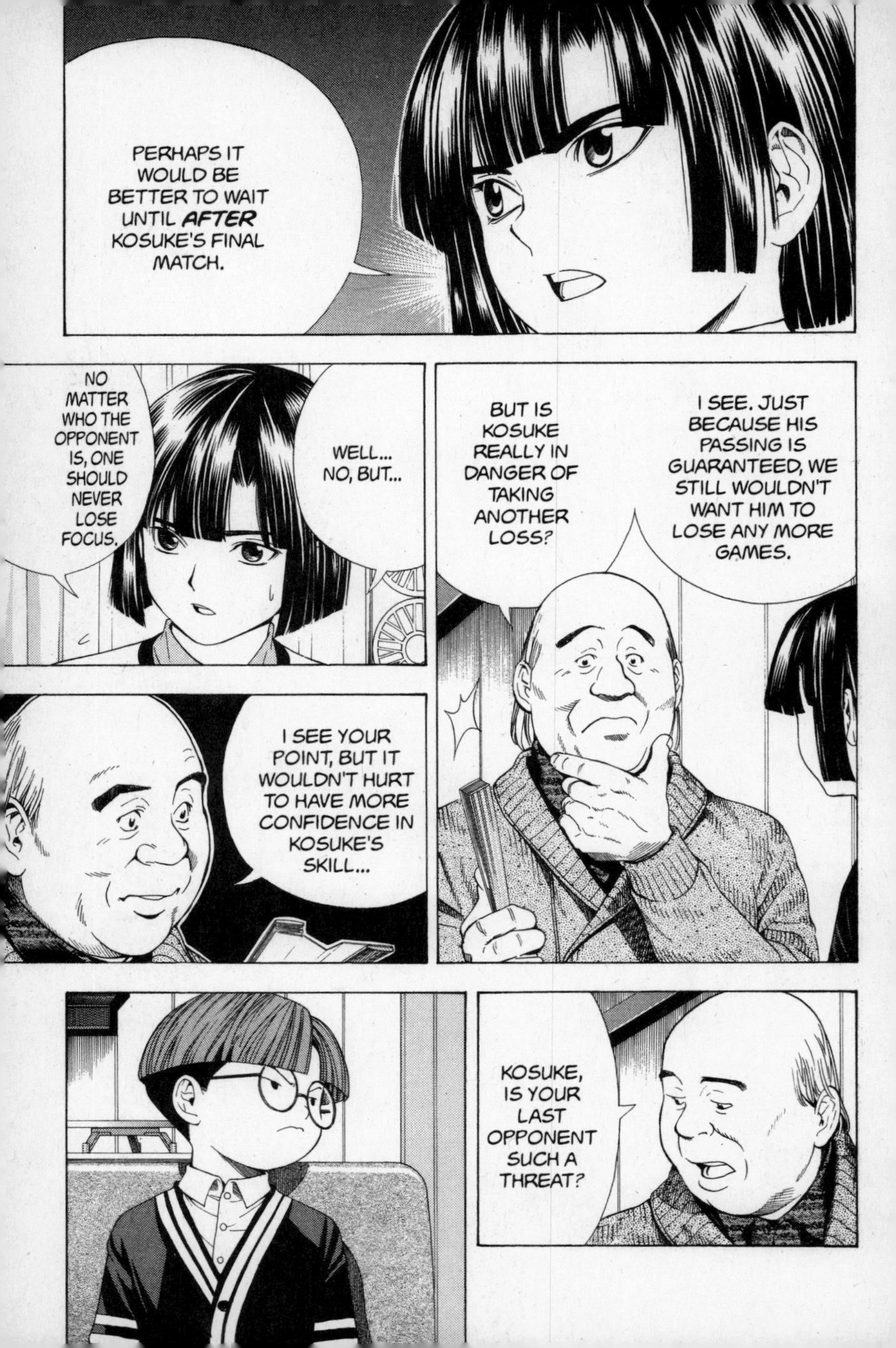
PERHAPS IT WOULD BE BETTER TO WAIT UNTIL AFTER KOSUKE'S FINAL MATCH.
I SEE. JUST BECAUSE HIS PASSING IS GUARANTEED, WE STILL WOULDN'T WANT HIM TO LOSE ANY MORE GAMES.
BUT IS KOSUKE REALLY IN DANGER OF TAKING ANOTHER LOSS?
WELL... NO, BUT...
NO MATTER WHO THE OPPONENT IS, ONE SHOULD NEVER LOSE FOCUS.
I SEE YOUR POINT, BUT IT WOULDN'T HURT TO HAVE MORE CONFIDENCE IN KOSUKE'S SKILL...
KOSUKE, IS YOUR LAST OPPONENT SUCH A THREAT?

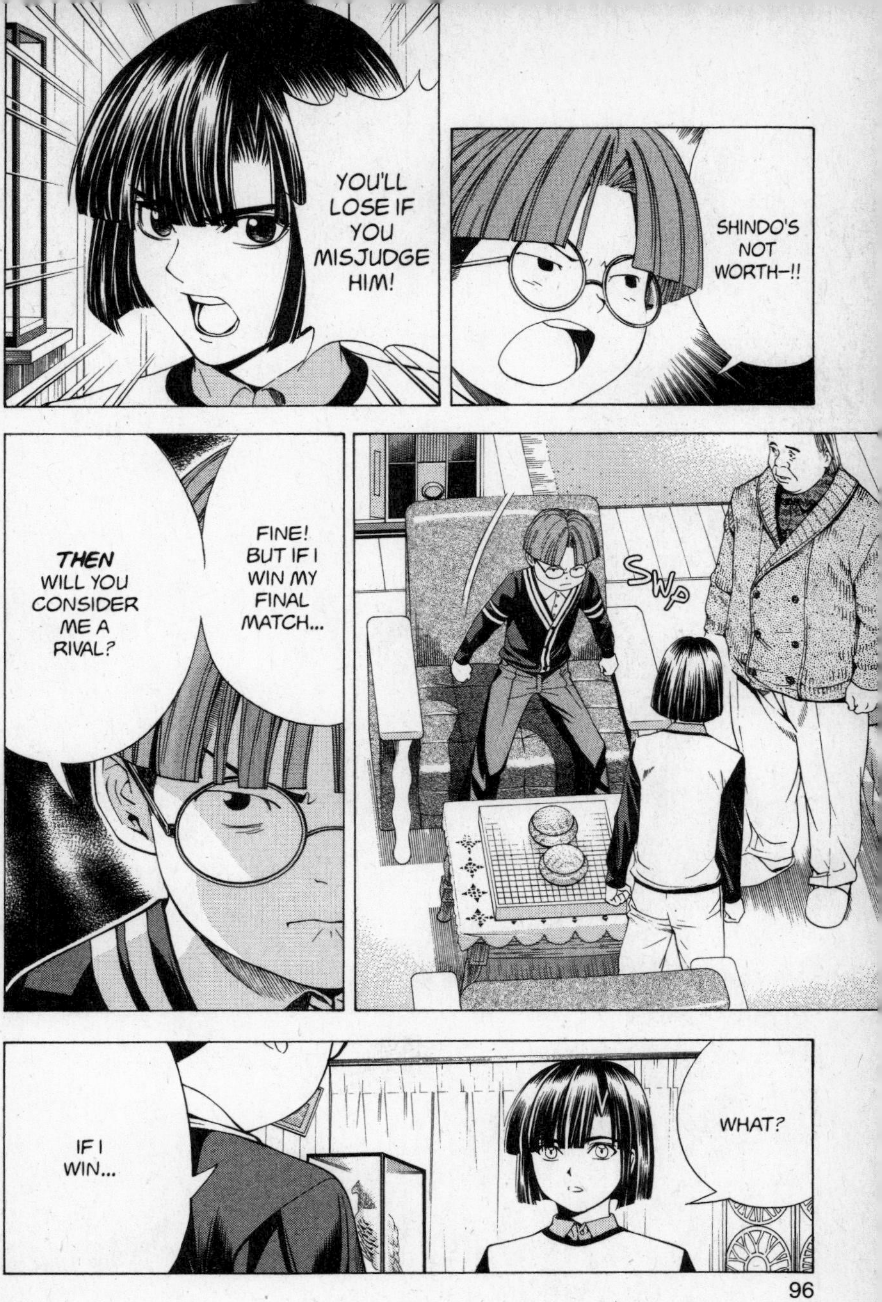
SHINDO'S NOT WORTH–!!
YOU'LL LOSE IF YOU MISJUDGE HIM!
SWP
FINE! BUT IF I WIN MY FINAL MATCH...
THEN WILL YOU CONSIDER ME A RIVAL?
IF I WIN...
WHAT?

READ THIS WAY

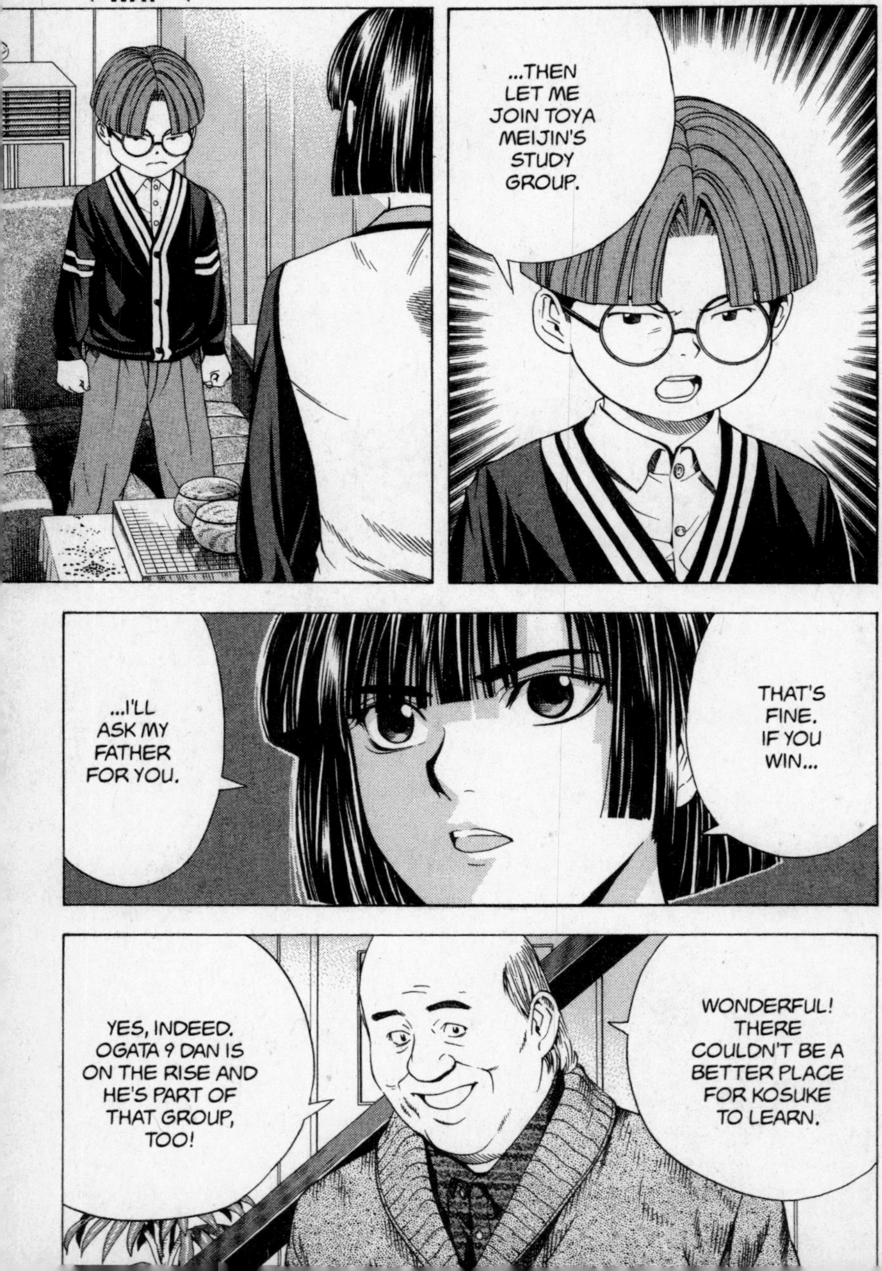
...THEN LET ME JOIN TOYA MEIJIN'S STUDY GROUP.
THAT'S FINE. IF YOU WIN...
...I'LL ASK MY FATHER FOR YOU.
WONDERFUL! THERE COULDN'T BE A BETTER PLACE FOR KOSUKE TO LEARN.
YES, INDEED. OGATA 9 DAN IS ON THE RISE AND HE'S PART OF THAT GROUP, TOO!

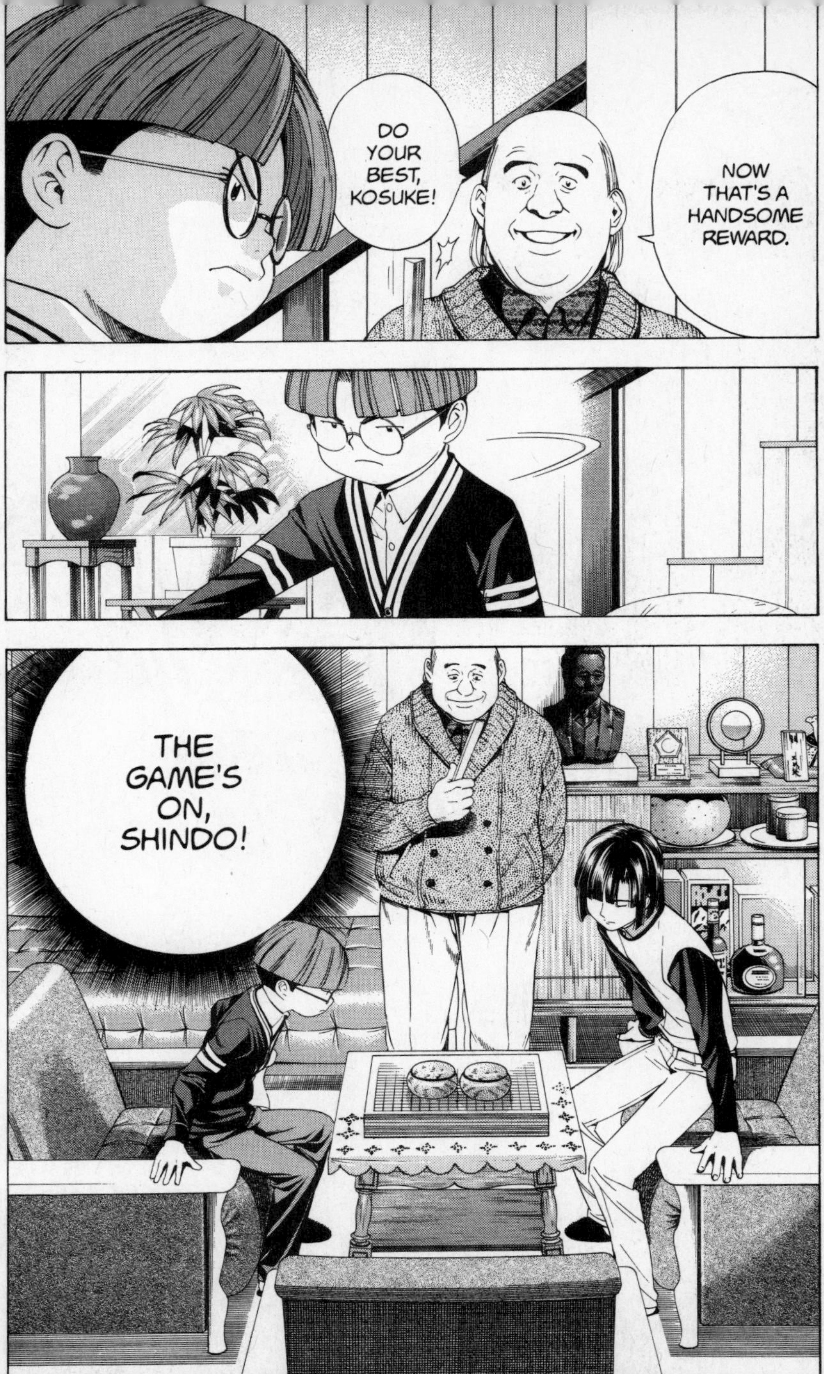
NOW THAT'S A HANDSOME REWARD.
DO YOUR BEST, KOSUKE!
THE GAME'S ON, SHINDO!

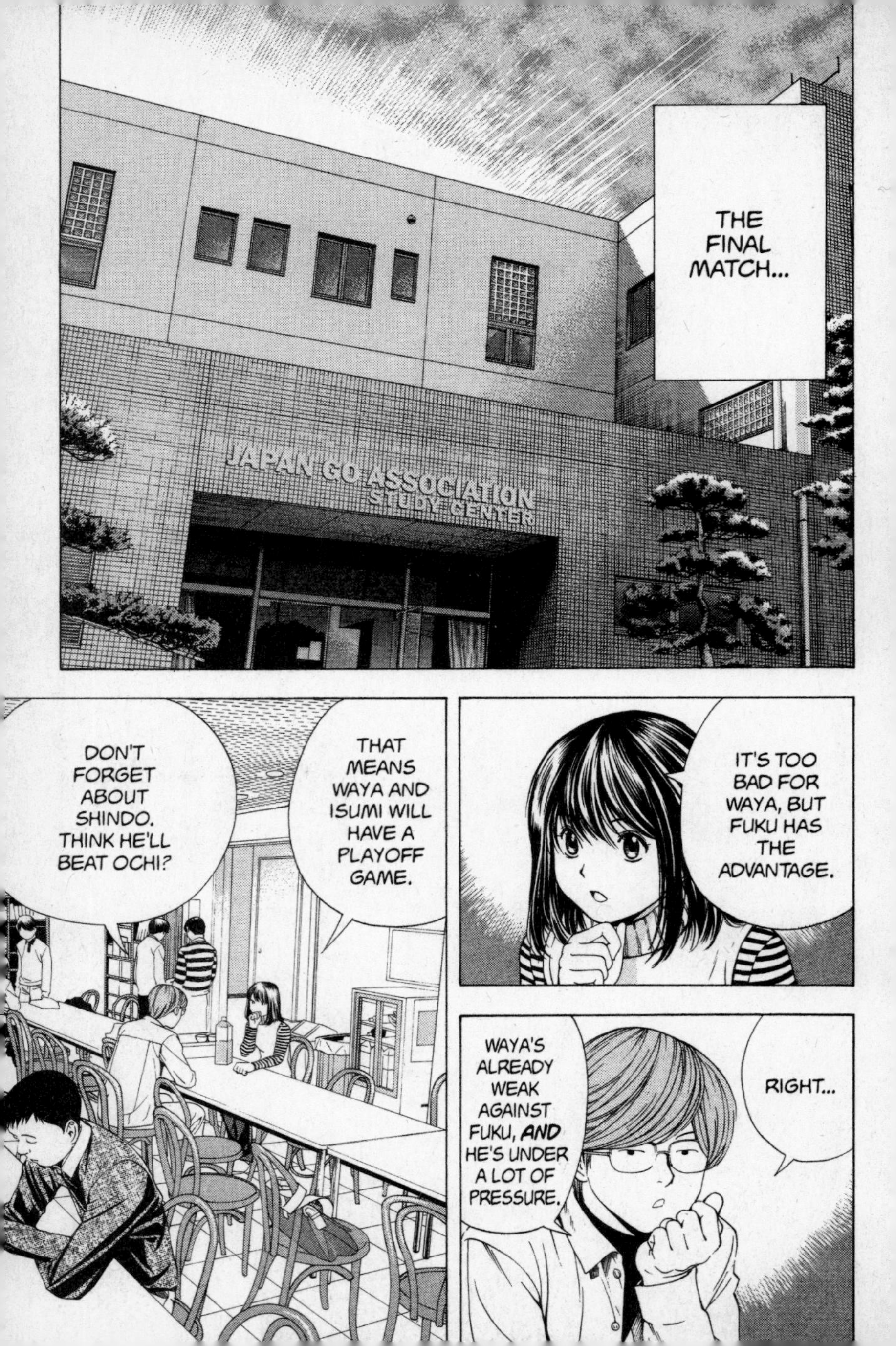
THE FINAL MATCH...
JAPAN GO ASSOCIATION
STUDY CENTER
IT'S TOO BAD FOR WAYA, BUT FUKU HAS THE ADVANTAGE.
RIGHT...
WAYA'S ALREADY WEAK AGAINST FUKU, AND HE'S UNDER A LOT OF PRESSURE.
THAT MEANS WAYA AND ISUMI WILL HAVE A PLAYOFF GAME.
DON'T FORGET ABOUT SHINDO. THINK HE'LL BEAT OCHI?

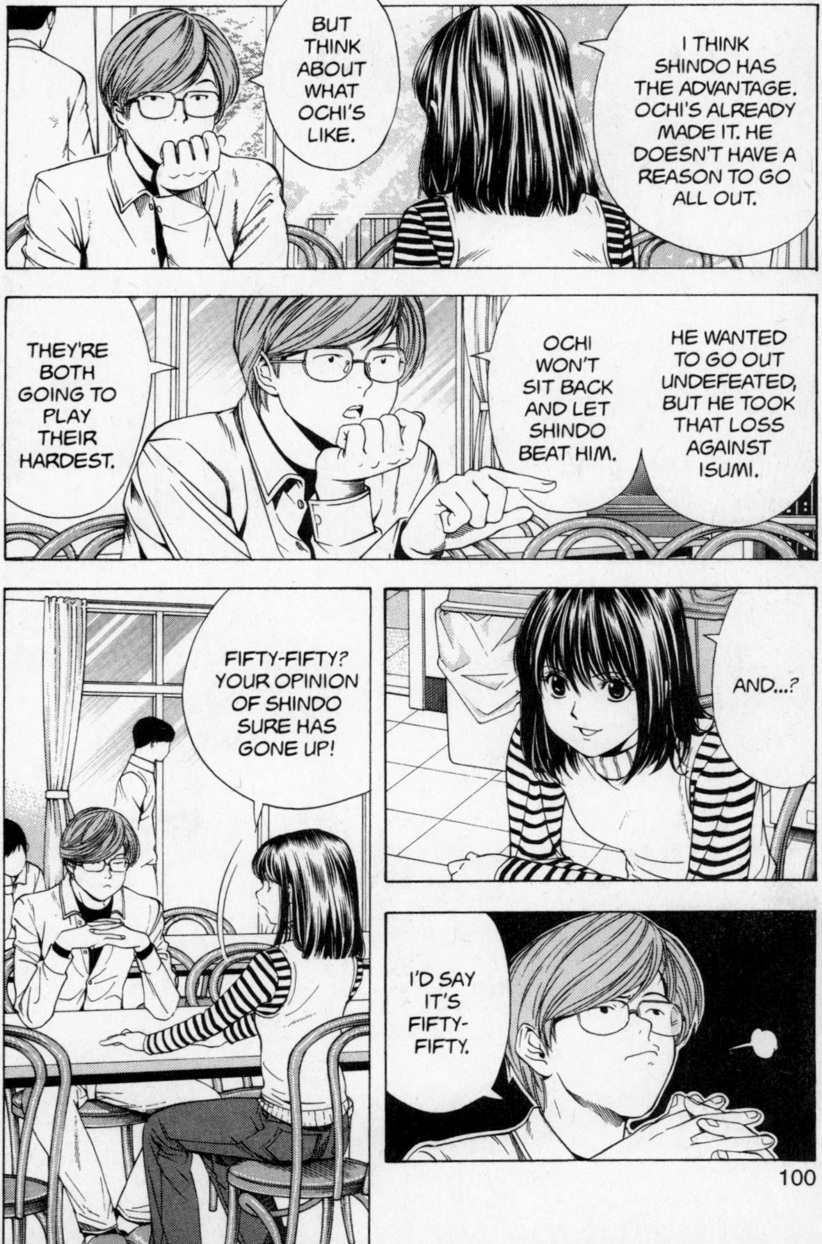
I THINK SHINDO HAS THE ADVANTAGE. OCHI'S ALREADY MADE IT. HE DOESN'T HAVE A REASON TO GO ALL OUT.
BUT THINK ABOUT WHAT OCHI'S LIKE.
HE WANTED TO GO OUT UNDEFEATED, BUT HE TOOK THAT LOSS AGAINST ISUMI.
OCHI WON'T SIT BACK AND LET SHINDO BEAT HIM.
THEY'RE BOTH GOING TO PLAY THEIR HARDEST.
AND...?
I'D SAY IT'S FIFTY-FIFTY.
FIFTY-FIFTY? YOUR OPINION OF SHINDO SURE HAS GONE UP!

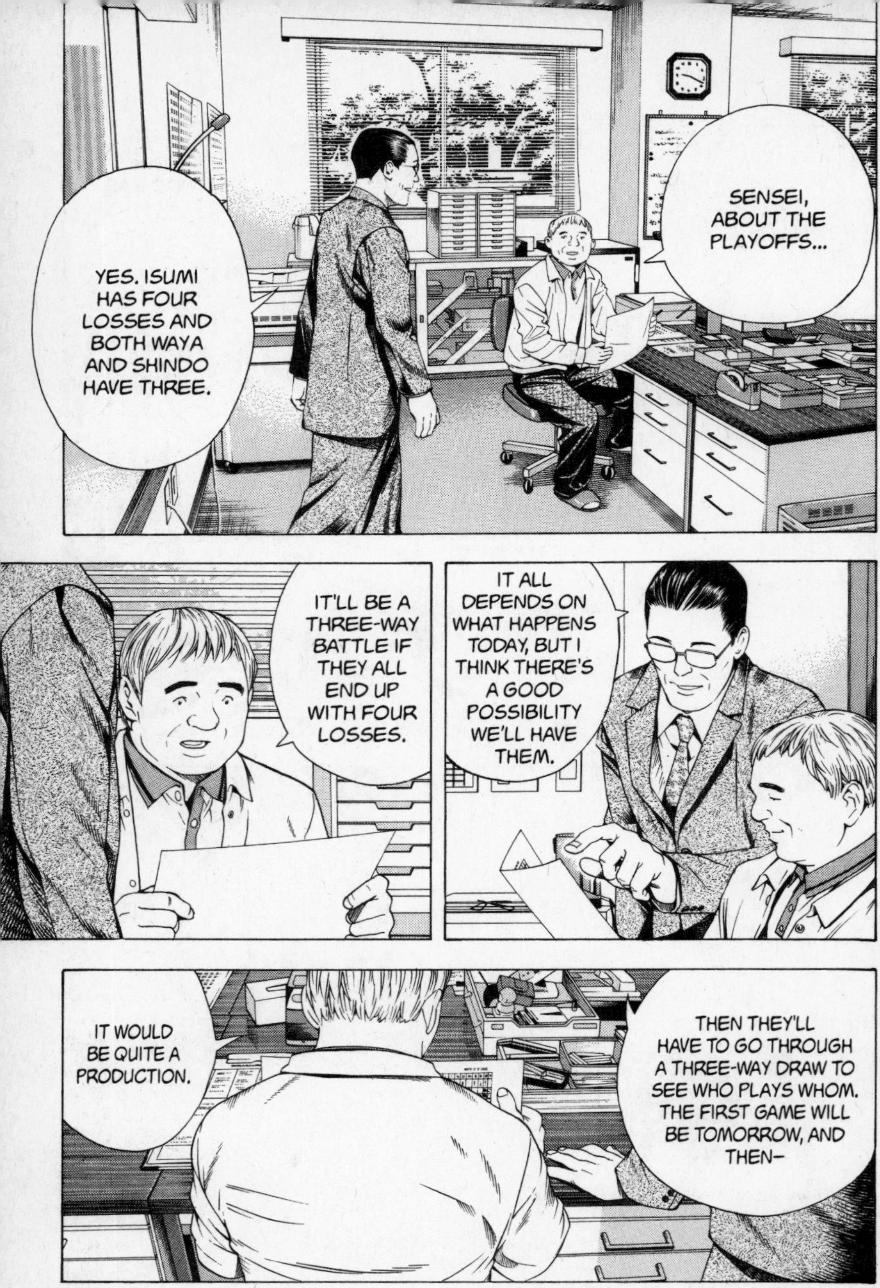
SENSEI, ABOUT THE PLAYOFFS...
YES. ISUMI HAS FOUR LOSSES AND BOTH WAYA AND SHINDO HAVE THREE.
IT ALL DEPENDS ON WHAT HAPPENS TODAY, BUT I THINK THERE'S A GOOD POSSIBILITY WE'LL HAVE THEM.
IT'LL BE A THREE-WAY BATTLE IF THEY ALL END UP WITH FOUR LOSSES.
THEN THEY'LL HAVE TO GO THROUGH A THREE-WAY DRAW TO SEE WHO PLAYS WHOM. THE FIRST GAME WILL BE TOMORROW, AND THEN–
IT WOULD BE QUITE A PRODUCTION.

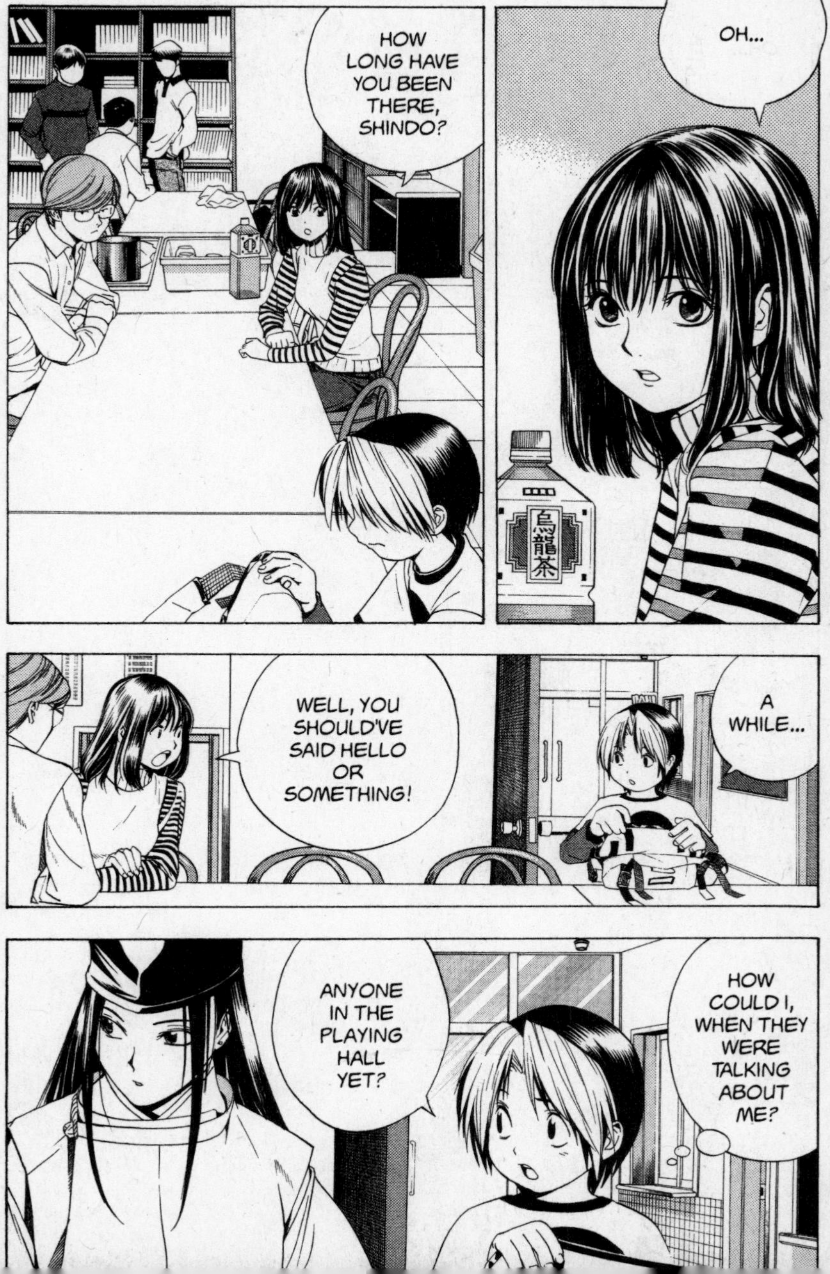
OH...
烏龍茶
HOW LONG HAVE YOU BEEN THERE, SHINDO?
A WHILE...
WELL, YOU SHOULD'VE SAID HELLO OR SOMETHING!
HOW COULD I, WHEN THEY WERE TALKING ABOUT ME?
ANYONE IN THE PLAYING HALL YET?

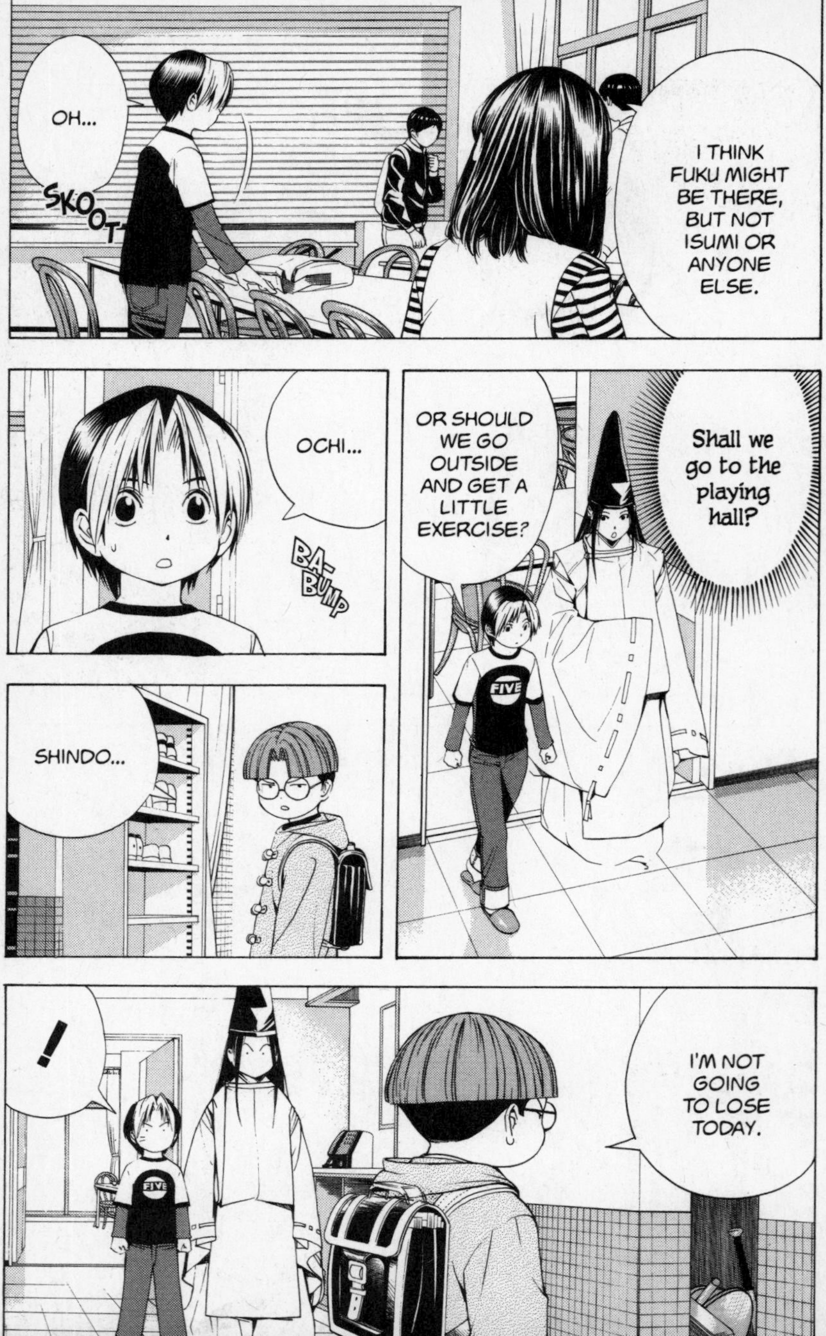
I THINK FUKU MIGHT BE THERE, BUT NOT ISUMI OR ANYONE ELSE.
OH...
SKOOT
Shall we go to the playing hall?
OR SHOULD WE GO OUTSIDE AND GET A LITTLE EXERCISE?
OCHI...
BA-BUMP
SHINDO...
I'M NOT GOING TO LOSE TODAY.
!

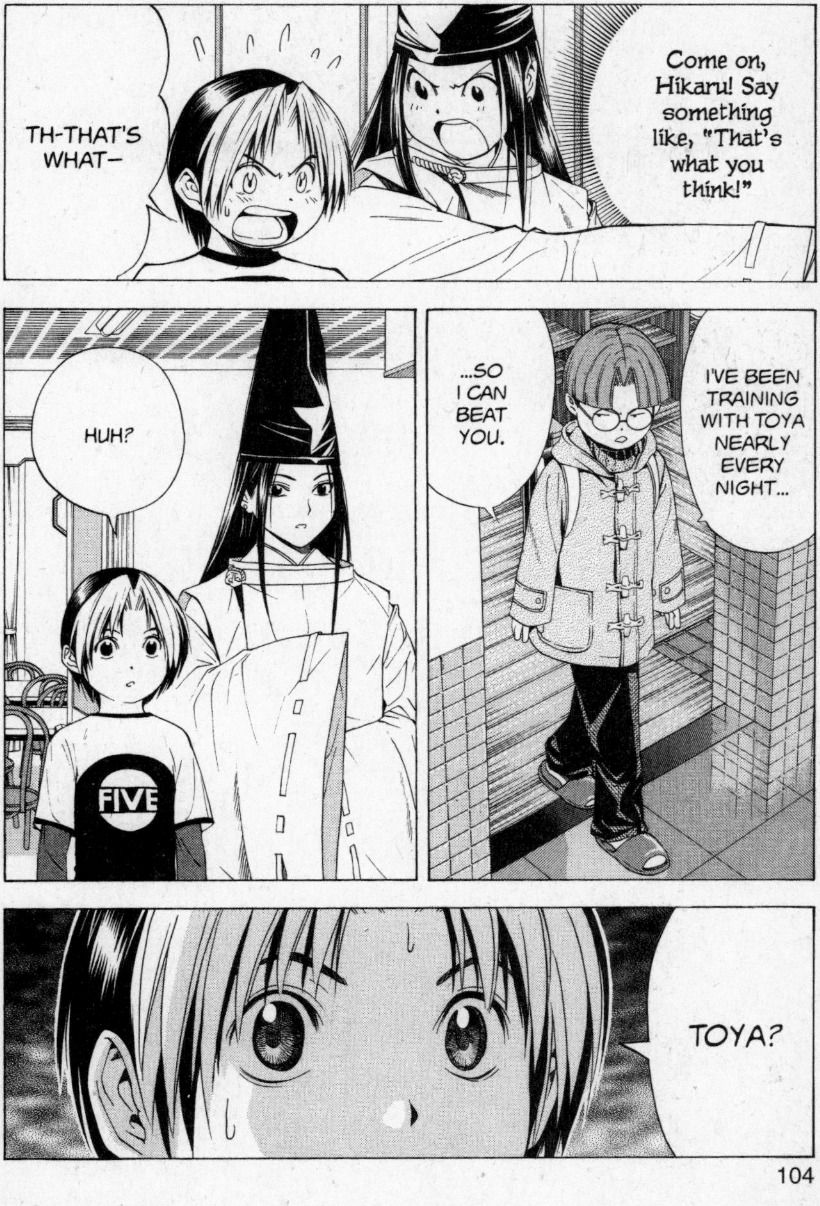
Come on, Hikaru! Say something like, "That's what you think!"
TH-THAT'S WHAT—
I'VE BEEN TRAINING WITH TOYA NEARLY EVERY NIGHT...
...SO I CAN BEAT YOU.
HUH?
FIVE
TOYA?

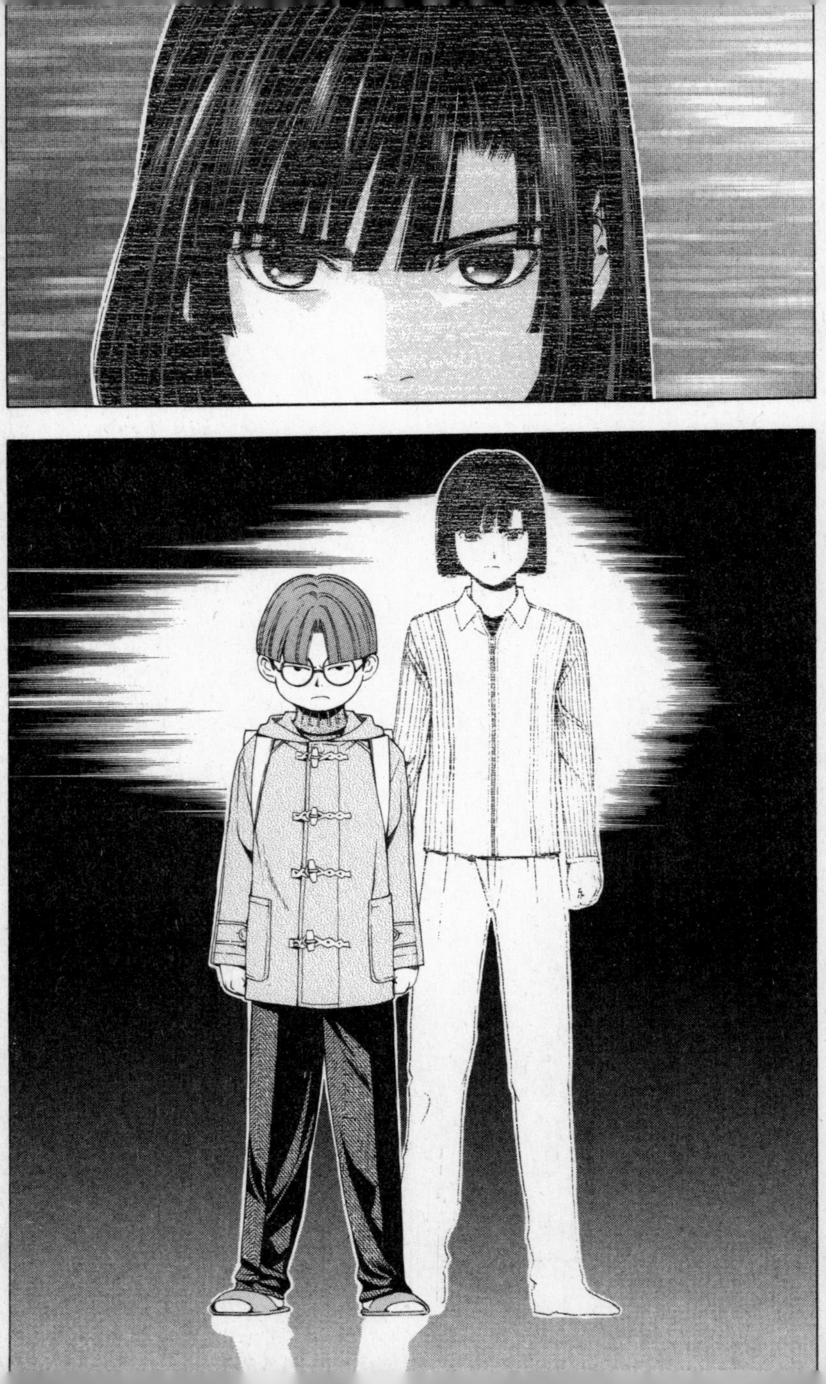

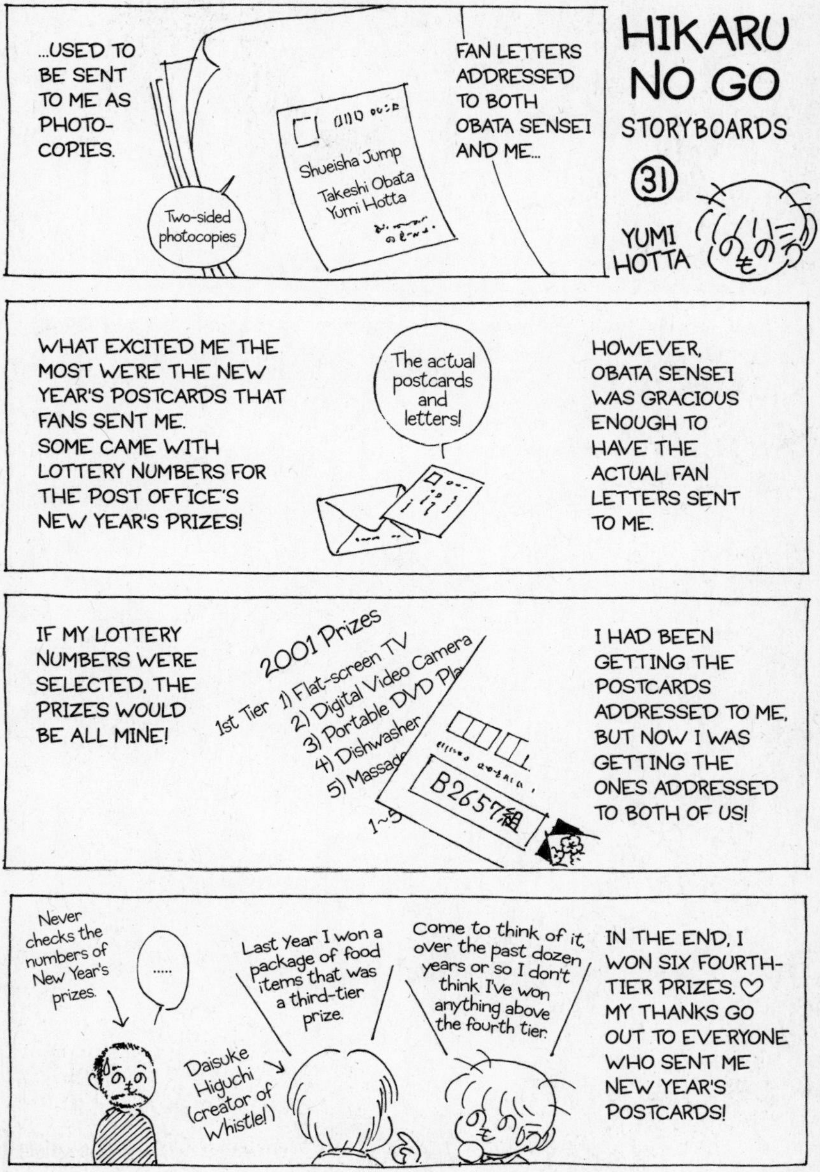

HIKARU NO GO STORYBOARDS 31
YUMI HOTTA
FAN LETTERS ADDRESSED TO BOTH OBATA SENSEI AND ME...
Shueisha Jump
Takeshi Obata
Yumi Hotta
...USED TO BE SENT TO ME AS PHOTO-COPIES.
Two-sided photocopies
HOWEVER, OBATA SENSEI WAS GRACIOUS ENOUGH TO HAVE THE ACTUAL FAN LETTERS SENT TO ME.
The actual postcards and letters!
WHAT EXCITED ME THE MOST WERE THE NEW YEAR'S POSTCARDS THAT FANS SENT ME. SOME CAME WITH LOTTERY NUMBERS FOR THE POST OFFICE'S NEW YEAR'S PRIZES!
I HAD BEEN GETTING THE POSTCARDS ADDRESSED TO ME, BUT NOW I WAS GETTING THE ONES ADDRESSED TO BOTH OF US!
B2657組
2001 Prizes
1st Tier 1) Flat-screen TV
2) Digital Video Camera
3) Portable DVD Pla
4) Dishwasher
5) Massage
1~5
IF MY LOTTERY NUMBERS WERE SELECTED, THE PRIZES WOULD BE ALL MINE!
IN THE END, I WON SIX FOURTH-TIER PRIZES. ♡ MY THANKS GO OUT TO EVERYONE WHO SENT ME NEW YEAR'S POSTCARDS!
Come to think of it, over the past dozen years or so I don't think I've won anything above the fourth tier.
Last Year I won a package of food items that was a third-tier prize.
Daisuke Higuchi (creator of Whistle!)
.....
Never checks the numbers of New Year's prizes.

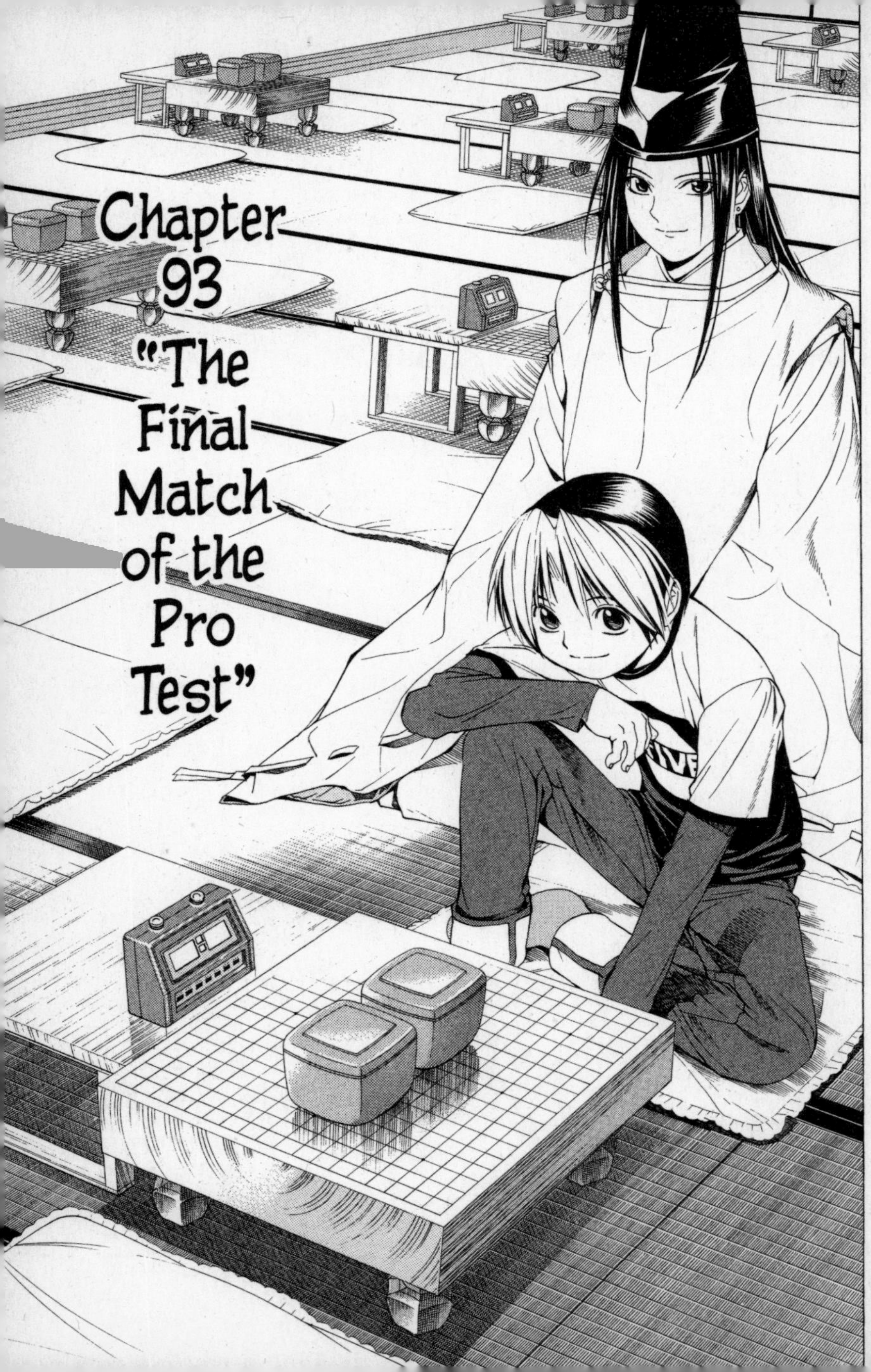
Chapter 93
"The Final Match of the Pro Test"

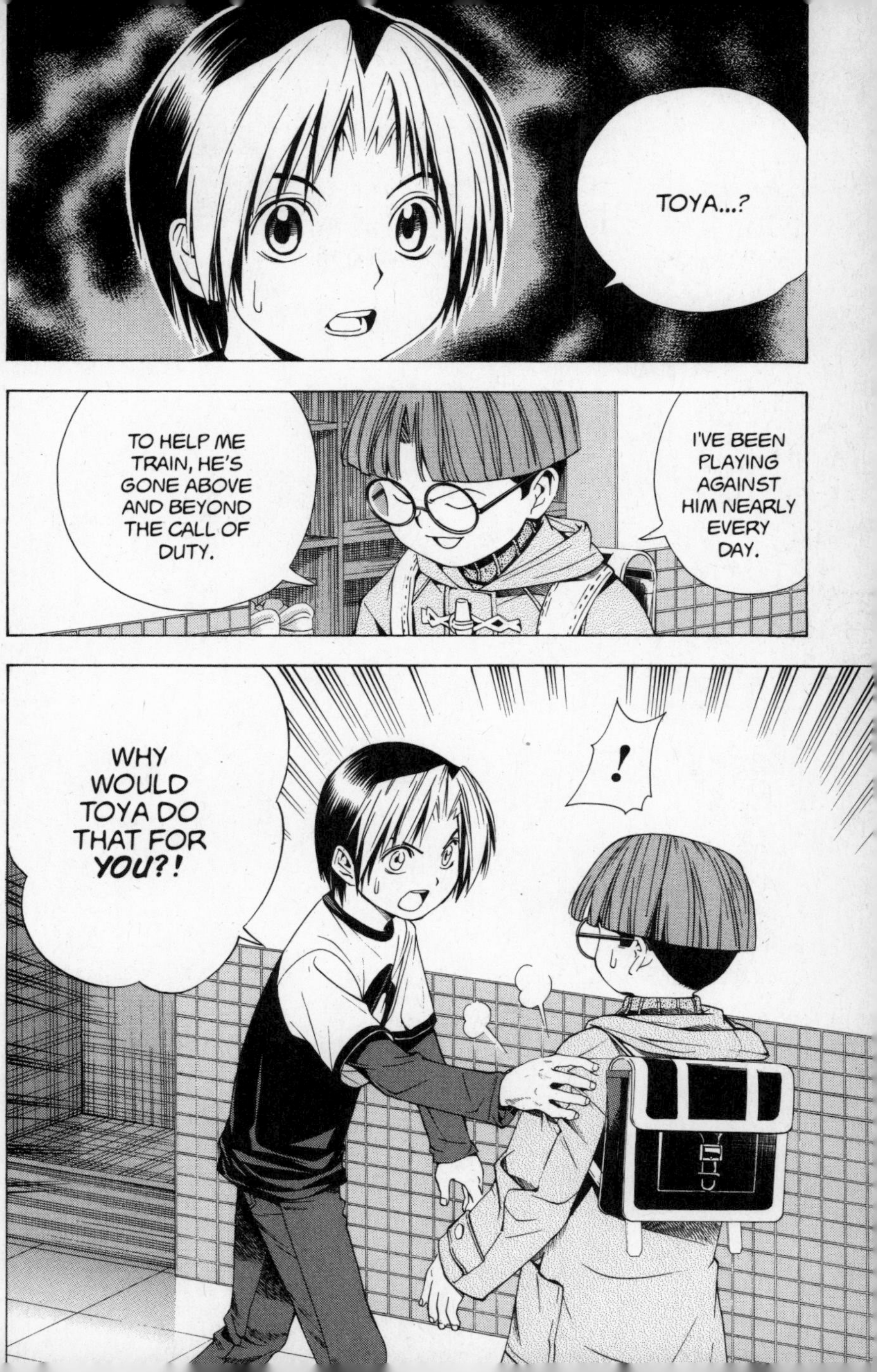
TOYA...?
I'VE BEEN PLAYING AGAINST HIM NEARLY EVERY DAY.
TO HELP ME TRAIN, HE'S GONE ABOVE AND BEYOND THE CALL OF DUTY.
!
WHY WOULD TOYA DO THAT FOR *YOU*?!

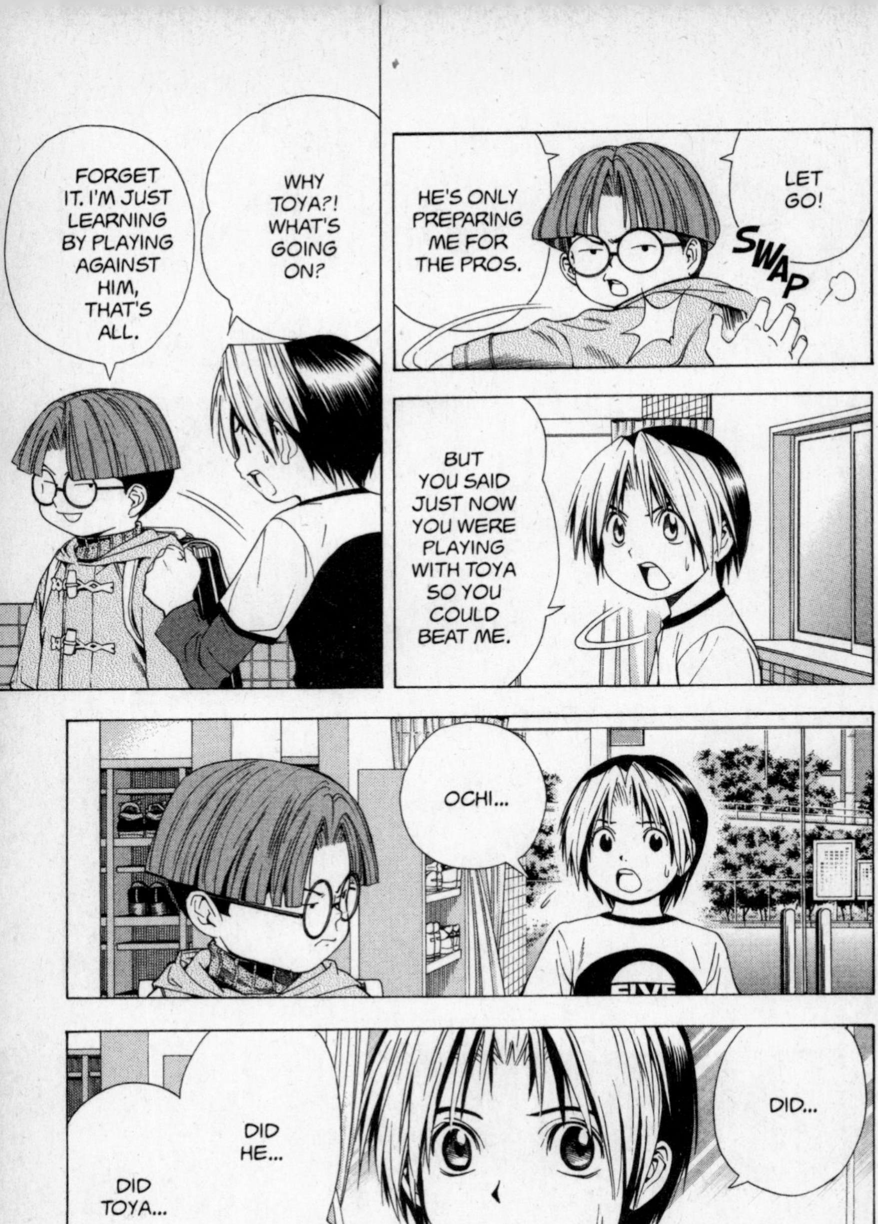

LET GO!
SWAP
HE'S ONLY PREPARING ME FOR THE PROS.
BUT YOU SAID JUST NOW YOU WERE PLAYING WITH TOYA SO YOU COULD BEAT ME.
WHY TOYA?! WHAT'S GOING ON?
FORGET IT. I'M JUST LEARNING BY PLAYING AGAINST HIM, THAT'S ALL.
OCHI...
FIVE
DID...
DID HE...
DID TOYA...

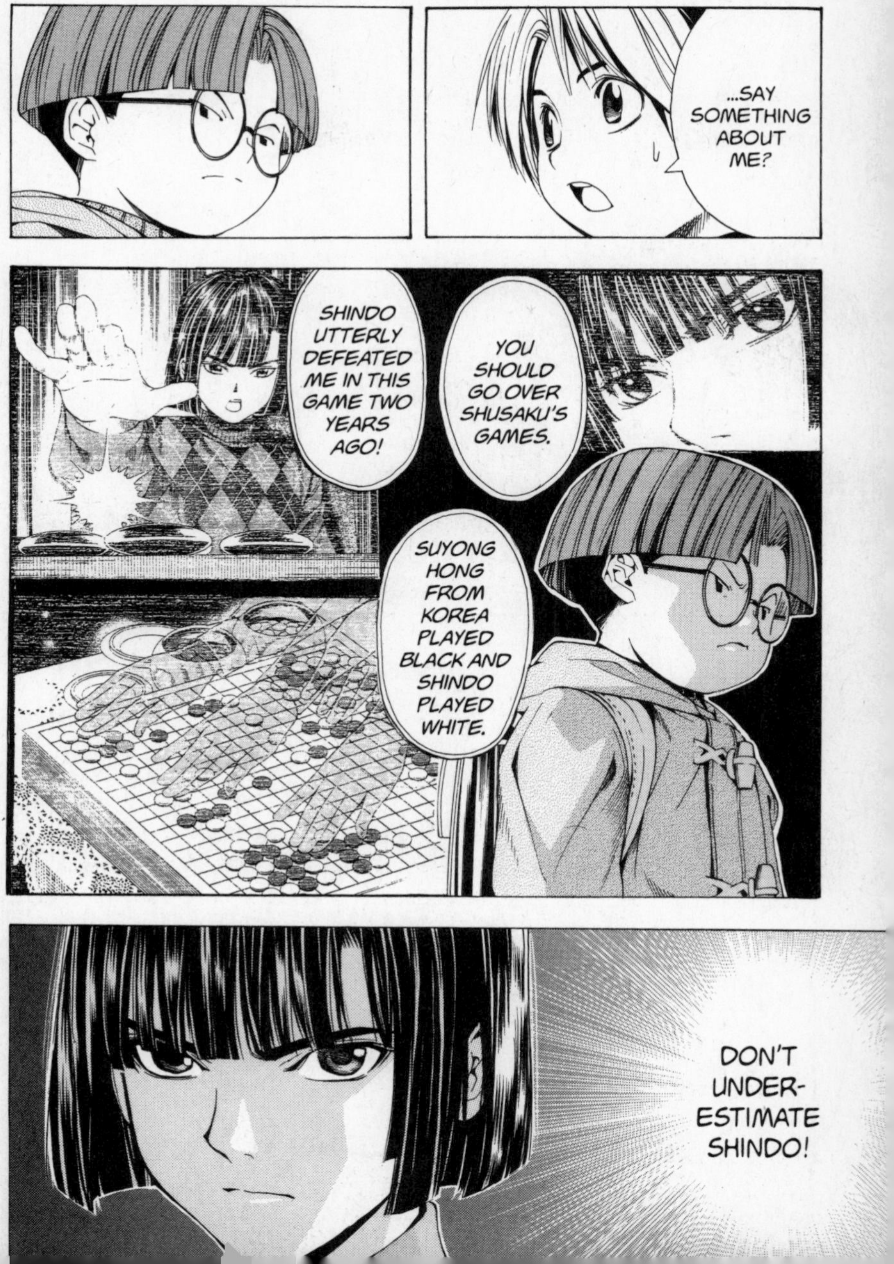
...SAY SOMETHING ABOUT ME?
YOU SHOULD GO OVER SHUSAKU'S GAMES.
SHINDO UTTERLY DEFEATED ME IN THIS GAME TWO YEARS AGO!
SUYONG HONG FROM KOREA PLAYED BLACK AND SHINDO PLAYED WHITE.
DON'T UNDER-ESTIMATE SHINDO!

READ THIS WAY

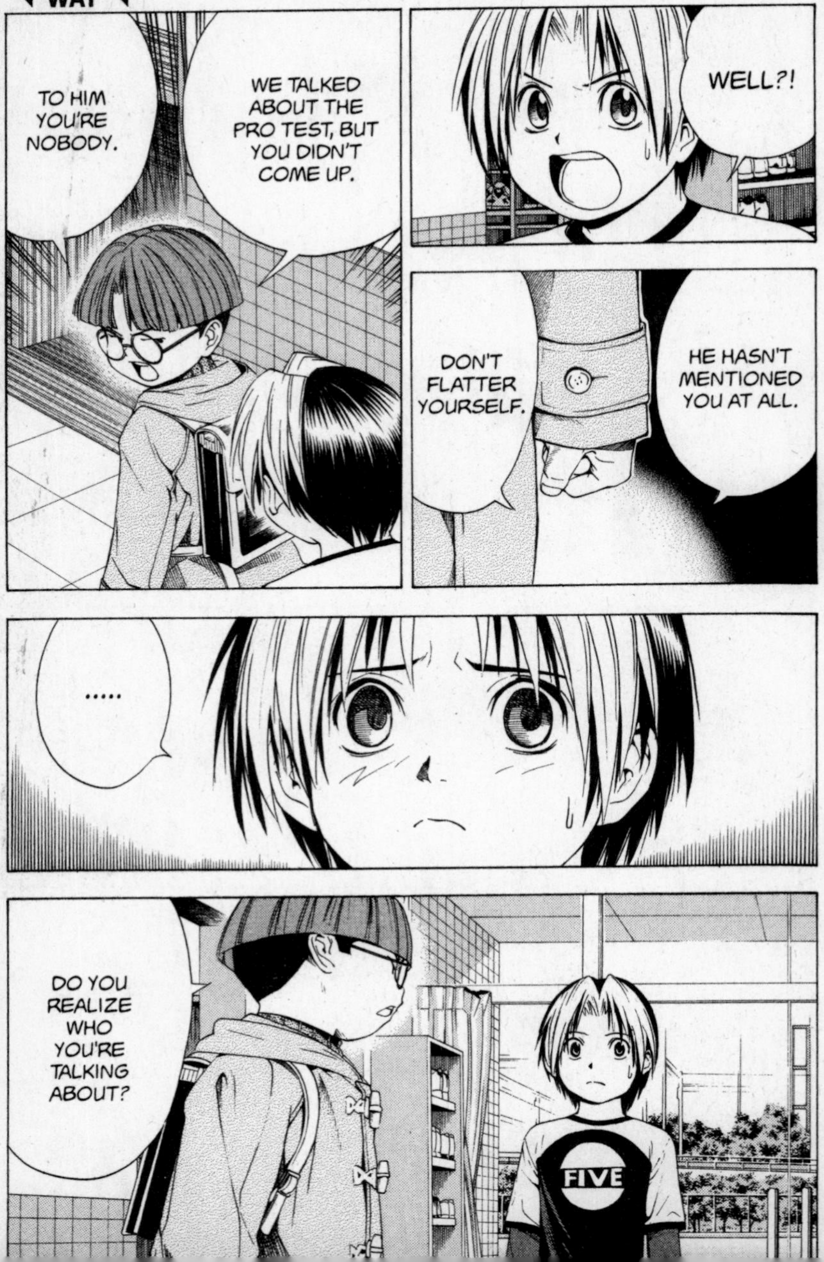

WELL?!
HE HASN'T MENTIONED YOU AT ALL.
DON'T FLATTER YOURSELF.
WE TALKED ABOUT THE PRO TEST, BUT YOU DIDN'T COME UP.
TO HIM YOU'RE NOBODY.
.....
DO YOU REALIZE WHO YOU'RE TALKING ABOUT?
FIVE

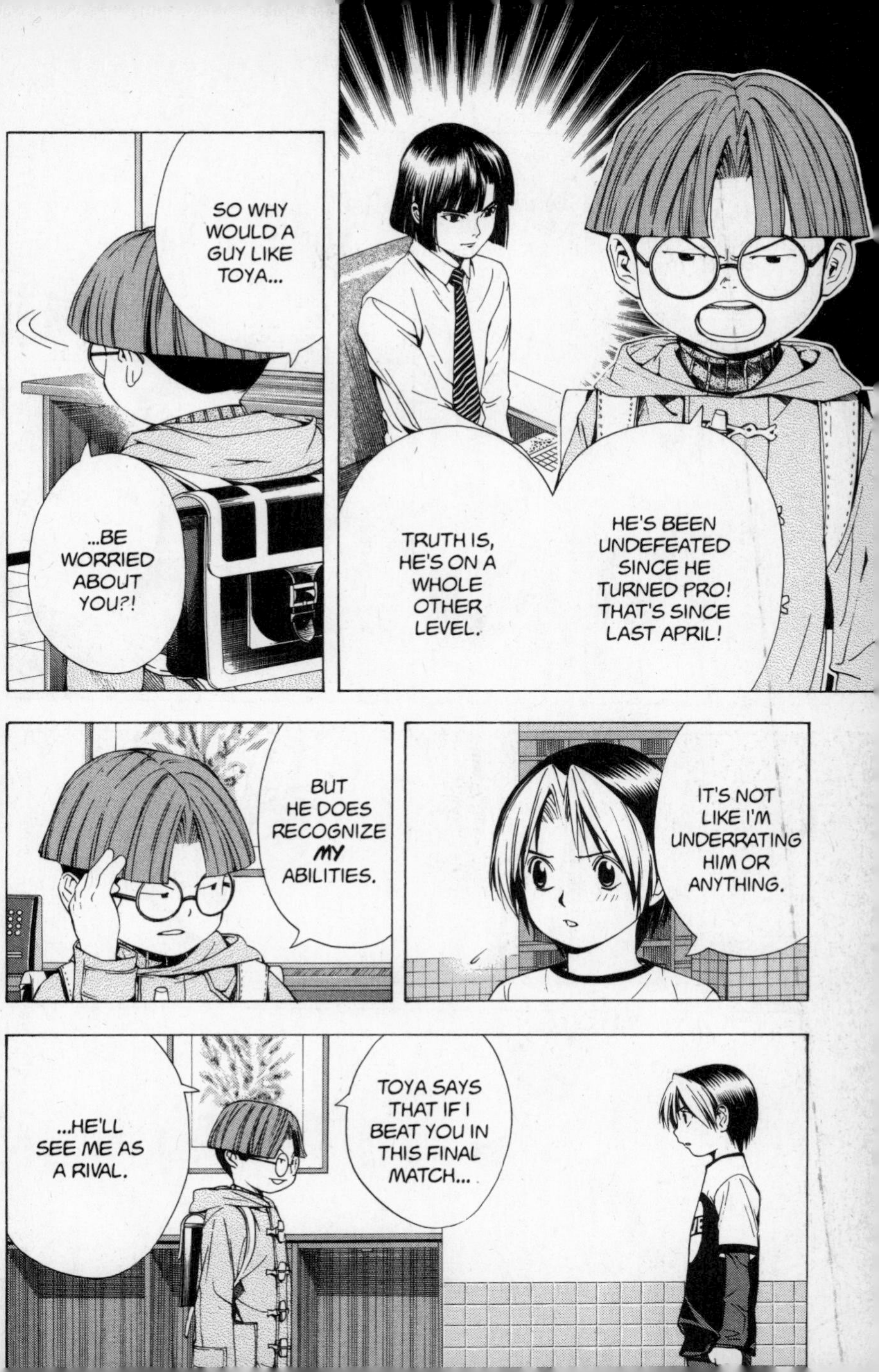
HE'S BEEN UNDEFEATED SINCE HE TURNED PRO! THAT'S SINCE LAST APRIL!
TRUTH IS, HE'S ON A WHOLE OTHER LEVEL.
SO WHY WOULD A GUY LIKE TOYA...
...BE WORRIED ABOUT YOU?!
IT'S NOT LIKE I'M UNDERRATING HIM OR ANYTHING.
BUT HE DOES RECOGNIZE *MY* ABILITIES.
TOYA SAYS THAT IF I BEAT YOU IN THIS FINAL MATCH...
...HE'LL SEE ME AS A RIVAL.

READ THIS WAY

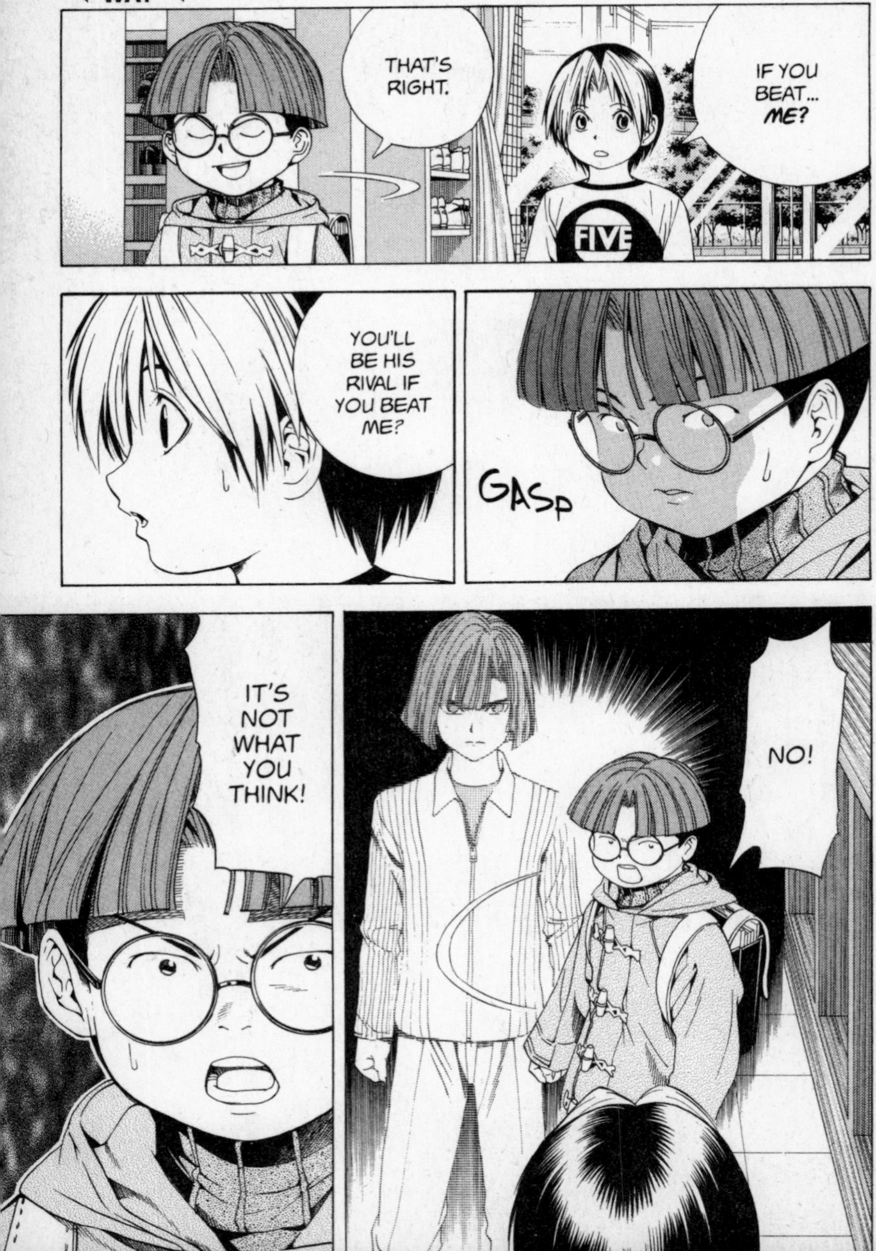
IF YOU BEAT... *ME?*
THAT'S RIGHT.
GASP
YOU'LL BE HIS RIVAL IF YOU BEAT ME?
NO!
IT'S NOT WHAT YOU THINK!

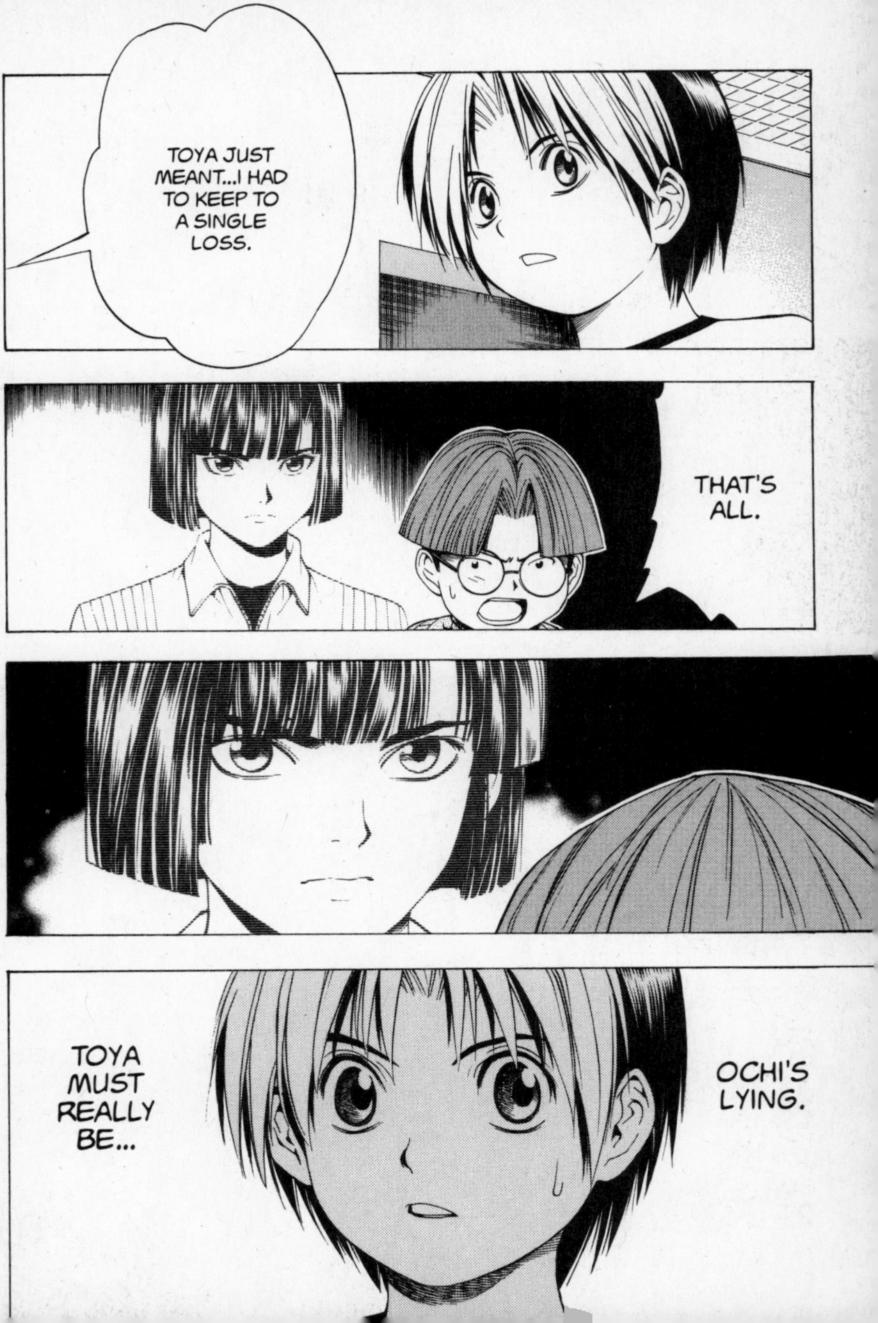
TOYA JUST MEANT...I HAD TO KEEP TO A SINGLE LOSS.
THAT'S ALL.
OCHI'S LYING.
TOYA MUST REALLY BE...

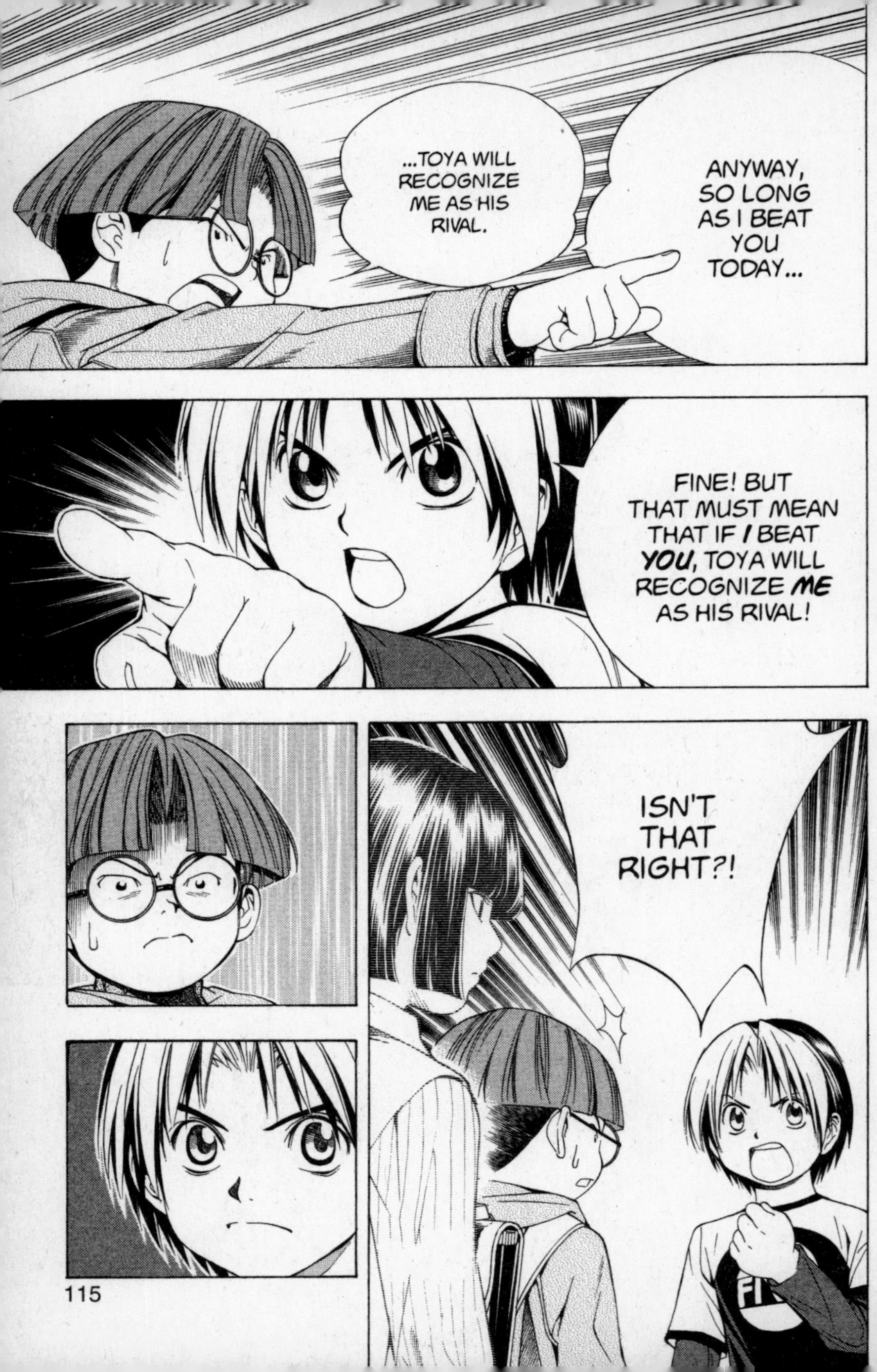
ANYWAY, SO LONG AS I BEAT YOU TODAY...
...TOYA WILL RECOGNIZE ME AS HIS RIVAL.
FINE! BUT THAT MUST MEAN THAT IF *I* BEAT ***YOU***, TOYA WILL RECOGNIZE ***ME*** AS HIS RIVAL!
ISN'T THAT RIGHT?!

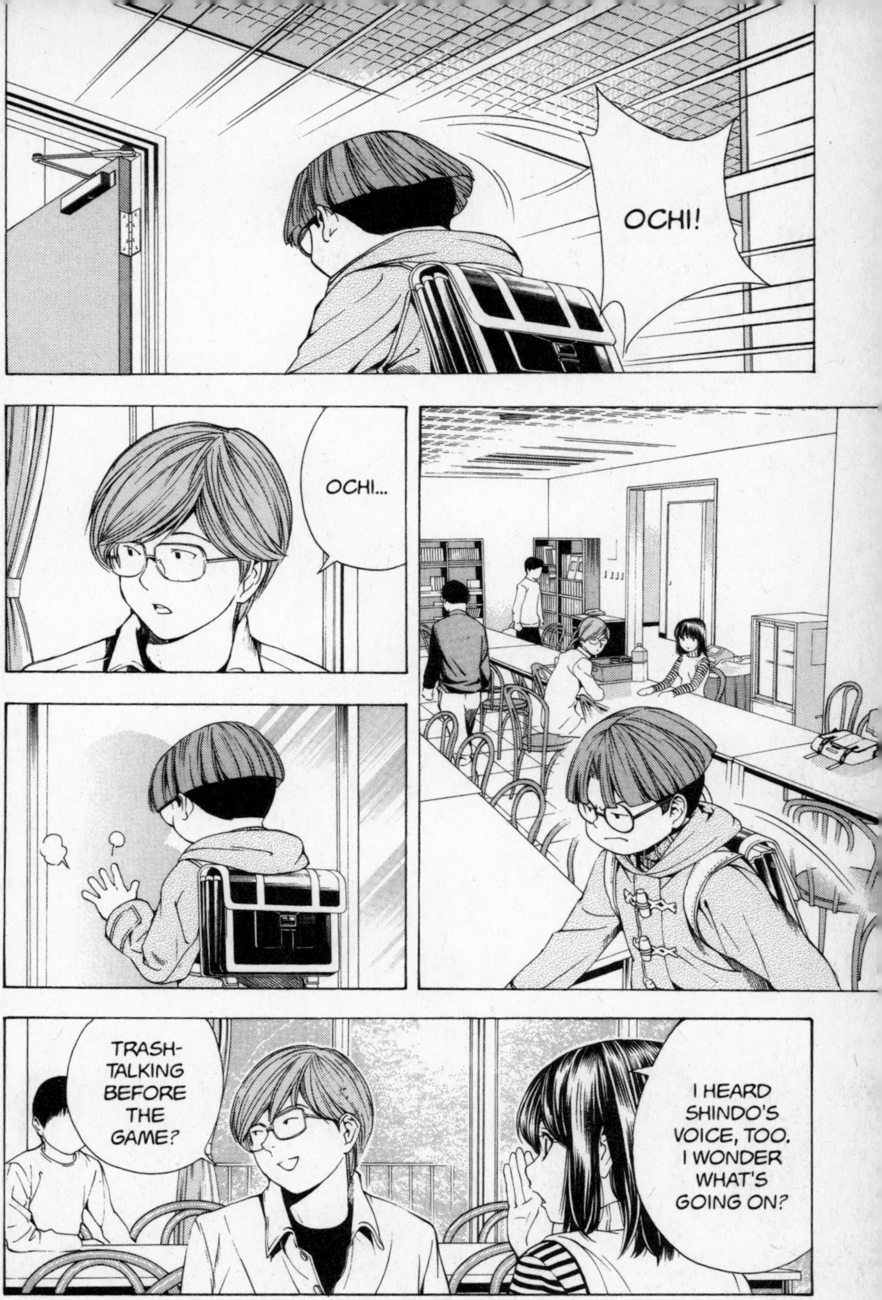
OCHI!
OCHI...
I HEARD SHINDO'S VOICE, TOO. I WONDER WHAT'S GOING ON?
TRASH-TALKING BEFORE THE GAME?

READ THIS WAY

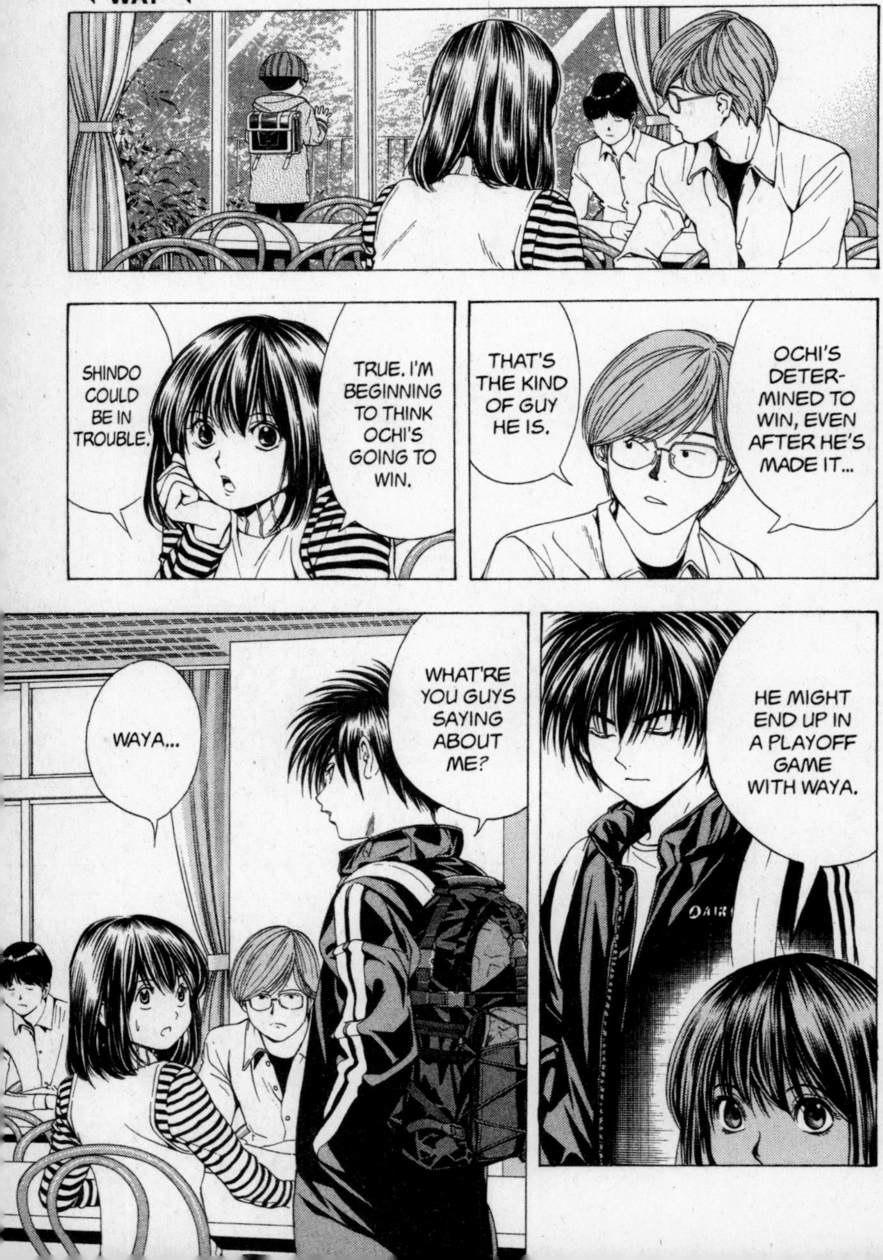
OCHI'S DETERMINED TO WIN, EVEN AFTER HE'S MADE IT...
THAT'S THE KIND OF GUY HE IS.
TRUE. I'M BEGINNING TO THINK OCHI'S GOING TO WIN.
SHINDO COULD BE IN TROUBLE.
HE MIGHT END UP IN A PLAYOFF GAME WITH WAYA.
WHAT'RE YOU GUYS SAYING ABOUT ME?
WAYA...

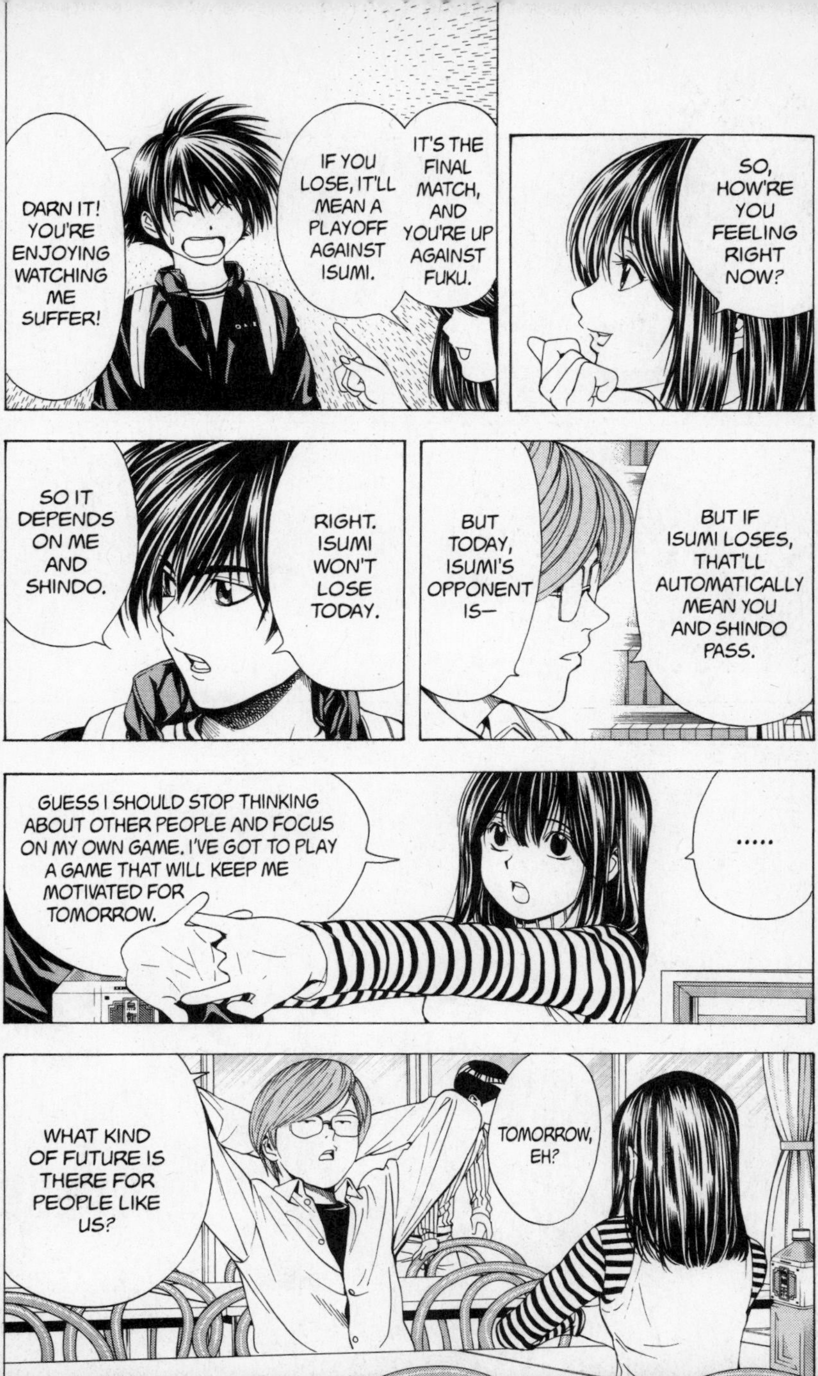
SO, HOW'RE YOU FEELING RIGHT NOW?
IT'S THE FINAL MATCH, AND YOU'RE UP AGAINST FUKU.
IF YOU LOSE, IT'LL MEAN A PLAYOFF AGAINST ISUMI.
DARN IT! YOU'RE ENJOYING WATCHING ME SUFFER!
BUT IF ISUMI LOSES, THAT'LL AUTOMATICALLY MEAN YOU AND SHINDO PASS.
BUT TODAY, ISUMI'S OPPONENT IS—
RIGHT. ISUMI WON'T LOSE TODAY.
SO IT DEPENDS ON ME AND SHINDO.
.....
GUESS I SHOULD STOP THINKING ABOUT OTHER PEOPLE AND FOCUS ON MY OWN GAME. I'VE GOT TO PLAY A GAME THAT WILL KEEP ME MOTIVATED FOR TOMORROW.
TOMORROW, EH?
WHAT KIND OF FUTURE IS THERE FOR PEOPLE LIKE US?

READ THIS WAY

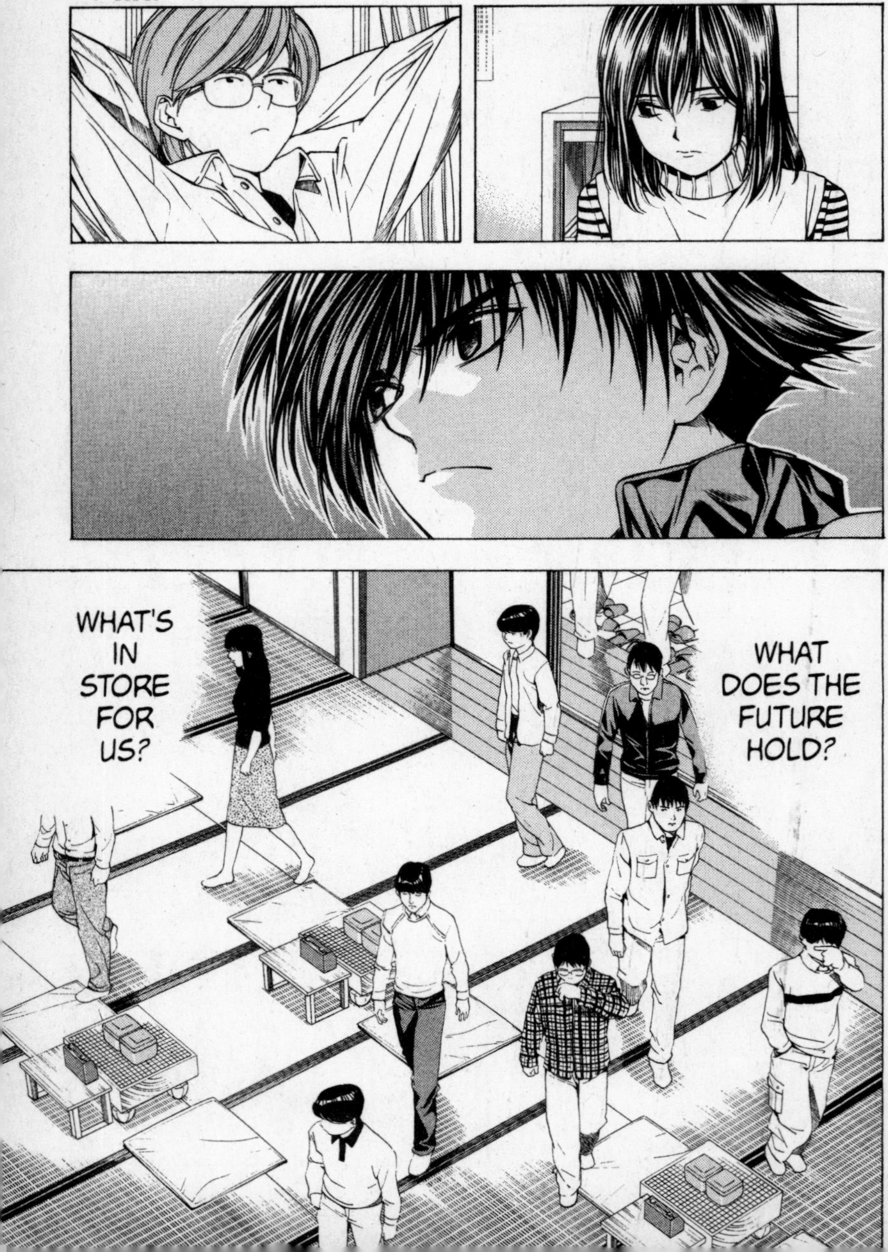
WHAT DOES THE FUTURE HOLD?
WHAT'S IN STORE FOR US?

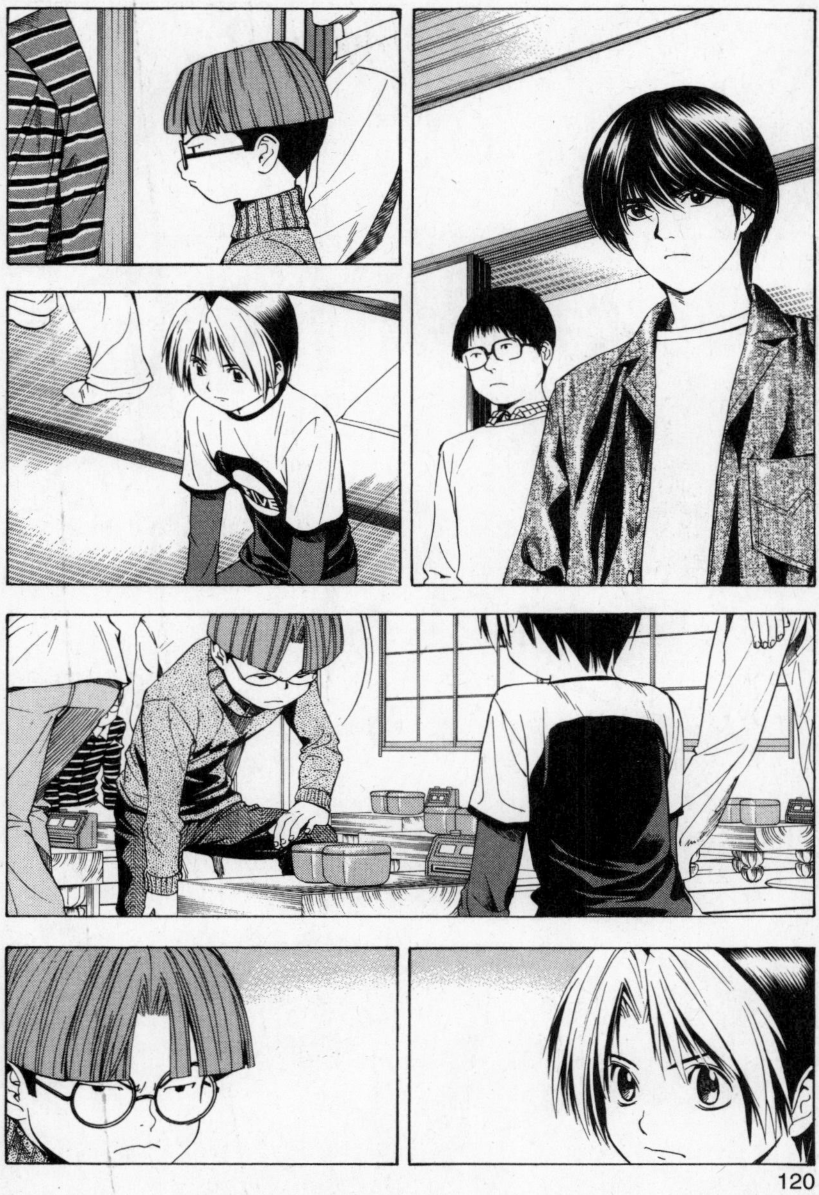

READ THIS WAY

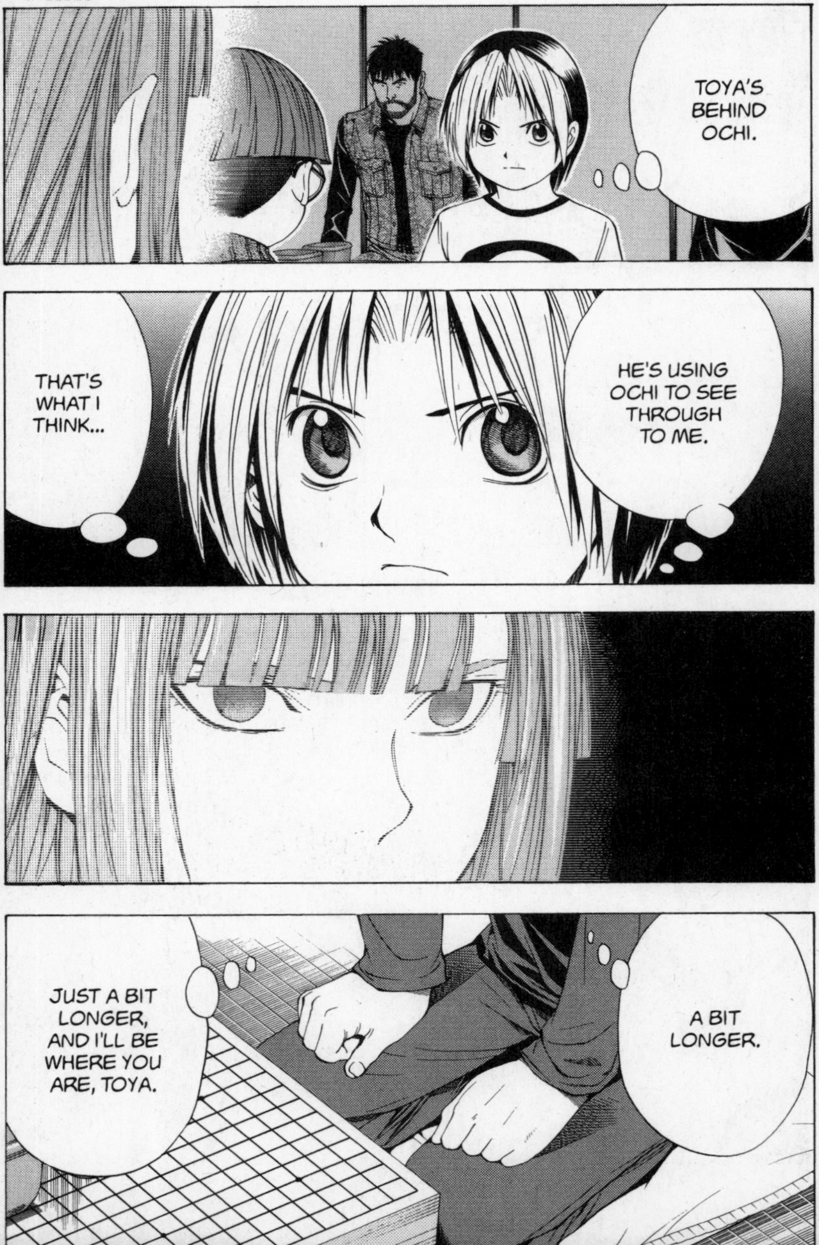
TOYA'S BEHIND OCHI.
HE'S USING OCHI TO SEE THROUGH TO ME.
THAT'S WHAT I THINK...
A BIT LONGER.
JUST A BIT LONGER, AND I'LL BE WHERE YOU ARE, TOYA.

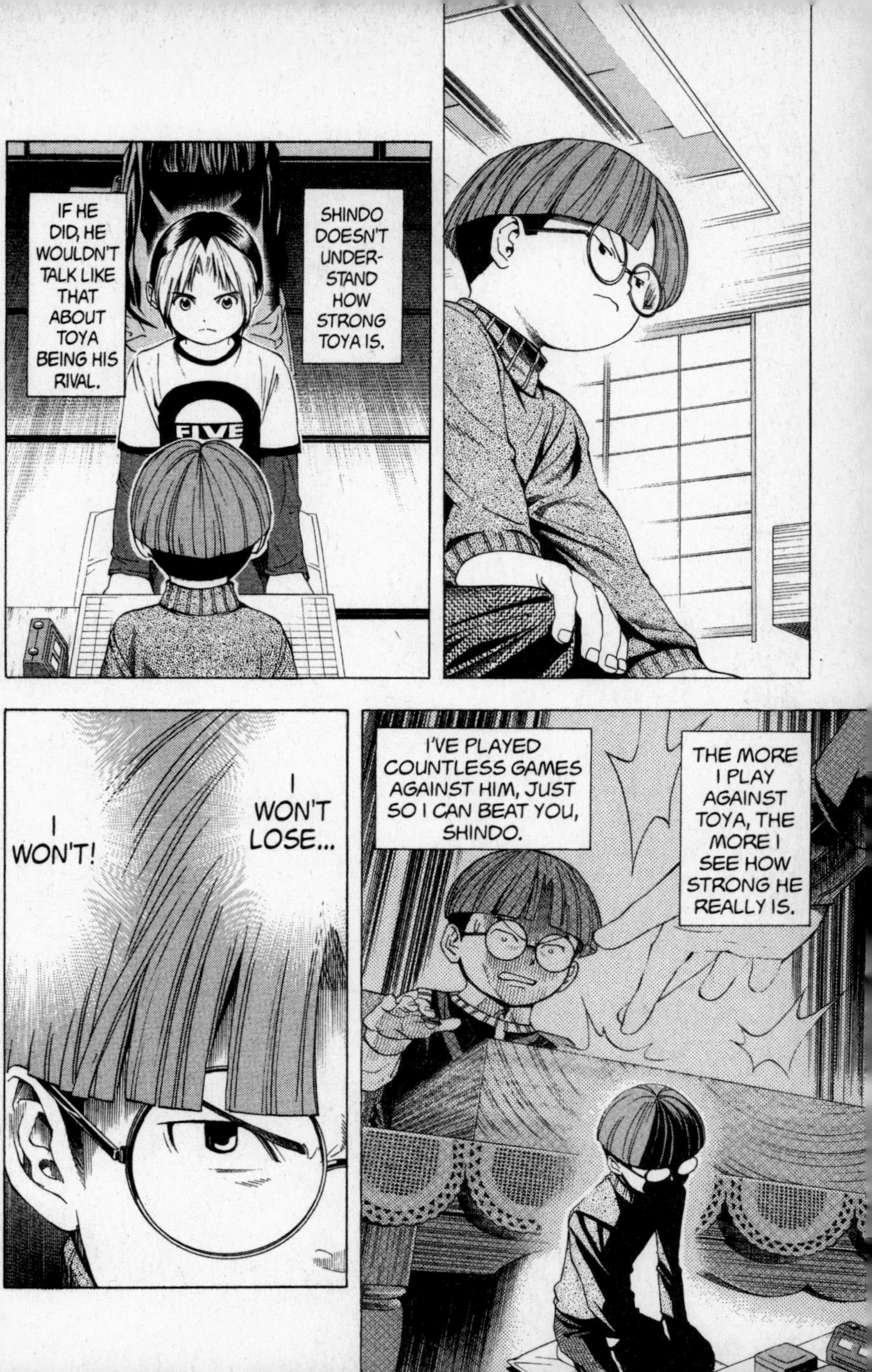
SHINDO DOESN'T UNDERSTAND HOW STRONG TOYA IS.
IF HE DID, HE WOULDN'T TALK LIKE THAT ABOUT TOYA BEING HIS RIVAL.
FIVE
THE MORE I PLAY AGAINST TOYA, THE MORE I SEE HOW STRONG HE REALLY IS.
I'VE PLAYED COUNTLESS GAMES AGAINST HIM, JUST SO I CAN BEAT YOU, SHINDO.
I WON'T LOSE...
I WON'T!

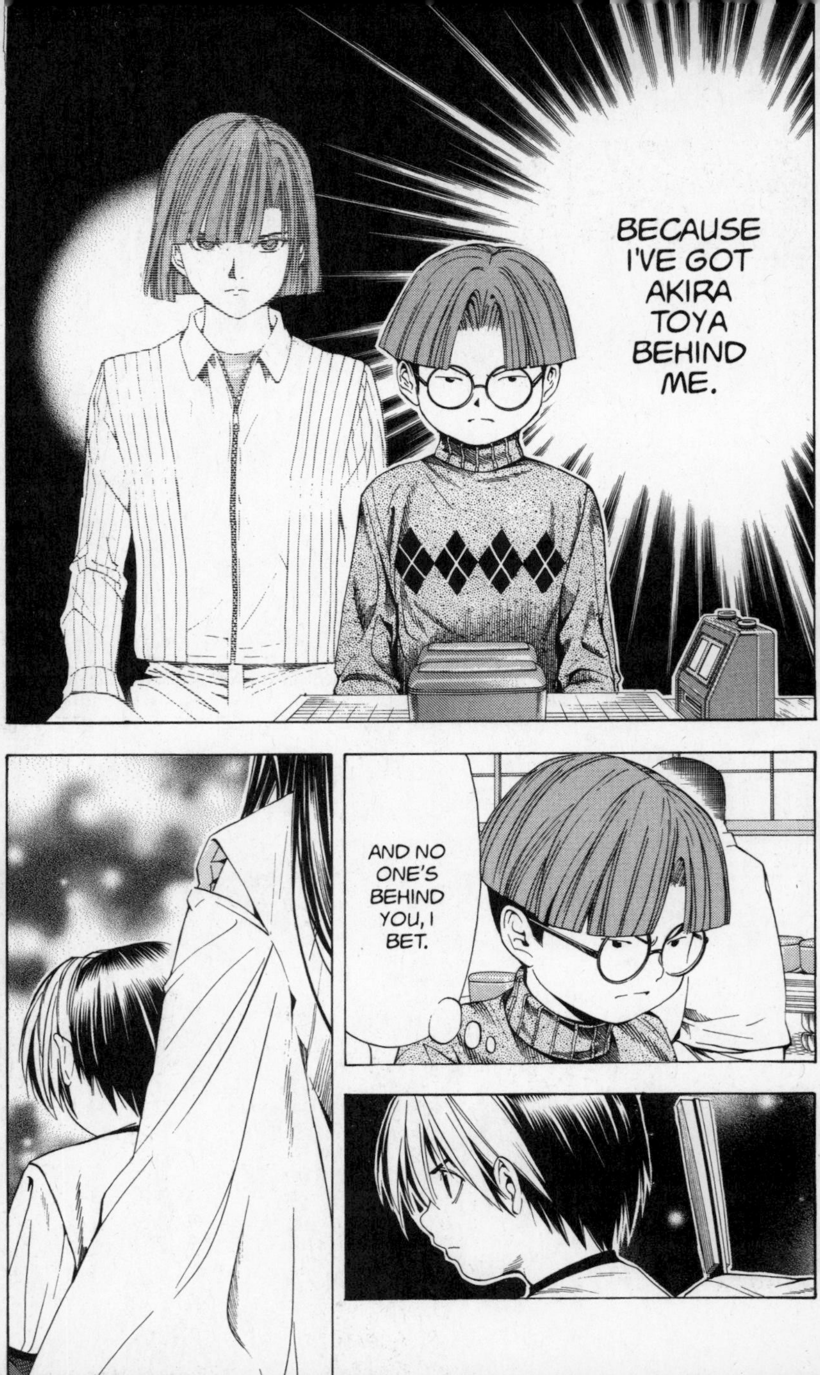
BECAUSE I'VE GOT AKIRA TOYA BEHIND ME.
AND NO ONE'S BEHIND YOU, I BET.

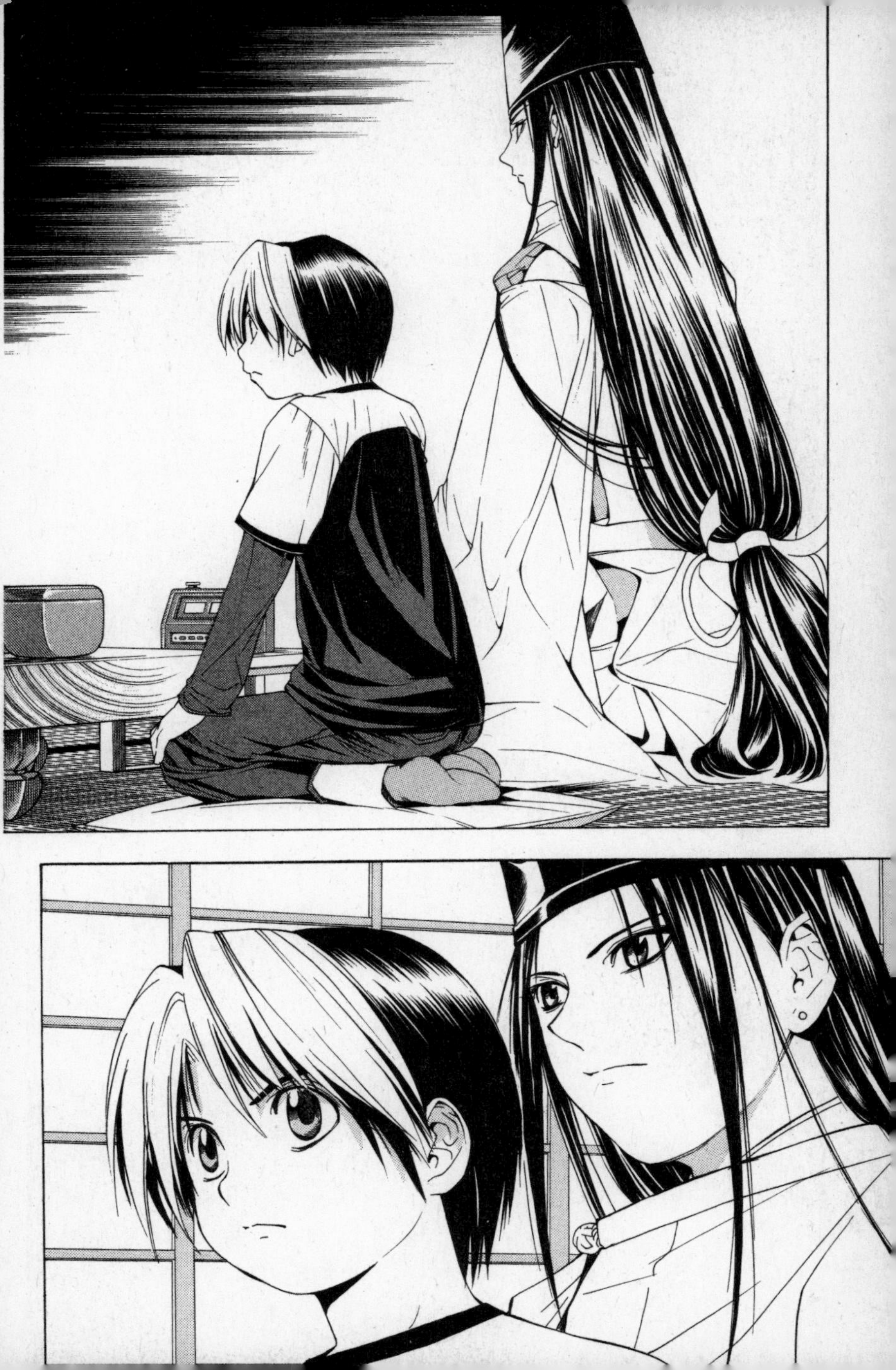

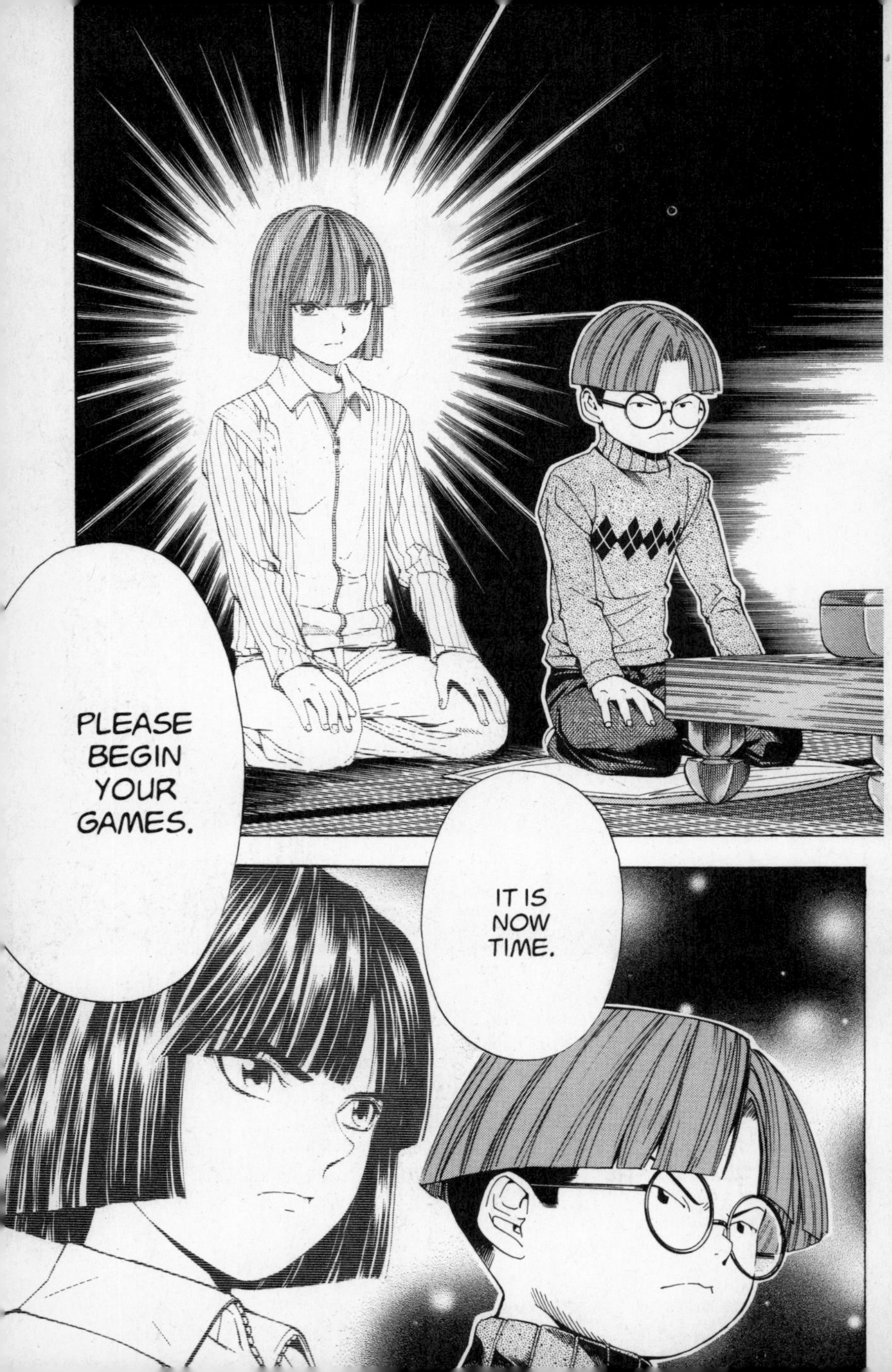
PLEASE BEGIN YOUR GAMES.
IT IS NOW TIME.

A WORD ABOUT HIKARU NO GO

THE EIGHT MAJOR TITLES

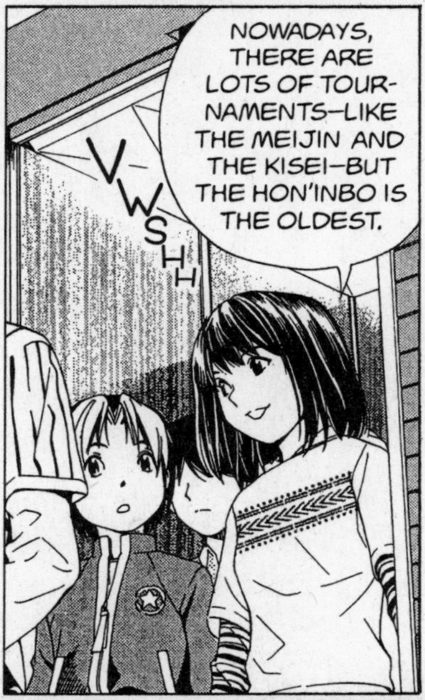
NOWADAYS, THERE ARE LOTS OF TOUR-NAMENTS—LIKE THE MEIJIN AND THE KISEI—BUT THE HON'INBO IS THE OLDEST.
VWSHH

THERE ARE EIGHT MAJOR GO TITLES: THE KISEI, MEIJIN, HON'INBO, JUDAN, TENGEN, OZA, WORLD FUJITSU CUP AND GOSEI. BESIDES THESE, THERE ARE OTHER TITLES, SUCH AS THE NHK CUP, THE NEC CUP, THE HAYAGO TOURNAMENT AND THE RYUSEI MATCH. AS A RESULT, THE TOP PLAYERS ARE VERY BUSY.

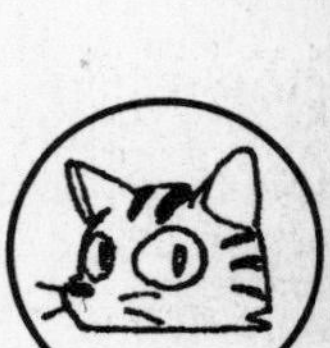

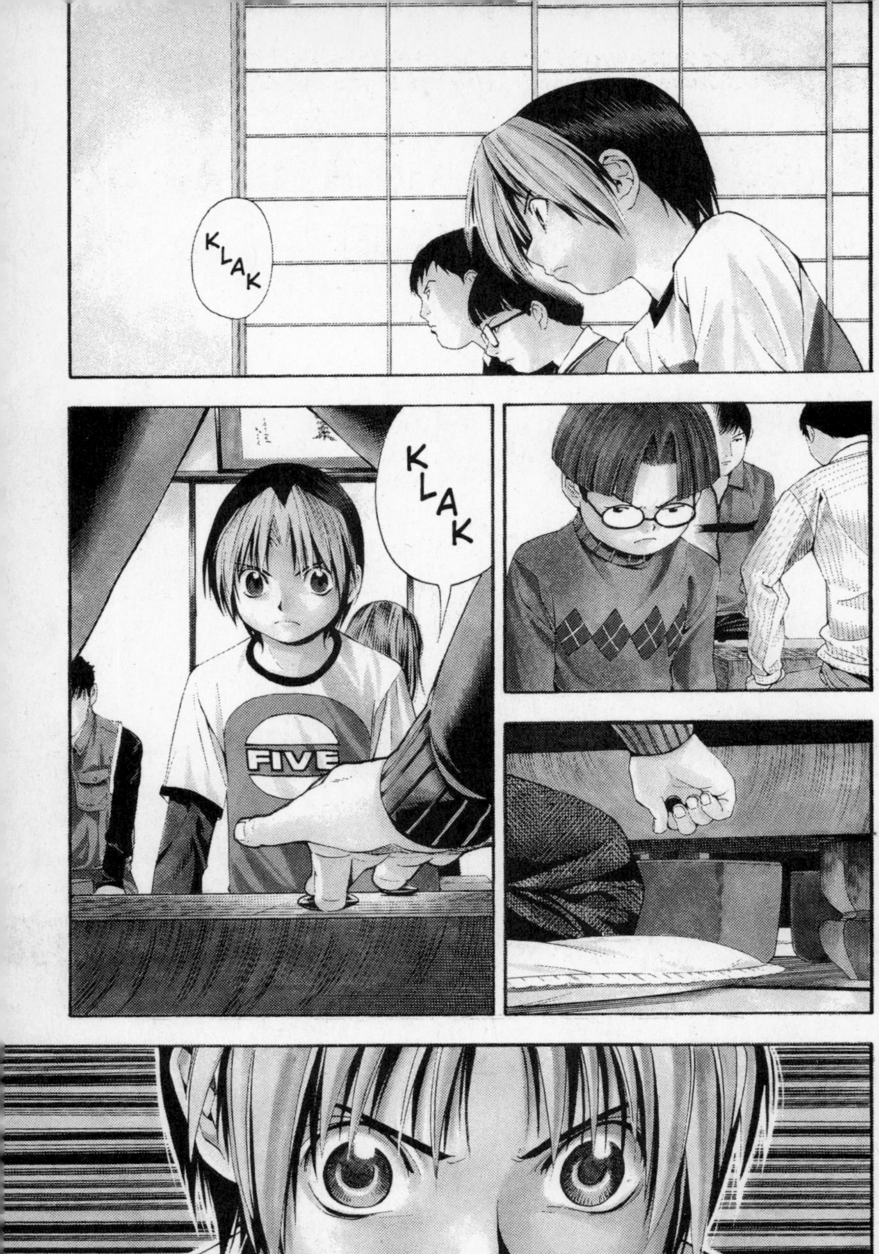
KLAK
KLAK

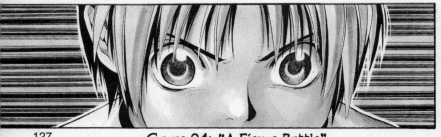

Game 94: "A Fierce Battle"

Game 94 "A Fierce Battle"

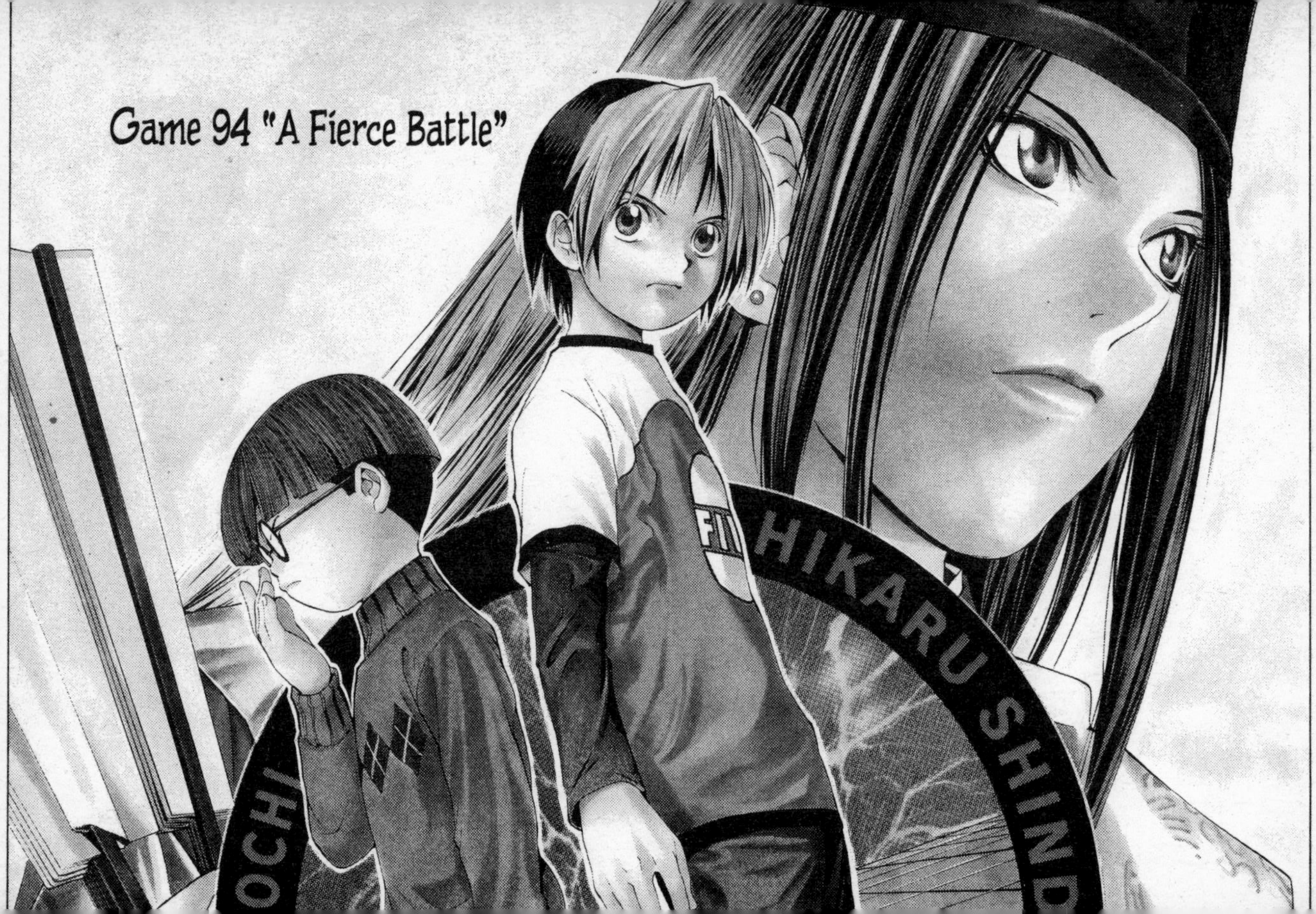
HIKARU SHIND
OCHI
FIT

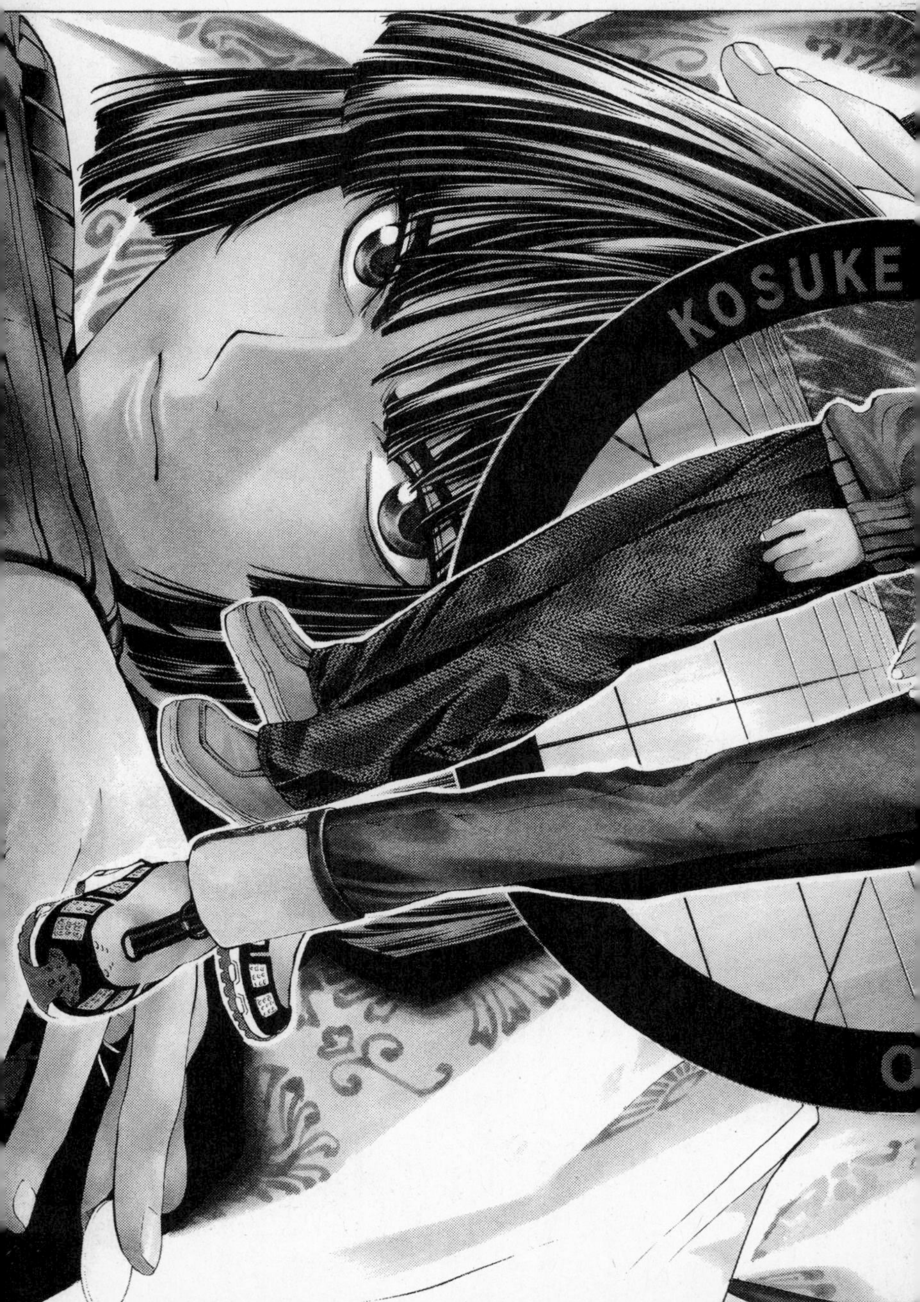
KOSUKE

5

SHINDO

HIKARU

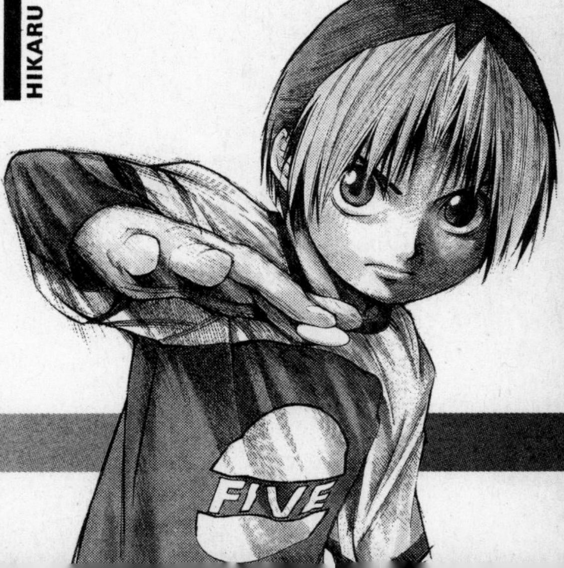
FIVE

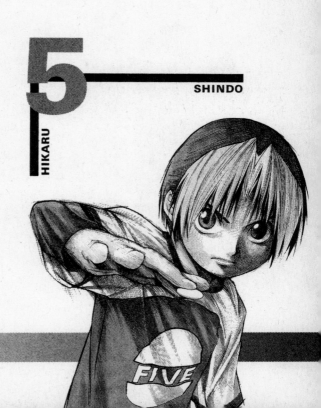

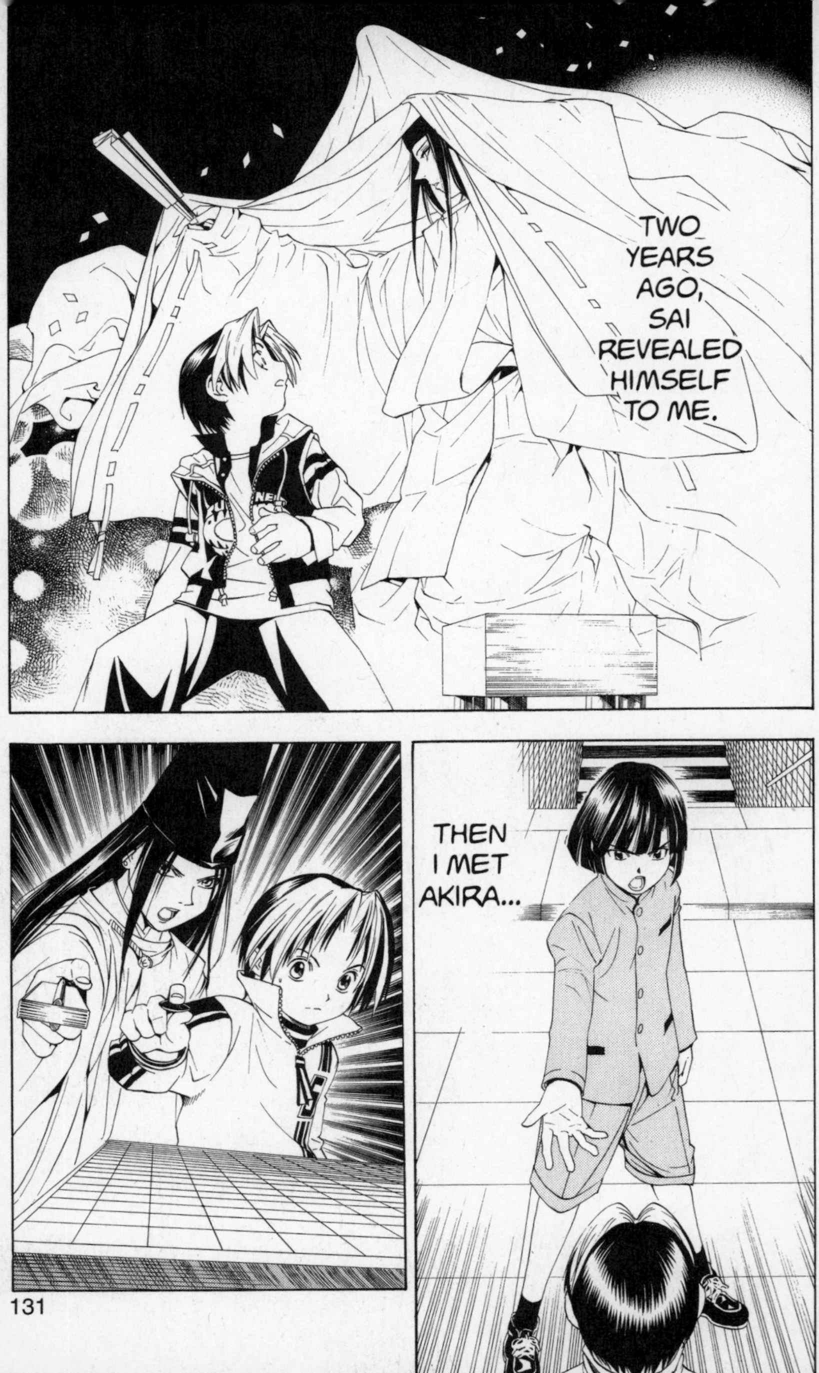
TWO YEARS AGO, SAI REVEALED HIMSELF TO ME.
THEN I MET AKIRA...

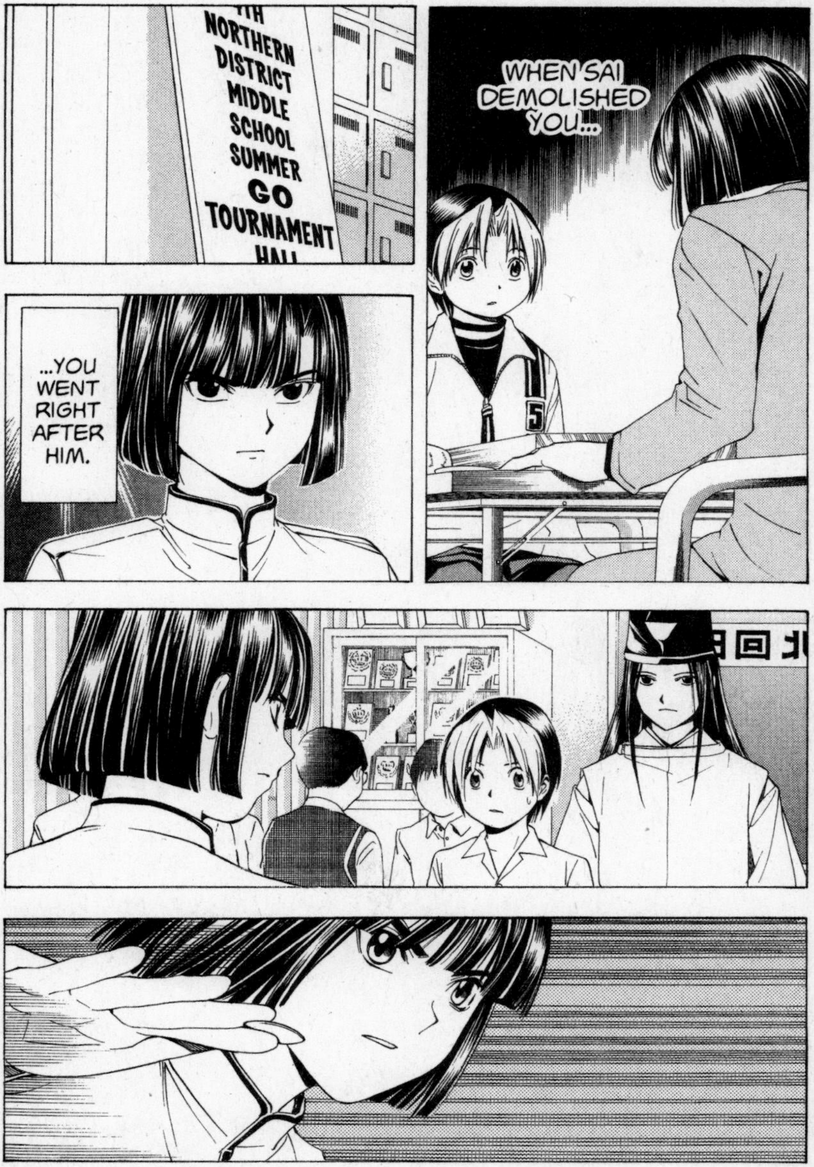
WHEN SAI DEMOLISHED YOU...
NORTHERN DISTRICT MIDDLE SCHOOL SUMMER GO TOURNAMENT
...YOU WENT RIGHT AFTER HIM.

READ THIS WAY

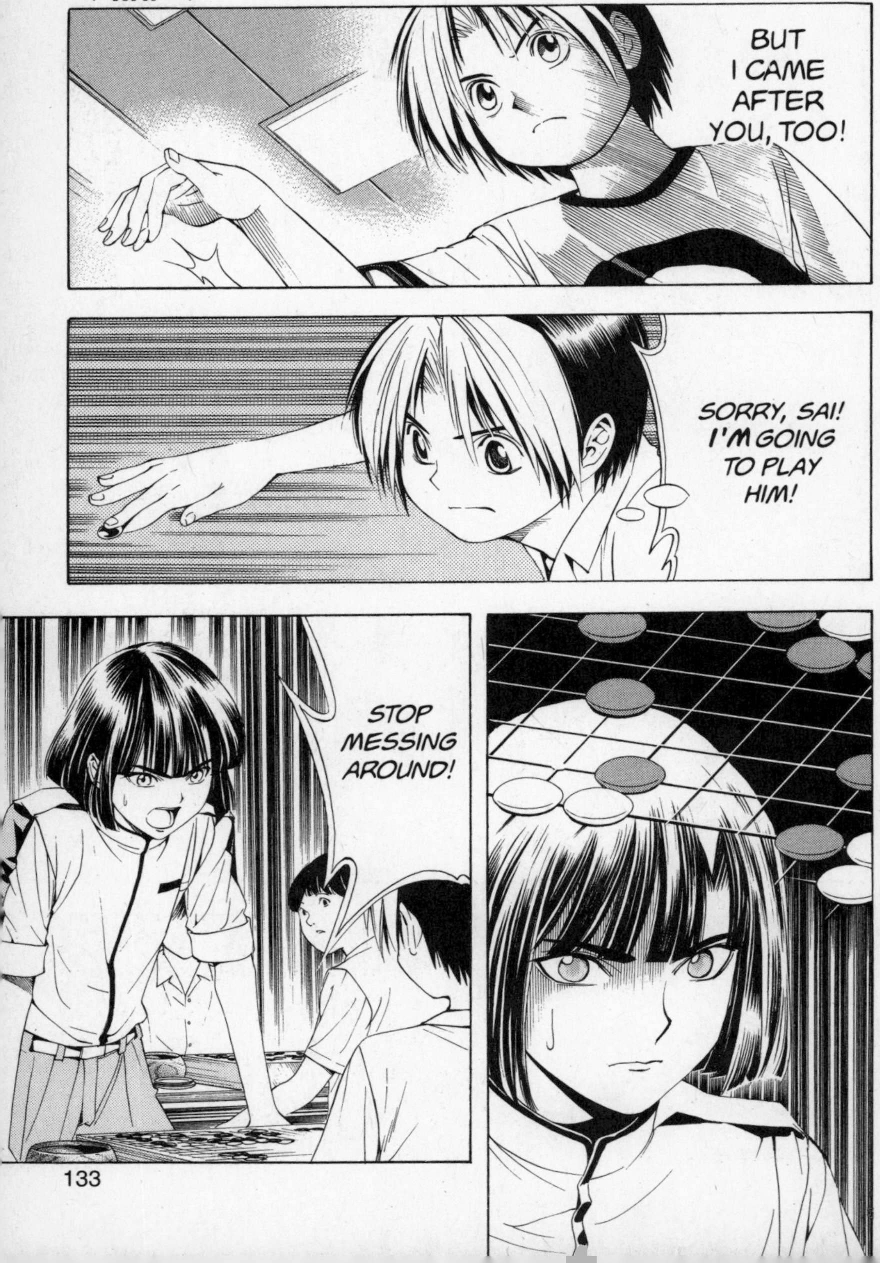
BUT I CAME AFTER YOU, TOO!
SORRY, SAI! I'M GOING TO PLAY HIM!
STOP MESSING AROUND!

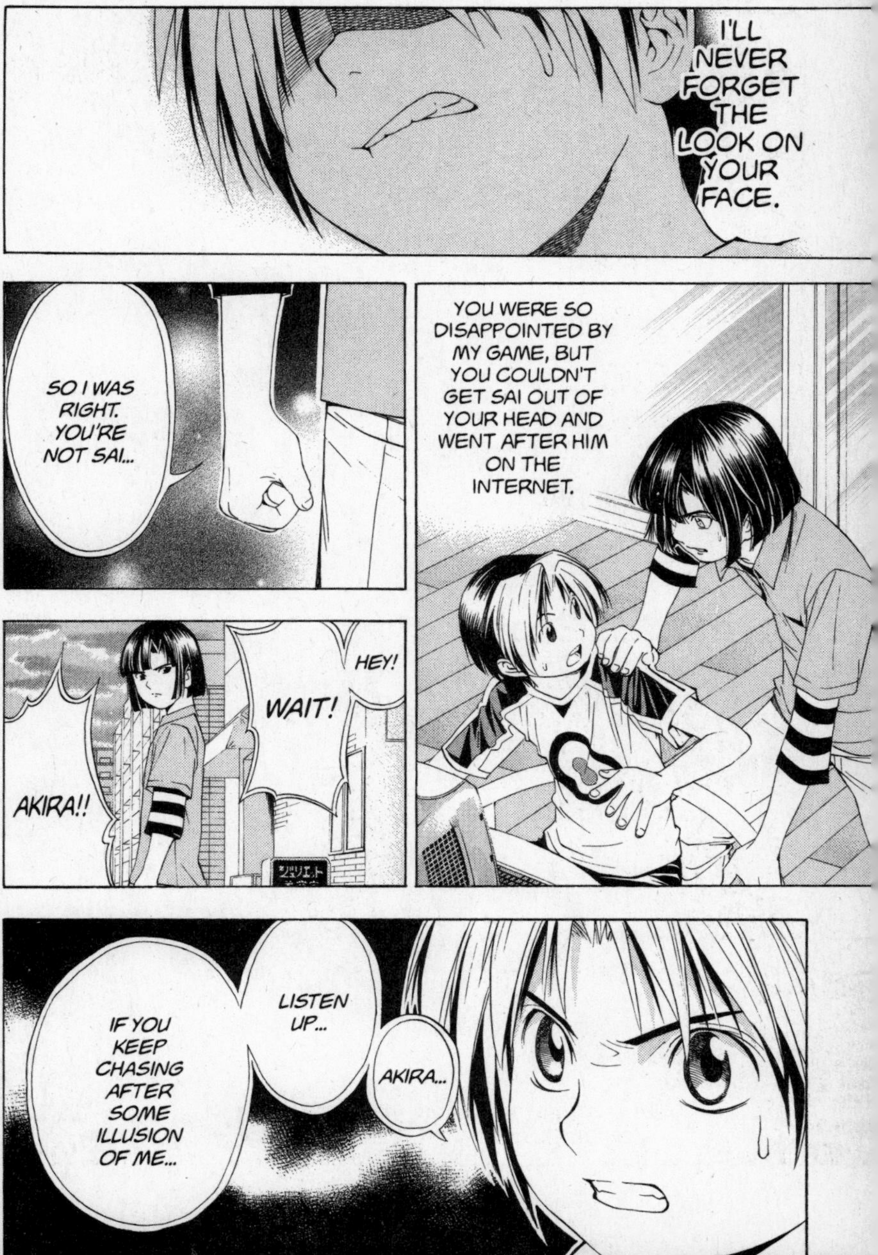
I'LL NEVER FORGET THE LOOK ON YOUR FACE.
YOU WERE SO DISAPPOINTED BY MY GAME, BUT YOU COULDN'T GET SAI OUT OF YOUR HEAD AND WENT AFTER HIM ON THE INTERNET.
SO I WAS RIGHT. YOU'RE NOT SAI...
HEY!
WAIT!
AKIRA!!
AKIRA...
LISTEN UP...
IF YOU KEEP CHASING AFTER SOME ILLUSION OF ME...

READ THIS WAY

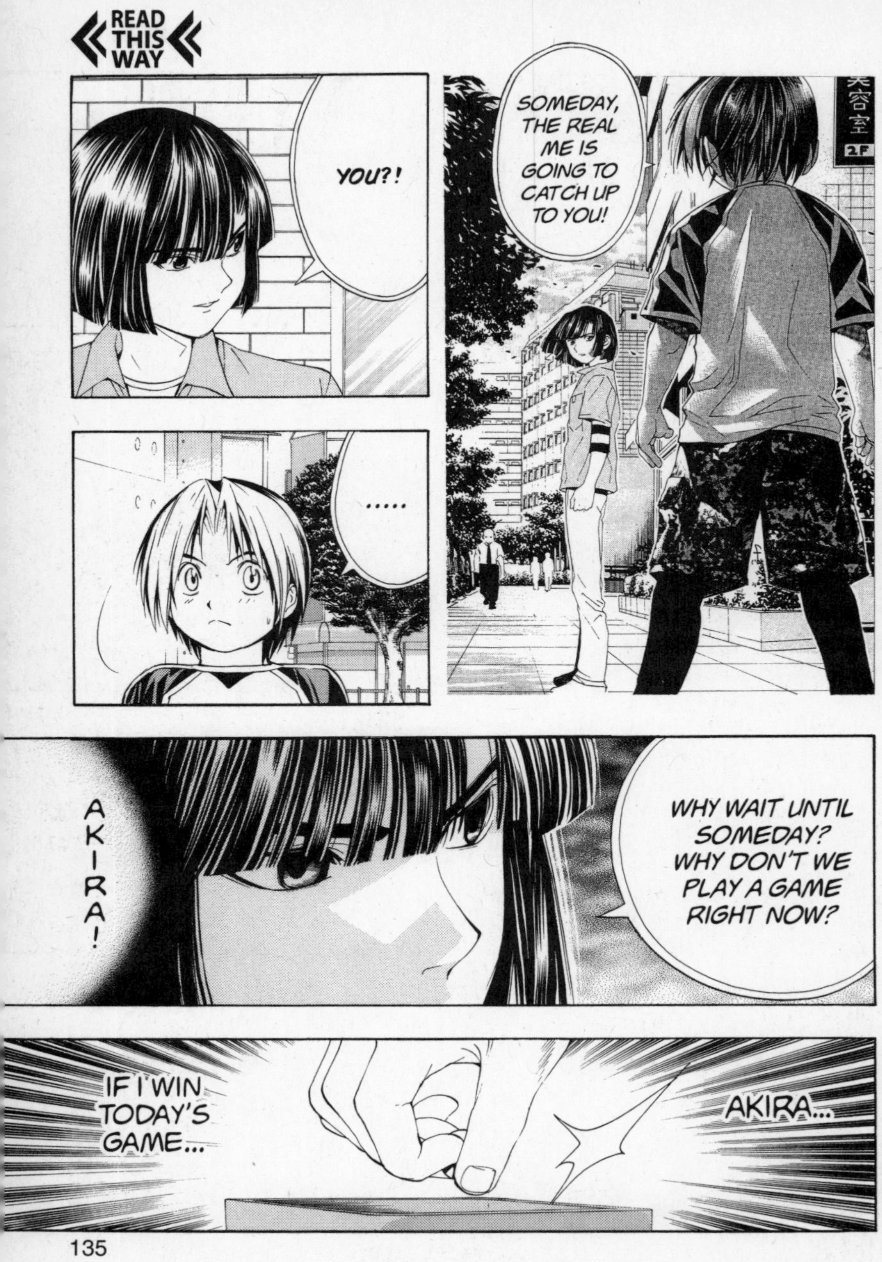

SOMEDAY, THE REAL ME IS GOING TO CATCH UP TO YOU!
YOU?!
.....
WHY WAIT UNTIL SOMEDAY? WHY DON'T WE PLAY A GAME RIGHT NOW?
AKIRA!
AKIRA...
IF I WIN TODAY'S GAME...

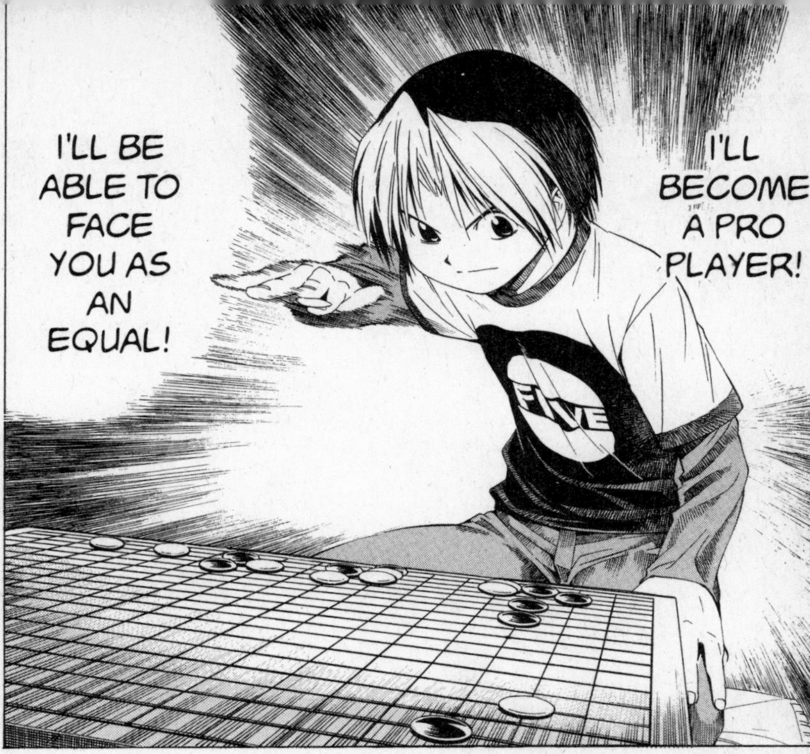
I'LL BECOME A PRO PLAYER!
I'LL BE ABLE TO FACE YOU AS AN EQUAL!
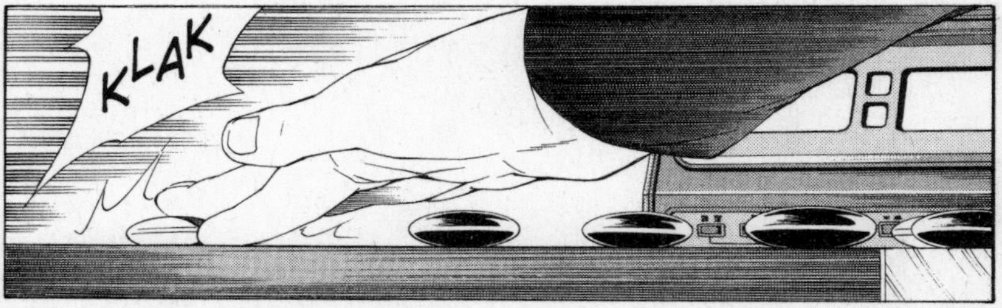
KLAK
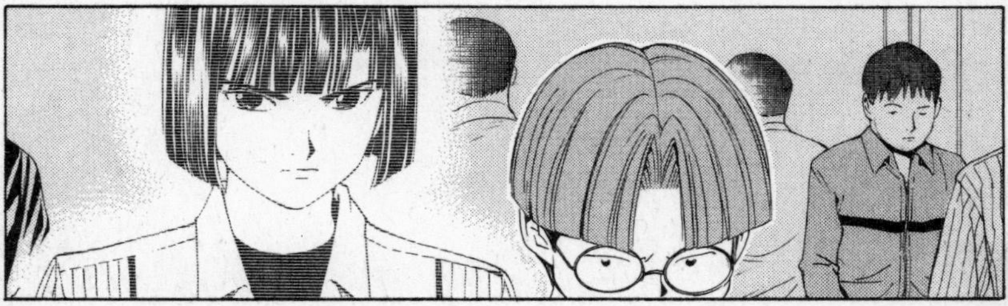

READ THIS WAY

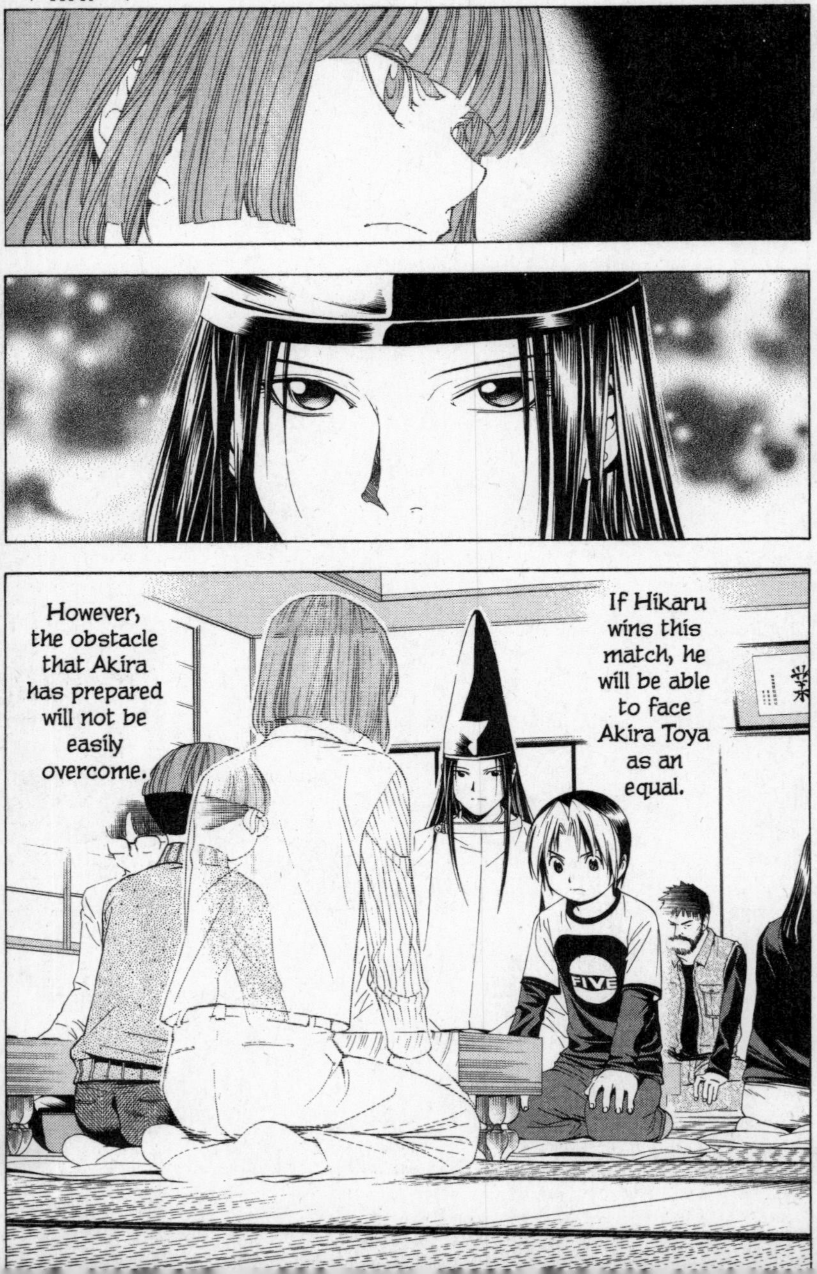
If Hikaru wins this match, he will be able to face Akira Toya as an equal.
However, the obstacle that Akira has prepared will not be easily overcome.

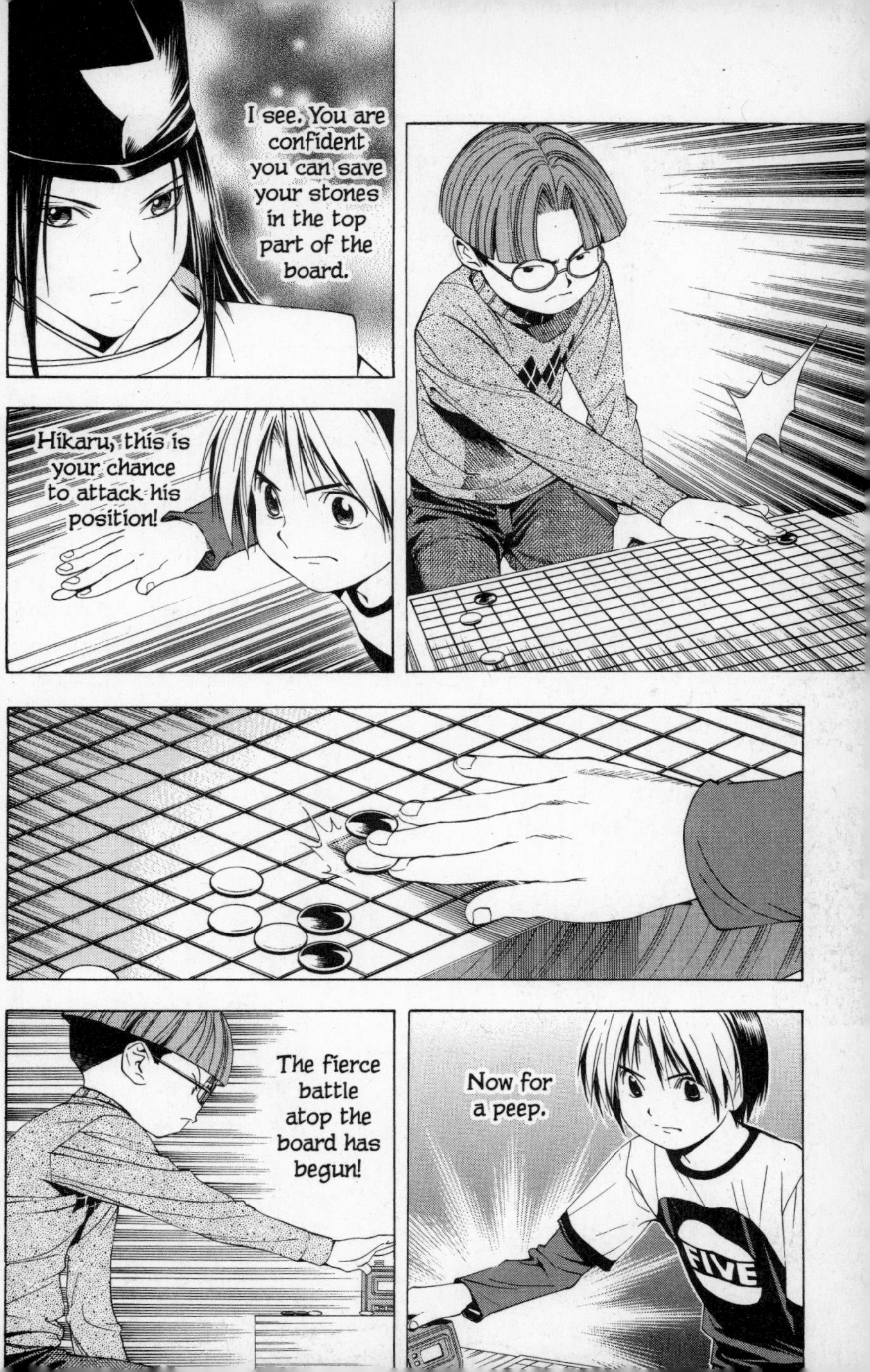
I see. You are confident you can save your stones in the top part of the board.
Hikaru, this is your chance to attack his position!
Now for a peep.
FIVE
The fierce battle atop the board has begun!

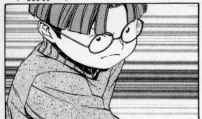

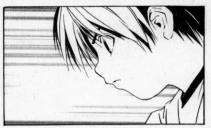

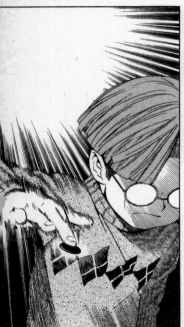

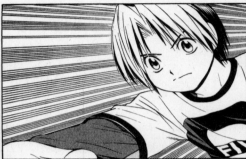

No good!
He's going
to attack!

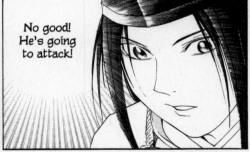

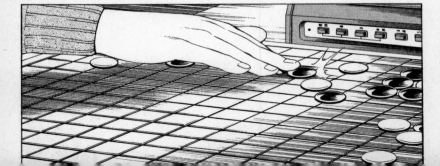

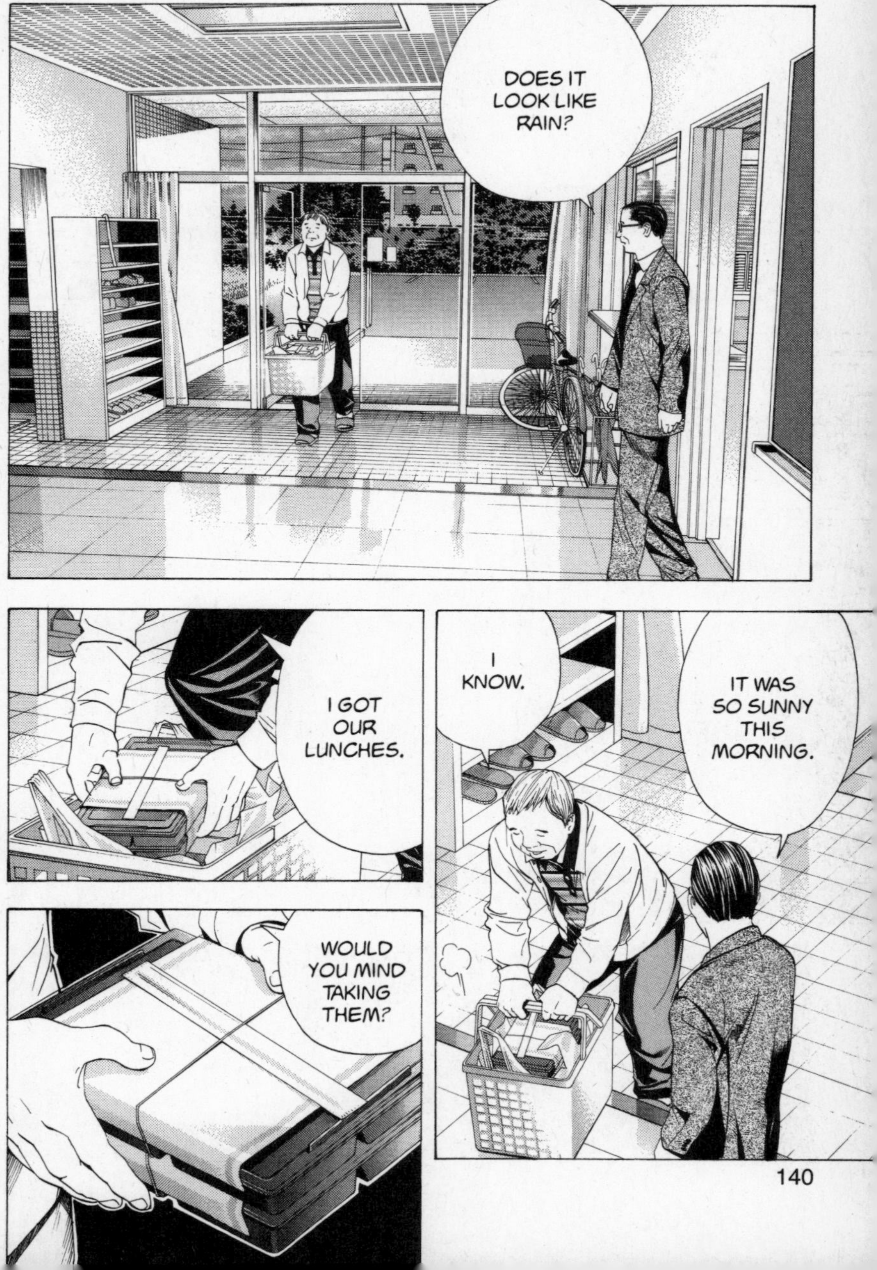
DOES IT LOOK LIKE RAIN?
IT WAS SO SUNNY THIS MORNING.
I KNOW.
I GOT OUR LUNCHES.
WOULD YOU MIND TAKING THEM?

READ THIS WAY

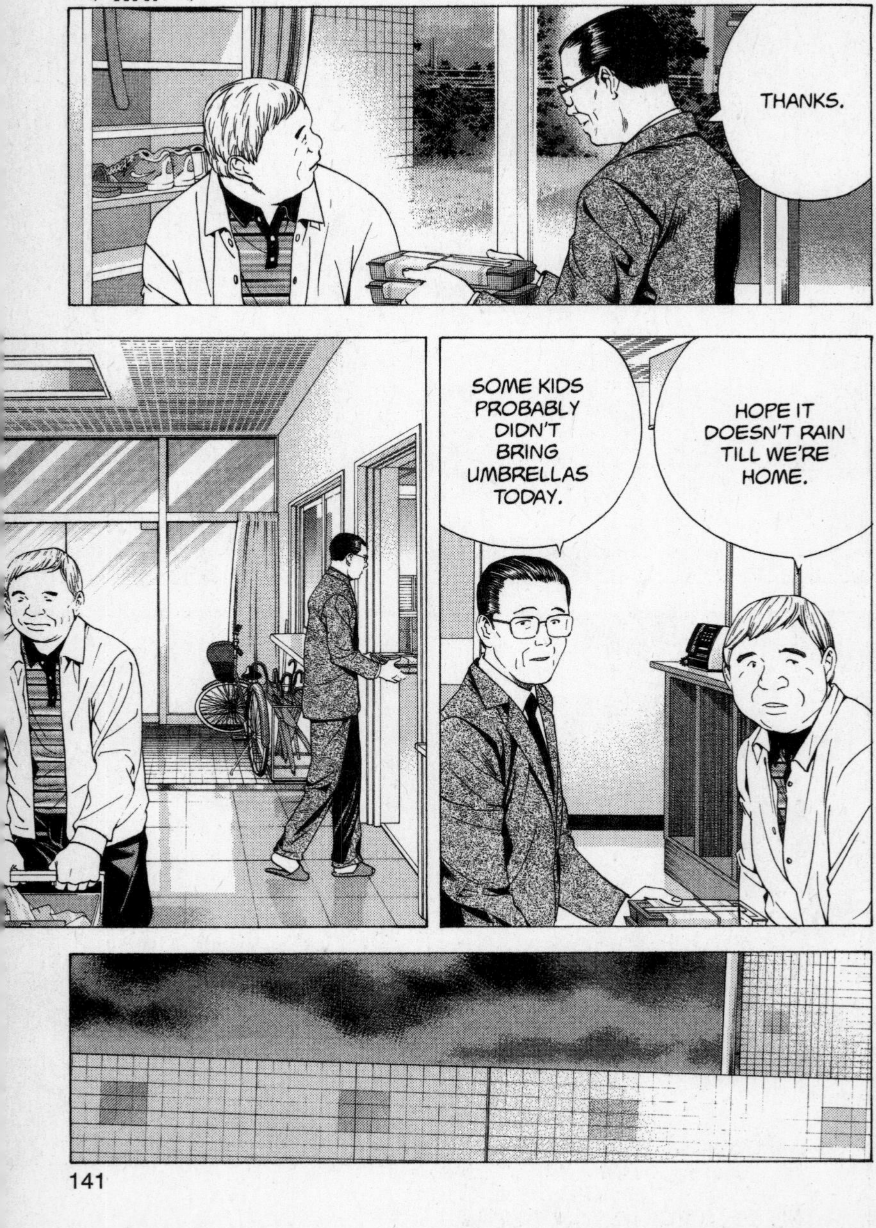
THANKS.
HOPE IT DOESN'T RAIN TILL WE'RE HOME.
SOME KIDS PROBABLY DIDN'T BRING UMBRELLAS TODAY.

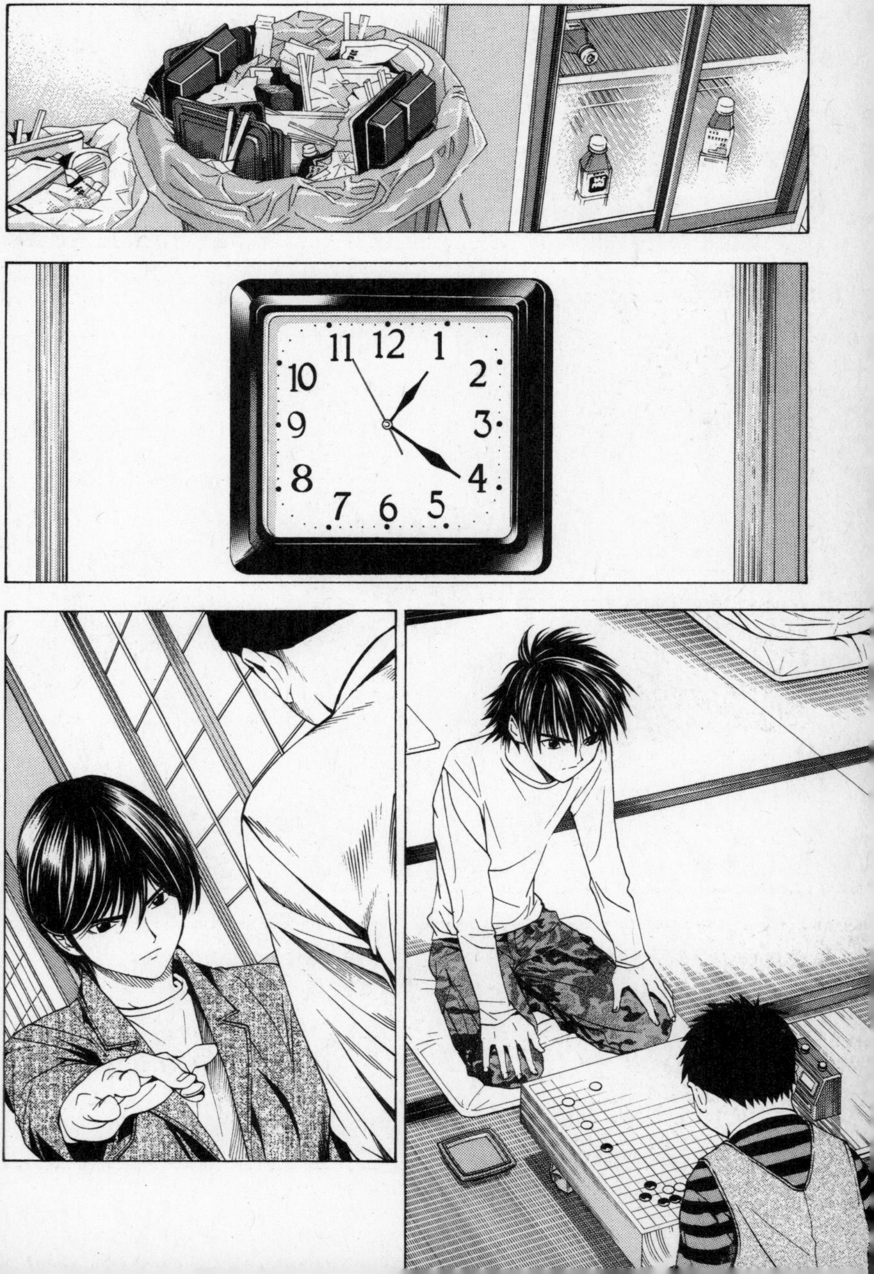

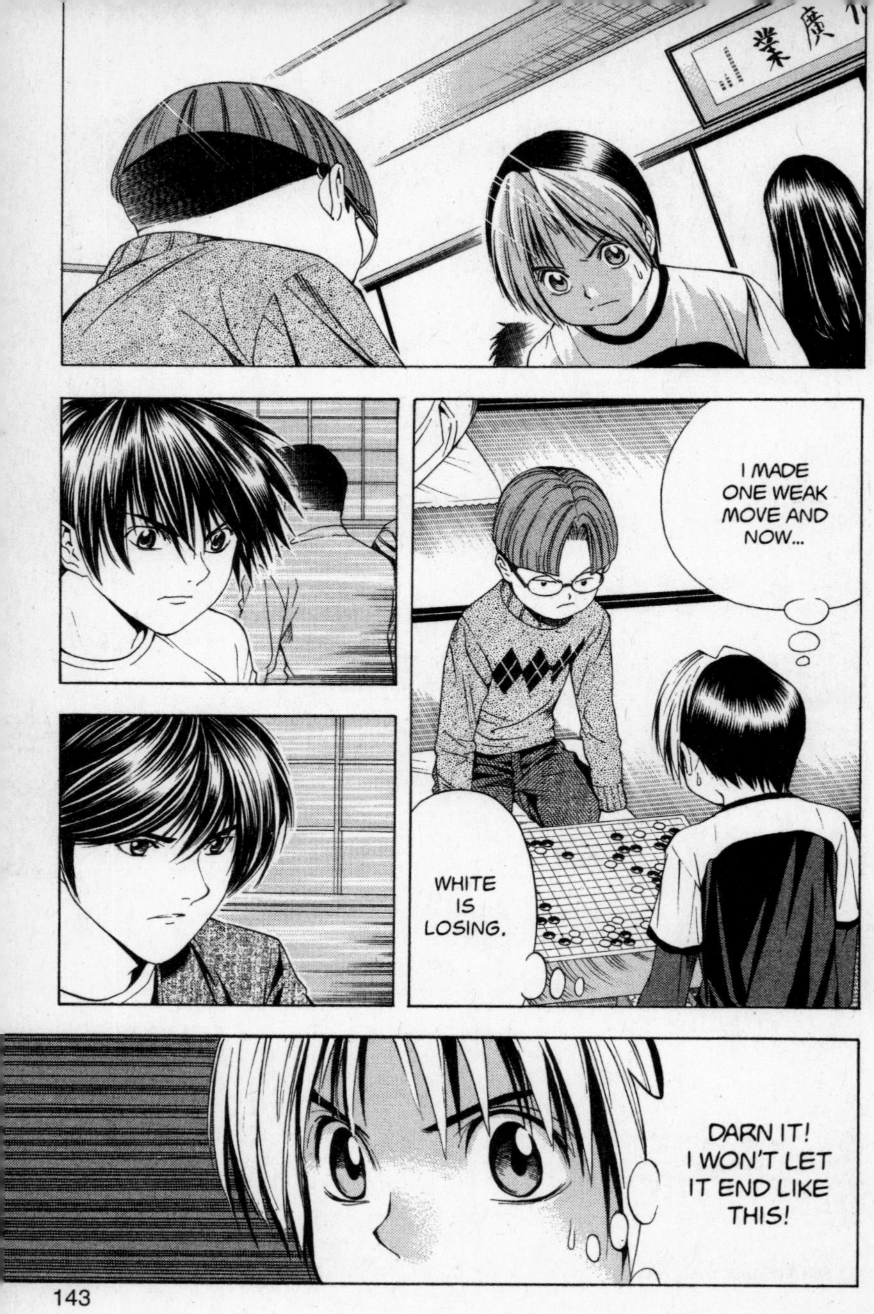
I MADE ONE WEAK MOVE AND NOW...
WHITE IS LOSING.
DARN IT! I WON'T LET IT END LIKE THIS!

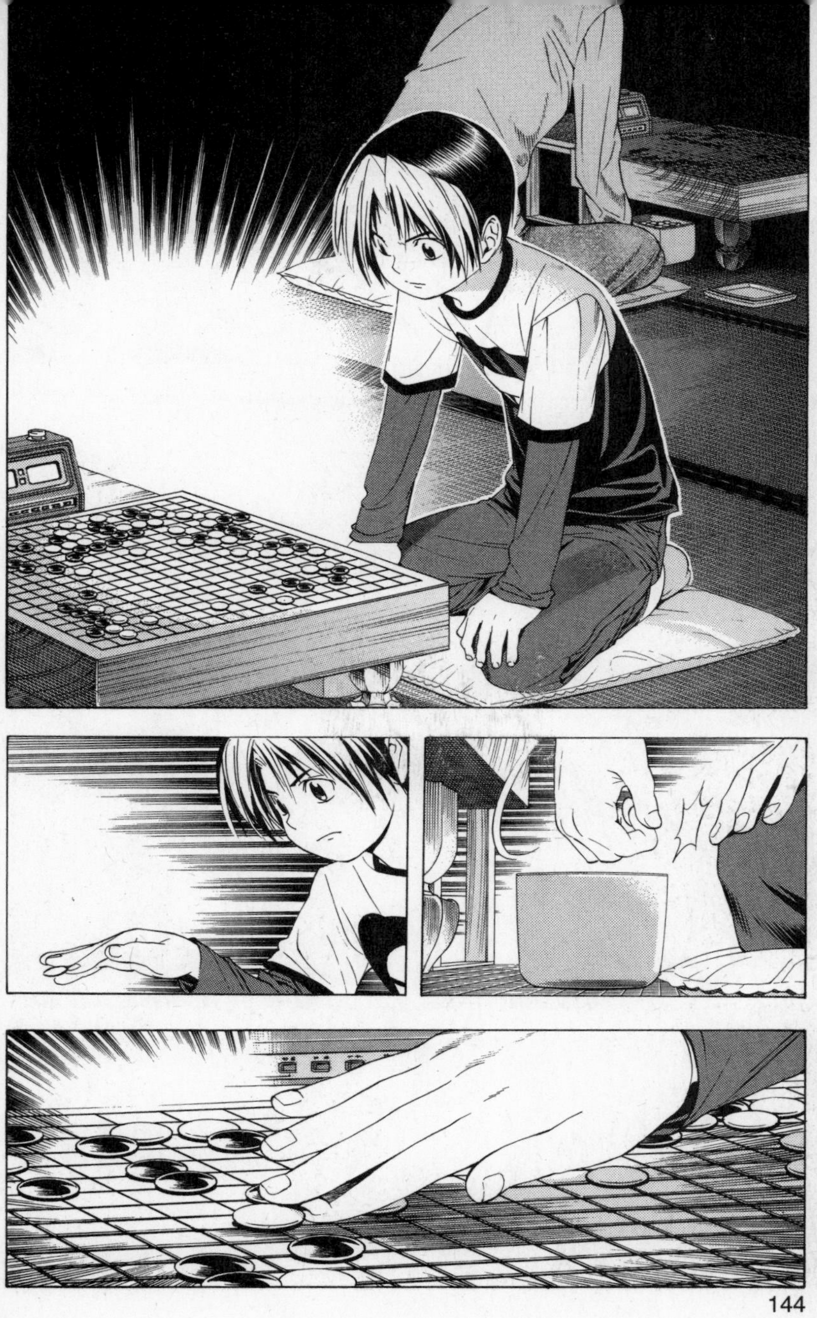

READ THIS WAY

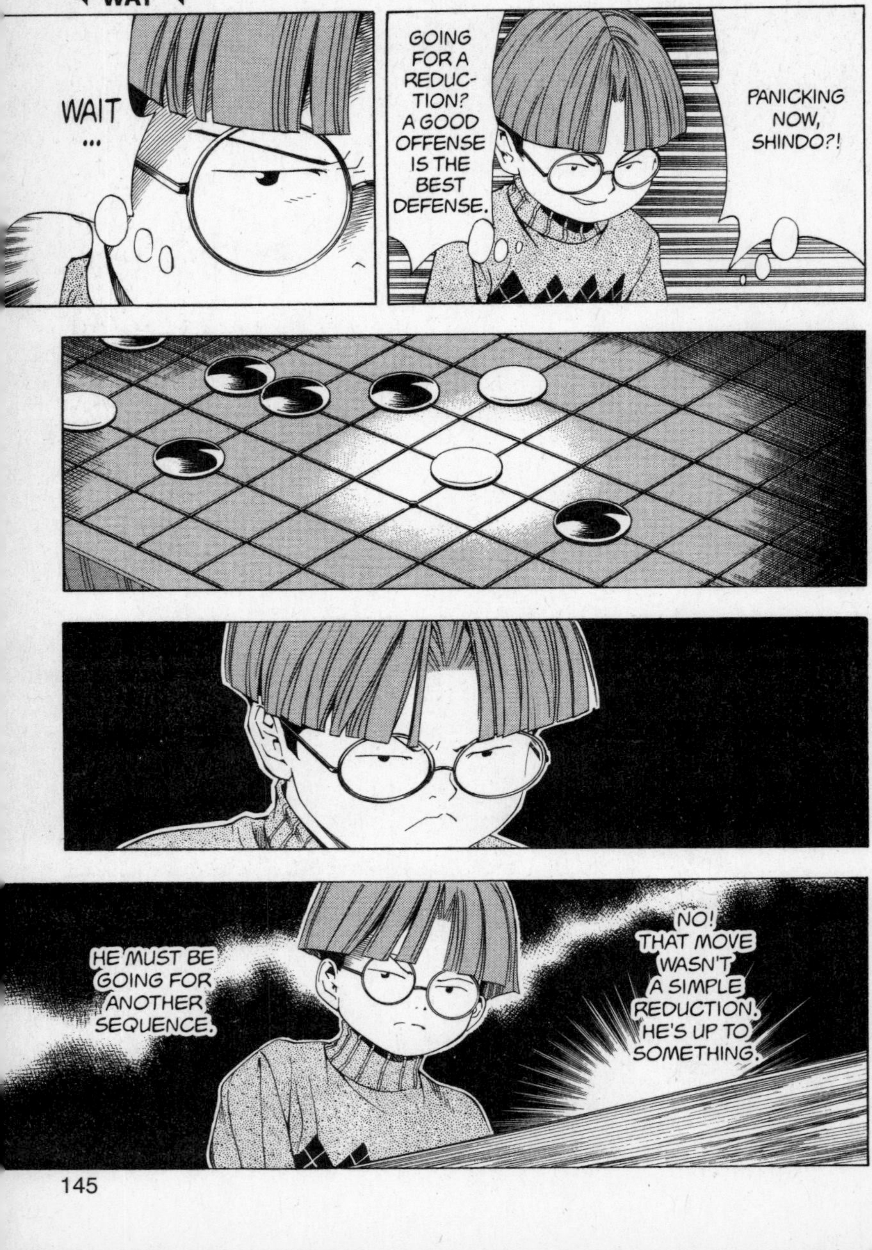
PANICKING NOW, SHINDO?!
GOING FOR A REDUCTION? A GOOD OFFENSE IS THE BEST DEFENSE.
WAIT ...
NO! THAT MOVE WASN'T A SIMPLE REDUCTION. HE'S UP TO SOMETHING.
HE MUST BE GOING FOR ANOTHER SEQUENCE.

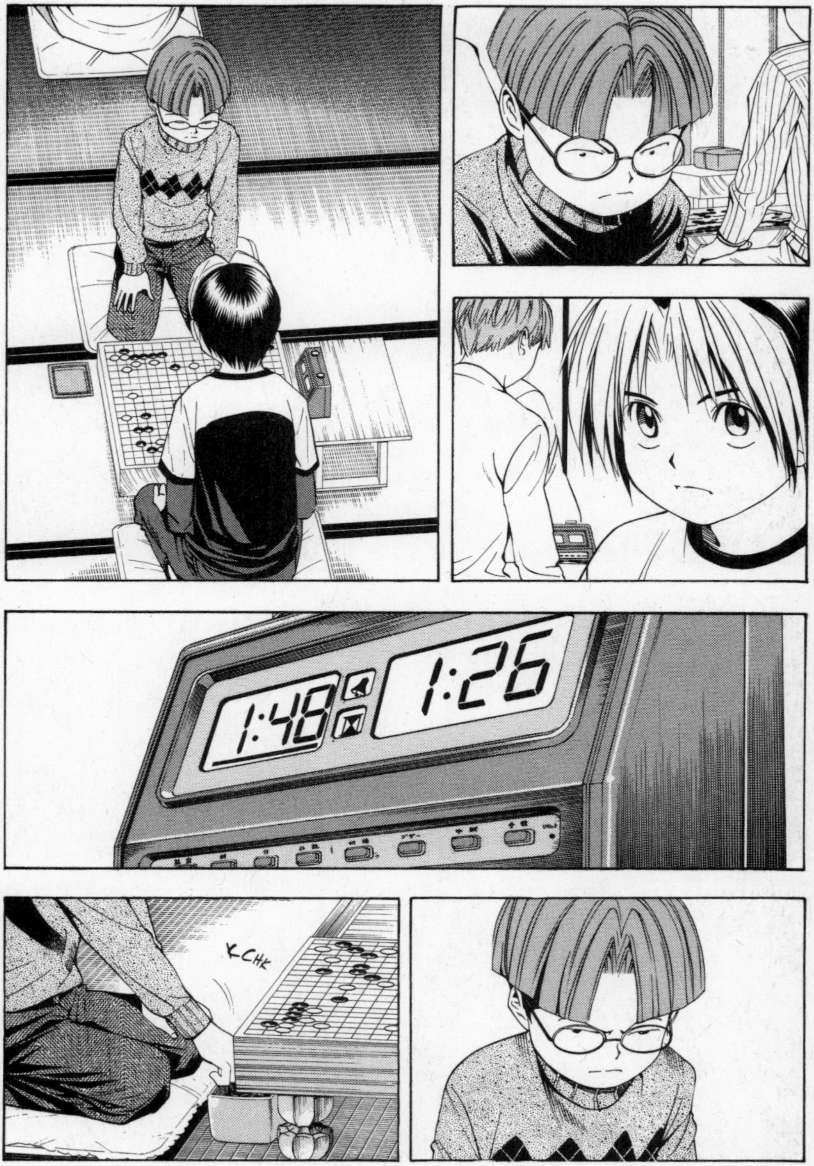
1:48
1:26
KCHK

READ THIS WAY

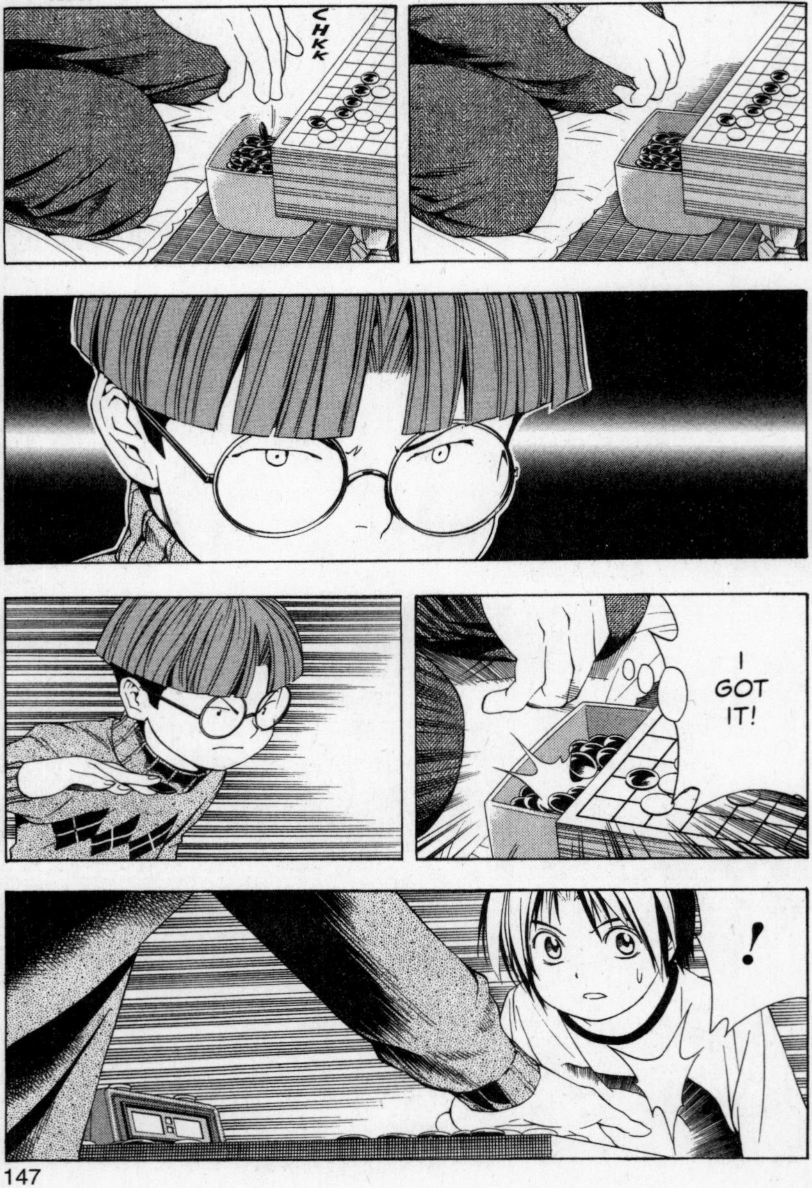
CHKK
I GOT IT!
!

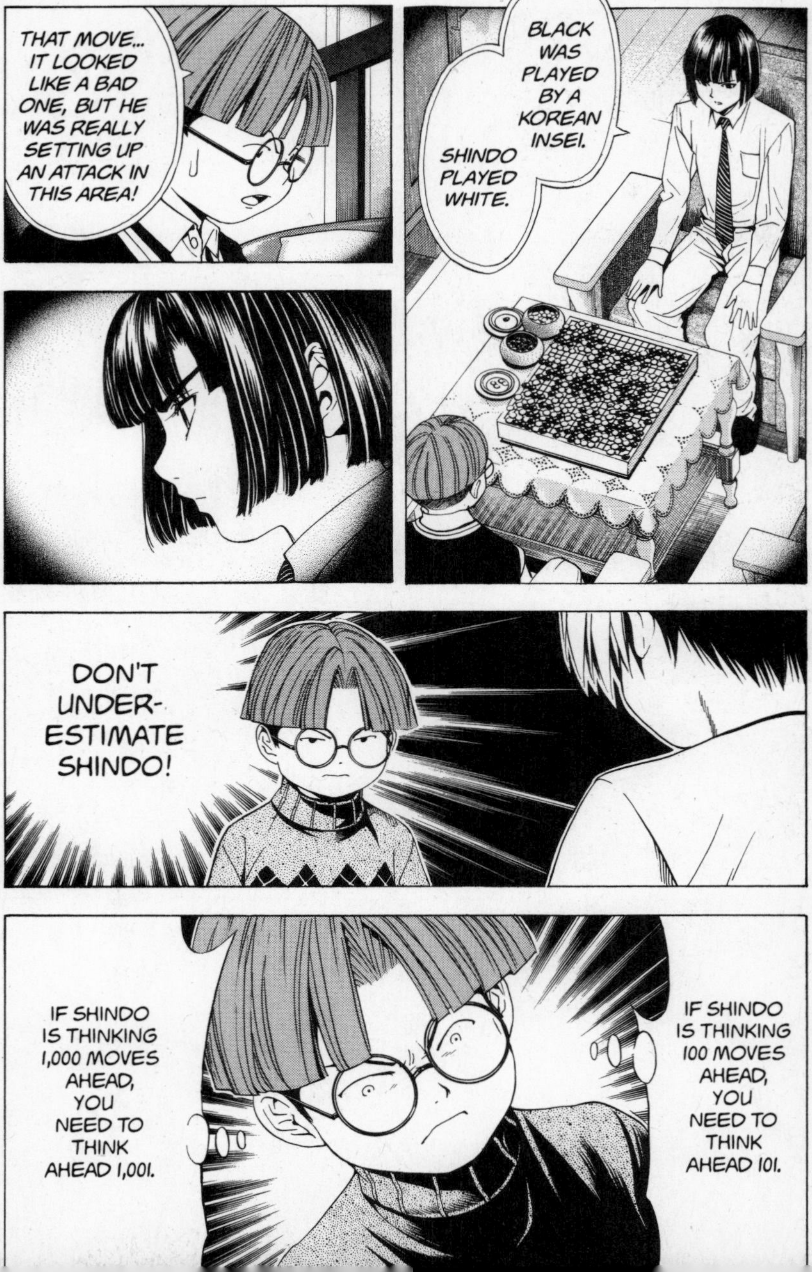
BLACK WAS PLAYED BY A KOREAN INSEI.
SHINDO PLAYED WHITE.
THAT MOVE... IT LOOKED LIKE A BAD ONE, BUT HE WAS REALLY SETTING UP AN ATTACK IN THIS AREA!
DON'T UNDER-ESTIMATE SHINDO!
IF SHINDO IS THINKING 100 MOVES AHEAD, YOU NEED TO THINK AHEAD 101.
IF SHINDO IS THINKING 1,000 MOVES AHEAD, YOU NEED TO THINK AHEAD 1,001.

READ THIS WAY

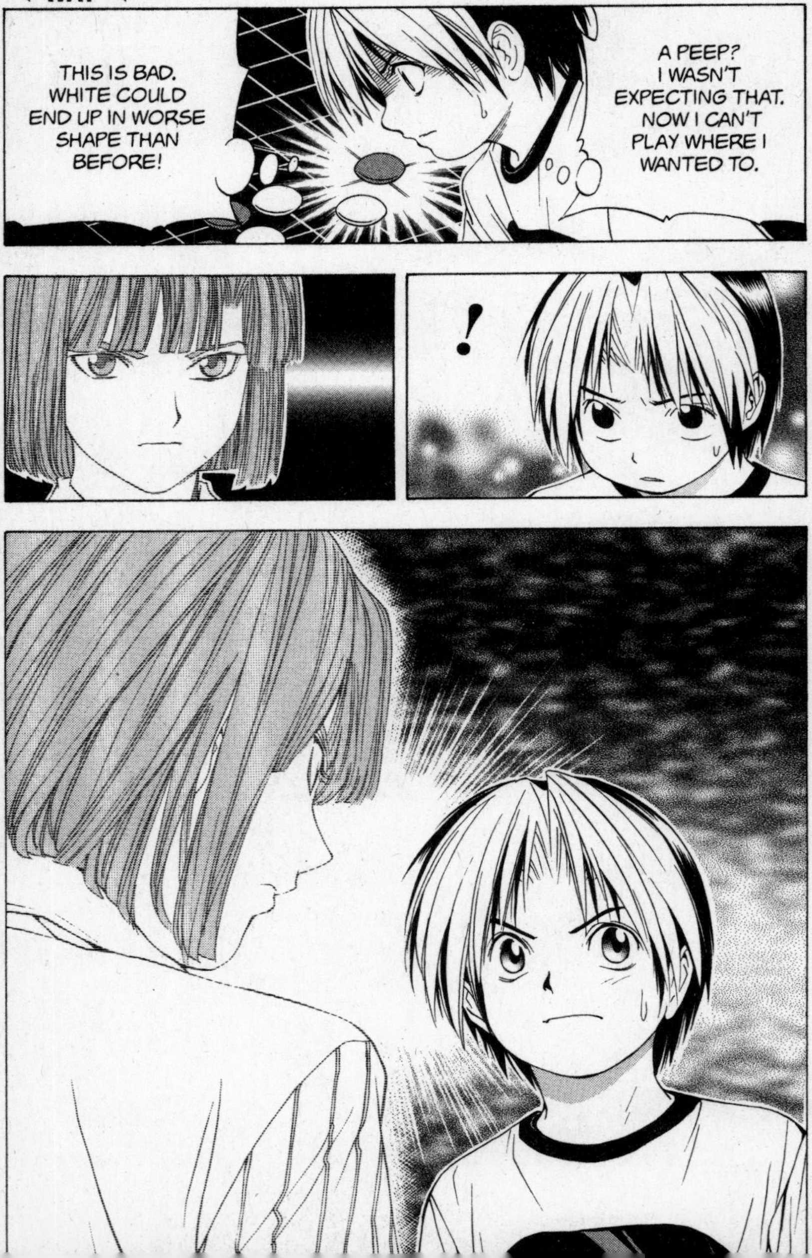
A PEEP? I WASN'T EXPECTING THAT. NOW I CAN'T PLAY WHERE I WANTED TO.
THIS IS BAD. WHITE COULD END UP IN WORSE SHAPE THAN BEFORE!
!

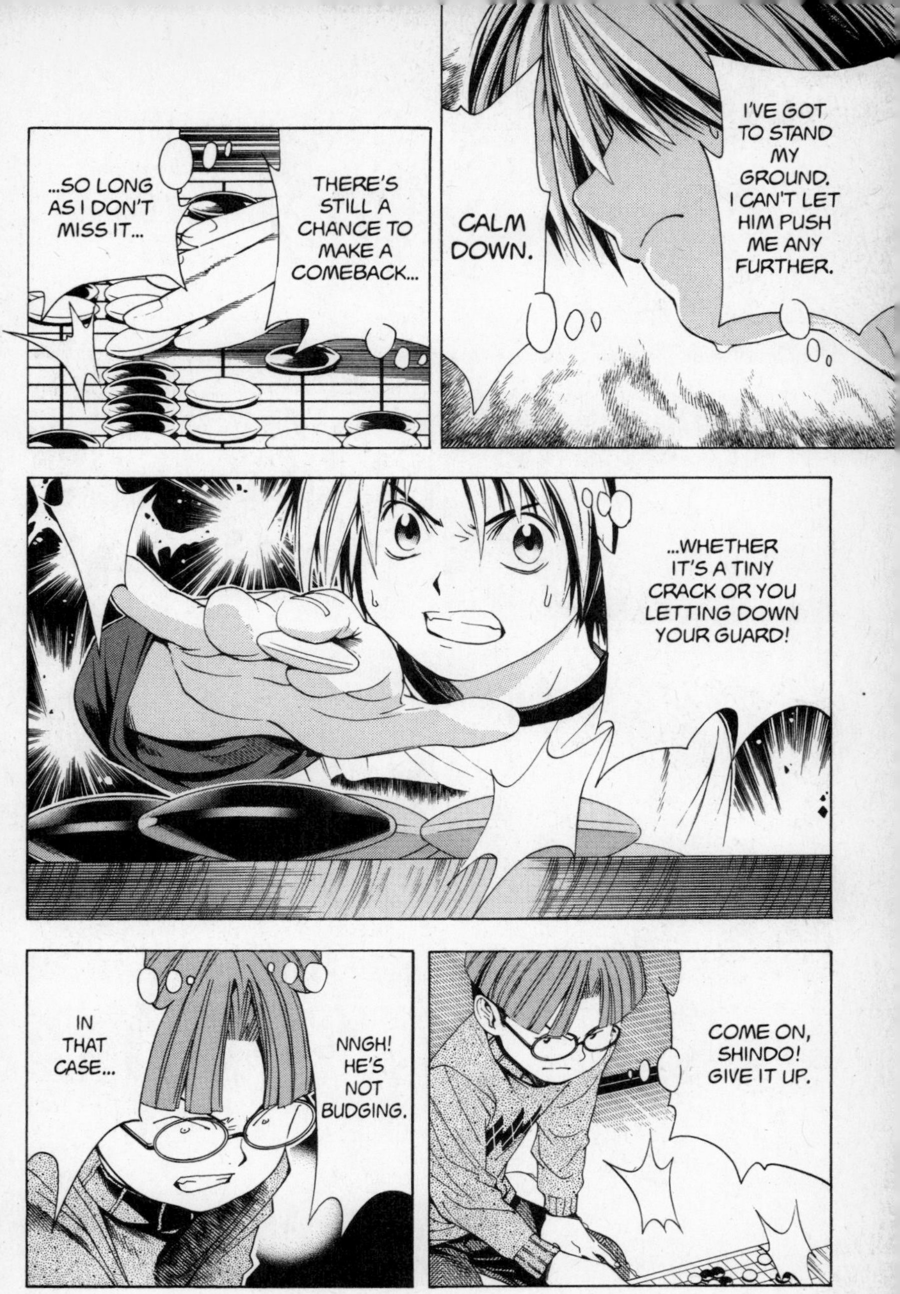
I'VE GOT TO STAND MY GROUND. I CAN'T LET HIM PUSH ME ANY FURTHER.
CALM DOWN.
THERE'S STILL A CHANCE TO MAKE A COMEBACK...
...SO LONG AS I DON'T MISS IT...
...WHETHER IT'S A TINY CRACK OR YOU LETTING DOWN YOUR GUARD!
COME ON, SHINDO! GIVE IT UP.
NNGH! HE'S NOT BUDGING.
IN THAT CASE...

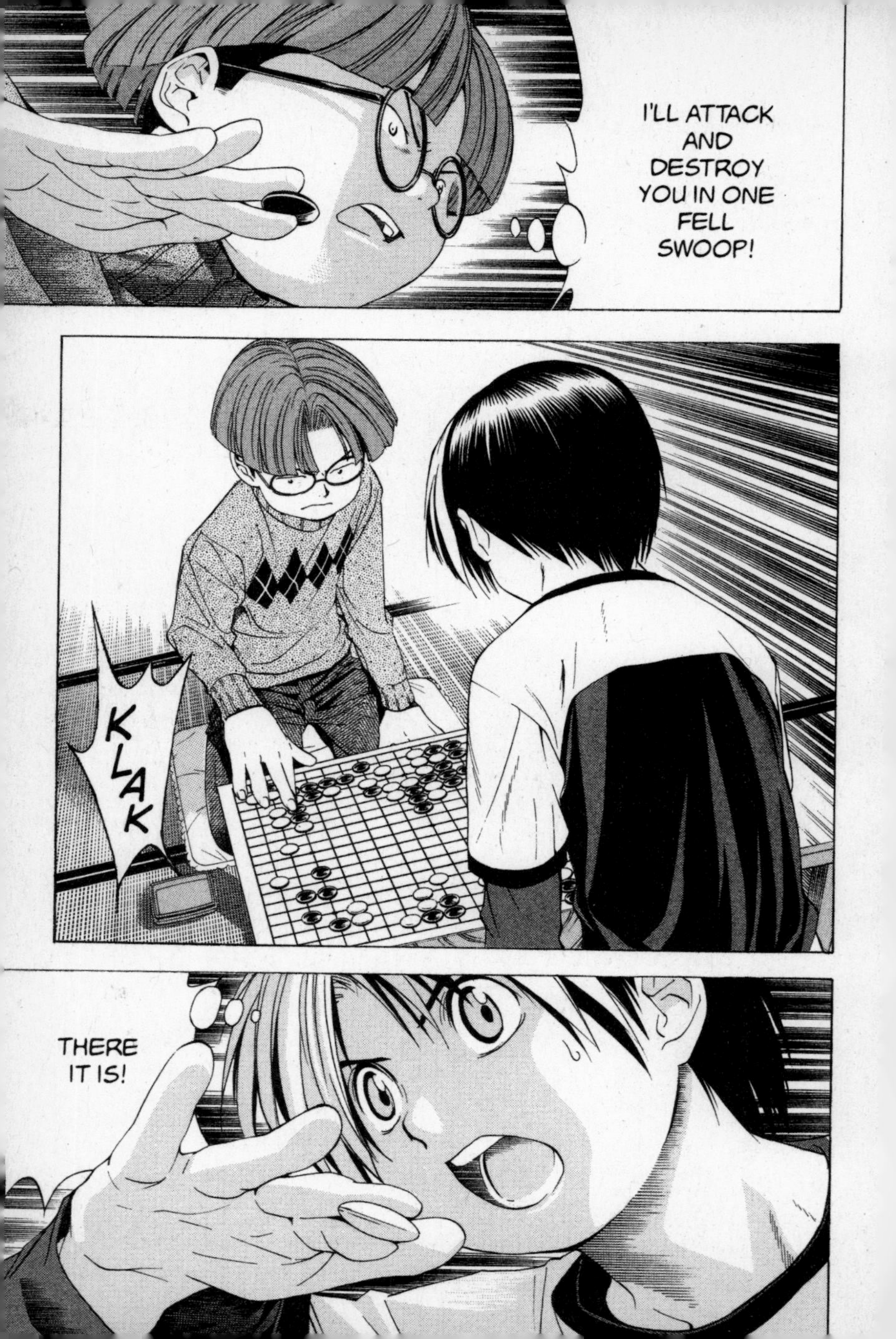
I'LL ATTACK AND DESTROY YOU IN ONE FELL SWOOP!
KLAK
THERE IT IS!

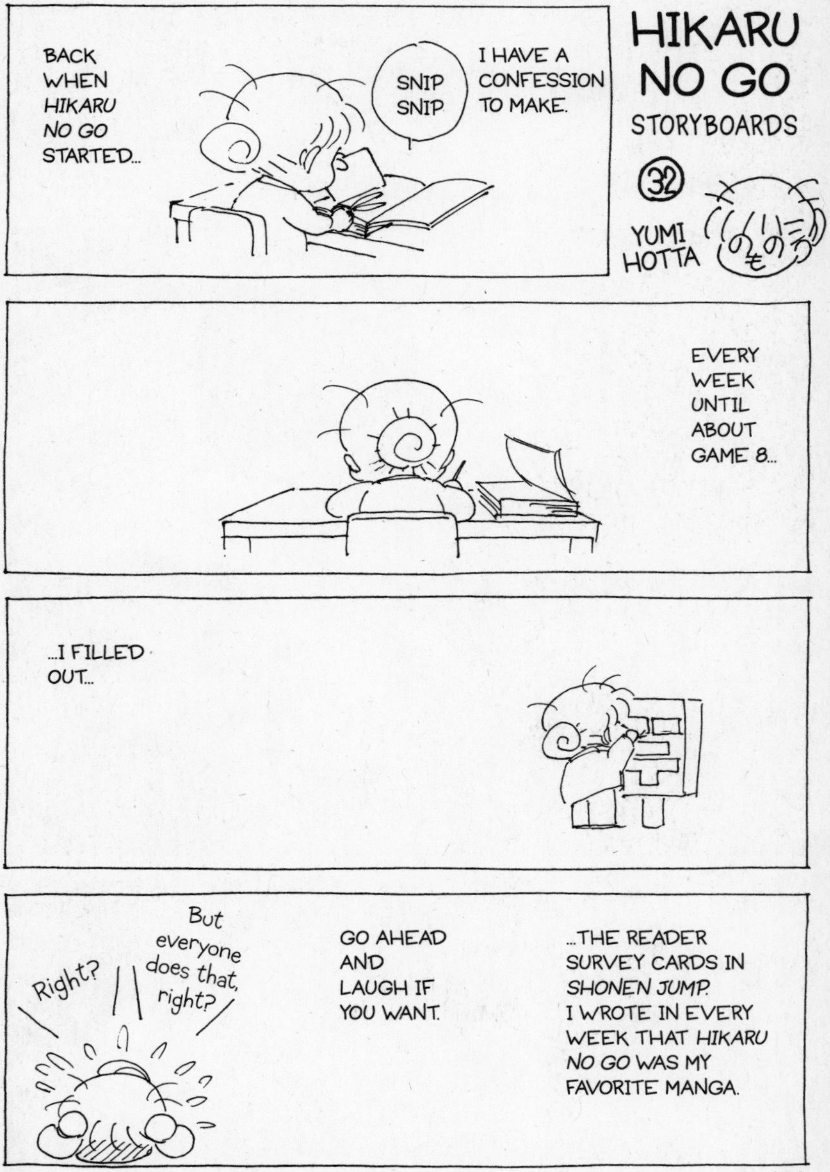
HIKARU NO GO STORYBOARDS
32
YUMI HOTTA
I HAVE A CONFESSION TO MAKE.
SNIP SNIP
BACK WHEN HIKARU NO GO STARTED...
EVERY WEEK UNTIL ABOUT GAME 8...
...I FILLED OUT...
...THE READER SURVEY CARDS IN SHONEN JUMP. I WROTE IN EVERY WEEK THAT HIKARU NO GO WAS MY FAVORITE MANGA.
GO AHEAD AND LAUGH IF YOU WANT.
But everyone does that, right?
Right?

Game 95 "The Second Player to Pass"

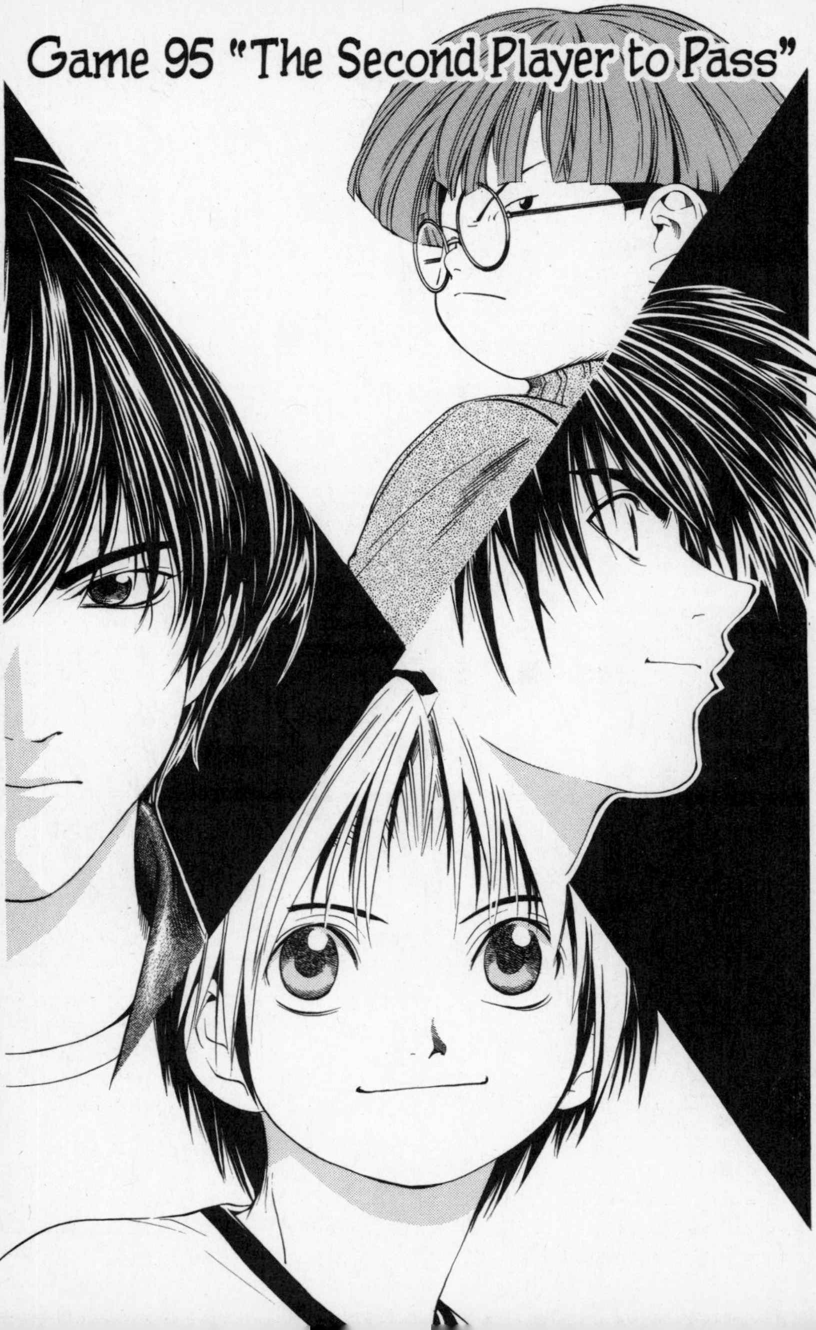

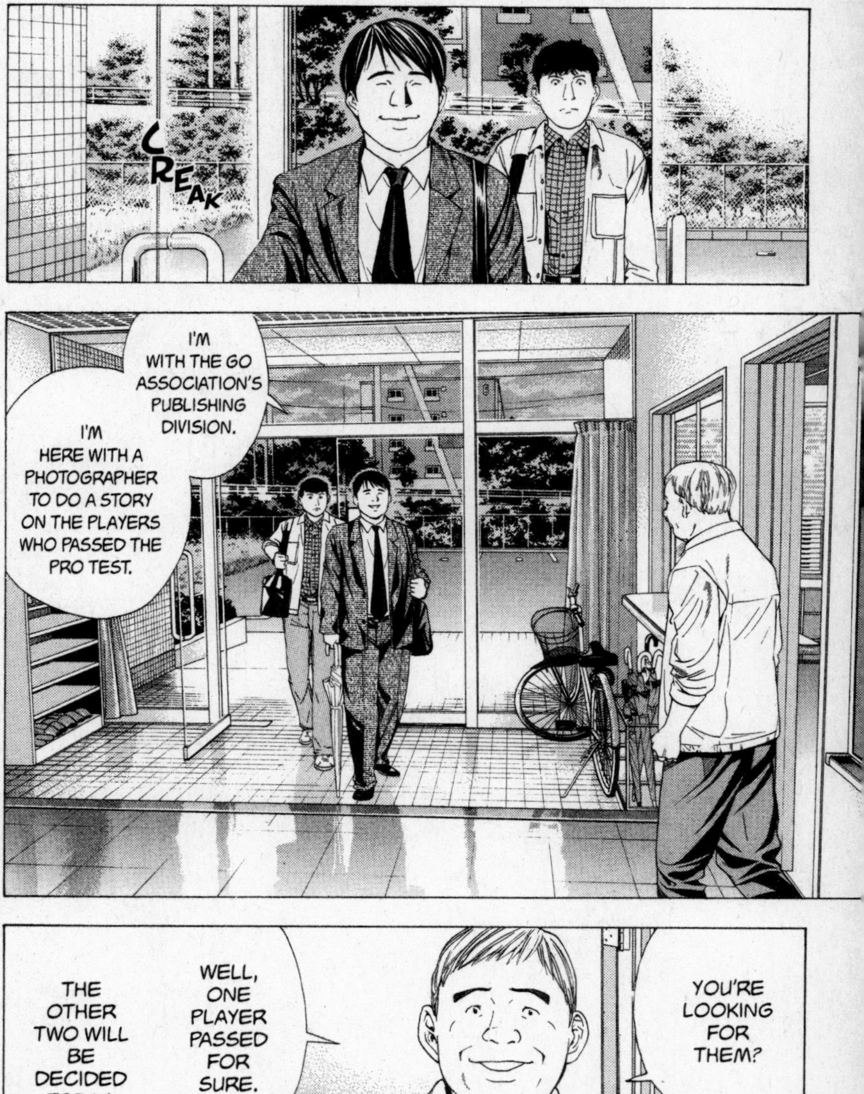
CREAK
I'M WITH THE GO ASSOCIATION'S PUBLISHING DIVISION.
I'M HERE WITH A PHOTOGRAPHER TO DO A STORY ON THE PLAYERS WHO PASSED THE PRO TEST.
YOU'RE LOOKING FOR THEM?
WELL, ONE PLAYER PASSED FOR SURE.
THE OTHER TWO WILL BE DECIDED TODAY.

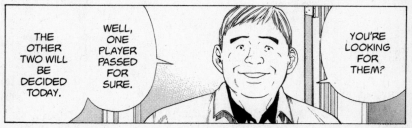

READ THIS WAY

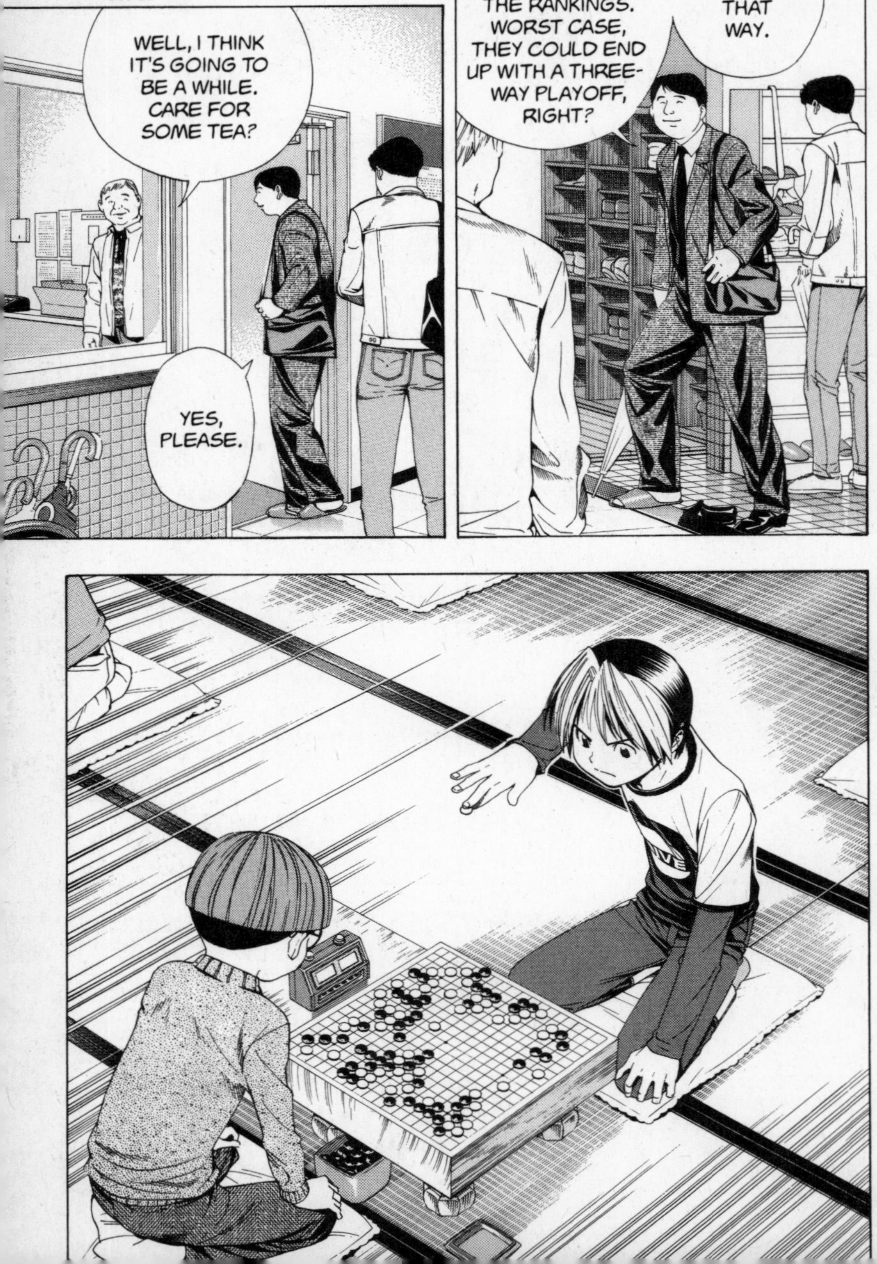
I'VE SEEN THE RANKINGS. WORST CASE, THEY COULD END UP WITH A THREE-WAY PLAYOFF, RIGHT?
SEEMS THAT WAY.
WELL, I THINK IT'S GOING TO BE A WHILE. CARE FOR SOME TEA?
YES, PLEASE.

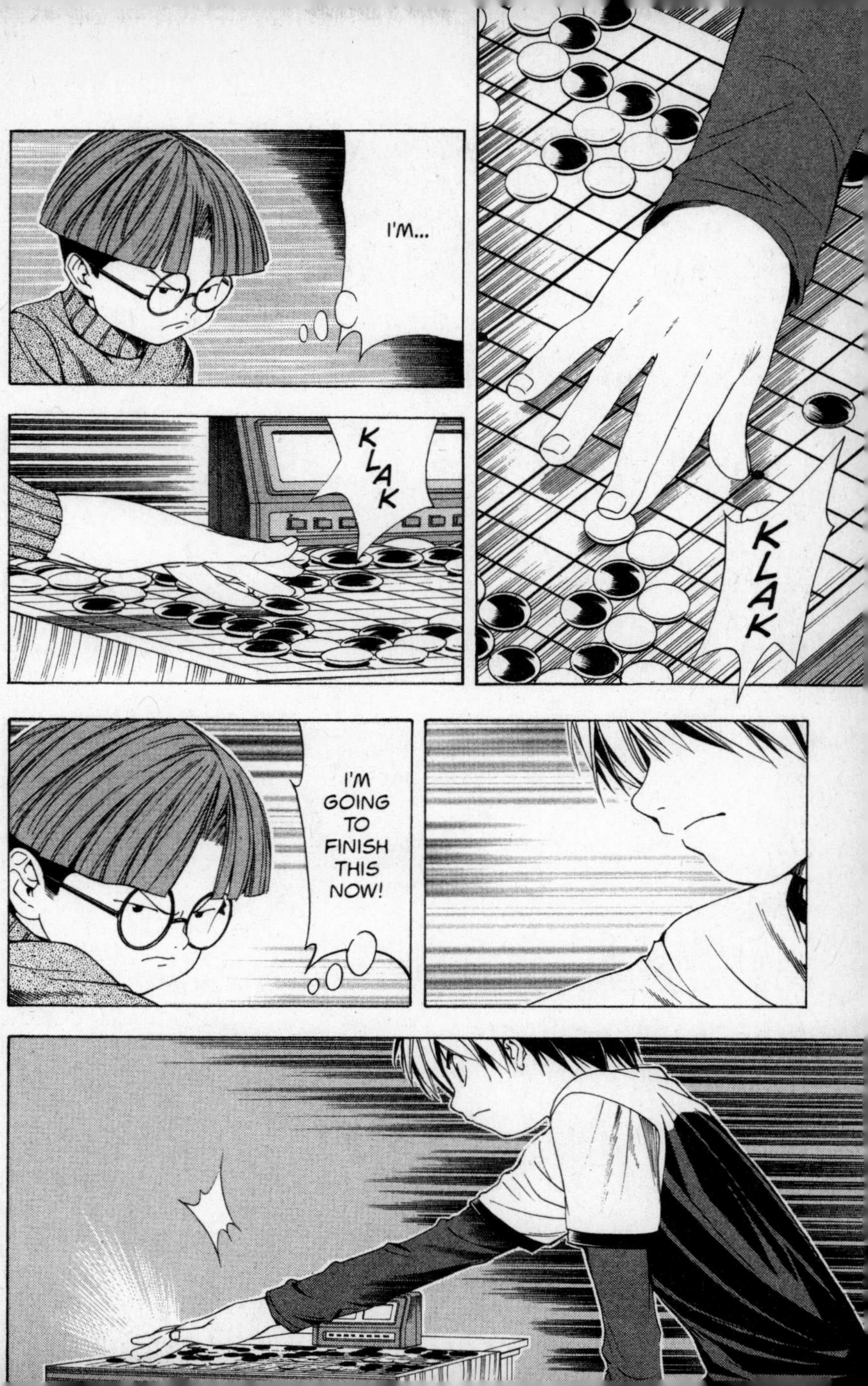
KLAK
I'M...
KLAK
I'M GOING TO FINISH THIS NOW!

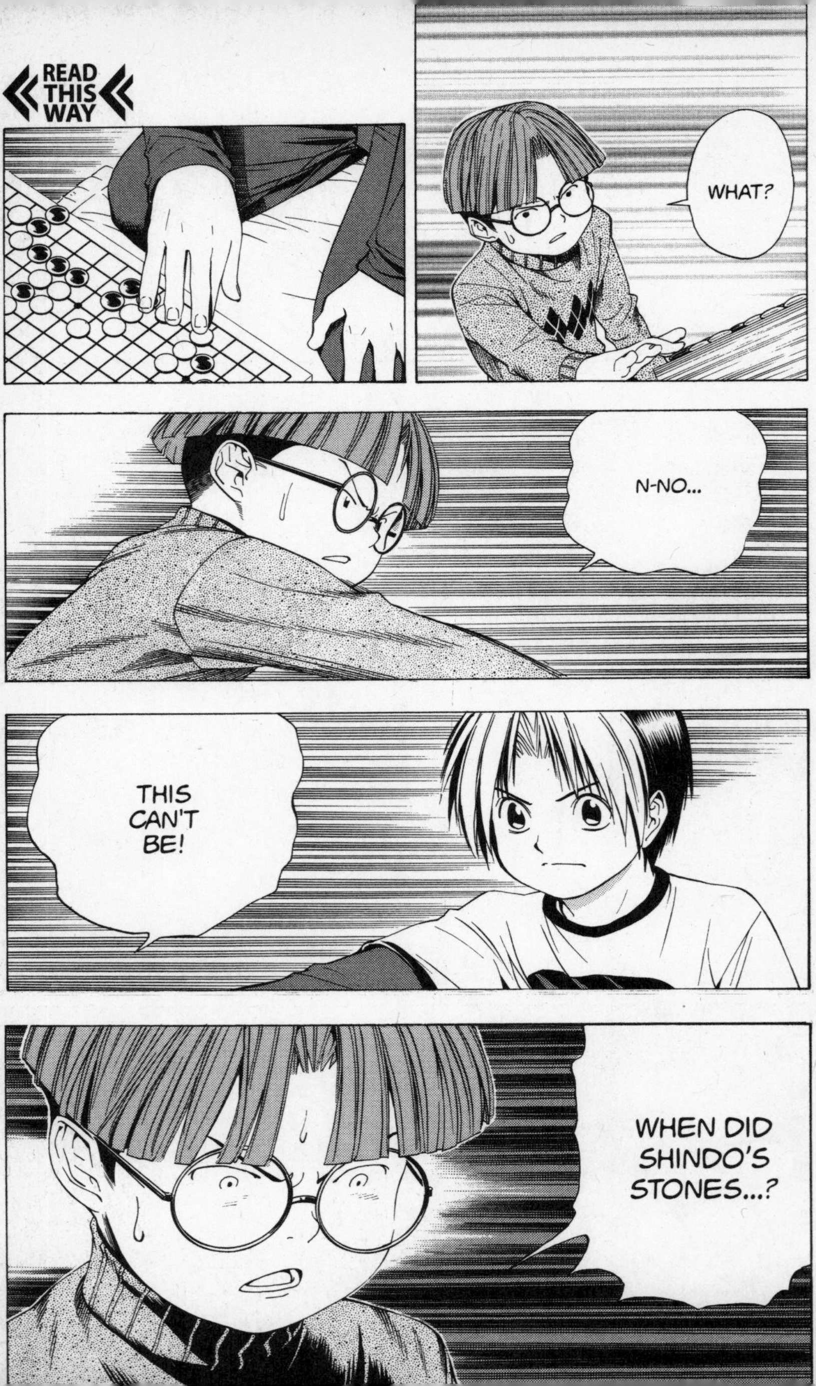
READ THIS WAY
WHAT?
N-NO...
THIS CAN'T BE!
WHEN DID SHINDO'S STONES...?

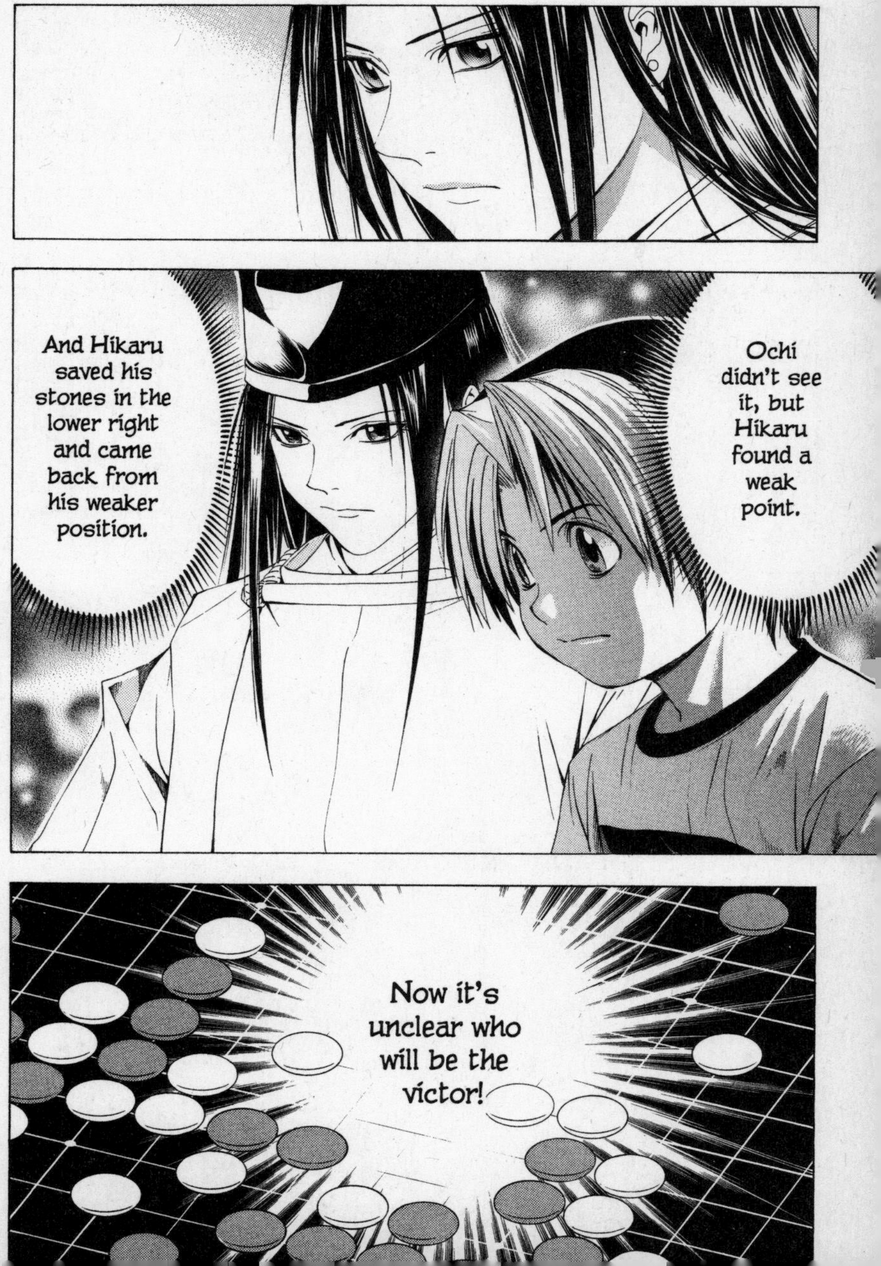
Ochi didn't see it, but Hikaru found a weak point.
And Hikaru saved his stones in the lower right and came back from his weaker position.
Now it's unclear who will be the victor!

READ THIS WAY

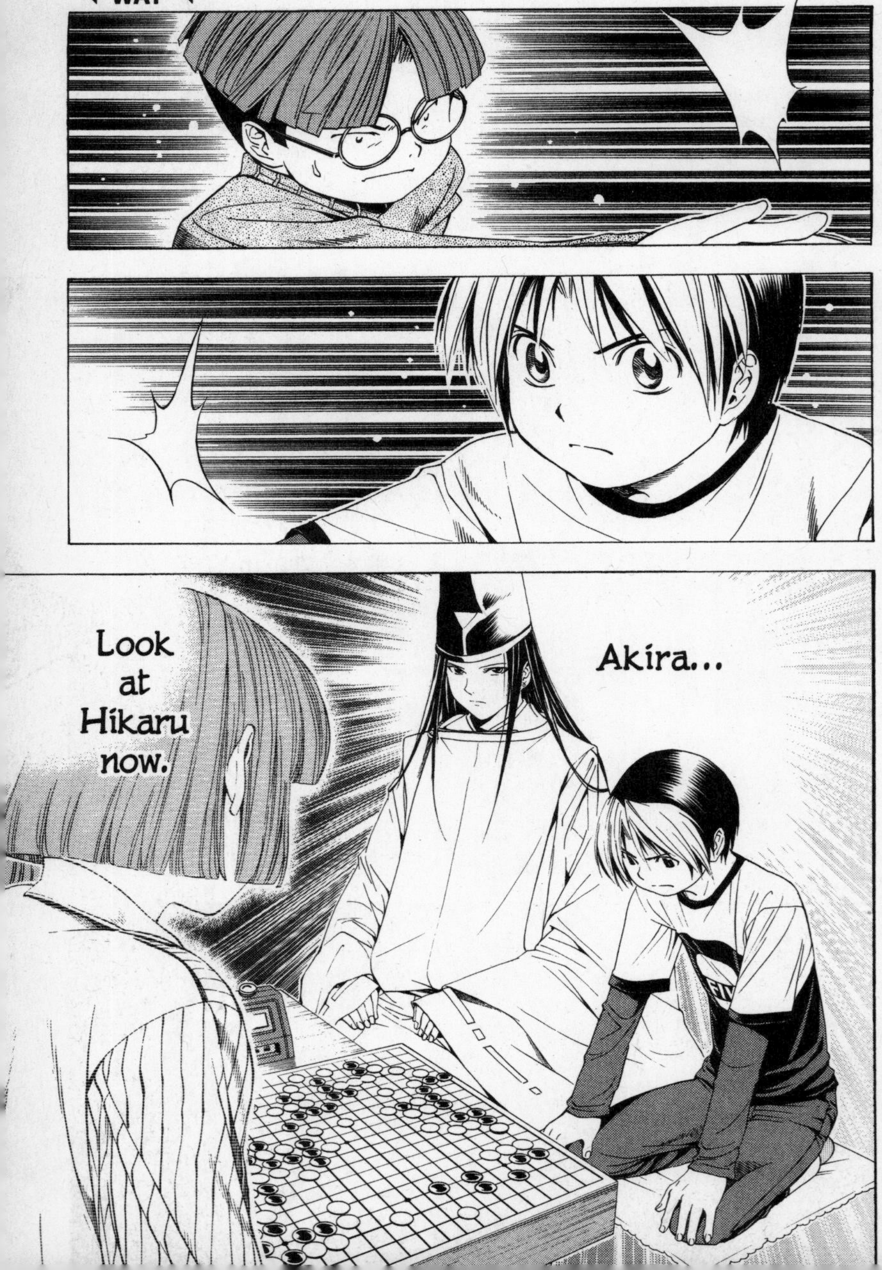
Akira...
Look at Hikaru now.

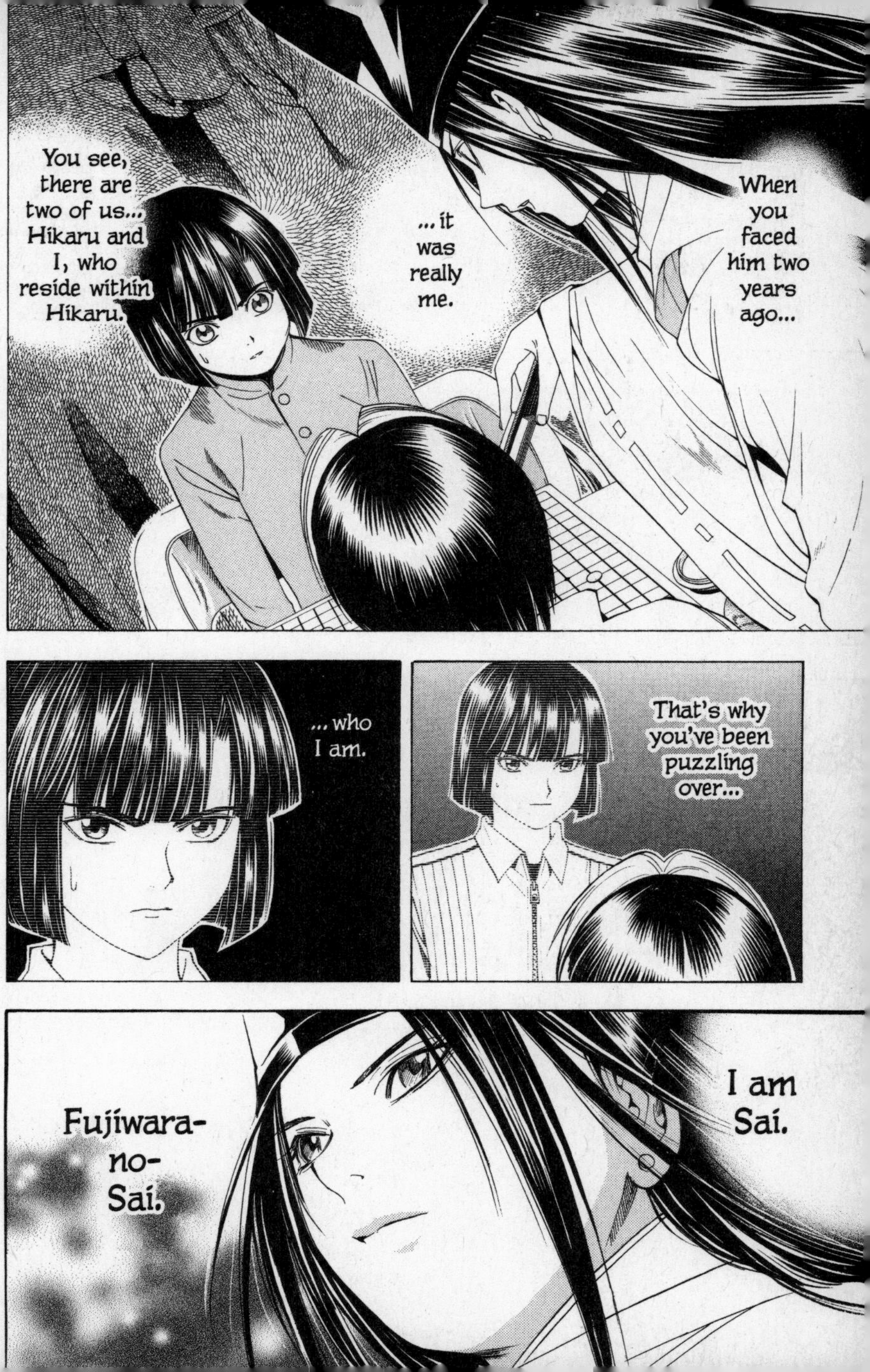
When you faced him two years ago...
...it was really me.
You see, there are two of us... Hikaru and I, who reside within Hikaru.
That's why you've been puzzling over...
...who I am.
I am Sai.
Fujiwara-no-Sai.

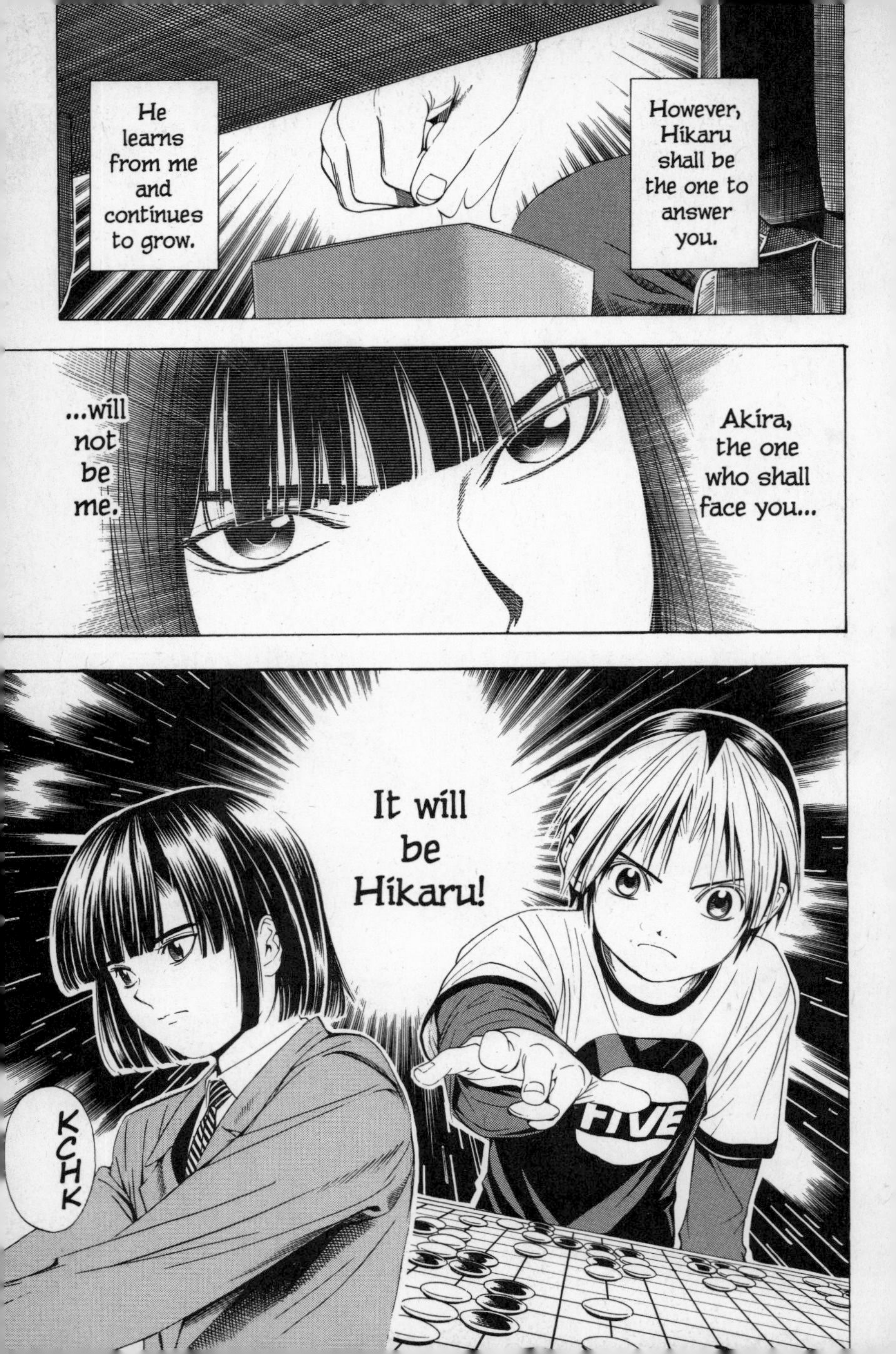
However, Hikaru shall be the one to answer you.
He learns from me and continues to grow.
Akira, the one who shall face you...
...will not be me.
It will be Hikaru!
KCHK

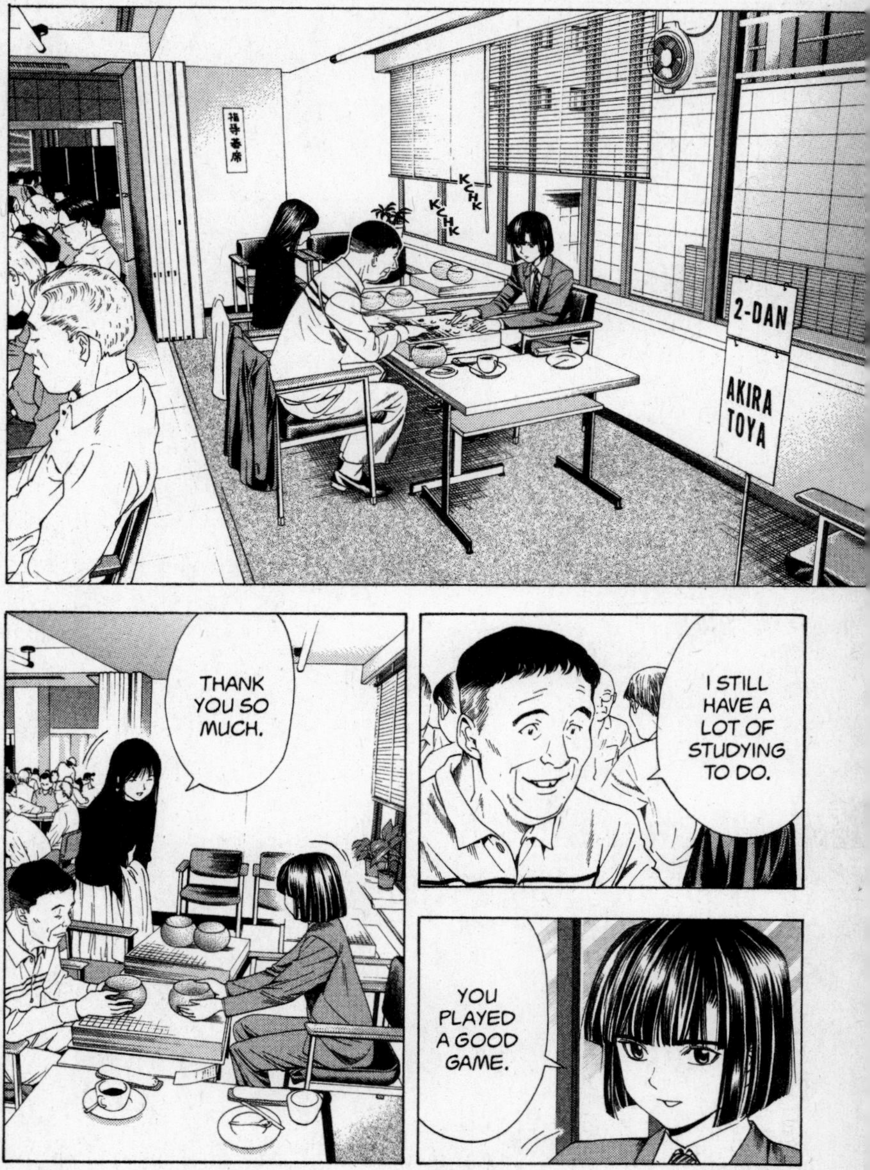
2-DAN
AKIRA TOYA
KCHK
KCHK
I STILL HAVE A LOT OF STUDYING TO DO.
YOU PLAYED A GOOD GAME.
THANK YOU SO MUCH.

READ THIS WAY

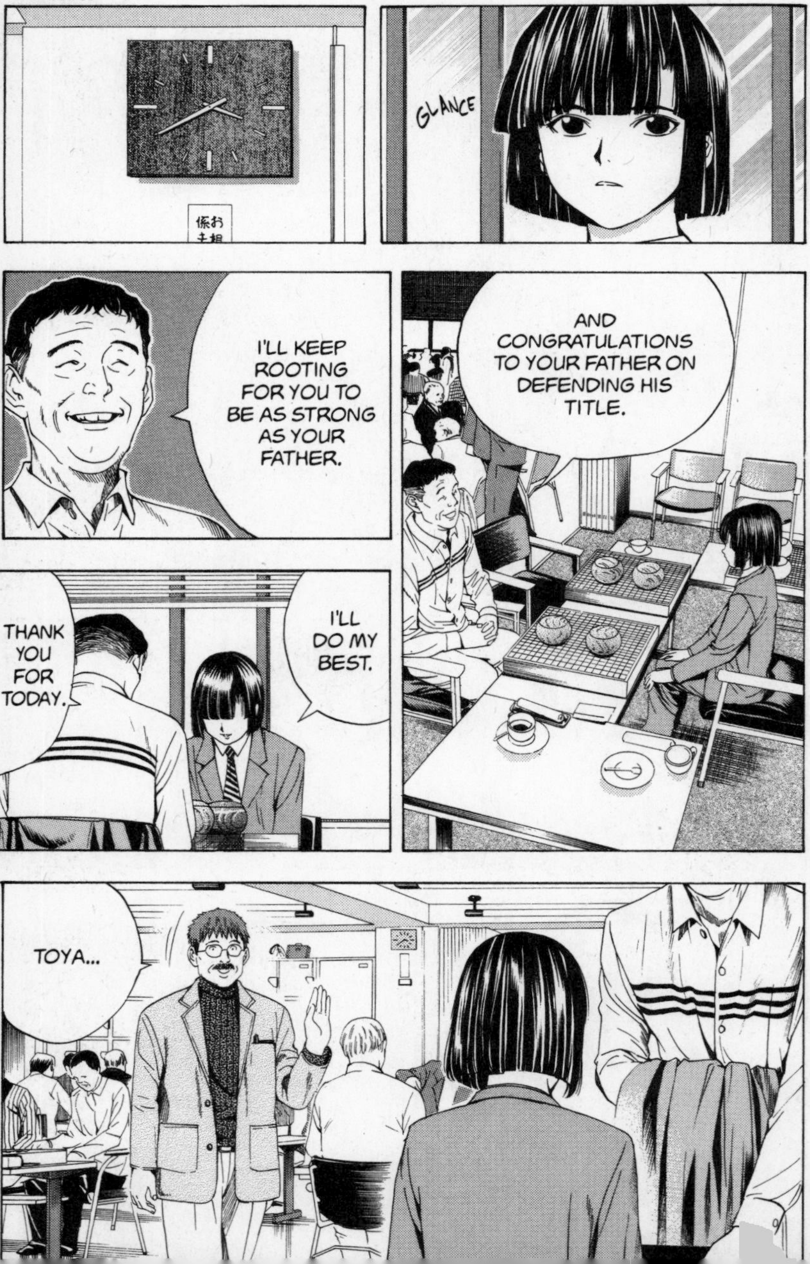
GLANCE
AND CONGRATULATIONS TO YOUR FATHER ON DEFENDING HIS TITLE.
I'LL KEEP ROOTING FOR YOU TO BE AS STRONG AS YOUR FATHER.
I'LL DO MY BEST.
THANK YOU FOR TODAY.
TOYA...

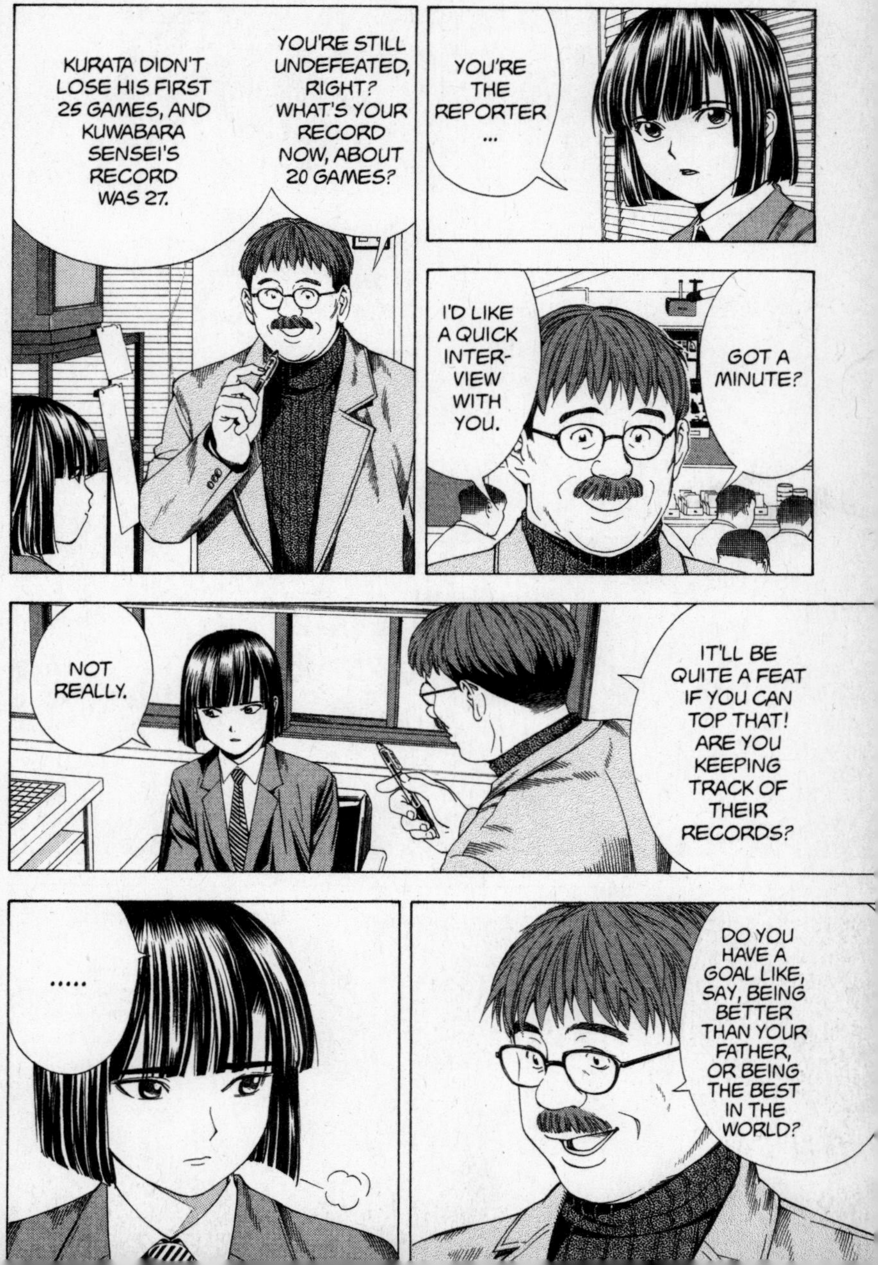
YOU'RE THE REPORTER ...
GOT A MINUTE?
I'D LIKE A QUICK INTER-VIEW WITH YOU.
YOU'RE STILL UNDEFEATED, RIGHT? WHAT'S YOUR RECORD NOW, ABOUT 20 GAMES?
KURATA DIDN'T LOSE HIS FIRST 25 GAMES, AND KUWABARA SENSEI'S RECORD WAS 27.
IT'LL BE QUITE A FEAT IF YOU CAN TOP THAT! ARE YOU KEEPING TRACK OF THEIR RECORDS?
NOT REALLY.
DO YOU HAVE A GOAL LIKE, SAY, BEING BETTER THAN YOUR FATHER, OR BEING THE BEST IN THE WORLD?
.....

READ THIS WAY

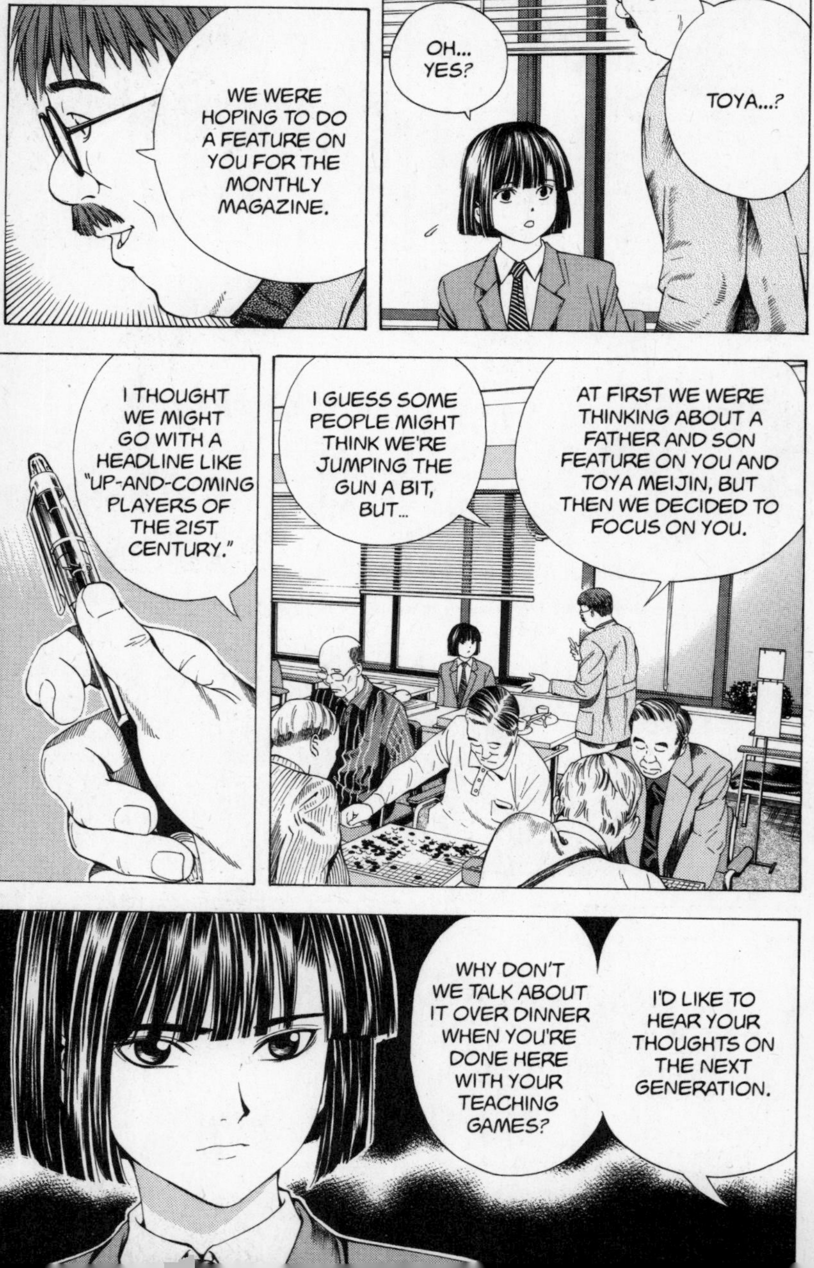
TOYA...?
OH... YES?
WE WERE HOPING TO DO A FEATURE ON YOU FOR THE MONTHLY MAGAZINE.
AT FIRST WE WERE THINKING ABOUT A FATHER AND SON FEATURE ON YOU AND TOYA MEIJIN, BUT THEN WE DECIDED TO FOCUS ON YOU.
I GUESS SOME PEOPLE MIGHT THINK WE'RE JUMPING THE GUN A BIT, BUT...
I THOUGHT WE MIGHT GO WITH A HEADLINE LIKE "UP-AND-COMING PLAYERS OF THE 21ST CENTURY."
I'D LIKE TO HEAR YOUR THOUGHTS ON THE NEXT GENERATION.
WHY DON'T WE TALK ABOUT IT OVER DINNER WHEN YOU'RE DONE HERE WITH YOUR TEACHING GAMES?

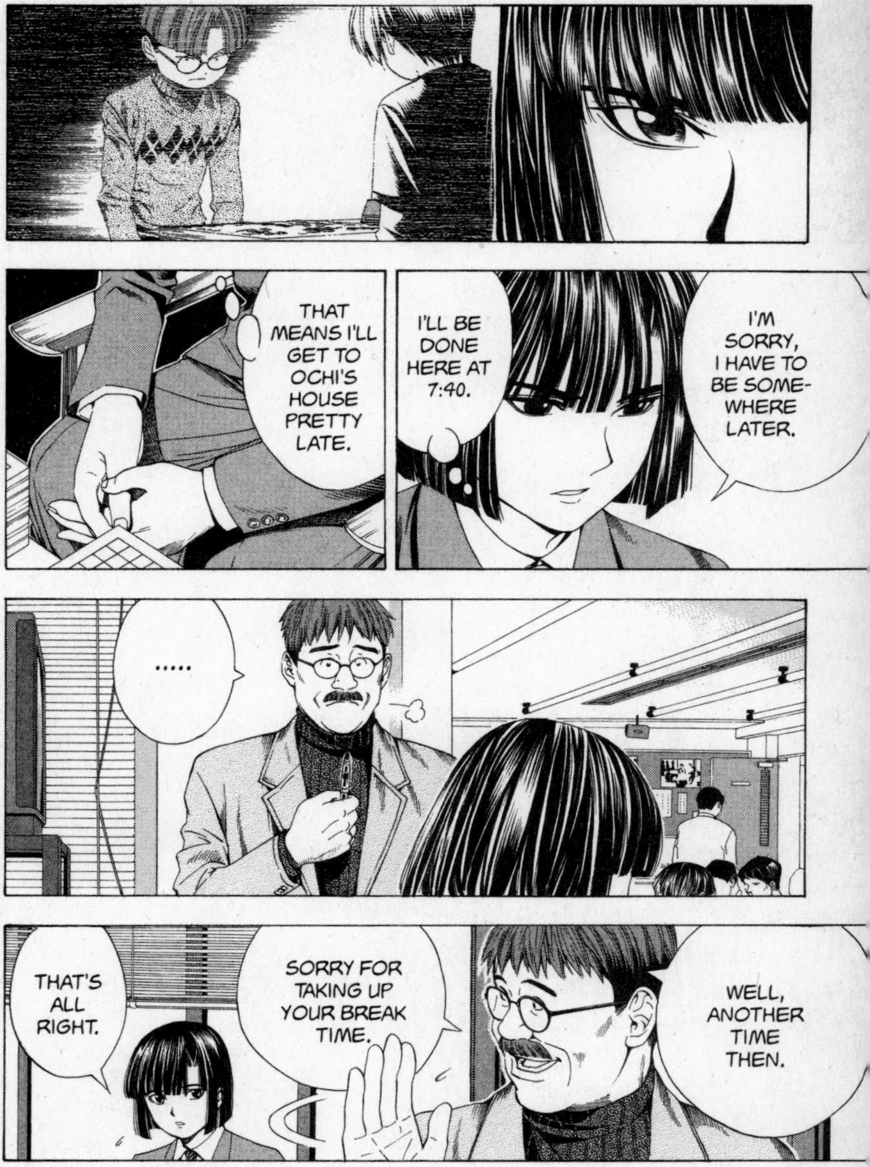
I'M SORRY, I HAVE TO BE SOME-WHERE LATER.
I'LL BE DONE HERE AT 7:40.
THAT MEANS I'LL GET TO OCHI'S HOUSE PRETTY LATE.
.....
WELL, ANOTHER TIME THEN.
SORRY FOR TAKING UP YOUR BREAK TIME.
THAT'S ALL RIGHT.

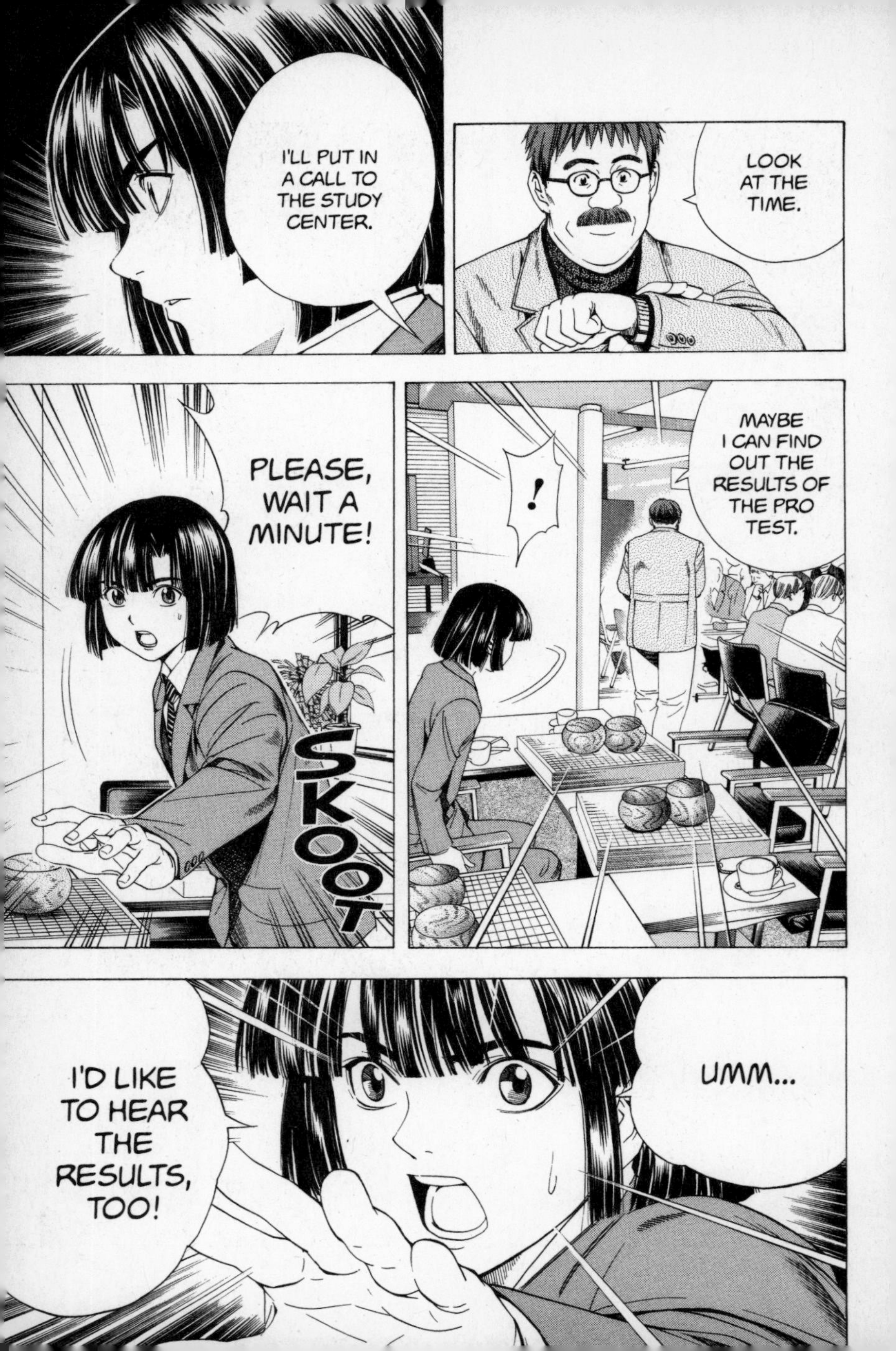
LOOK AT THE TIME.
I'LL PUT IN A CALL TO THE STUDY CENTER.
MAYBE I CAN FIND OUT THE RESULTS OF THE PRO TEST.
!
PLEASE, WAIT A MINUTE!
SKOOT
UMM...
I'D LIKE TO HEAR THE RESULTS, TOO!

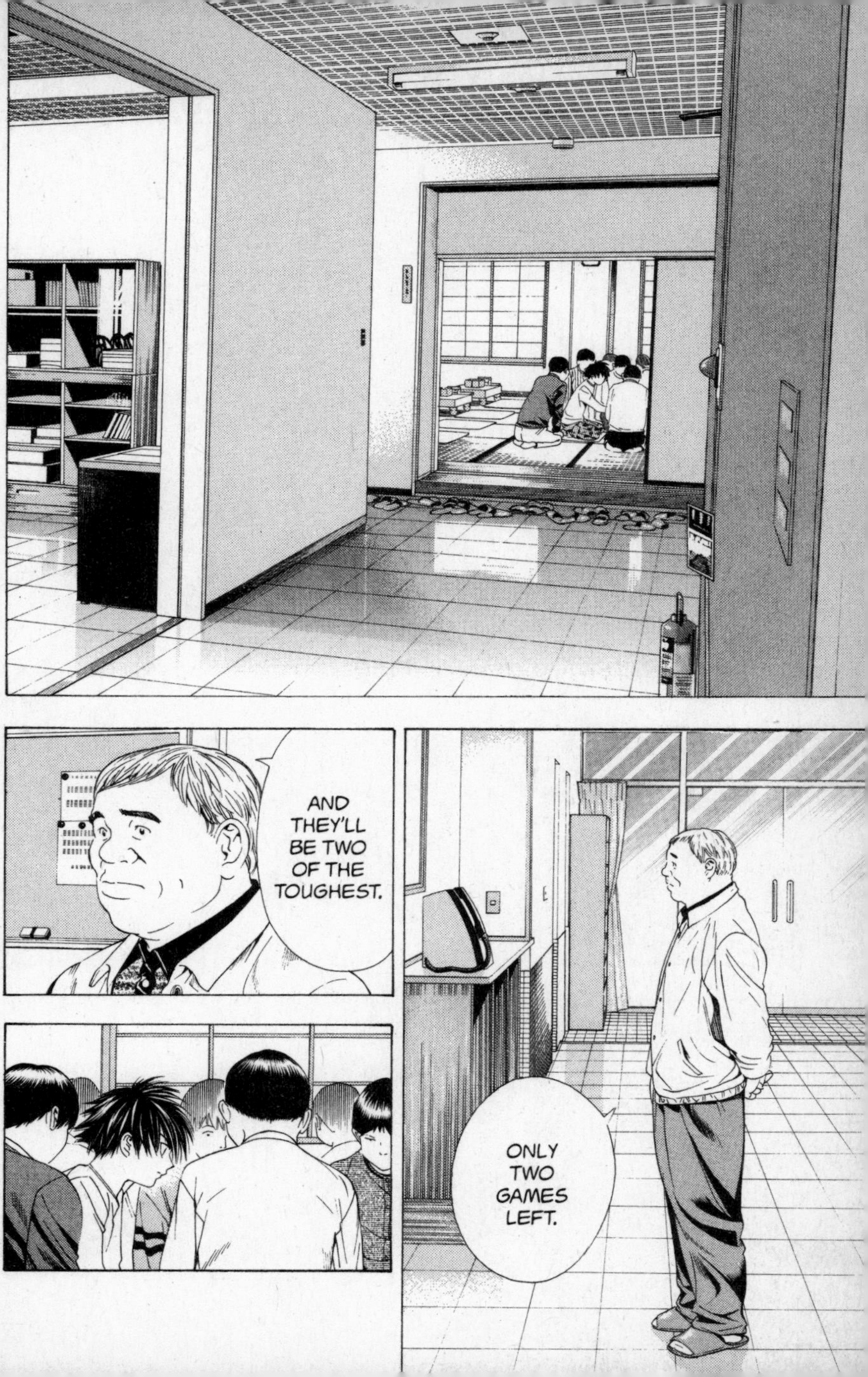
ONLY TWO GAMES LEFT.
AND THEY'LL BE TWO OF THE TOUGHEST.

READ THIS WAY

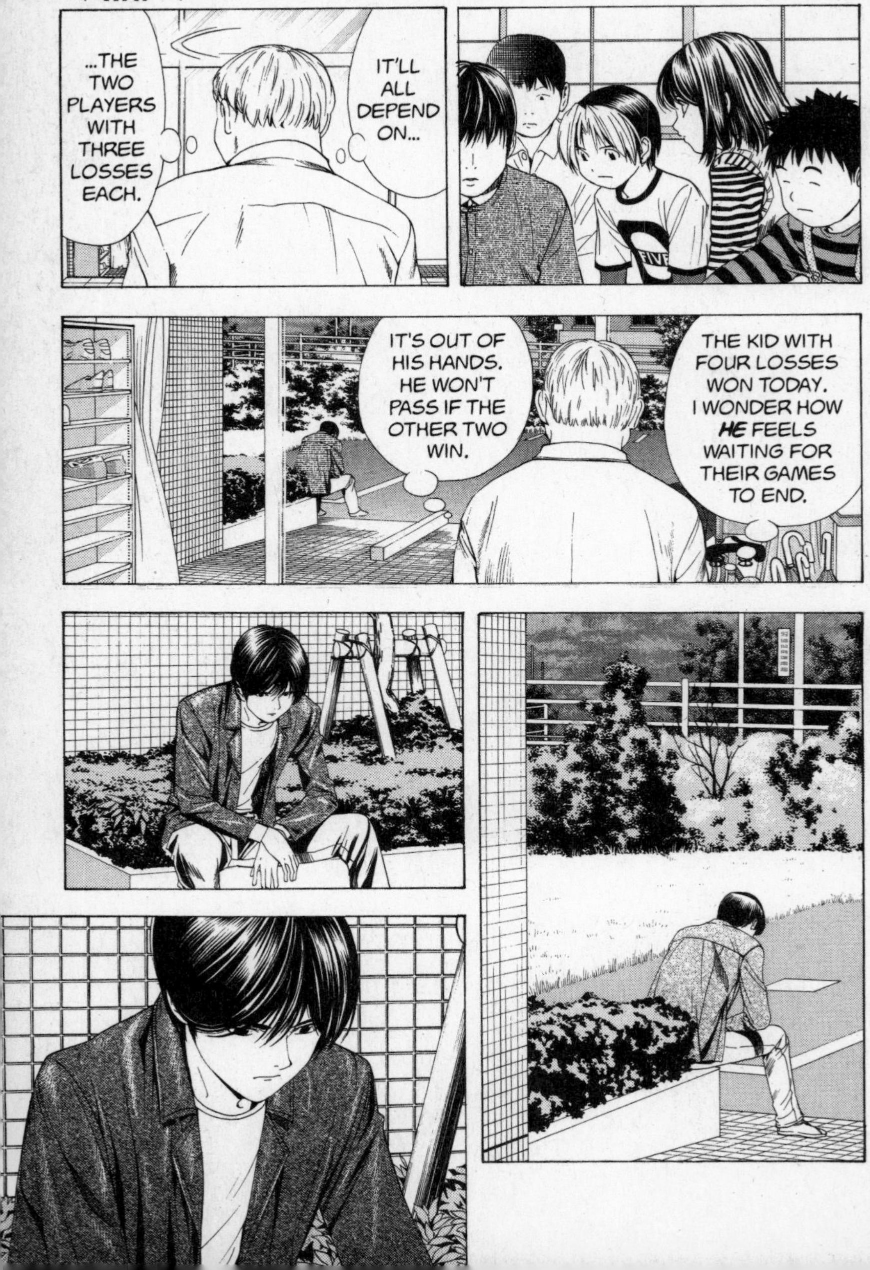
IT'LL ALL DEPEND ON...
...THE TWO PLAYERS WITH THREE LOSSES EACH.
THE KID WITH FOUR LOSSES WON TODAY. I WONDER HOW *HE* FEELS WAITING FOR THEIR GAMES TO END.
IT'S OUT OF HIS HANDS. HE WON'T PASS IF THE OTHER TWO WIN.

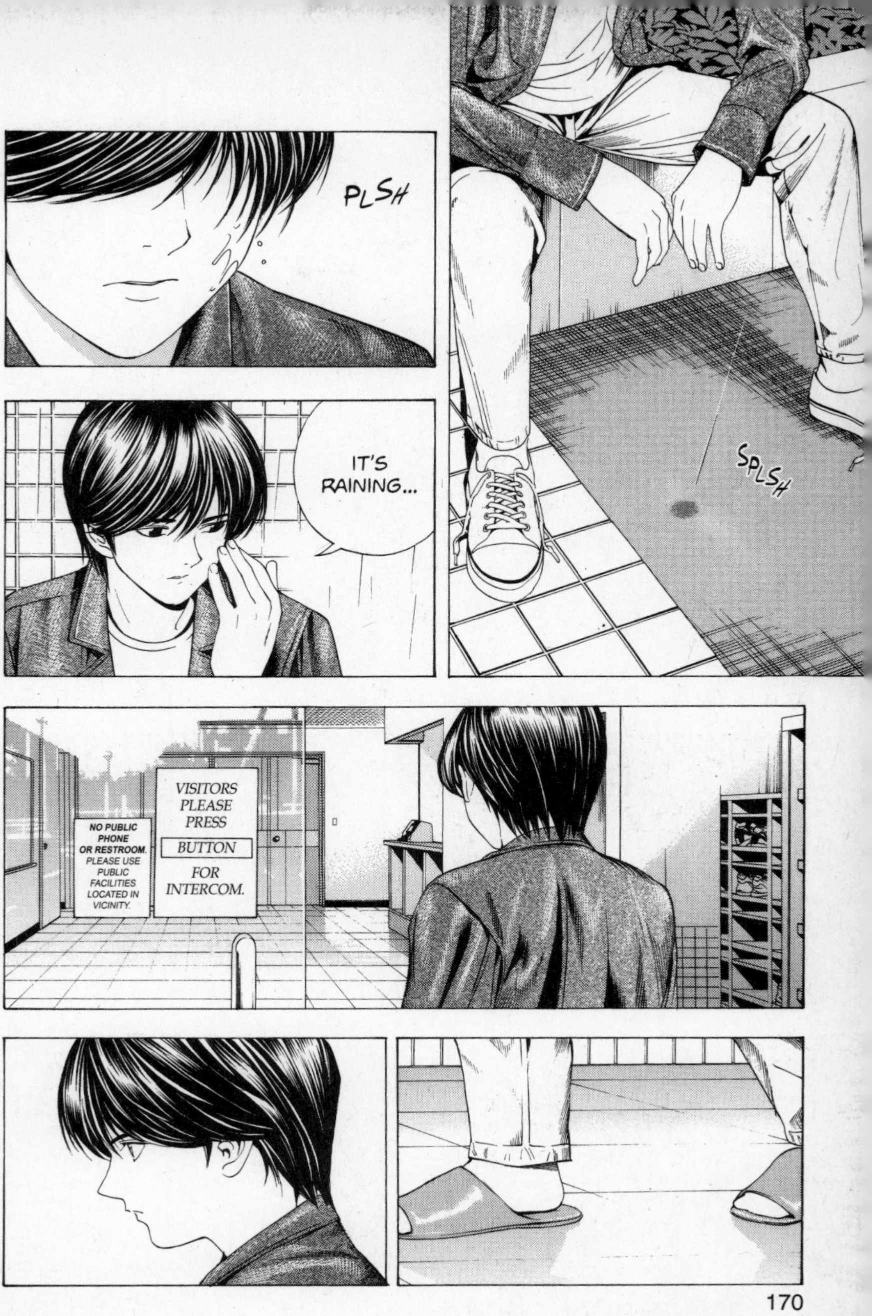
SPLSH
PLSH
IT'S RAINING...
VISITORS PLEASE PRESS BUTTON FOR INTERCOM.
NO PUBLIC PHONE OR RESTROOM. PLEASE USE PUBLIC FACILITIES LOCATED IN VICINITY.

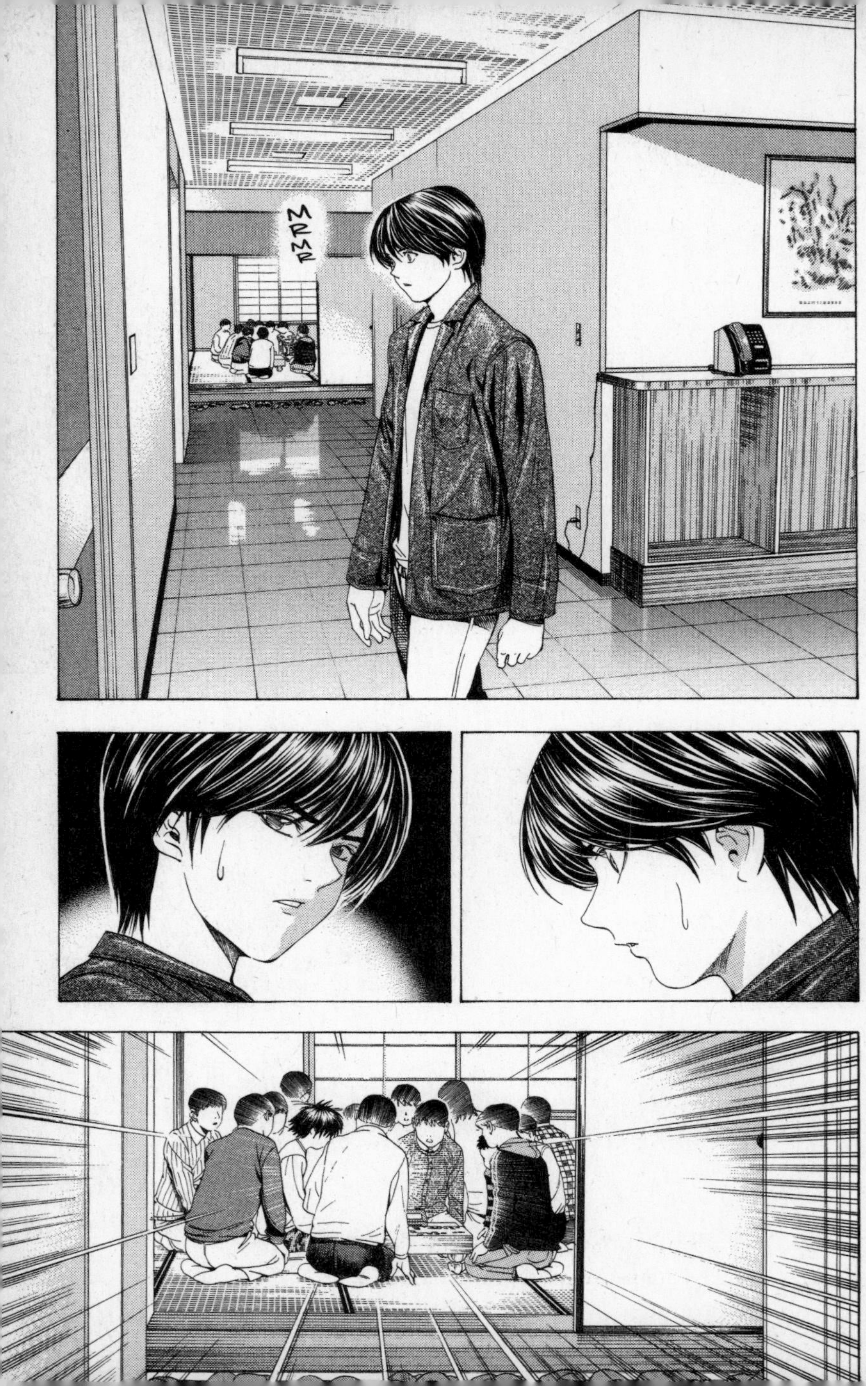
MRMR

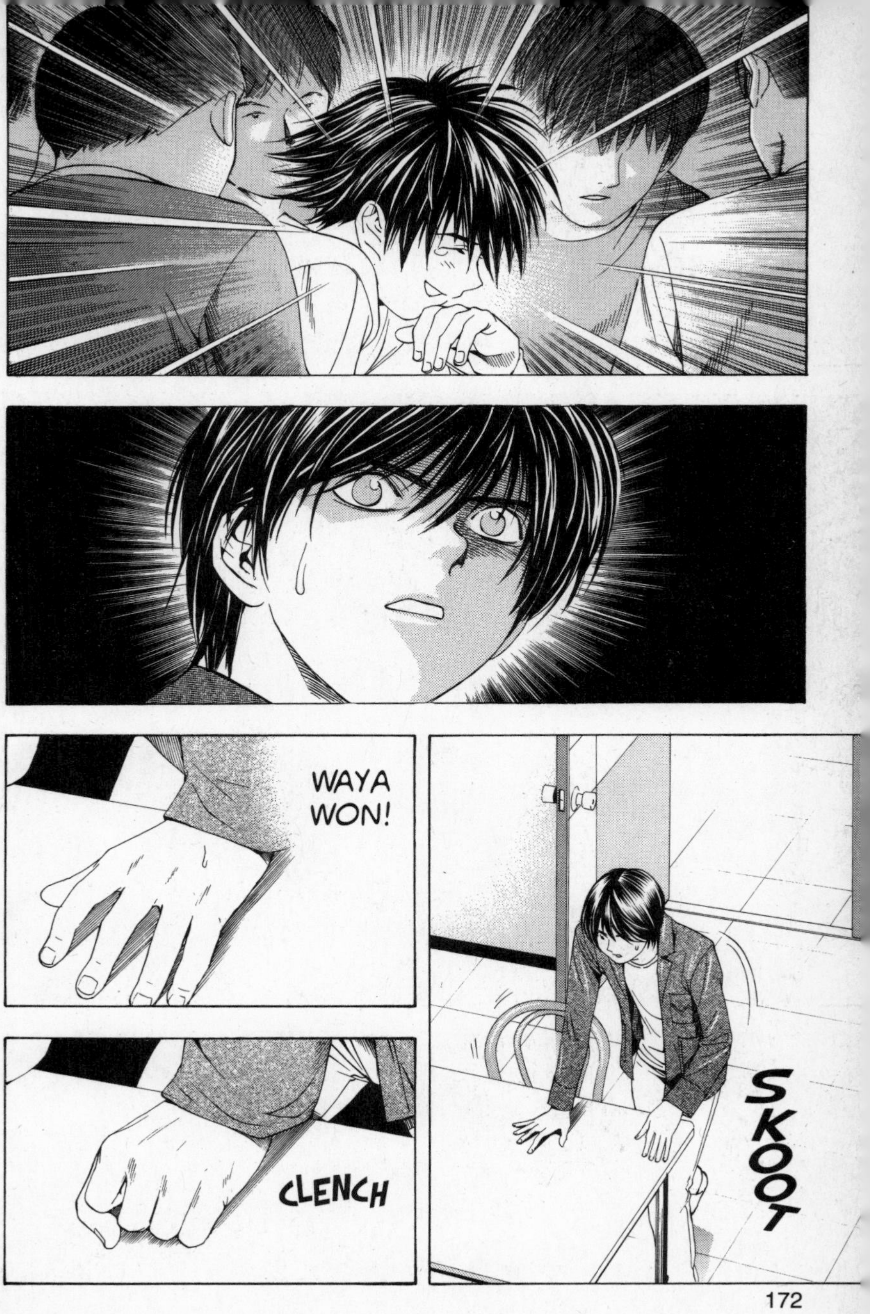
SKOOT
WAYA WON!
CLENCH

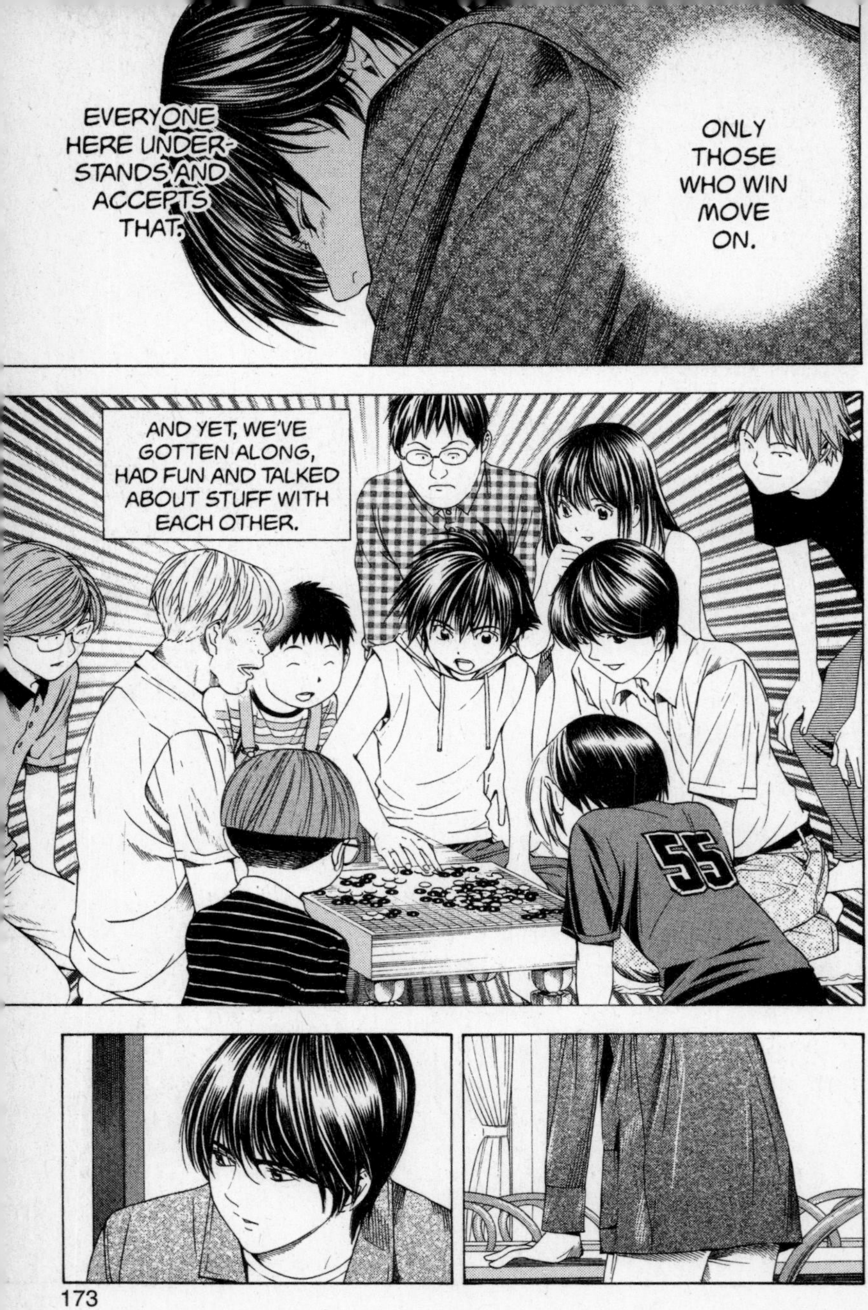
ONLY THOSE WHO WIN MOVE ON.
EVERYONE HERE UNDER-STANDS AND ACCEPTS THAT.
AND YET, WE'VE GOTTEN ALONG, HAD FUN AND TALKED ABOUT STUFF WITH EACH OTHER.

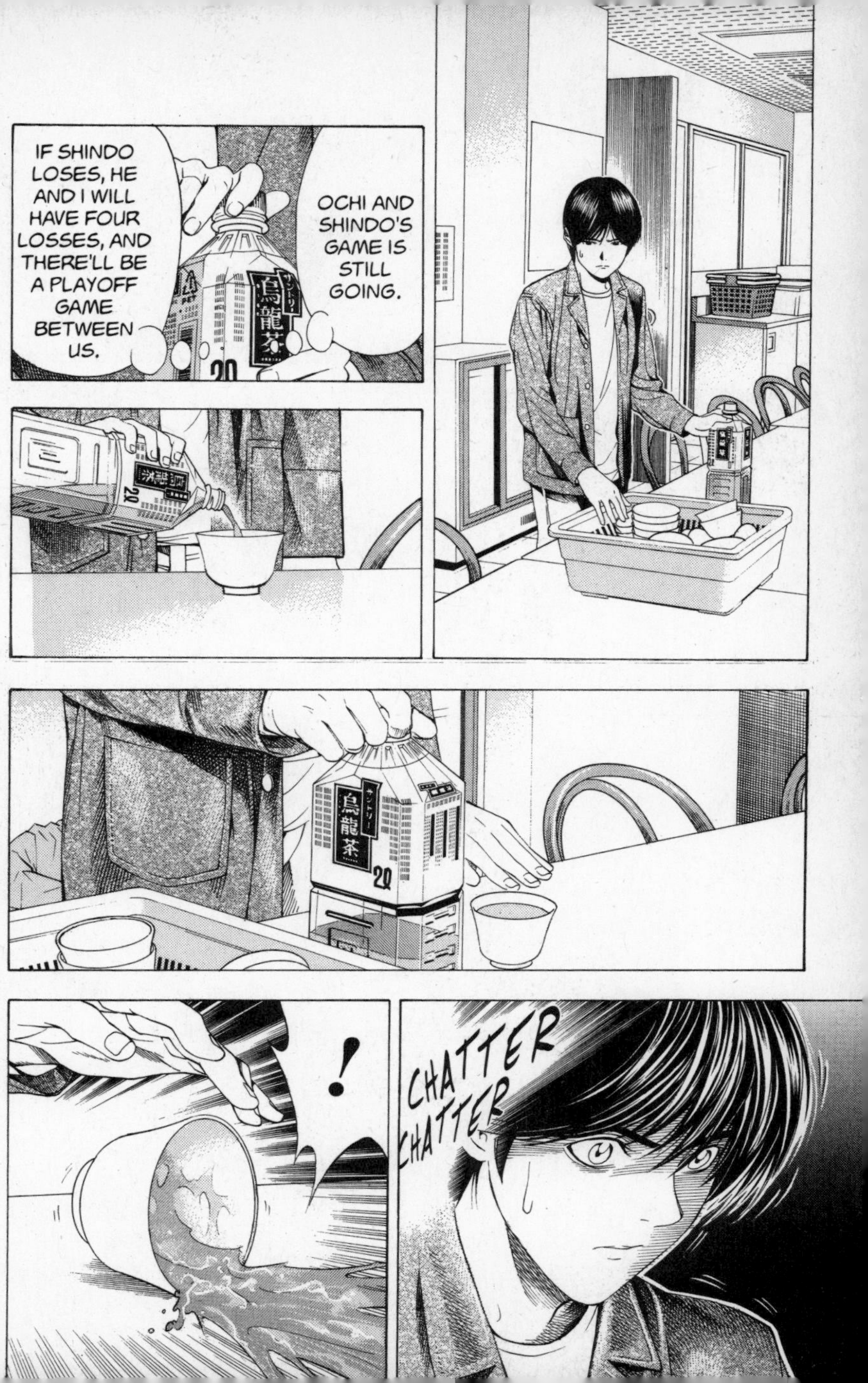
OCHI AND SHINDO'S GAME IS STILL GOING.
IF SHINDO LOSES, HE AND I WILL HAVE FOUR LOSSES, AND THERE'LL BE A PLAYOFF GAME BETWEEN US.
CHATTER
CHATTER
!

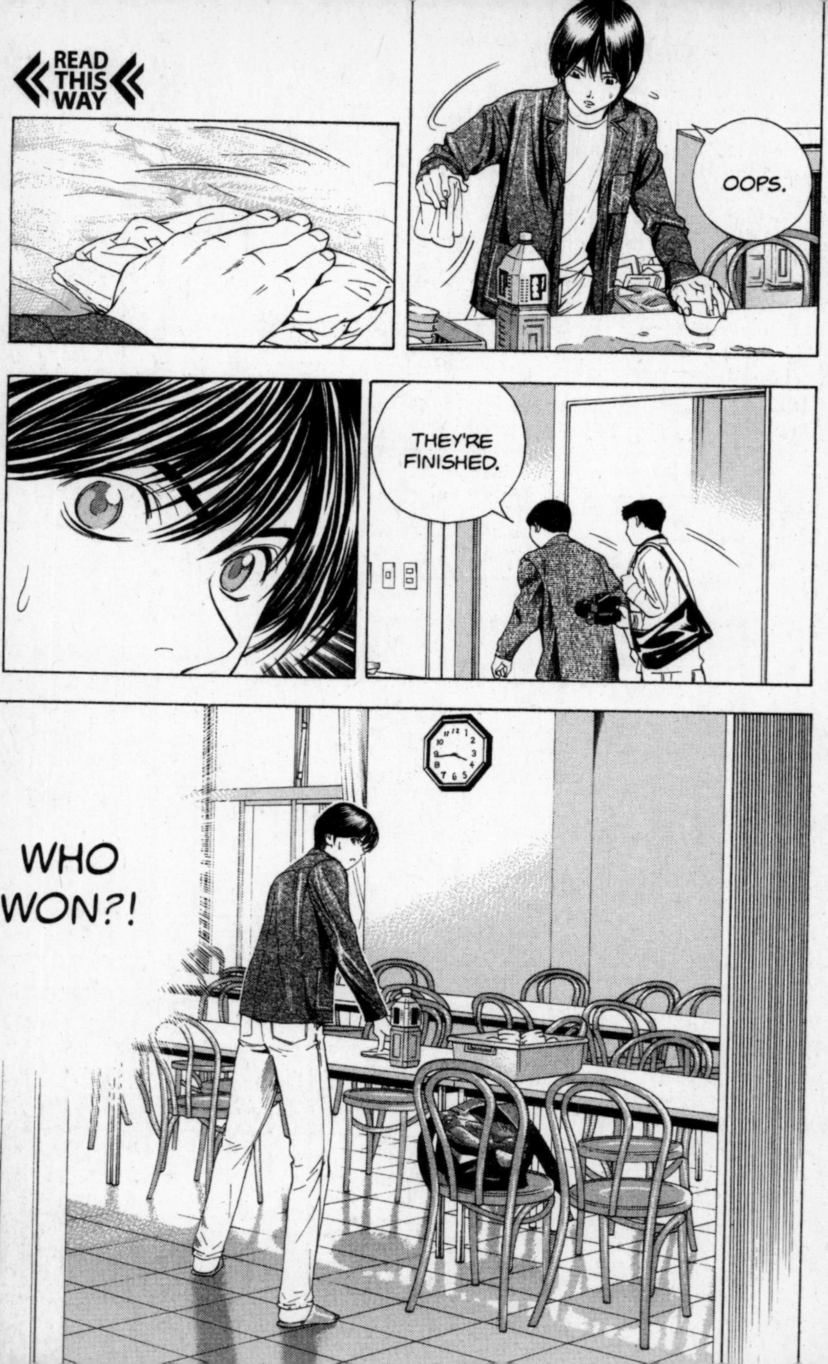
READ THIS WAY
OOPS.
THEY'RE FINISHED.
WHO WON?!

PRO TEST STANDINGS FOR GAMES 16-27

ENTRY NO.		NAME	AGE	16 10/1	17 10/3	18 10/7	19 10/8	20 10/10	21 10/14	22 10/15	23 10/17	24 10/21	25 10/22	26 10/24	27 10/28
1	outside	Kazuhiko Hino	24	● 17	● 18	○ 19	○ 20	● 21	● 22	● 23	○ 24	● 25	● 26	○ 27	● 28
2	outside	Toshiro Tsubaki	29	● 16	● 17	○ 18	○ 19	○ 20	● 21	● 22	○ 23	○ 24	● 25	○ 26	○ 27
3	insei	Eiji Komiya	16	○ 15	○ 16	○ 17	○ 18	○ 19	○ 20	● 21	● 22	○ 23	○ 24	● 25	○ 26
4	insei	Takashi Nakamura	14	● 14	○ 15	● 16	● 17	○ 18	○ 19	○ 20	● 21	● 22	● 23	● 24	● 25
5	outside	Hiroshi Oshima	20	● 13	○ 14	○ 15	● 16	● 17	○ 18	● 19	○ 20	● 21	● 22	○ 23	● 24
6	insei	Nobuyuki Takakura	15	● 12	○ 13	○ 14	○ 15	● 16	● 17	● 18	● 19	○ 20	● 21	● 22	● 23
7	insei	Hikaru Shindo	13	○ 11	● 12	○ 13	○ 14	○ 15	○ 16	○ 17	○ 18	○ 19	○ 20	○ 21	22
8	insei	Yuta Fukui	12	○ 10	● 11	● 12	○ 13	● 14	○ 15	○ 16	● 17	● 18	○ 19	● 20	● 21
9	insei	Jun Kaneda	17	● 28	○ 10	● 11	● 12	○ 13	● 14	● 15	● 16	● 17	● 18	○ 19	○ 20
10	outside	Koji Tachiyama	22	● 8	● 9	● 28	● 11	● 12	○ 13	● 14	○ 15	● 16	● 17	● 18	● 19
11	insei	Asumi Nase	16	● 7	○ 8	○ 9	○ 10	● 28	○ 12	● 13	● 14	○ 15	● 16	● 17	● 18
12	insei	Toshinori Honda	17	○ 6	○ 7	○ 8	○ 9	○ 10	● 11	○ 28	○ 13	○ 14	○ 15	● 16	● 17
13	outside	Yasutoshi Sugishita	20	○ 5	● 6	● 7	● 8	● 9	● 10	○ 11	● 12	● 28	● 14	○ 15	○ 16
14	insei	Shogo Nozaki	16	○ 4	● 5	● 6	● 7	○ 8	○ 9	○ 10	○ 11	● 12	○ 13	● 28	● 15
15	outside	Kazunari Ishikawa	23	● 3	● 4	● 5	● 6	● 7	● 8	○ 9	● 10	● 11	● 12	● 13	○ 14
16	outside	Kyohei Katagiri	25	○ 2	● 3	○ 4	○ 5	○ 6	● 7	● 8	○ 9	○ 10	○ 11	○ 12	● 13
17	insei	Toshiki Adachi	16	○ 1	○ 2	● 3	○ 4	○ 5	○ 6	● 7	○ 8	○ 9	○ 10	○ 11	○ 12
18	insei	Tatsuya Hayashi	14	● 27	○ 1	● 2	● 3	● 4	● 5	○ 6	● 7	○ 8	○ 9	○ 10	○ 11
19	insei	Mai Sasaki	16	● 26	○ 27	● 1	● 2	● 3	● 4	○ 5	○ 6	● 7	● 8	● 9	○ 10
20	outside	Masahiro Hatanaka	27	● 25	○ 26	● 27	● 1	● 2	● 3	● 4	● 5	● 6	● 7	○ 8	● 9
21	insei	Yoshitaka Waya	15	○ 24	○ 25	○ 26	○ 27	○ 1	○ 2	○ 3	○ 4	○ 5	○ 6	● 7	○ 8
22	insei	Kosuke Ochi	12	○ 23	○ 24	○ 25	○ 26	○ 27	○ 1	○ 2	○ 3	○ 4	○ 5	○ 6	7
23	insei	Ryo Iijima	17	● 22	● 28	○ 24	○ 25	○ 26	○ 27	○ 1	● 2	● 3	○ 4	● 5	○ 6
24	outside	Saki Miura	20	● 21	● 22	● 23	● 28	● 25	○ 26	○ 27	● 1	● 2	● 3	○ 4	○ 5
25	insei	Naoto Isobe	16	○ 20	● 21	● 22	● 23	○ 24	● 28	○ 26	● 27	○ 1	○ 2	○ 3	○ 4
26	outside	Yuriko Kitahara	22	○ 19	● 20	● 21	● 22	● 23	● 24	● 25	● 28	● 27	○ 1	● 2	● 3
27	insei	Mitsuru Sawai	16	○ 18	● 19	○ 20	● 21	● 22	● 23	● 24	○ 25	○ 26	● 28	● 1	● 2
28	insei	Shinichiro Isumi	18	○ 9	○ 23	○ 10	○ 24	○ 11	○ 25	● 12	○ 26	○ 13	○ 27	○ 14	○ 1

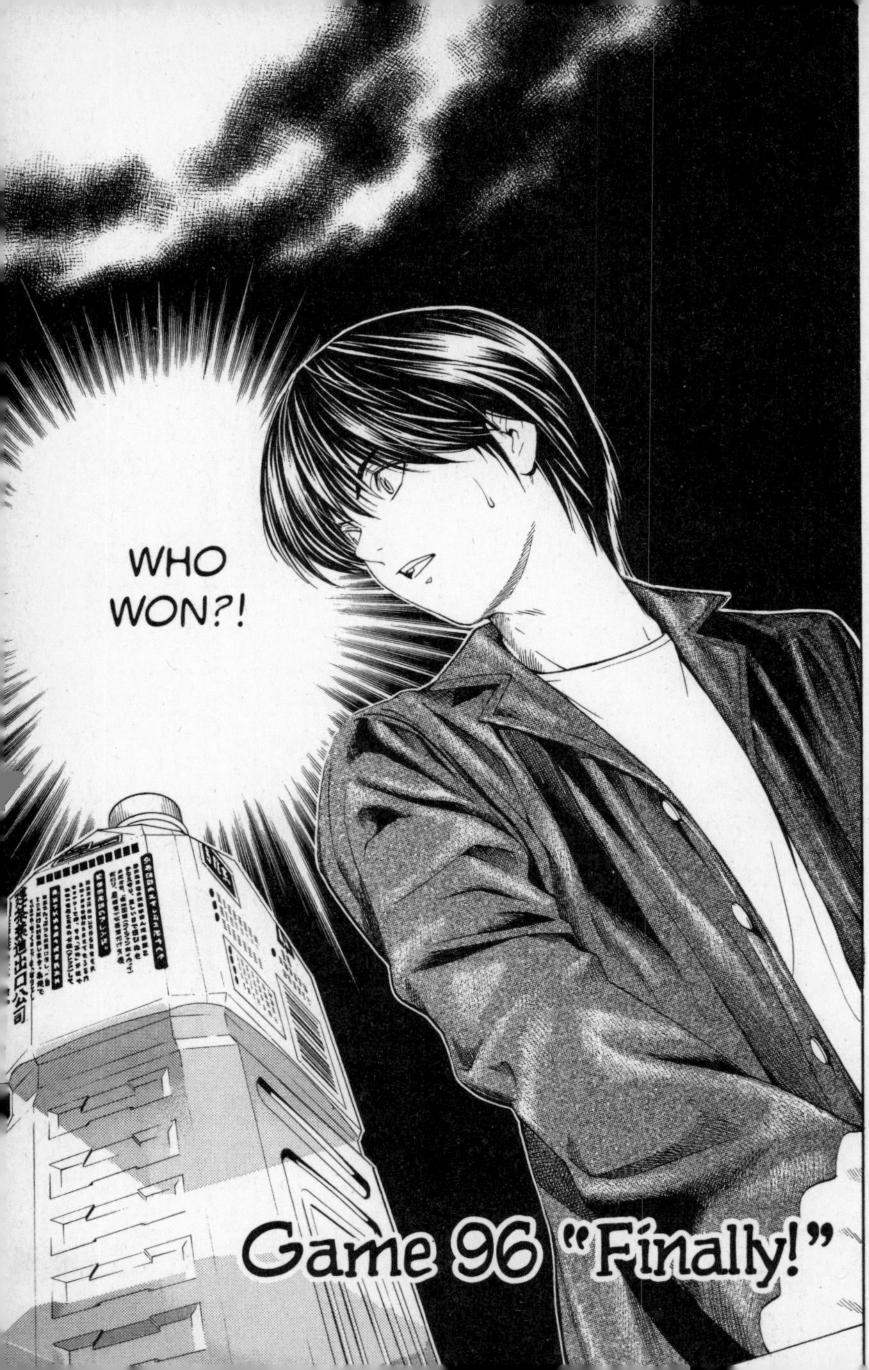
WHO WON?!
Game 96 "Finally!"

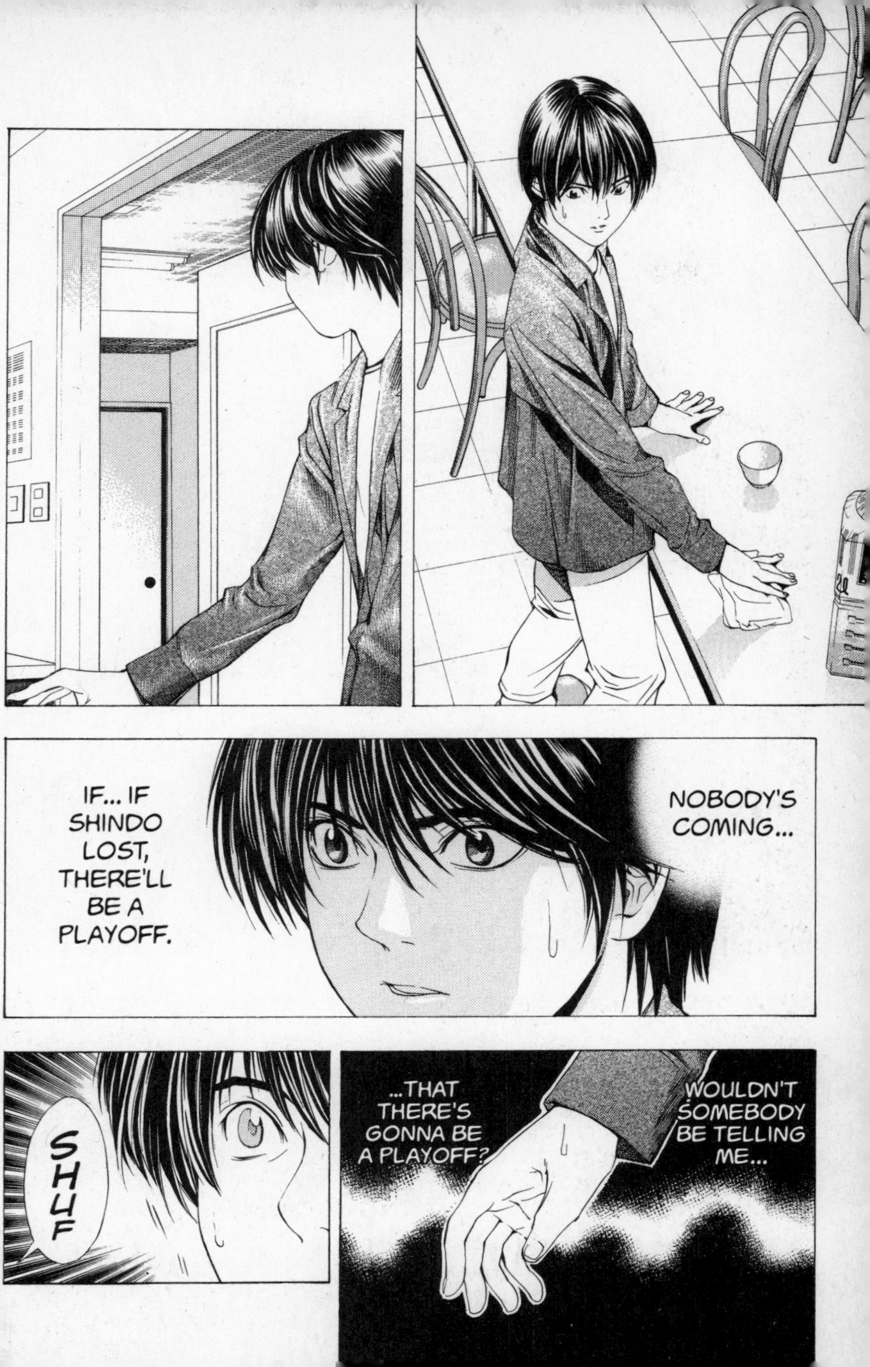
NOBODY'S COMING...
IF... IF SHINDO LOST, THERE'LL BE A PLAYOFF.
WOULDN'T SOMEBODY BE TELLING ME...
...THAT THERE'S GONNA BE A PLAYOFF?
SHUF

READ THIS WAY

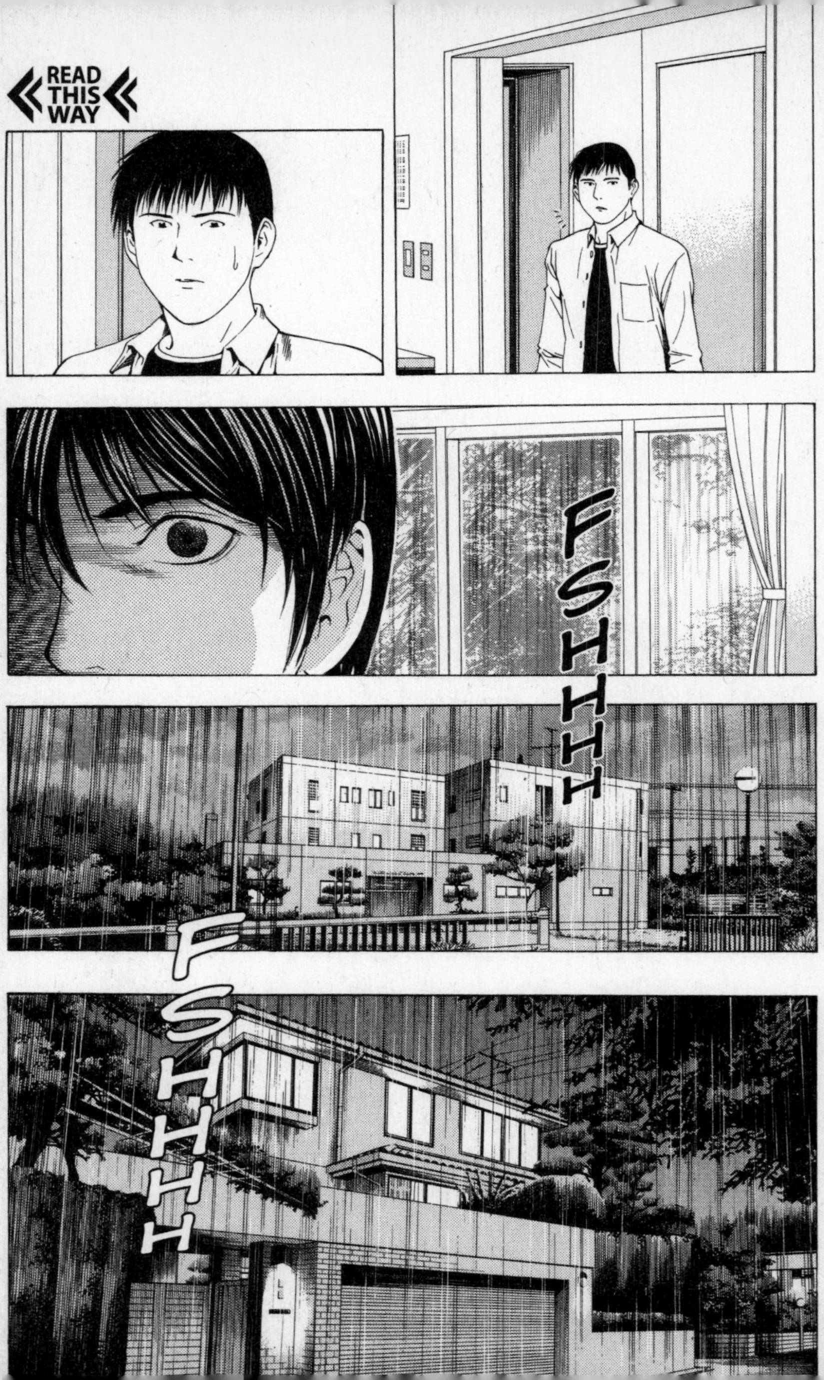
FSHHHH
FSHHHH

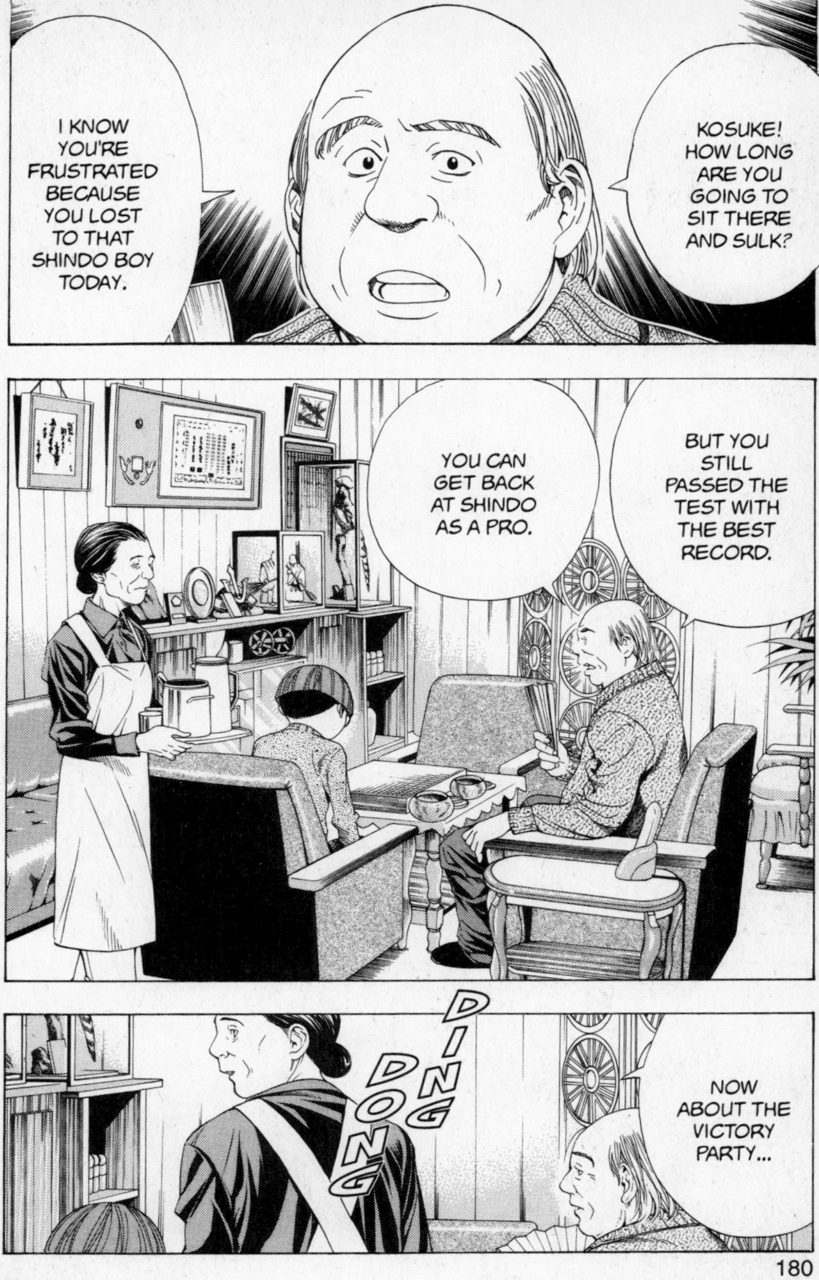
KOSUKE! HOW LONG ARE YOU GOING TO SIT THERE AND SULK?
I KNOW YOU'RE FRUSTRATED BECAUSE YOU LOST TO THAT SHINDO BOY TODAY.
BUT YOU STILL PASSED THE TEST WITH THE BEST RECORD.
YOU CAN GET BACK AT SHINDO AS A PRO.
NOW ABOUT THE VICTORY PARTY...
DING DONG

READ THIS WAY

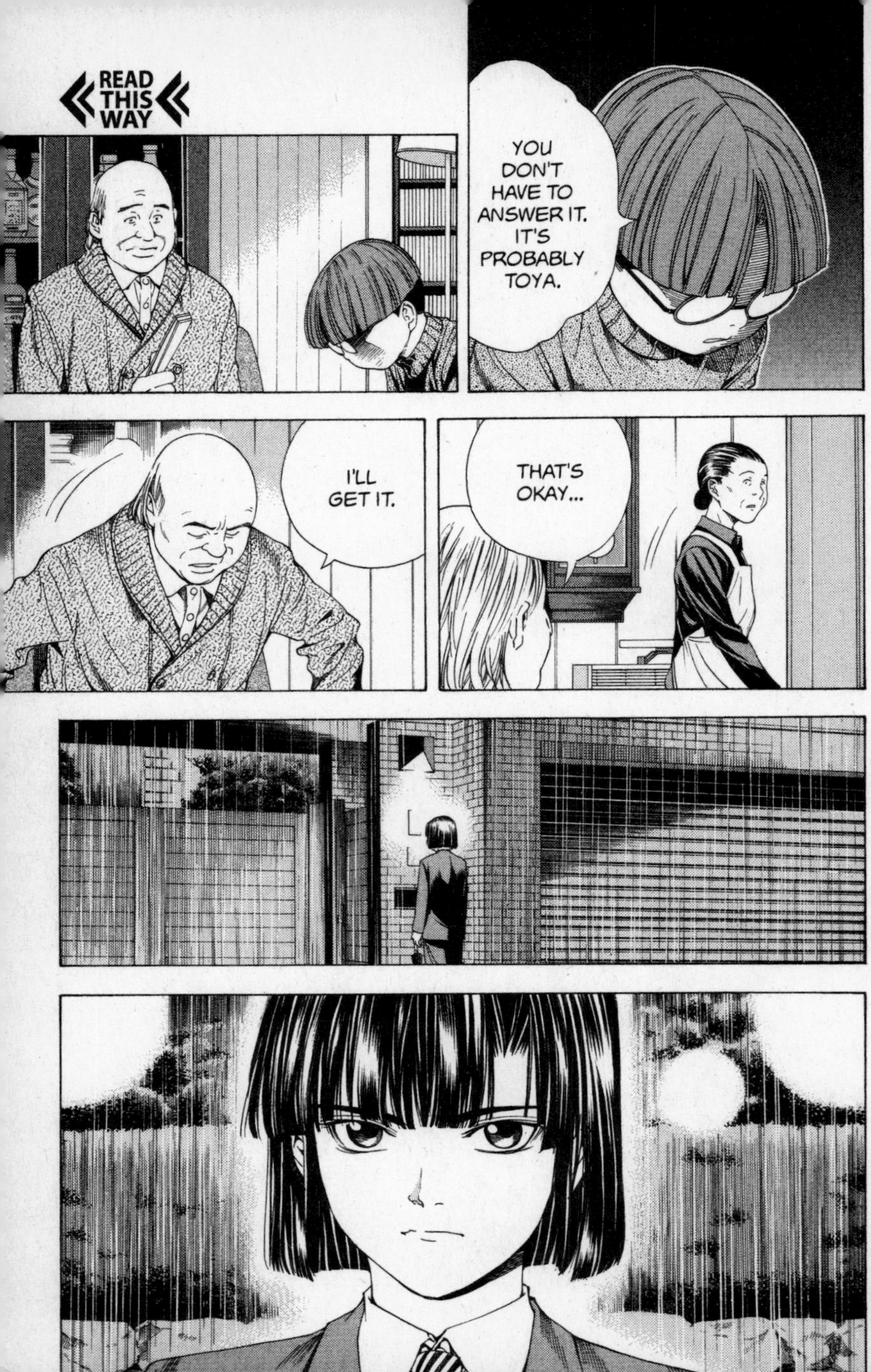
YOU DON'T HAVE TO ANSWER IT. IT'S PROBABLY TOYA.
THAT'S OKAY...
I'LL GET IT.

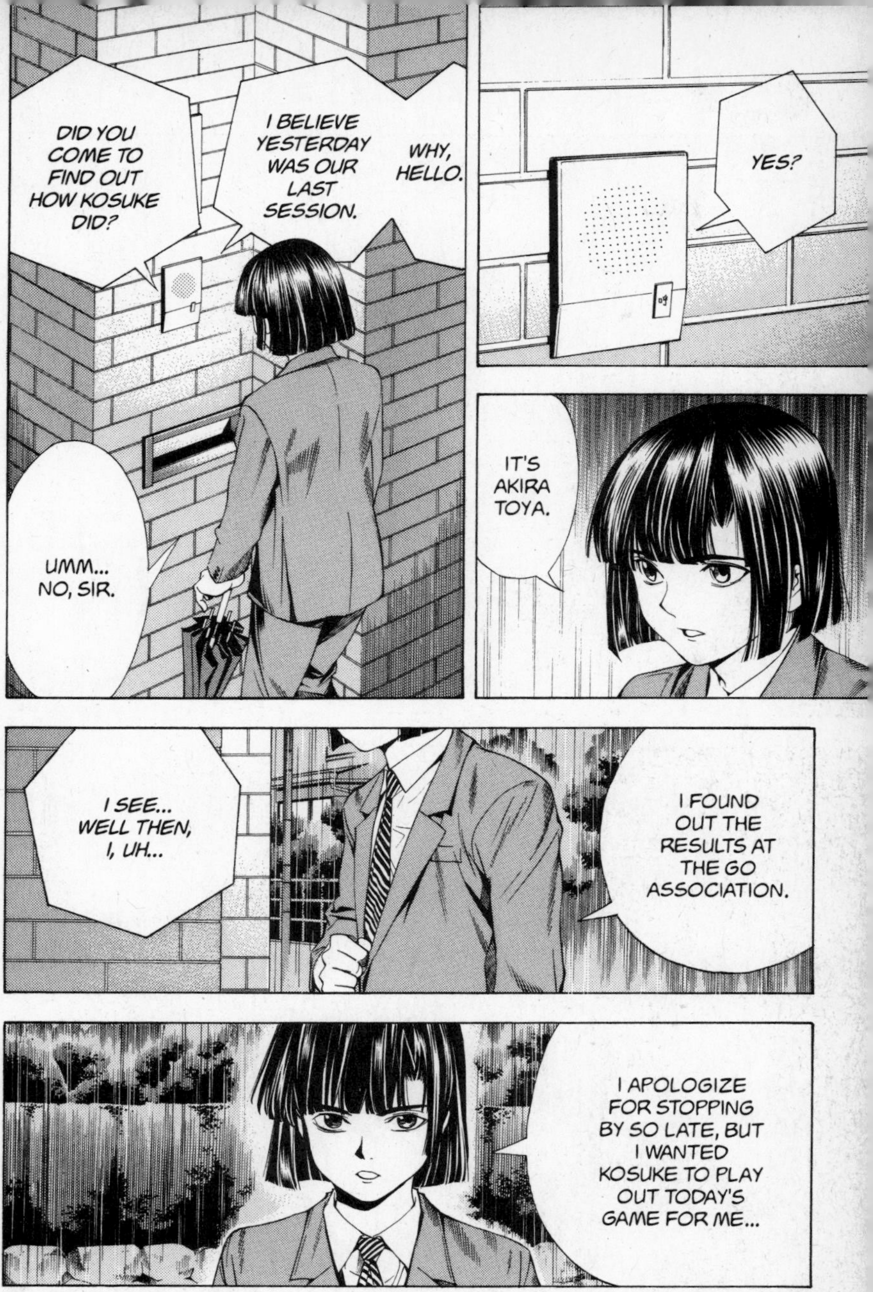
YES?
IT'S AKIRA TOYA.
WHY, HELLO.
I BELIEVE YESTERDAY WAS OUR LAST SESSION.
DID YOU COME TO FIND OUT HOW KOSUKE DID?
UMM... NO, SIR.
I FOUND OUT THE RESULTS AT THE GO ASSOCIATION.
I SEE... WELL THEN, I, UH...
I APOLOGIZE FOR STOPPING BY SO LATE, BUT I WANTED KOSUKE TO PLAY OUT TODAY'S GAME FOR ME...

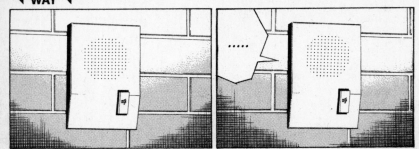

.....

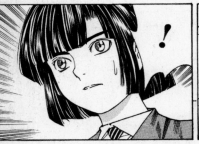

!

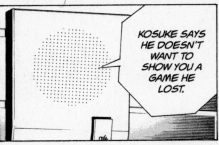

KOSUKE SAYS HE DOESN'T WANT TO SHOW YOU A GAME HE LOST.

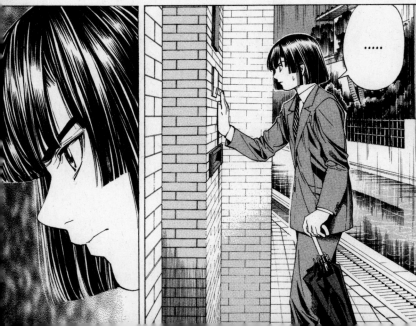

.....

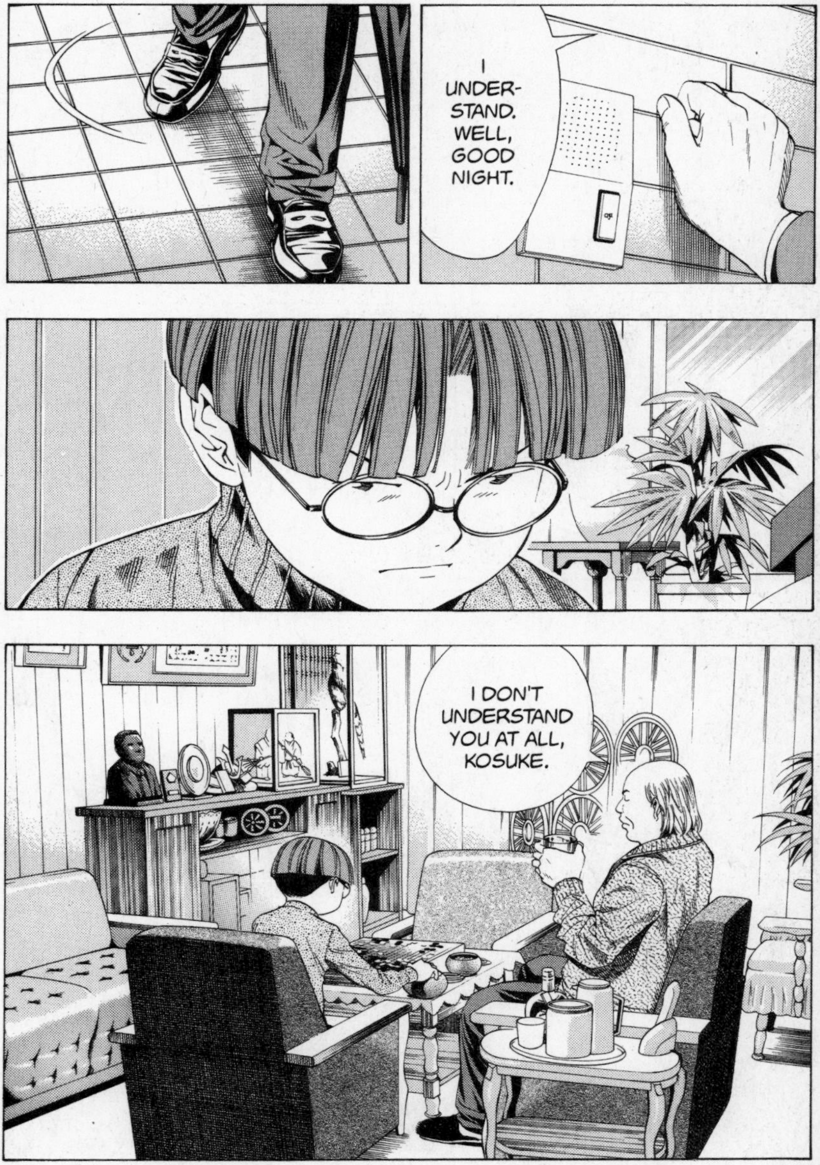
I UNDER-STAND. WELL, GOOD NIGHT.
I DON'T UNDERSTAND YOU AT ALL, KOSUKE.

READ THIS WAY

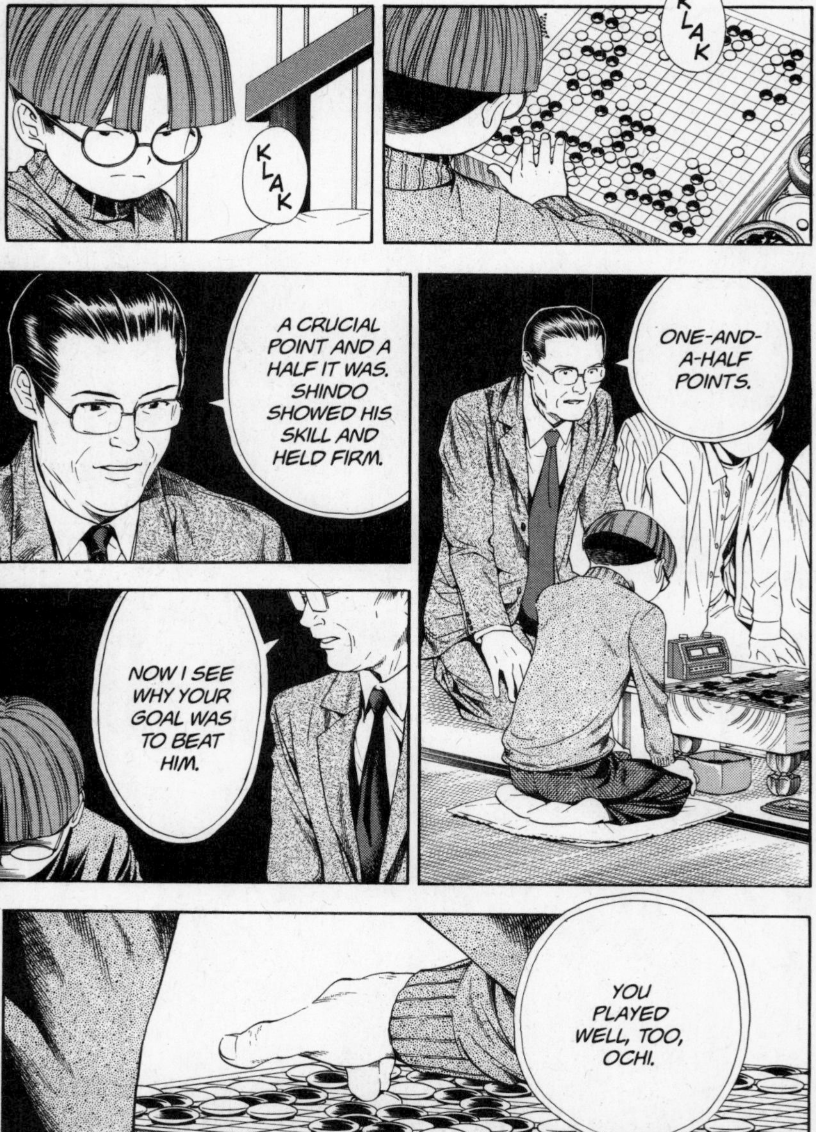
KLAK
KLAK
ONE-AND-A-HALF POINTS.
A CRUCIAL POINT AND A HALF IT WAS. SHINDO SHOWED HIS SKILL AND HELD FIRM.
NOW I SEE WHY YOUR GOAL WAS TO BEAT HIM.
YOU PLAYED WELL, TOO, OCHI.

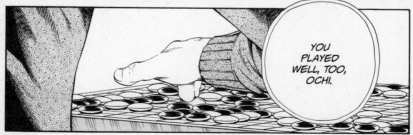

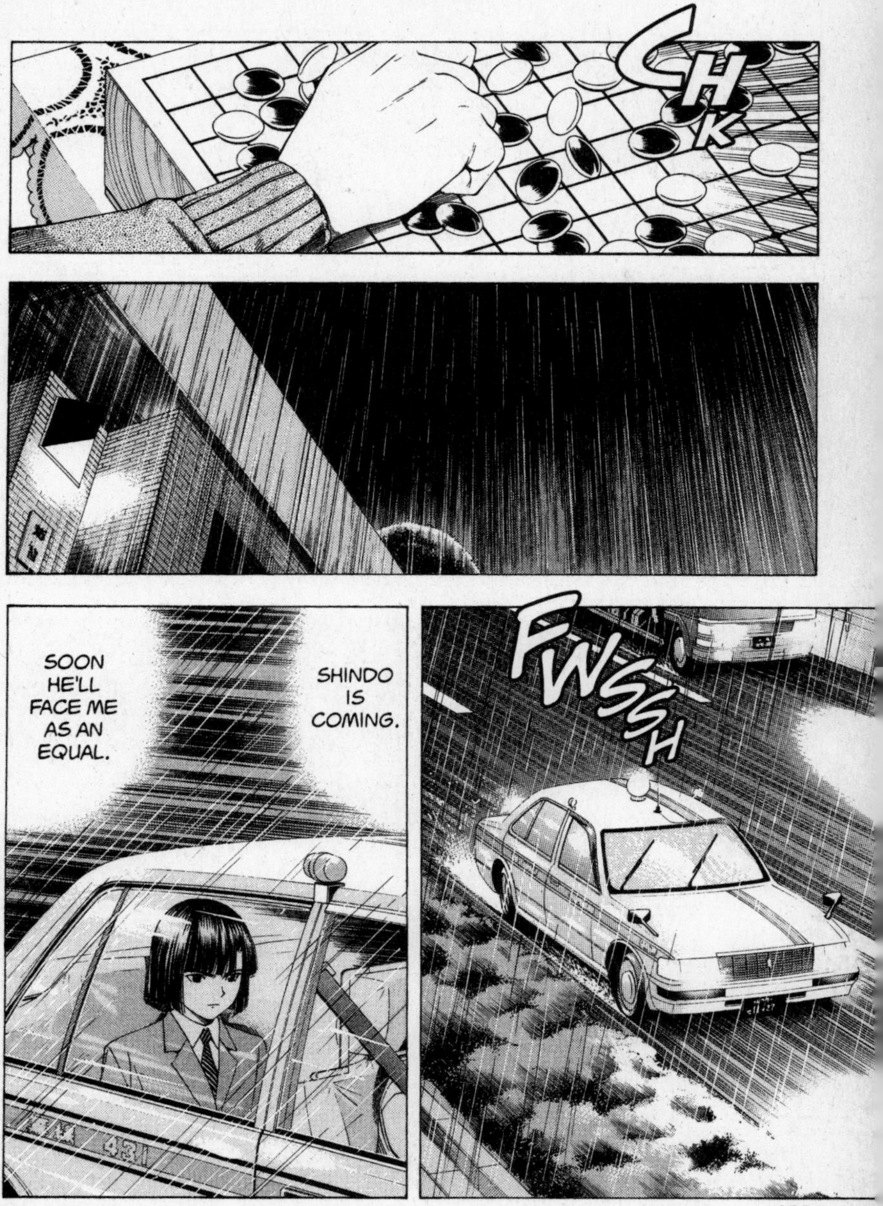
CHK
FWSSH
SHINDO IS COMING.
SOON HE'LL FACE ME AS AN EQUAL.

READ THIS WAY

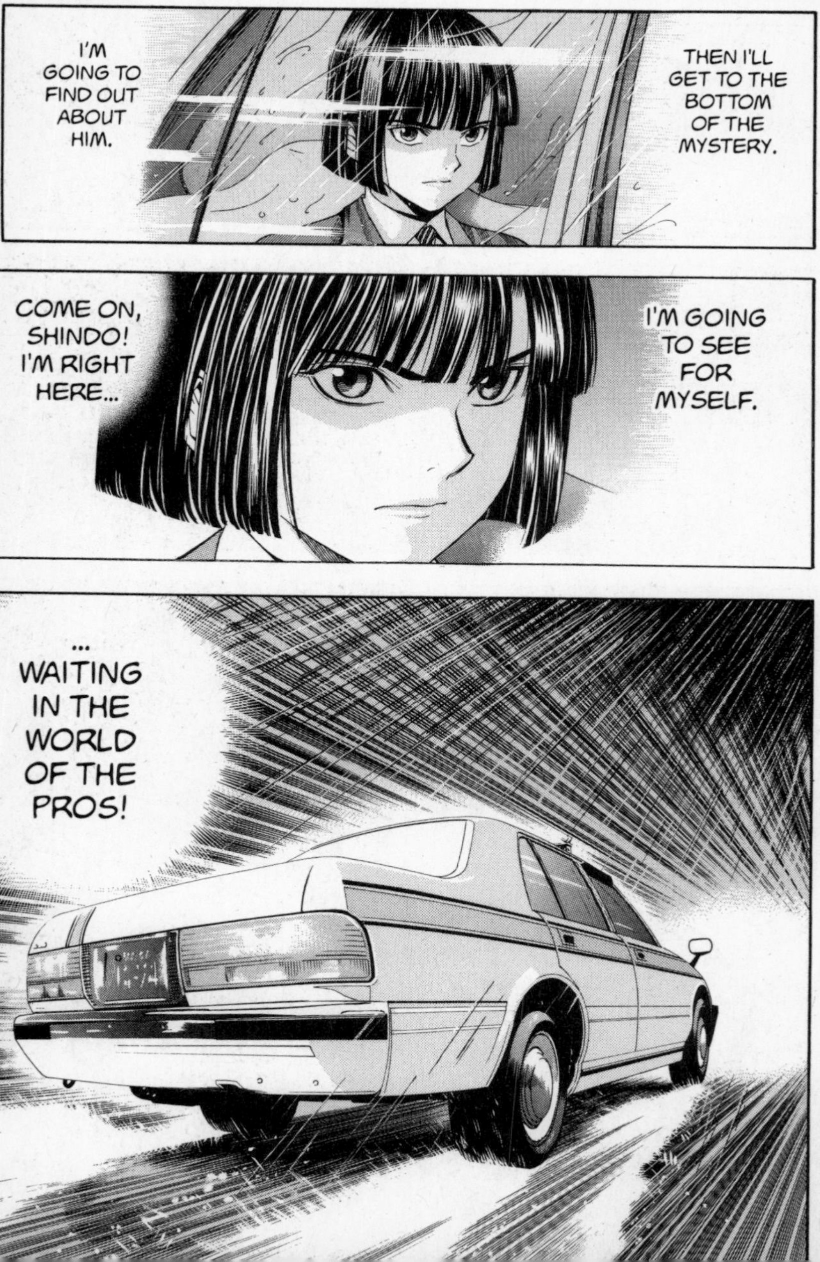
THEN I'LL GET TO THE BOTTOM OF THE MYSTERY.
I'M GOING TO FIND OUT ABOUT HIM.
I'M GOING TO SEE FOR MYSELF.
COME ON, SHINDO! I'M RIGHT HERE...
... WAITING IN THE WORLD OF THE PROS!

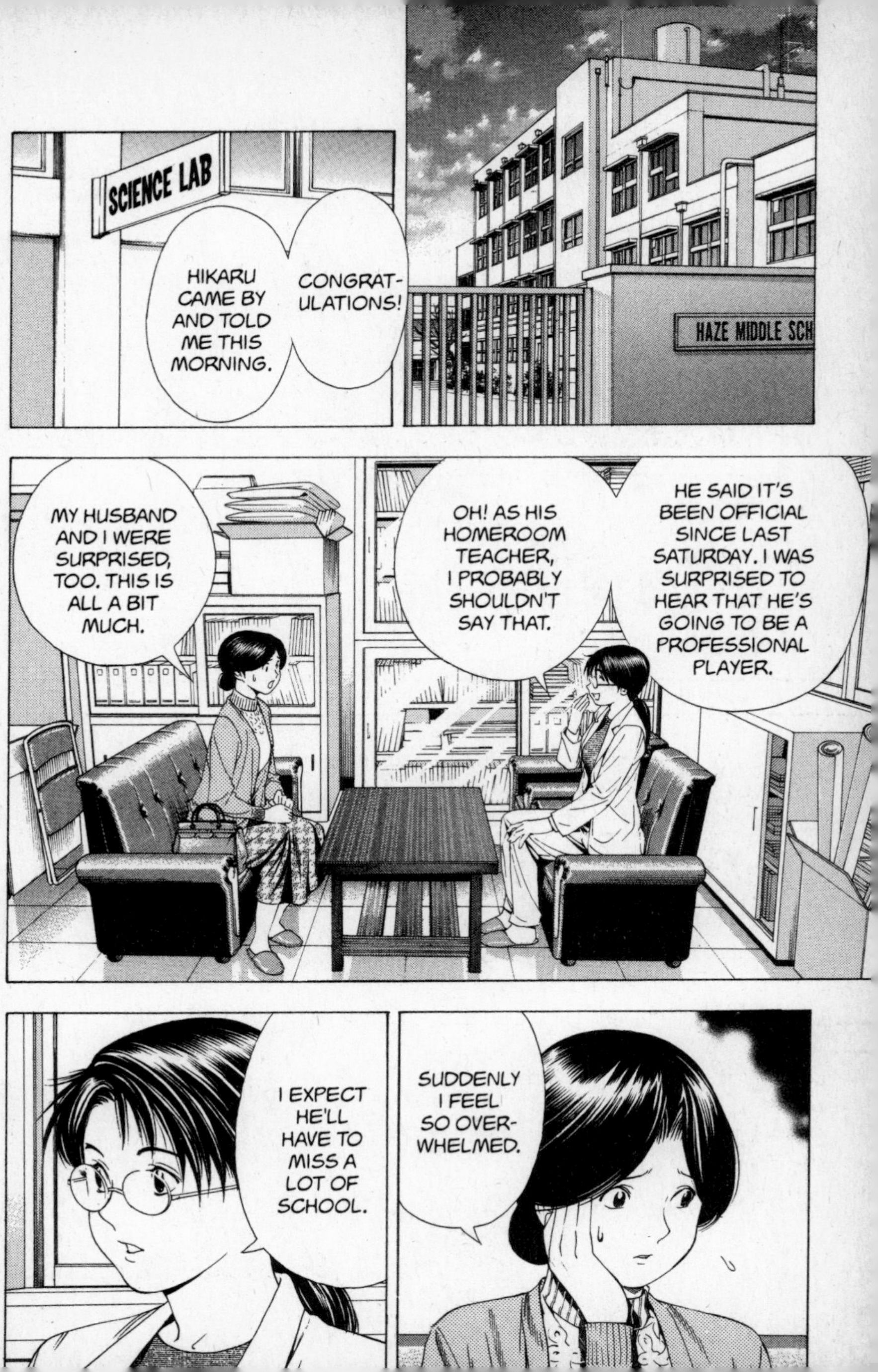
HAZE MIDDLE SCH
SCIENCE LAB
CONGRAT-ULATIONS!
HIKARU CAME BY AND TOLD ME THIS MORNING.
HE SAID IT'S BEEN OFFICIAL SINCE LAST SATURDAY. I WAS SURPRISED TO HEAR THAT HE'S GOING TO BE A PROFESSIONAL PLAYER.
OH! AS HIS HOMEROOM TEACHER, I PROBABLY SHOULDN'T SAY THAT.
MY HUSBAND AND I WERE SURPRISED, TOO. THIS IS ALL A BIT MUCH.
SUDDENLY I FEEL SO OVER-WHELMED.
I EXPECT HE'LL HAVE TO MISS A LOT OF SCHOOL.

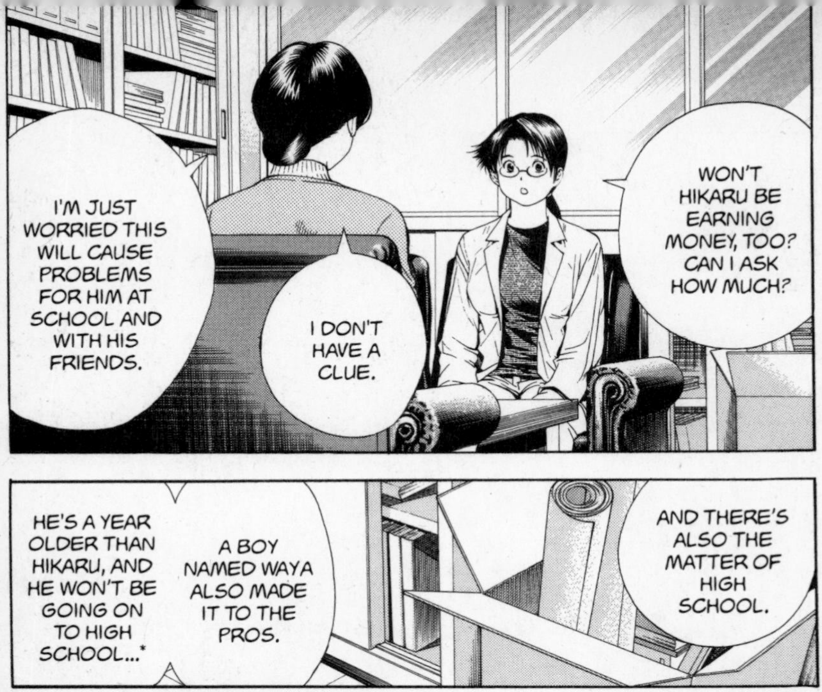
WON'T HIKARU BE EARNING MONEY, TOO? CAN I ASK HOW MUCH?
I DON'T HAVE A CLUE.
I'M JUST WORRIED THIS WILL CAUSE PROBLEMS FOR HIM AT SCHOOL AND WITH HIS FRIENDS.
AND THERE'S ALSO THE MATTER OF HIGH SCHOOL.
A BOY NAMED WAYA ALSO MADE IT TO THE PROS.
HE'S A YEAR OLDER THAN HIKARU, AND HE WON'T BE GOING ON TO HIGH SCHOOL...*

*High school isn't compulsory in Japan.

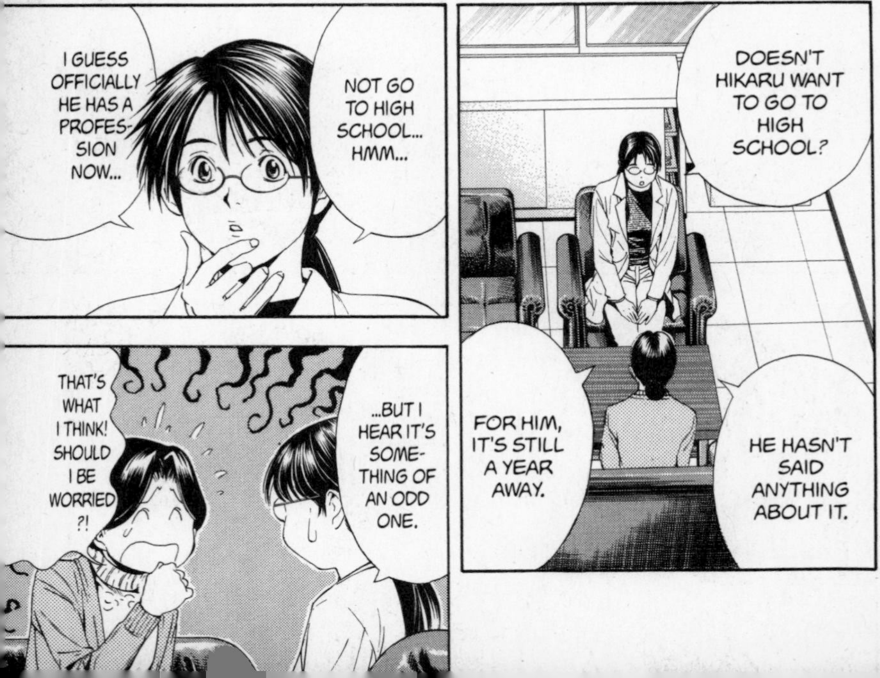
DOESN'T HIKARU WANT TO GO TO HIGH SCHOOL?
HE HASN'T SAID ANYTHING ABOUT IT.
FOR HIM, IT'S STILL A YEAR AWAY.
NOT GO TO HIGH SCHOOL... HMM...
I GUESS OFFICIALLY HE HAS A PROFES-SION NOW...
...BUT I HEAR IT'S SOME-THING OF AN ODD ONE.
THAT'S WHAT I THINK! SHOULD I BE WORRIED?!

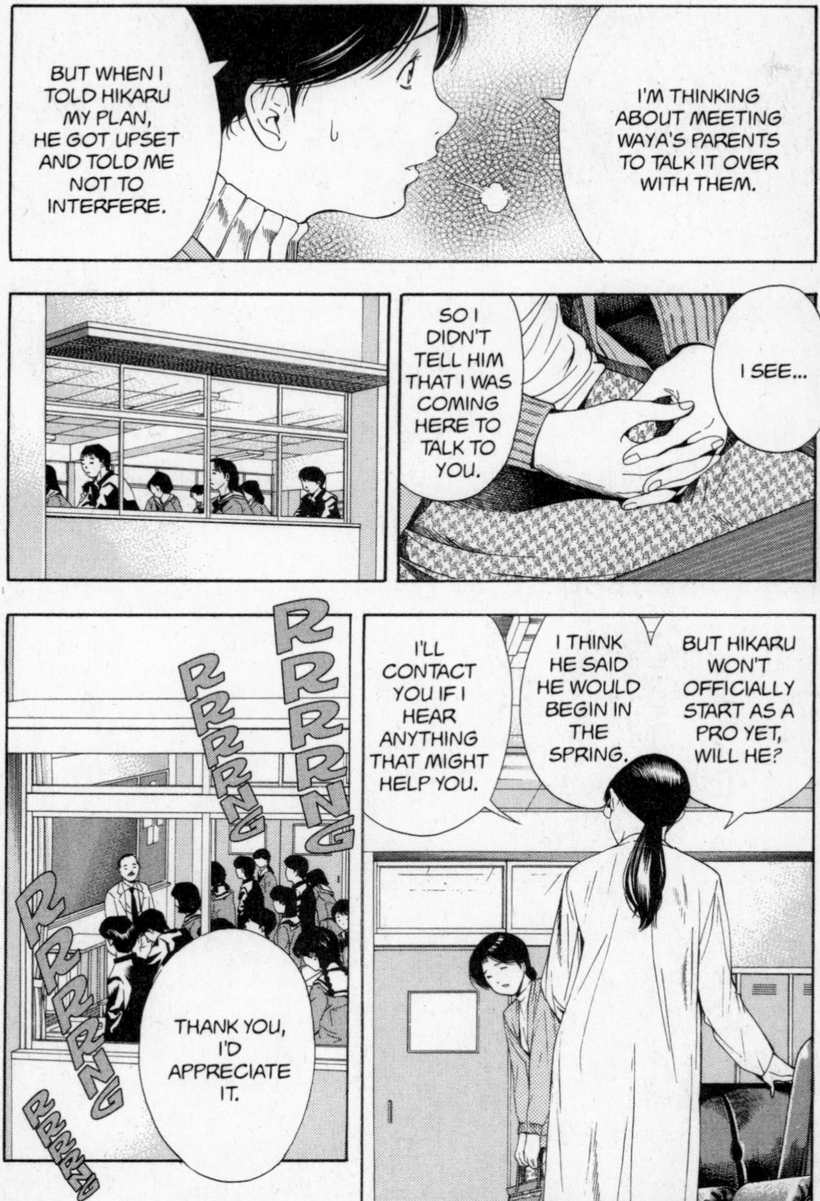
I'M THINKING ABOUT MEETING WAYA'S PARENTS TO TALK IT OVER WITH THEM.
BUT WHEN I TOLD HIKARU MY PLAN, HE GOT UPSET AND TOLD ME NOT TO INTERFERE.
I SEE...
SO I DIDN'T TELL HIM THAT I WAS COMING HERE TO TALK TO YOU.
BUT HIKARU WON'T OFFICIALLY START AS A PRO YET, WILL HE?
I THINK HE SAID HE WOULD BEGIN IN THE SPRING.
I'LL CONTACT YOU IF I HEAR ANYTHING THAT MIGHT HELP YOU.
RRRRNG
RRRRNG
RRRRNG
THANK YOU, I'D APPRECIATE IT.

READ THIS WAY

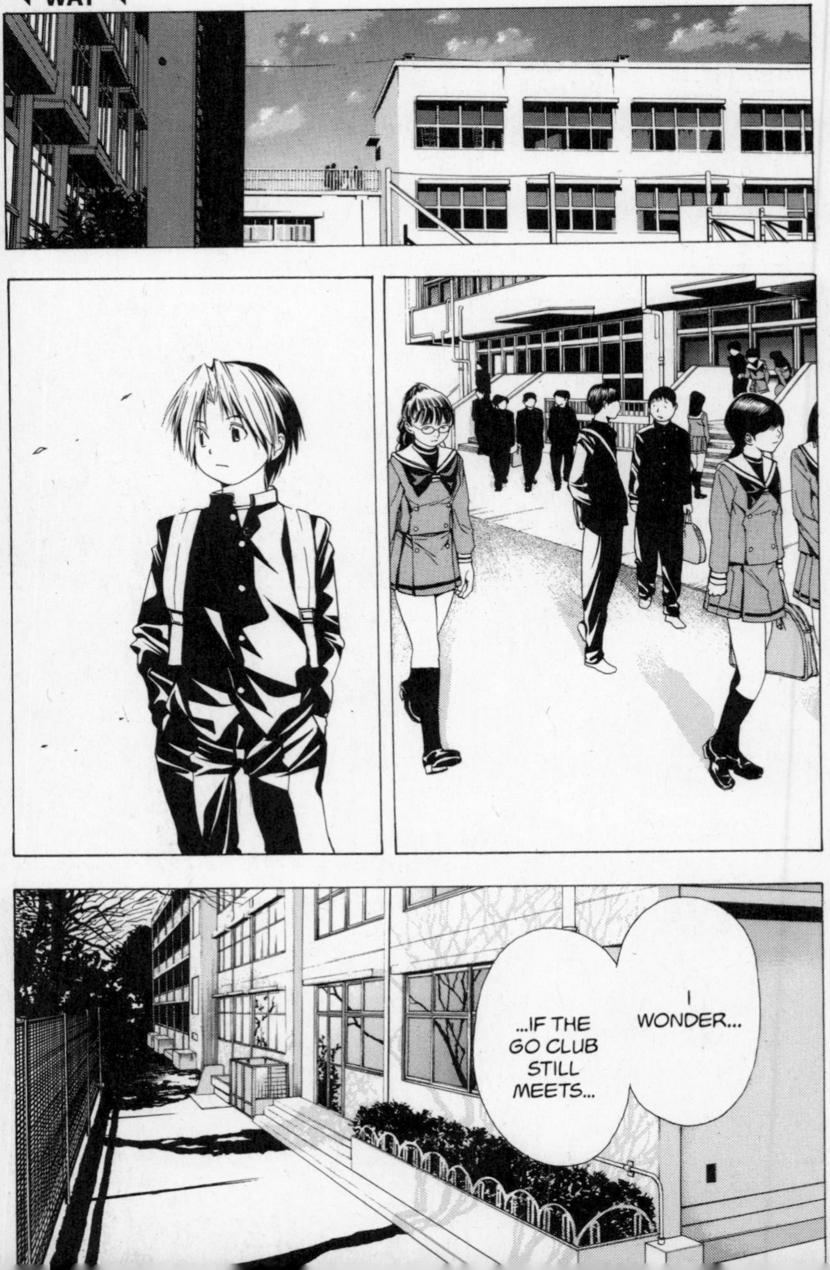

I WONDER...
...IF THE GO CLUB STILL MEETS...

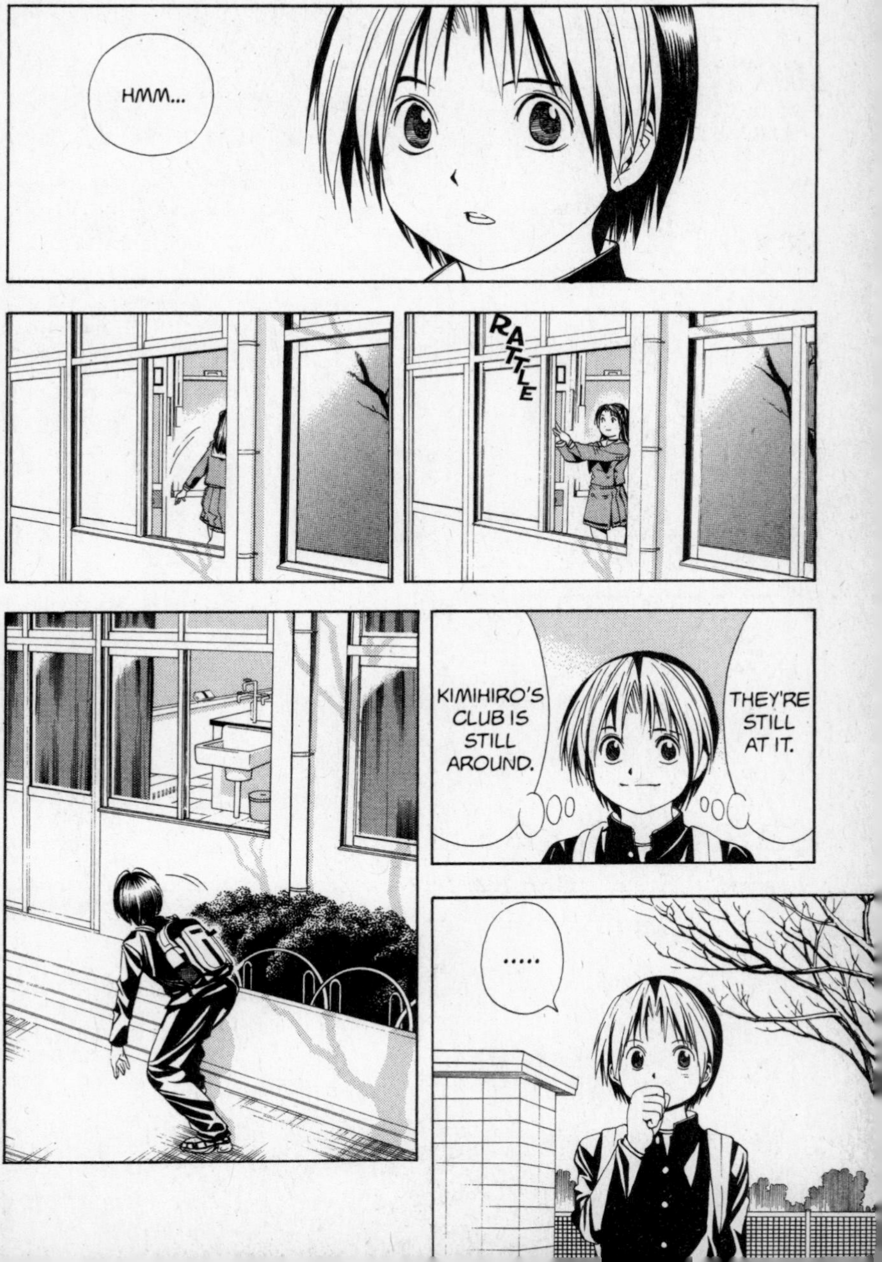
HMM...
RATTLE
THEY'RE STILL AT IT.
KIMIHIRO'S CLUB IS STILL AROUND.
.....

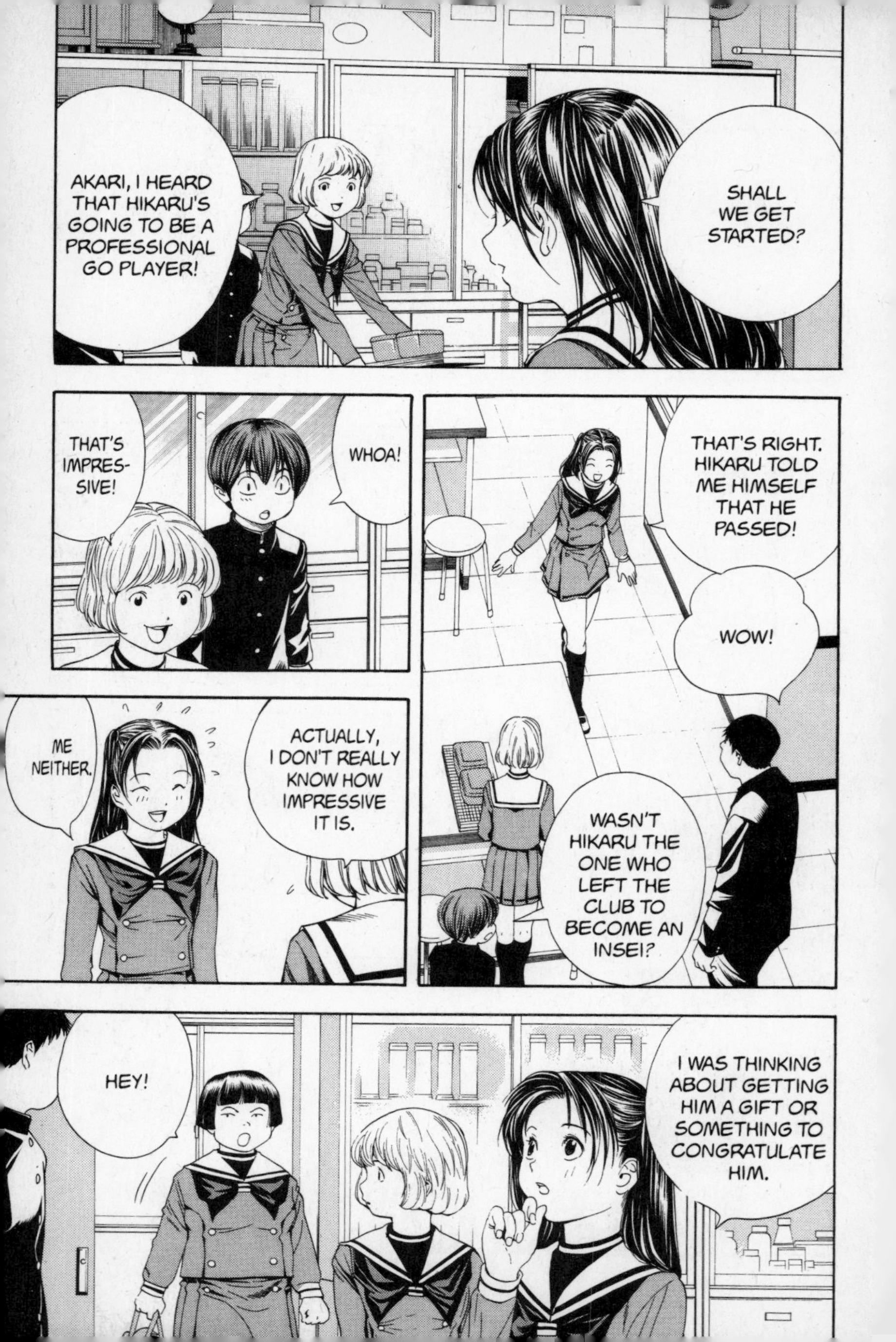
SHALL WE GET STARTED?
AKARI, I HEARD THAT HIKARU'S GOING TO BE A PROFESSIONAL GO PLAYER!
THAT'S RIGHT. HIKARU TOLD ME HIMSELF THAT HE PASSED!
WOW!
WASN'T HIKARU THE ONE WHO LEFT THE CLUB TO BECOME AN INSEI?
WHOA!
THAT'S IMPRES-SIVE!
ACTUALLY, I DON'T REALLY KNOW HOW IMPRESSIVE IT IS.
ME NEITHER.
I WAS THINKING ABOUT GETTING HIM A GIFT OR SOMETHING TO CONGRATULATE HIM.
HEY!

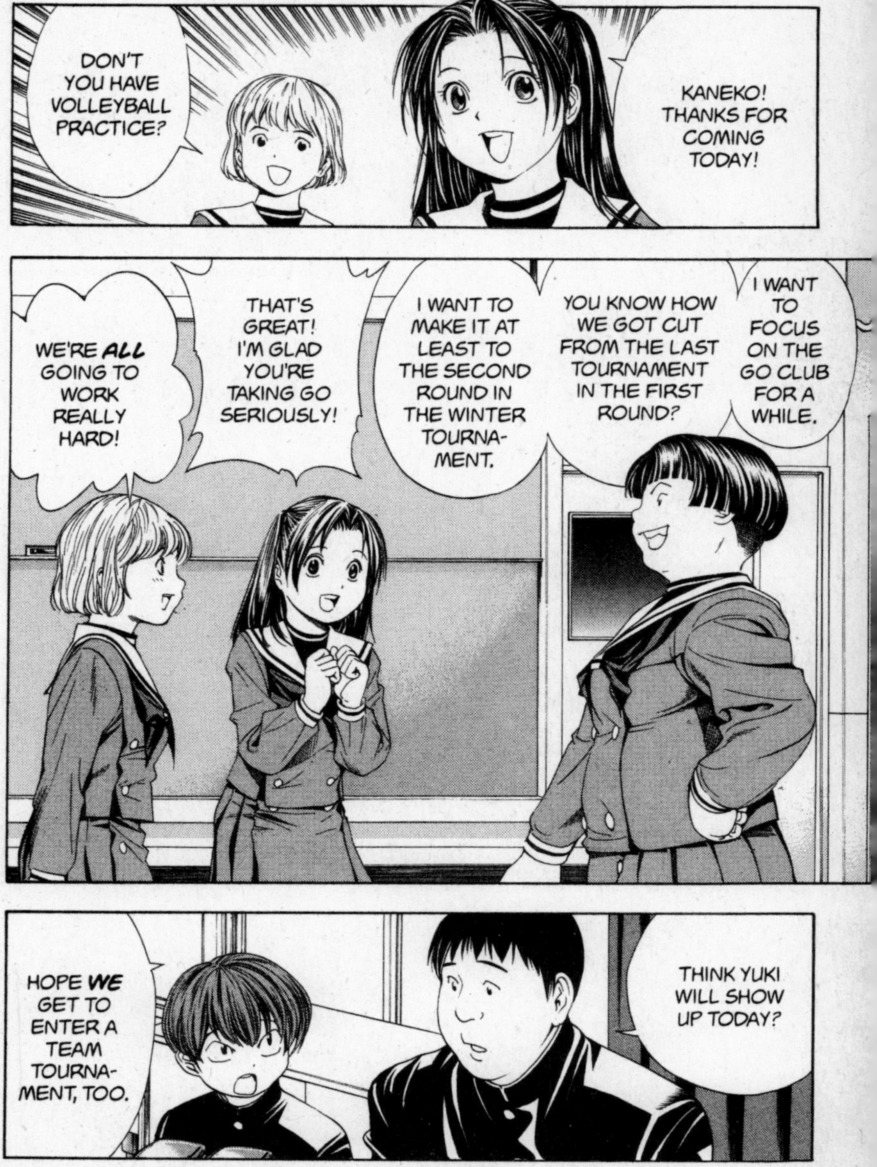
KANEKO! THANKS FOR COMING TODAY!
DON'T YOU HAVE VOLLEYBALL PRACTICE?
I WANT TO FOCUS ON THE GO CLUB FOR A WHILE.
YOU KNOW HOW WE GOT CUT FROM THE LAST TOURNAMENT IN THE FIRST ROUND?
I WANT TO MAKE IT AT LEAST TO THE SECOND ROUND IN THE WINTER TOURNA-MENT.
THAT'S GREAT! I'M GLAD YOU'RE TAKING GO SERIOUSLY!
WE'RE ***ALL*** GOING TO WORK REALLY HARD!
THINK YUKI WILL SHOW UP TODAY?
HOPE ***WE*** GET TO ENTER A TEAM TOURNA-MENT, TOO.

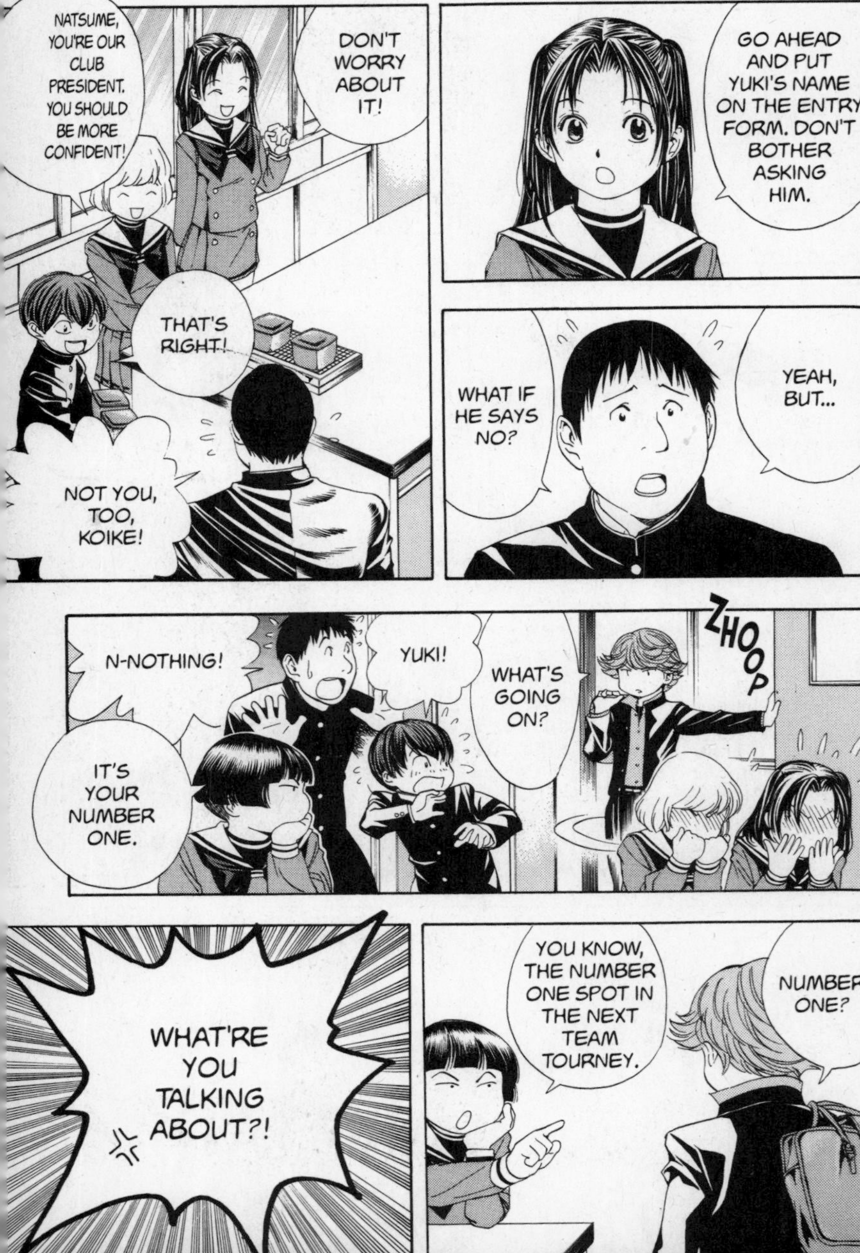
GO AHEAD AND PUT YUKI'S NAME ON THE ENTRY FORM. DON'T BOTHER ASKING HIM.
YEAH, BUT...
WHAT IF HE SAYS NO?
DON'T WORRY ABOUT IT!
NATSUME, YOU'RE OUR CLUB PRESIDENT. YOU SHOULD BE MORE CONFIDENT!
THAT'S RIGHT!
NOT YOU, TOO, KOIKE!
ZHOOP
WHAT'S GOING ON?
YUKI!
N-NOTHING!
IT'S YOUR NUMBER ONE.
NUMBER ONE?
YOU KNOW, THE NUMBER ONE SPOT IN THE NEXT TEAM TOURNEY.
WHAT'RE YOU TALKING ABOUT?!

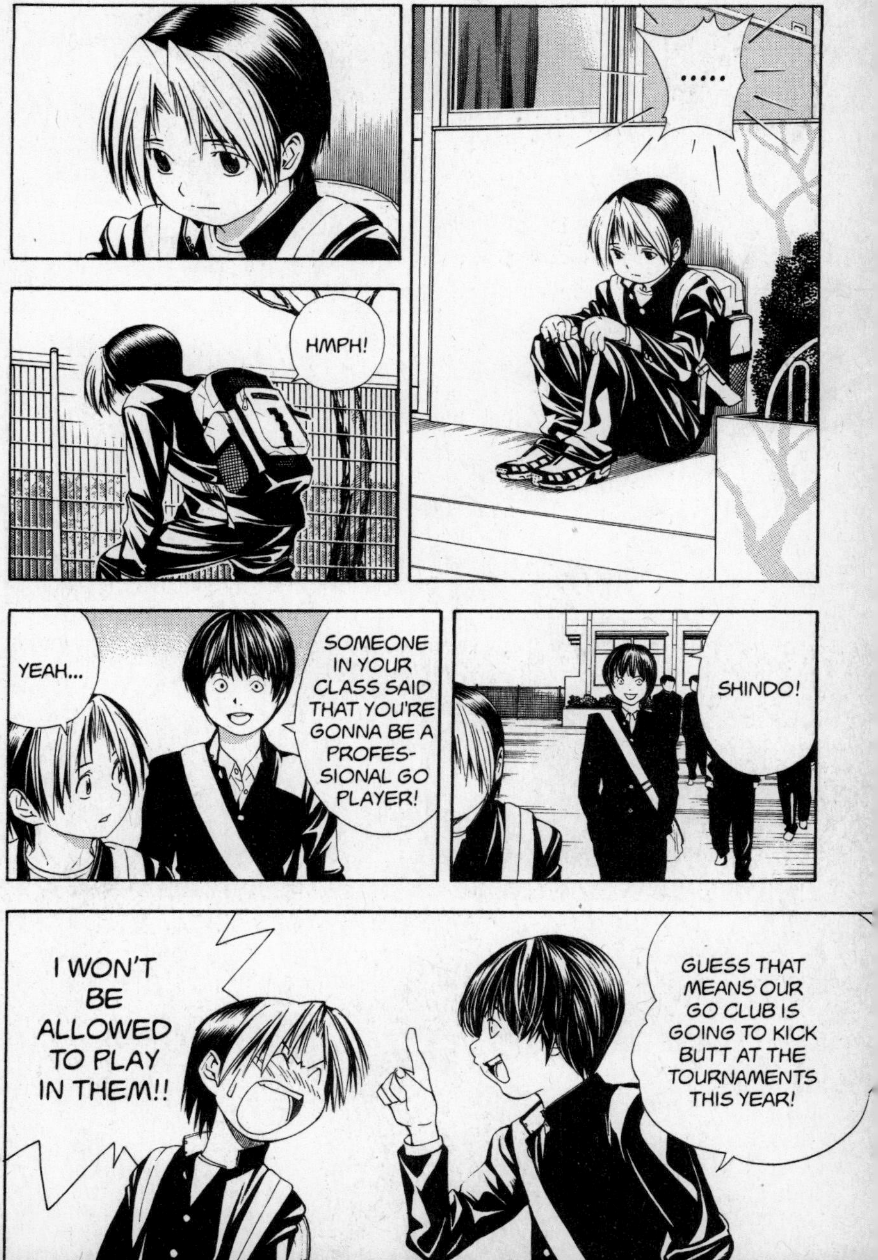
.....
HMPH!
SHINDO!
SOMEONE IN YOUR CLASS SAID THAT YOU'RE GONNA BE A PROFES- SIONAL GO PLAYER!
YEAH...
GUESS THAT MEANS OUR GO CLUB IS GOING TO KICK BUTT AT THE TOURNAMENTS THIS YEAR!
I WON'T BE ALLOWED TO PLAY IN THEM!!

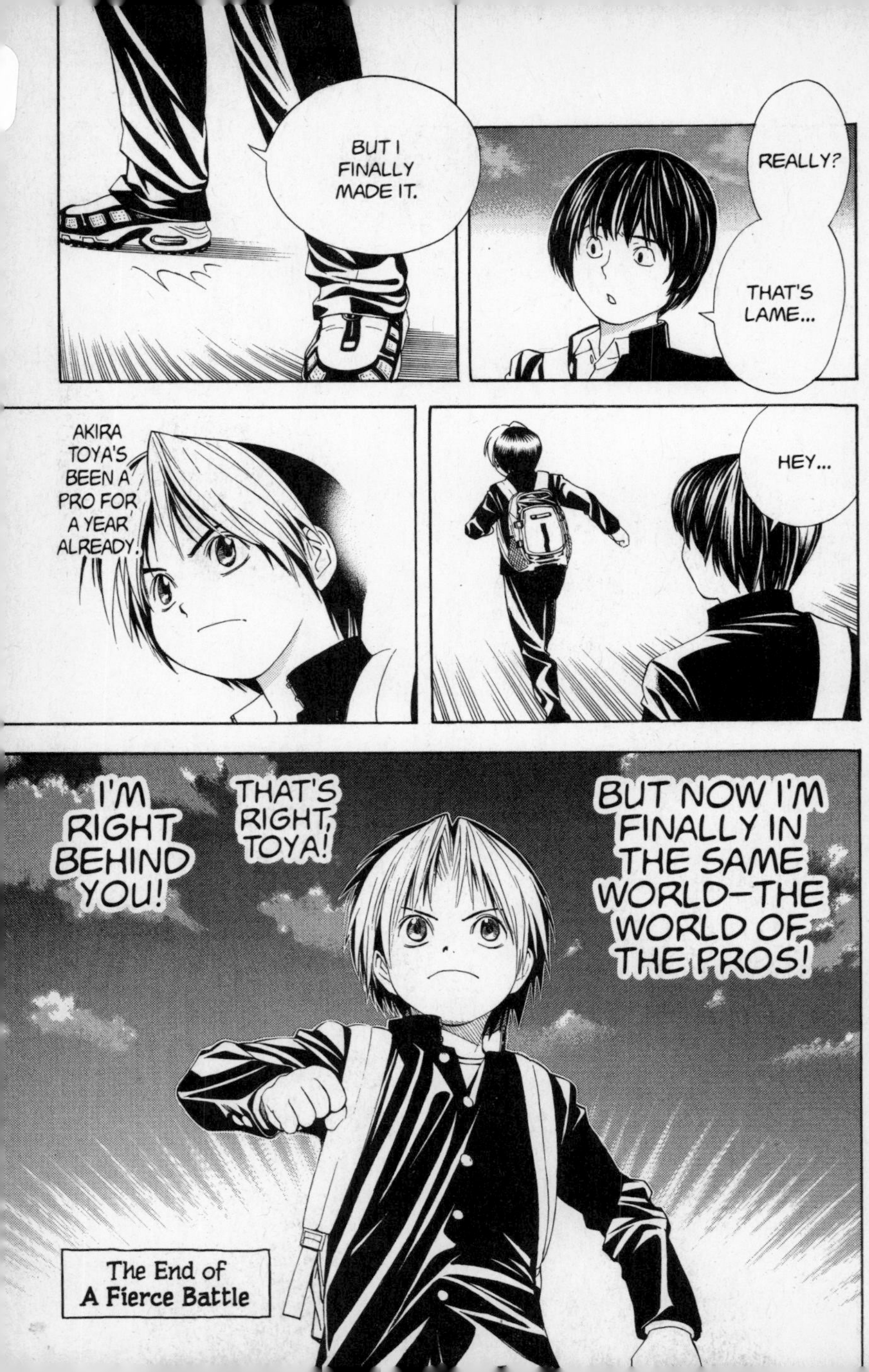
REALLY?
THAT'S LAME...
BUT I FINALLY MADE IT.
HEY...
AKIRA TOYA'S BEEN A PRO FOR A YEAR ALREADY.
BUT NOW I'M FINALLY IN THE SAME WORLD—THE WORLD OF THE PROS!
THAT'S RIGHT, TOYA!
I'M RIGHT BEHIND YOU!
The End of A Fierce Battle

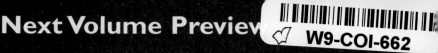

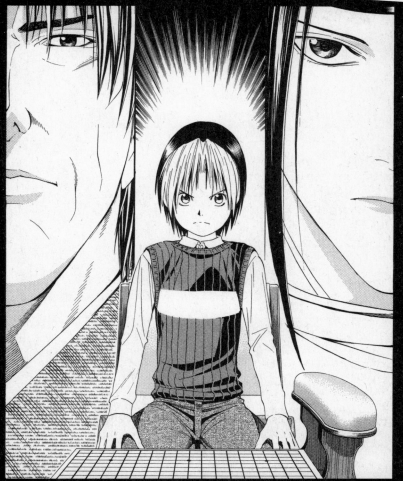

Hikaru's career as a professional go player begins! In his first game he must face veteran player Toya Meijin, none other than Akira's father. But to Sai, this round is *personal*. Then Sai attempts to teach a cheating go player a lesson he'll never forget... Will Hikaru's ghostly master do him proud, or make him look like an amateur?

COMING MAY 2008

Read it first in SHONEN JUMP magazine!